SMILE of DISCONTENT

Women in Culture and Society
A series edited by Catharine R. Stimpson

SMILE OF DISCONTENT

Humor, Gender, and Nineteenth-Century British Fiction

Eileen Gillooly

THE
UNIVERSITY OF CHICAGO PRESS
Chicago & London

Eileen Gillooly teaches English and comparative literature at Columbia University, where she is director of the Core Curriculum. This is her first book.

The University of Chicago Press, Chicago 60637
The University of Chicago Press, Ltd., London
© 1999 by The University of Chicago
All rights reserved. Published 1999
08 07 06 05 04 03 02 01 00 99   5 4 3 2 1

ISBN (cloth): 0-226-29401-3
ISBN (paper): 0-226-29402-1

Library of Congress Cataloging-in-Publication Data

Gillooly, Eileen.
    Smile of discontent : humor, gender, and nineteenth-century
British fiction / Eileen Gillooly.
        p.   cm.
    Includes bibliographical references and index.
    ISBN 0-226-29401-3. — ISBN 0-226-29402-1 (pbk.)
    1. English fiction—Women authors—History and criticism.
2. Women and literature—Great Britain—History—19th century.
3. English fiction—19th century—History and criticism.
4. Humorous stories, English—History and criticism.   5. Comic, The,
in literature.   6. Discontent in literature.   7. Sex role in
literature.   8. Narration (Rhetoric).   I. Title.
PR868.H85G55   1999
823'.8099287—dc21   98-46167
                                                                CIP

⊗ The paper used in this publication meets the minimum requirements of
the American National Standard for Information Sciences—Permanence
of Paper for Printed Library Materials, ANSI Z39.48-1992.

For
Dan, Kate, and Ben

and
in memory of my parents

Contents

A gallery of illustrations follows page 76

FOREWORD

In Shakespeare's *The Taming of the Shrew,* Petruchio seeks to establish his rule over Katherina, the rich but "rough" woman he has married. On his wedding night he vows to a friend, ". . . I'll curb her mad and headstrong humour" (IV, i, 212). Through sleep deprivation and other charmless techniques of behavior modification, he succeeds. Broken and remade, Kate becomes a paragon of—and apparent mouthpiece for—a woman's submissiveness, sweetness, and obedience.

Eileen Gillooly's *Smile of Discontent* is aware of the extent of the fear of a woman's mad and headstrong humours. She is equally alert to the power of the picture of the ideal woman as a post-marital Kate, which reached a climax in middle-class, nineteenth-century Britain. However, Gillooly argues persuasively, not every subject in Petruchio's patriarchal domain was wholly submissive, sweet, and obedient. One subtle, even sly, technique of resistance is discursive: a way of writing and speaking that Gillooly names "feminine humor." Crucially, both women and men were and can be feminine humorists. For humor represents an attitude and a linguistic turn, the software of the mind, not a genetic dictate, the hardware of the body.

A fearless writer, Gillooly takes on one of the hardest of cultural questions, "What is humor?," and one of the hardest of psychological questions, "Why do we laugh?" We often duck them, not only because they are hard, but because we fear that humor and laughter will wilt as a source of pleasure if we strap them down under the hot light of hyperrational analysis. Gillooly is too deft, agile, and nuanced a writer to permit this to happen. She also loves literature too openly and strongly. "Many years ago," *Smile of Discontent* begins, "I noticed that as I read novels—especially nineteenth-century British novels, for which I had a keen, and still unsatisfied appetite—I would inscribe the margins with tiny private notations indicating where humor lay" (xvii).

And where does humor lie? Gillooly argues that it "signifies both a cognitive, psychological process and its textual product" (xxi). They make us aware that a particular sociocultural stimulus provokes at least two conflicting interpretative contexts. This doubled reading in turn breeds a sense of incongruity and amusement. To be sure, irony also demands a double reading. When I am being ironic, I say one thing but mean another—I might murmur to a companion, "I just *love* parsnips," but actually be warning, "No parsnips welcome here."

Gillooly distinguishes feminine humor from irony for a number of reasons, among them a frequent association of irony with masculinity. In contrast, feminine humor deploys a set of narrative strategies that are associated with "traits, behaviors, perspectives, preoccupations, and dispositions that have . . . been both historically and cross-culturally constructed as appropriate to or descriptive of women" (xix). Among these are passivity, indirection, and self-effacement. *Smile of Discontent* then makes two striking claims for feminine humor.

The first concerns its effect. It invites the alert reader to take tea with subversion. Unlike the far brasher carnivalesque, which momentarily overthrows convention and order, feminine humor is understated. It sews its stitches in nooks, crannies, and corners of a narrative. It carefully patrols and controls its aggressive impulses—in part to disarm any counterattack. Deliberately cultivating a low profile, it has been critically overlooked, unlike the more flamboyant hysteria and masochism, two well-mapped pathologies that bear some family resemblances. No matter how decorously and shyly, feminine humor mocks "the disproportions and incongruities *within* the (masculinized) norm, the traditional locus of cultural authority, which internalized carries the weight and force of Law" (xx). Even the sweetest of womanly smiles can query Petruchio's regime—perhaps even that of Kate, his wife.

The second claim concerns the affect of this humor. It also invites the reader to experience, not anger and outrage, but more benign feelings. Here Gillooly originally revises both other feminist explorations of women's humor and Sigmund Freud's *Wit and Its Relation to the Unconscious* (1905), that invaluable exploration of the comic. The humorist, Freud suggests, transforms potential pain into pleasure through appeals to our superego. The feminine humorist, Gillooly counterargues, calls not on the internalized father but the internalized mother. In so doing, she or he evokes a pre-Oedipal dynamic of playfulness, the dyad of mother/child, and protective sympathy for the child against the rigors of paternal orders.

If scientific theories must be tested against the realities of nature, so literary theories must be tested against the realities of the text. Gillooly's poetics and paradigms of feminine humor must help us interpret a poem or a novel or a letter. They do. Persuasively, she shows how feminine humor works in Fanny Burney, Jane Austen, Elizabeth Gaskell, Anthony Trollope, George Eliot, and, in an intriguing section, in the relationship between

Henry James and Edith Wharton. In a brief Coda, Gillooly notes that twentieth-century women writers have access to more kinds of humor than their nineteenth-century predecessors. Yet, feminine humor persists—in part because contemporary writers use their predecessors and bring them into their work; in part because contemporary writers, even if they have lost faith in the power of maternal consolation, retain their capacity for weaving empathetic bonds between narrators and characters and between text and reader.

I must confess that I began *Smile of Discontent* with some suspicion. Would there really be, I asked myself, some important general idea about humor? Could I be asked to follow once again close readings of canonical or near-canonical women writers? I am now ashamed that my doubting was so simple. Fortunately, no one can wholly curb the subjects of humor and comedy, for they are by nature too rough, independent, headstrong, anarchic, and polyvocal. They can, however, be illuminated. This Gillooly has done crisply, elegantly, solidly, wittily. People can now adapt her theory of feminine humor to other traditions. This is a book that should leave all of us with an appetite for literature content.

Catharine R. Stimpson
New York University

ACKNOWLEDGMENTS

Any book that takes shape over the course of nearly two decades accumulates a debt of gratitude that simple acknowledgment, however heartfelt, cannot possibly repay. Steven Marcus, who directed the dissertation from which this book has emerged, not only gently guided me to many of the sources, musings, and arguments offered in these pages, but did so with such sympathy of purpose that I was sometimes fooled into thinking their discovery my own. Together with Ann Douglas, Jonathan Arac, and Priscilla Parkhurst Ferguson—whose intellectual generosity and tireless writing of recommendations continue to deepen my sense of obligation to them and to their example—he remains among the most treasured of readers. The Pachymamacowcow warrants special thanks for her wise counsel and ever-cheerful efforts on my behalf, as does Catharine R. Stimpson, for responding—with what I've come to learn is characteristic magnanimity—to Martha Howell's urging that she look at my manuscript. I'm most grateful to them all.

I have benefited from the blessedly precise suggestions of my two readers at the University of Chicago Press, as well as from Susan Bielstein's delightfully reassuring editorship. I am especially grateful for the sustaining interest and astute advice of many whose friendship I value even more highly. Among these are Ina Lipkowitz Buzard, Carla Cappetti, Kathy Eden, Margaret Ferguson, Wallace Gray, Dan and Helen Horowitz, Amy Edith Johnson, David Johnston, Jonathan Levin, James Mirollo, Zita Nunes, Cathy Popkin, Ellen Ross, Maura Spiegel, and Zvjezdana Vržić. Martha Fay, Peggy Sradnick, Stuart Kramer, Jo Ann Walthal, Suzanne Boorsch, Allan Appel, Marion and Edward Mongan, and Sacha and Nat Lord in other ways made writing possible. Joseph Wiesenfarth, Robyn Warhol, and Jean Wyatt were kind enough to make presents of books at crucial moments (the latter a recommendation as well), and Mary Poovey deserves thanks for the great pleasure I had in delivering a fifty-minute version of this book at New York University. For assistance in obtaining illustrations, I owe much to the efforts of Pat Kennedy, David Carmac, and Meg Perlman.

One of the more attractive features of my mostly administrative appointment at Columbia is its having brought me into sympathetic relation with a great many faculty in departments other than my own. Too numerous to name here, these—along with several of my colleagues in English and Comparative Literature—have demonstrated an apparently inexhaustible willingness to help me talk this book into being. Without the financial support of an American Council of Learned Societies Fellowship, a Charlotte Newcombe Dissertation Fellowship (and the moral support of a proffered Whiting Fellowship), however, my project would have remained strictly conversational.

My deepest and broadest appreciation goes to Dan, Kate, and Ben Polin, who in their various ways facilitated writing and made life joyful in the process. Dan, in particular, cannot be thanked enough: sensitive reader, syntax unsnarler, superlative co-parent, major breadwinner, and willing target of my pent-up aggression and lasting affection. Kate and Ben teach me daily the strength and abiding pleasure of the maternal bond. Watching their passion for reading and delight in humor supersede my own has been one of the greatest of satisfactions. This book is dedicated to them and to their father.

Portions of this book have been previously published, in slightly or moderately revised form. Many of the ideas and some of the prose of Chapter 1, "The Poetics of Frustration," were first presented in "Women and Humor," *Feminist Studies* 17, no. 3 (Winter 1991). Chapter 3 contains a version of "Rehabilitating Mary Crawford: Mansfield Park and the Relief of 'Throwing Ridicule,'" in *Feminist Nightmares/Women at Odds: Feminism and the Problem of Sisterhood,* ed. Susan Ostrov Weisser and Jennifer Fleischner (New York: New York University Press, 1994). And Chapter 4, "Humor as Daughterly Defense: *Cranford,*" appeared more concisely in *ELH* 59 (1992). All are reprinted here by the permission of the publishers.

ABBREVIATIONS

BG   *A Backward Glance.* By Edith Wharton. New York: Charles Scribner's Sons, 1933.

CP   *Collected Papers.* By Sigmund Freud. Vols. 1–5. New York: Basic Books, 1959.

DT   *Doctor Thorne.* By Anthony Trollope. Oxford: Oxford University Press, 1980.

EC   *Essence of Christianity.* By Ludwig Feuerbach. Translated by George Eliot. New York: Harper and Row, 1957.

EGL   *The Letters of Mrs. Gaskell.* Edited by J. A. V. Chapple and Arthur Pollard. Manchester: Manchester University Press, 1966.

FP   *Framley Parsonage.* By Anthony Trollope. Harmondsworth: Penguin, 1984.

GEL   *The George Eliot Letters.* 8 vols. Edited by Gordon Haight. New Haven: Yale University Press, 1954–78.

JAL   *Jane Austen's Letters to Her Sister Cassandra and Others.* Edited by R. W. Chapman. 2d ed. London: Oxford University Press, 1952.

MP   *Mansfield Park.* By Jane Austen. Harmondsworth: Penguin, 1966.

P   *Persuasion.* By Jane Austen. Edited by R. W. Chapman. New York: Norton, 1958.

PR   *Playing and Reality.* By D. W. Winnicott. Harmondsworth: Penguin, 1980.

SH   *Studies in Hysteria.* By Josef Breuer and Sigmund Freud. New York: Basic Books, n.d.

SMAA   *The Small House at Allington.* By Anthony Trollope. Oxford: Oxford University Press, 1980.

PREFACE

The tongues of mocking wenches are as keen
As is the razor's edge invisible,
Cutting a smaller hair than may be seen;
Above the sense of sense, so sensible
Seemeth their conference, their conceits have wings
Fleeter than arrows, bullets, wind, thought, swifter things.
—*Love's Labour's Lost*, 5.2.256–61

Many years ago I noticed that as I read novels—especially nineteenth-century British novels, for which I had a keen, and still unsatisfied, appetite—I would inscribe the margins with tiny private notations indicating where humor lay. Soon my copies, not only of *Pickwick Papers* and *Vanity Fair* but of *The Heart of Midlothian, Middlemarch,* and *Jane Eyre,* were covered with obscure marginal symbols that threatened to outnumber every other critical marking. Sitting in a graduate seminar perhaps two years after I first became aware of this obsession with signs of humor, I mentioned in a discussion of Jane Austen that I was especially fond of *Mansfield Park* and *Persuasion* because, though less witty than *Pride and Prejudice,* less parodic than *Northanger Abbey,* and less comic than *Emma,* they seemed to me to be the most deeply and devastatingly humorous of Austen's novels. This comment met with puzzled silence. Two of my fellow students—both women—were inclined to agree with me but, like me, found more precise explanation elusive. The rest of the class either sided openly with or appeared to acquiesce in the opinion of one bright and collegial (male) student who suggested that what I probably meant by "humor" was what was then uniformly called "irony" in Austen criticism: in *Pride and Prejudice, Emma,* and *Northanger Abbey* her irony was witty; in the rest of the novels it was simply ironic.

This pronouncement seemed to miss my point. Labeling what was quietly, obliquely, often evasively derisive or subversively funny in Austen's narrative discourse as "irony" struck me as reductive and debilitating. Austen's power to provoke silent laughter—not so much at specific characters (as is generally the case in Scott or Dickens) as at a social structure that her narrative in other ways apparently supported (in contrast, for example, to Thackeray's unrelenting satire)—not only exceeded ironic bounds but, indeed, upon consideration, every standard classification of the comic.

Equally dismaying was to find that the difficulty in naming what was amusing about Austen applied to almost an entire century of (mostly) female novelists who followed her.[1] Classification was particularly problematic in texts where the "humor" was restricted to brief, discrete, often fleeting moments instead of constituting a primary narrative strategy. No traditional category of humor was sufficient to describe, for example, the funny, sexually charged banter of Jane and Mr. Rochester, or to account for the sudden, surprising deflation of the passionate betrothal scene of *The Tenant of Wildfell Hall*—in which the narrating heroine, responding to her future husband's bullying insistence that she admit she loves him, comments: "This was unendurable. I made an effort to rise, but he was kneeling on my dress."[2] Such instances of humor (the latter borders on farce), hidden among the folds of otherwise thoroughly sober novels, have, when noticed at all, received nothing more than perfunctory acknowledgment.

Following the critical path of such readers as Margaret Homans and Mary Poovey, who have investigated other discursive tactics that have similarly gone unidentified and unexplored in women's writing, I have come to think that the humor of nineteenth-century British middle-class women has been largely overlooked because it so seldom fits comfortably into the inherited nomenclature of the comic.[3] From Aristotle to Freud and beyond, theories of humor have been almost exclusively based on examples of humor authored by men.[4] Not surprising, then, however well standard taxonomies—with their rigid, often conflicting, subdivisions into wit, comedy, satire, and so forth—may serve in the study of Scott's, Dickens's, or Thackeray's humor, they generally fail to describe the subtlety and diffuseness of their female contemporaries' humorous practice. Gaskell's *Cranford* is exemplary: in being funny without being a clear case of wit, irony, satire, "high" or "low" comedy, it defies precise placement within the schema by which (masculine) humor is customarily identified, hierarchized, and, in some cases, canonized. Indeed, one might argue that the intercategorical nature of this novel's humor—added to its cultural liability as an ahistorical chronicle of feminine domesticity—is largely responsible for its relatively uncelebrated literary status.

Instead of lobbying for a new category within the established hierarchy of humor to account for the amusing quality of many nineteenth-century women's texts, I want to interrogate existing categories in order to expose the concealed presence of the feminine. My interest, that is, lies not in establishing *generic* boundaries to demarcate "women's" humor from "men's," but in exploring those narrative, rhetorical, and affective tactics that—because of their passivity, indirection, and self-effacement—have been *gendered* feminine in nineteenth-century British culture and have consequently been ignored almost entirely in considerations of humor. Collectively, these tactics comprise a discourse that is both textually and culturally distinctive. Rather, for example, than characterizing the narrative tone of an entire novel (as does Thackeray's penetrating satire or Dickens's vigorous comedy), humor often occurs in Austen, Eliot, the Brontës, and their less illustrious colleagues as an assortment of barely perceptible punctures in the narration—what Bruce Robbins in another context has called "the local transgressive workings of comic rhetoric."[5] Here it furtively undermines both the "authorized" reading of the text and sociocultural values that often are overtly endorsed by the plots. Although highly subversive, such humor is only remotely related to the better-studied carnivalesque, which momentarily overturns the social order in narrative fact or imagination. Its method, rather, reflects its gendered status: it works with extreme subtlety and delicately nuanced gestures to confound the political and affective meaning of the text. Because critics by and large have focused on the ways in which humor reinforces an author's broad political and moral allegiances (Swift's or Pope's satire, for example), this subversive aspect of much of nineteenth-century women's humor, residing as it does in scattered local details, largely has been missed or dismissed.

While the ends to which the writers considered in this study put humor are certainly diverse, their humorous tactics are strikingly similar; what is even more impressive perhaps, given their common nineteenth-century development, is that such tactics are widely employed by other women in other periods and places.[6] These tactics might best be called "feminine" in being associated with traits, behaviors, perspectives, preoccupations, and dispositions that have—with remarkable continuity and integrity—been both historically and cross-culturally constructed as appropriate to or descriptive of women. (It should, of course, be understood that such a discourse is neither *necessarily* employed by women nor is it unavailable to men).[7] Although resisting easy or clear definition, "feminine" humor may be cumulatively distinguished from more widely recognized forms of traditional or "masculine" humor in production and consumption, in form, content, occasion, and psychological function. For instance, rather than conceptualizing humor as the disjunction between the norm and its transgression, as theorists of humor-as-incongruity have done, feminine humor inverts the paradigm by mocking the disproportions and incongruities *within* the (masculinized) norm, the traditional locus of cultural authority, which internalized carries the weight and force of Law. Thus, the humor of *Persuasion,* in protecting Anne Elliot, mocks the implicitly phallocratic notion, dominant in the culture of the text, that agency is deviant when femininely embodied. Moreover, because its production and content are noticeably marked by gender, the audience for such humor is also likely to be gender-marked: to be most appreciated by, and to have special collusive import for, readers whose experiences and resentments resemble those engaged in the humor.[8] Feminine humor in this way functions as a tactic of cultural as well as textual resistance. Although working quietly and locally within a text, it nevertheless participates in a culturally pervasive discourse of gendered protest that, due to prevailing historical conditions, becomes peculiarly audible in the greater nineteenth century. This seems to me especially important to remember when considering canonized writers like Austen who are generally reputed to have "transcended" both their subject matter and their gender in successfully attracting a large male readership. For no matter how "universal" the appeal of Austen, Gaskell, Eliot, and others like them may be, their writing retains the imprint of their feminine experience in a masculine culture.

Subsequent chapters—particularly those in Part I: Theory and Praxis—elaborate and refine the formulation of "feminine humor" that is sketched out here and culturally situated in the Introduction. However, because of the semantic confusion that inevitably arises in any discussion of humor—where "definitions," Dr. Johnson reminds us, are particularly "hazardous"[9]—some preliminary comments are in order.

First of all, I use "humor" generically—as the broadest term possible for what is amusing. Others have sometimes employed "comedy" or "the comic" in this capacity, but since comedy is even heavier with connotations than is humor (whatever else, comedy is also a dramatic or narrative form—the counterpart to tragedy—traditionally culminating in marriage, regeneration, or reintegration), I have decided to opt for the less freighted term.[10] Certainly, humor carries its own particular connotations—of "good humor," of affective rather than intellectual investment—but these, as we shall see, are more compatible with my understanding of how the feminine variety operates. In its least restricted sense, humor signifies both a cognitive, psychological process and its textual product, whereby any sociocultural stimulus capable of interpretation (a statement, an image, a sound) is read bisociationally—that is, with an awareness of at least two conflicting interpretive contexts—and in being so read is found to be both incongruous and amusing. The double awareness required of humor is parallel to that required of irony but affectively different from it. In Chapter 1, I consider the ways in which "feminine humor"—a gender-marked offspring of the parent category—not only differs from certain subcategories of humor as they have customarily been defined (particularly tendentious jokes) but is, in fact, more closely associated with the traditional subcategory of "humor" than we generally acknowledge.[11]

Although feminine humor approximates what might be tonally described as "subtle comic irony," I'm uncomfortable hauling in the idea (and intellectual baggage) of "irony" even with the tempering modifiers. "Irony" is less a concept than a portmanteau term. It refers to both comic and tragic strategies: in the first, it functions as an aggressive, mastering tactic; in the second, as a momentary or sustained recognition of existential dissonance. It encompasses in practice, if not theory, sarcasm and satire as well as a host of otherwise unspecified and not necessarily funny incongruities in life and representation. And it materializes variously as a rhetorical trope, a psychological capacity (as in "a sense of irony"), and a structure of comprehension. Furthermore, it calls forth certain specific associations that I want very much to avoid. As Kierkegaard first noted, irony—at least in the Hegelian sense that has come to dominate—is founded upon a logic of binary distinctions (ideal/real, intention/expression) that not only assumes a universal consensus about the particular value and meaning of such distinctions, but that privileges one term at the expense of the other (ideal over real, intention over expression). Consequently, irony of this sort works through negation to *affirm* the ontological integrity of language, even when words fail adequately to express their meaning: indeed, the disparity between the idea and the word (or between normative and individual action) is what constitutes the "irony."[12] Certainly, what is amusing in Austen is not ironic in this sense (so much less does the term apply to the other authors in this study); and although calling Austen's humor "multi-perspectival irony" would perhaps avoid the unwanted association of simple binarism, it would still fail to address the fact that irony is often not the least bit amusing.

A further problem with the term "irony" is that it is troped, if not gendered, as masculine. In its comic incarnation, irony presumes not only an *alazon* but an *eiron* or figure of disguised authority: an awkward posture for the feminine to maintain in almost any existent culture. Moreover, in seeking to dominate signification, to cancel out or "cut off" all other entertainable meaning, irony might be called not only tyrannous but even oedipal—an association that is further enforced by irony's being, like jokes, structurally triadic (if epistemologically binary), requiring at least theoretically a third party who, devalued by the ironist and listener, is deaf to the ironic utterance. Humor, on the other hand, working by meticulous representation of the cultural text and characterized by a dispersion and fluidity of meaning, offers its female practitioners a more compatible relation to self (the feminine ego being culturally constructed as obedient, dispersed, relational, and renunciative) than does the reinforcement of ego through relatively open revolt that is characteristic of irony.[13] Indeed, one might say that if irony is "masculine," being a direct, negative response to the Law, then "feminine irony"—impeded by the feminine position from active rebellion—can only, as Cordelia famously demonstrated, be expressed as silence. For such reasons as these, I have opted for "humor," despite its limitations, as the term that most nearly accommodates the characteristic subtlety, the intercategorical, polyvalent and gendered nature of the discourse I am intent on describing.

The use of "feminine" requires explanation as well. What may be considered feminine in one culture at one time may not necessarily hold for another at a different moment—though in Western culture, at any rate, the early Greek construction of the feminine has proved to be alarmingly resilient. I use the term to indicate those values and qualities that culture (in this case nineteenth-century British middle-class culture) has deemed to be appropriate to or characteristic of women—qualities like passivity, submission, dutifulness, gratitude, selflessness, maternal feeling, and sympathy. Conversely, I try to reserve "female" to indicate what is actually produced or possessed by *women,* regardless of how feminine or unfeminine such agency might be. I am sorely aware that in calling the discourse I analyze "feminine" I am—despite disclaimers—vulnerable to charges of essentialism. I can only stress that I use the word cautiously, not as a bodily marker but as a theoretical one, to suggest a gender-marked distinction in the humorous affect, rhetoric, and content of the writing I consider. To name such a distinction may be reductionist, but it also bestows a discursive identity upon—and thus brings to cultural consciousness—what might otherwise be sensed as only faint textual muttering. In theory, "feminine" and "maternal" (which are often culturally conflated) are not biologically determined attributes but tropes for indicating gender difference within discourse and—to the extent that such difference constitutes social relations—within culture as well.[14] By this (phallocentric) logic, internalization is a feminine activity, penetration a masculine one; and sympathy—no matter how often performed by men—is psychologically derived from the empathic relation between mother and child. Although nineteenth-century men rarely avail themselves of it, "feminine humor" is, by my definition, open to male users. Indeed, as Chapter 2—"The Feminine Difference: Three Paradigms"—seeks in part to demonstrate, Anthony Trollope and Henry James at least occasionally employ humor that passes for the feminine variety.

Finally, I want to stress that my object of investigation is a particular *discourse* of humor and to do so for two reasons. The first is to distinguish it from humor of plot and humor of character. Although the humor of the narrative discourse may draw upon the jokes or eccentricities of particular characters or contribute to the overall affect of a comic plot, it is, formally speaking, an independent phenomenon, often appearing in texts (like *The Mill on the Floss*) that are otherwise seldom thought to be terribly funny. The second reason is that I want to benefit from the Bakhtinian notion of discourse as a polyphonic expression of many competing textual "voices." In this sense, a femininely humorous narrative discourse occurs simultaneously and in tension with the sober discourse(s) of the text. My intention in part is to disclose how it dialogically qualifies and resists the text's dominant ideological expression.[15]

*   *   *

The three main writers in my study—besides being white, British, middle-class, nineteenth-century women—have all attained more or less canonical status. This common fate, though perhaps not essential to qualify for a study of feminine humor, is nevertheless critical in assessing its power. For if Austen and Eliot especially enjoy a privileged position within English literature that few male authors share and that no other female writers besides Virginia Woolf or the Brontës have come close to achieving, it is in some degree due to their successfully disguising both their "difference" and their differences with their culture. Austen and Eliot, despite the feminist sympathies many recent critics have claimed for them, remain the darlings of Great Books courses everywhere. They do so largely by confining their frustration and resentment (and sometimes even their concern) about such issues as the sociocultural treatment of daughters almost exclusively within the limits of their humor. In this way, humor not only camouflages their attack on cherished nineteenth-century values like female passivity but, by charming its readers, disarms any possible objection to their insurrection as well.

Although Austen is extremely cautious about her subversive activity—her plots are conventionally feminine; her heroines (even the spunky ones), pleasant and unthreatening—her humor nonetheless functions, as we shall see in Chapter 3, to undermine traditional constructions of gender. Passivity, submission, usefulness, and gratitude are deconstructed, so to speak, as "feminine" values in *Mansfield Park,* despite the fact that the heroine herself embodies them. And though Fanny Price may be rewarded for daughterly dutifulness with her husband of choice, such behavior is humorously assailed throughout the novel for being destructive of female selfhood. Similarly, instances of humor in *Persuasion* that explicitly ridicule the cultural overvaluation of romantic love at the very least compromise narrative approval of the Eliot-Wentworth marriage, which so crucially depends upon it.

Gaskell joins Austen in quietly dismantling conventional constructions of femininity but, in addition, experiments with a narrative poetics that reveals the markings of gender. Chapter 4 examines the ways in which the humor of the young female narrator of *Cranford* works to defend her from internalized cultural expectations of daughterly selflessness, while allowing her to retaliate against representatives of cultural authority who embody such expectations—retaliation that occurs most strikingly in the text's language of mutilation. Moreover, the narrative itself, being associatively rather than logically structured, somewhat uncannily recalls the semiotic communication attributed to the infant-mother dyad.

The influence of the maternal likewise pervades *The Mill on the Floss.* On the one hand, longing for the lost mother generates Eliot's plot; on the other, maternally sympathetic humor informs the narrator's relationship to her heroine. Chapter 5 considers the ways in which the narrator's humorous discourse protects Maggie Tulliver from the demands and failures of her environment (in part by reducing parental figures to child status), while offering itself as an interpretive alternative to Maggie's frustrations, so long, that is, as she remains a child. Once she achieves nubility, the narrator's maternal bond to Maggie is severed, and the humor not only ceases to protect her but, indeed, with minor exceptions, ceases altogether. In consequence, Maggie's innate masochistic tendencies—fostered by her culture's insistence upon female selflessness—develop unchecked, eventually becoming the primary affective force of the novel. While this chapter makes the strongest case for the complex relation between masochism and feminine humor (wherein the latter acts as a negotiation of and defense against the former), the discussion of the Wharton/James relationship in Chapter 2 considers how humor itself under a particular set of pressures can become masochistic.

The goals and tactics of feminine humor—notably its subversiveness, diffuseness, and self-deprecation—have much in common with the humor of others who are similarly marginalized (and consequently gendered feminine) in a culture dominated by white, heterosexual, able-bodied, Christian, middle-class masculinity. Indeed, for Kierkegaard, the distinguishing characteristic of the humorist is precisely "feel[ing] for a time like the other."[16] However, without, I hope, treating feminine humor as a restrictive critical category, I limit my discussion in this study to the methods by which gender as an isolated variable—rather than in context with other components of identity such as race, class, religion, ethnicity, or sexuality, with which it culturally occurs—makes its presence felt in humor through its choice of targets, rhetoric, and affects.[17] Because not only most forms of humor but sober expression itself is troped masculine, feminine humor—hiding in the interstices of such expression—is even less likely than other varieties to garner much textual authority. Rarely evoking more than a smile or a smirk, such humor nevertheless allows its practitioners to express what would otherwise be repressed or prohibited. In so doing, it enacts a healthy resistance to the cultural frustrations that provoke it into being—a resistance that, for the most part, has taken place in critical obscurity.

Positioning the Feminine, 1778–1913[1]

Christ was saying something to the people one day, which interested Him very much, and interested them very much; and Mary and his brothers came in the middle of it, and wanted to interrupt Him, and take Him home to dinner, very likely . . . , and He . . . answers, "Who is my mother? and who are my brethren? Whosoever shall do the will of my Father which is in heaven, the same is my brother and sister and mother." But if *we* were to say that, we should be accused of "destroying the family tie," of diminishing the obligation of the home duties . . . If He had said, "Tell them I am engaged at this moment in something very important; that the instruction of the multitude ought to go before any personal ties; that I will remember to come when I have done," no one would have been impressed . . . Christ, if He had been a woman, might have been nothing but a great complainer.

—Florence Nightingale, *Cassandra* (1852)[2]

At the head of this paper I have placed the four categories ["Criminals, Idiots, Women, and Minors"] under which persons are now excluded from many civil, and all political rights in England. They were complacently quoted this year by the *Times* as every way fit and proper exceptions; but yet it has appeared to not a few, that the place assigned to Women among them is hardly any longer suitable. To a woman herself who is aware that she never committed a Crime; who fondly believes that she is not an Idiot; and who is alas! only too sure she is no longer a Minor, there naturally appears some incongruity in placing her, for such important purposes, in an association wherein otherwise she would scarcely be likely to find herself.

—Frances Power Cobbe, "Criminals, Idiots, Women, and Minors" (1868)[3]

In 1882, Margaret Oliphant—critic, essayist, historian, novelist; mother of five and wage-earning mainstay of a dozen or so mostly male relatives—wryly observed that while British culture proudly celebrated the masculine "flood of noble poetry at the meeting-point" of the eighteenth and nineteenth centuries, it was unrepentantly "negligent of . . . the sudden development of purely feminine genius at the same great era."[4] Of course, "female writers have never been wanting," she was quick to add. Even "in the dimmest ages," there had "always been one here and there adding a mild, often a feeble, soprano to the deeper tenor of the concert." Yet, because the cultural antagonism to women's voices rising "to the higher notes" and leading "the strain" had ever been vehement, those voices were fated, if not to silence then to being—in the "flood" of masculine sound—continually drowned out. Nevertheless, and in the midst of the male-identified Romantic Movement, "an entirely feminine strain of the highest character and importance—a branch of art worthy and noble, and in no way inferior, yet quite characteristically feminine" (206)—struggled successfully to be heard, finding its surest expression, Oliphant maintained, not in sublime or ironic poetry but in the domestic novels of Maria Edgeworth, Jane Austen, and Susan Ferrier: each of whom represented "the characteristics of her race [Irish, English, Scottish, respectively] in a manner as *amusing* as it is instructive" (203; my emphasis).

To gender the domestic novel feminine hardly constituted a bold departure from received standards of judgment on Oliphant's part. At least since Aristotle, values, behaviors, and personality traits, qualities of intellect and moral understanding, have regularly been subjected along with physiological characteristics to such binary classification.[5] Indeed, despite the occasional, muted cry of a George Henry Lewes that gender is "a categorization of mental and physical manifestations rather than . . . a biological given,"[6] nineteenth-century England witnessed an escalation and intensification of gendering both in social conduct and in fields of knowledge where social scientists in particular worked diligently to conflate the (female) natural and cultural. Darwin and Freud, to cite only the two most familiar examples, structure their epoch-making thought upon naturalized gender distinctions.

What *is* extraordinary about Oliphant's formulation of the feminine novel is the pride of place it awards to humor. Historically staked out as masculine territory, humor has rarely tolerated even female trespassers, much less claims to possession. Jest books by women in the Elizabethan era, full of phallus-deflating humor, and the bawdy post-Restoration wit of Aphra Behn, Delarivier Manley, and Eliza Haywood are clear evidence that a woman, when given the proper historical moment, could be as licentiously funny as the next man. But such moments have been, until the latter part of the twentieth century, remarkably infrequent in British middle-class culture, and the cost in reputation to the individuals who engaged in public displays of wit or satire, often exceedingly heavy. Furthermore, because both sex and humor have traditionally been identified as masculine activities (the proper feminine position being, in these instances, the passive receptacle or butt), female ribaldry registered as a double violation of gender. Swift and Pope are merely the most famous of the cultural powers who vilified the "female wits" of the late seventeenth and early eighteenth centuries: these gender-crossing women were not only "scandalous" scribblers but, given the *double entendre* of female publication (public woman = prostitute), suspiciously whorish as well. As Robert Gould quipped in *A Satirical Epistle to the Female Author of a Poem called "Sylvia's Revenge"* (1691): "Punk and Poesie agree so pat, / You cannot well be *this,* and not be *that.*"[7]

By the close of the eighteenth century, even this grudging toleration of humor-wielding females had drastically declined. The intellectual and personal freedoms apparently enjoyed by a number of English women writers from the Restoration through the Age of Johnson were abruptly rescinded when threats to the order of things (civil unrest at home, revolution abroad) incited a reactionary rigidification of social codes, conspicuous along gender lines, promoted by the likes of Edmund Burke.[8] Transgressors such as Behn and Manley, once fashionable if risqué, became bywords for female abomination—and remained so long into the present century. As Woolf ruefully notes in *A Room of One's Own,* despite (or, indeed, because of) her "humour, vitality and courage," Behn's reputation cast an ominous shadow on the efforts of women writers for many years to come: "Aphra Behn!" parents would wail to daughters with literary aspirations. "Death would be better!"[9]

Women, however, were not the only ones to find their humorous activity newly regulated. A middle-class, evangelically influenced shift in taste toward politer, more restrained forms of expression resulted in the virtual disappearance of the picaresque and bawdy from both the masculine and feminine sides of the literary landscape by about 1800. Even Fielding and Smollett, those "'robust' masters of the art of fiction," as Oliphant calls them, were no longer "considered suitable for domestic reading"—that is, for consumption by "an ever-increasing audience" that was, in reputation at any rate, becoming disproportionately female. In fact, it was the market for "pure-minded and delicate art" that "call[ed] into being" the feminine novel—a species that "was found to the amazement of all beholders to be capable of delighting and amusing the public without infringing the highest standard of morals" (*Literary History,* 204). Of course, there were male novelists who similarly succeeded in delighting without offense. Richardson was certainly one, although, lacking an active sense of humor, he failed precisely to *amuse* in his presentation of virtue.[10] And Scott was another, interpolating into his historical romances a variety of dim-witted but diverting "humor characters" whose genealogy might be traced to Shakespeare's Pistol and Dogberry. But as Scott himself magnanimously noticed, the greatest innovations in novelistic humor were being achieved by the women: by Edgeworth, whose "rich humour, pathetic tenderness, and admirable tact" he found personally inimitable; by Ferrier, whose "gentle but powerful" satire earned his championship and "generous applause"; and perhaps most of all by Austen, whose "talent for describing the involvement and feelings and characters of ordinary life . . . is to me the most wonderful I ever met with. The Big Bow-wow strain I can do myself like any now going, but the exquisite touch . . . is denied me."[11]

Appreciation like Scott's—together with the cultural demand for comic products more decorous than recent decades had supplied—encouraged some women writers not simply to exercise (with caution) their sense of humor but to develop a form of humorous expression that was, by contemporary social standards, identifiably as well as acceptably feminine. While political satire, comic drama, and the "Big Bow-wow strain" remained off limits to female users for most of the nineteenth century, "scenes of domestic life, treated humorously"—that is, with humor that was sympathetic and restrained, tender and tactful—came to signal "the feminine note in fiction."[12] Oliphant describes the phenomenon in terms that stress the paradoxical—even oxymoronic—nature of its difference: it is "genial humour, satirical yet kind" (*Literary History,* 288); a "mocking love" that takes the heroine "to pieces with an affectionate and caressing hand" (241) and lets "us laugh at her indeed, but tenderly, as we do at the follies of our favourite child" (229); a "keen and smiling derision" (232); a "laughing assault" full of "general fun and tender ridicule" (229); an "amiable contempt" (232). "Derision, "contempt," and "assault"—which are embedded, however unconsciously, in our normative understanding of humor— are here domesticated by modifiers ("tender," "affectionate and caressing") that declare their femininity. For Hazlitt and Freud among others (as I shall later discuss), to modify humor meant to compromise it: subtlety, sympathy, maternal affection weakened humorous pleasure. Humor thus emasculated or effeminized, however, might be safely practiced by women when more virile forms were deemed inappropriate for their use. Affectively sympathetic (though often infused with a trace of bitter sarcasm), rhetorically self-effacing, and intellectually (if covertly) preoccupied with the injuries, inconveniences, and injustices of gender, feminine humor not only offered nineteenth-century women a socially acceptable means of voicing their discontent but, with ironic aptness, employed virtues and wiles traditionally gendered feminine in doing so.

Maria Edgeworth's *The Modern Griselda* (1805) nicely illustrates the point. In spirit a dramatization of her "Essay on the Noble Science of Self-Justification" (1795)—which satirizes female conduct books by advising women to use such assigned traits as weakness, timidity, innocence, and, most of all, silence as argumentative artillery in the battle of the sexes—*The Modern Griselda* is the only one of Edgeworth's novels besides *Castle Rackrent* written without the knowledge and critical oversight of her father.[13] It is an amusing (at moments, hilarious) tale of an upper-middle-class bride who initially gains dominance over her husband by "acting to perfection the part of a dutiful wife"—that is, by passively-aggressively practicing the behaviors of the contemporary model woman (hence, the title).[14] Like the eponymous heroine of Oliphant's *Miss Marjoribanks*, who advertises her commandeering of the paternal household as simply fulfilling "the duty of an only child to devote herself to her father's comfort," Griselda engages in a "species of wilfulness" that for a time passes with her husband, Bolingbroke, as "the strongest proof of her solicitude about his good opinion" (193).[15] Indeed, her "charms of beauty are heightened by the anguish of sensibility" she displays; there is "something so amiable, so flattering to his vanity" in her excessive feeling that he finds it difficult to "complain of the killing pleasure" (187). Expounding a hyper-romanticized doctrine of the marital relation ("true love creates perfect sympathy in taste, and an absolute identity of opinion upon all subjects, physical, metaphysical, moral, political, and economic") and professing herself incapable of reasoning (the feminine realm of love being "far, far above the jurisdiction of reason" [191]), Griselda nevertheless cavils with her husband about everything from the proper pronunciation of the noun "winds" to the quality of basket straw. Like his progenitor in *Richard II*, Bolingbroke eventually rebels against the capricious behavior of his ruler, prompting Griselda to counterattack with the most annoyingly servile submission: "'You have taught me my duty; the duty of a wife is to submit; and submit I hope I shall in future, without reply or reasoning, to your sovereign will and pleasure'" [212]).[16]

In an attempt to escape the constant battle and to remove Griselda from the pernicious influence of her friend Mrs. Nettleby (who preaches that "'a wife must be a tyrant or a slave'" [209]), Bolingbroke takes his wife to the country house of the Granbys, another newly married couple, whose marriage—built upon an "equality of rights" (207)—is narratively presented as blissful. Despite the Granbys' example, Griselda persists in trying to gain power over her husband through femininized means (she cites "scenes in novels and plays" as evidence of their efficacy [258]), eventually alienating him so completely that when she threatens separation in a final attempt to gain his submission, he calls her bluff and agrees to one. The story concludes with two quotations. The first, from Book IX of *Paradise Lost,* addresses the foolishness of "Him who to worth in woman overtrusting / Lets her will rule." The second—from *The Taming of the Shrew,* IV.i, and constituting the final words of Edgeworth's novel—implies not only that any possible marital reconciliation would now depend upon Griselda's subjugation but also that, like Petruchio, Bolingbroke may employ his wife's own tactics against her in such taming, and with greater masculine success.

Reasonably enough, critics have tended in their interpretation of *The Modern Griselda* to be guided by the trajectory of the main plot. For Marilyn Butler, Edgeworth's novel is "a light comedy about a silly wife who wears out her husband's patience"; for Elizabeth Harden, it is a chronicle of "a disintegrating marriage," which begins in "comic absurdity" and ends in "the absurdly tragic."[17] Although both readings note the presence of humor in the tale, neither studies its performance. What makes Griselda's overwrought feminine behavior so funny, I would urge, is not that she fails to achieve the ideal (as humor-in-incongruity proponents might explain it), but rather that she so alarmingly fulfills it. The values she has inculcated—weakness, caprice, hypersensibility, public submission—are laughable, that is, not simply because she misappropriates them as weapons against her natural ruler, but because they possess in early nineteenth-century culture the power and status of feminine *virtue.* Griselda herself is thoroughly ludicrous, of course, and the narrative dwells with manifest pleasure on her antics. Her utter absurdity, however, also functions less obviously (and more subversively) to camouflage the narrator's "amiable contempt" for popular notions of femininity.

Emma Granby, half of the happy couple whose example Bolingbroke tries vainly to impress upon Griselda, participates in the narrative subterfuge. Reasonable, respectful, even-tempered, and sympathetic, Emma exemplifies the sort of feminine traits required of a truly modern Griselda. Indeed, according to Butler, she is "introduced into the action solely to show how a sensible wife behaves."[18] Yet, under cover of her didactic function, Emma harbors other ideas and values that are less identifiably feminine. She insists, for example, that marriage be based upon "mutual sacrifice and mutual compromise" (208) rather than upon a wife's deference to her husband. And her considerable personal appeal has much less to do with her highly praised good sense than it does with the irresistible "magic of her good-humour" (216)—humor that both defends her against Griselda's rancor and charms her own husband into a state of somewhat comical devotion. (When the masons employed to build a new cottage, "by mistake, followed the plan which Mr. Granby proposed, instead of that which Emma had suggested," he not only "desired that it might be pulled down and altered to suit Emma's taste" but impetuously "ran to assist the masons" [227] in doing so.) Although the plot of *The Modern Griselda* may peg it as a cautionary tale, ending with a paean to feminine submission, the wife it softly praises is neither subservient nor humorless. On the contrary, humor is the true Griselda's finest feature, the false Griselda's greatest lack: the latter, indeed, is "afflicted with an absolute incapacity of distinguishing jest from earnest" (219), and some of the funniest moments of the tale address her typically feminine inability to get a joke. Moreover, far from compromising her femininity, Emma's humor—restrained, good-natured, tactful, and tender—actually enhances its expression: aiding her to ease the discomfort of others ("her whole desire was to conciliate" [208]), to exercise her seemingly inexhaustible "powers of pleasing" (217), and to indulge—with the slightest *frisson* of masochistic gratification—her putatively gender-innate capacity for sympathy (for "from sympathy arose the greatest pleasure and pain of her existence" [208]).

* * *

Women are soft, mild, pitiful, and flexible.

—*3 Henry VI*, I.iv.141

Although Jean-Jacques Rousseau was certainly not the first to propose a plan of specifically female education, his notions about how best to rear Sophy had extraordinary, if indirect, influence on the way femininity came to be defined in England during the greater nineteenth century.[19] True, his educational plan was impracticable, by British standards at any rate, and his assertion that "everything that characterizes the fair sex" in a state of civilization "ought to be respected as established by *nature*" bewildering, given that he considered almost everything that characterized *men* in the civilized state to indicate quite the opposite (emphasis added).[20] Nevertheless, it was his articulation (and universalization) of woman as the dependent counterpart of the male subject—naturally, and thus rightfully, "weak and passive"; "gentle" and "timid"; "modest, devoted, retiring"; "made to obey" and "to please"; to endure "patiently the wrong-doing of others" while being "eager to atone for her own"—that bolstered his arch-enemy Burke's similar suppositions about the feminine and that, coming from a political ally, so infuriated Wollstonecraft.[21]

Rousseau's ideal woman lost almost nothing in her translation into English conduct literature and advice manuals. Applicable with variations to either the dutiful daughter or the faithful wife and mother, her virtues ("delicate observation," "taste," "charm," and "self-control"), her duties ("to tend," "to counsel," "to console"), and her constraints (to be "enslaved" to "proprieties" and ever "subjected either to a man or to the judgments of men") not only survived the change of culture but, moreover, thrived hardily for well over a century in a British middle-class environment. Woolf, who was eighteen years of age in 1900, complained with "smiling derision" of the tenacity of the conduct-book model and its suffocating hold on the female psyche:

> I discovered that if I were going to review books I should need to do battle with a certain phantom . . . [:] The Angel in the House . . . It was she who bothered me and wasted my time and so tormented me that at last I killed her . . . She was intensely sympathetic. She was immensely charming. She was utterly unselfish. She excelled in the difficult arts of family life. She sacrificed herself daily. If there was chicken, she took the leg; if there was a draught she sat in it—in short she was so constituted that she never had a mind or a wish of her own, but preferred to sympathize always with the minds and wishes of others.[22]

Although it was hardly his intention that it should do so, there was one trait acknowledged by Rousseau to be acutely feminine that worked to resist the power of the icon Woolf found so menacing. "A woman's real resource is her wit; not that foolish wit which is so greatly admired in society" (335) (to the contrary, "a female wit is a scourge to . . . everybody" and "makes herself ridiculous" (371–2]), "but that wit which is adapted to her condition, *the art of taking advantage of our position and controlling us through our own strength*" (335; my emphasis). For Rousseau, this "pleasant easy wit" (327)—full of "gentleness, tact, and kindness" (370)—was properly employed in "check[ing] the petulant child and restrain[ing] the brutal husband," in making the home an "abode of happiness" (335). Yet, given its undeniably subversive nature, such wit might also be enlisted for less domestically supportive purposes. When combined, for instance, with well-timed "caresses" and "tears," it might enable a woman to gain unofficial authority over her household, "contriving to be ordered to do what she wants" done (370). It might be used not simply to charm and cajole men but to "disconcert" (361) them on occasion, to resist the representation of femininity they tended to promulgate, or, more protectively, to alleviate the frustration provoked by "the strictest and most enduring restraints" (332) culturally imposed upon women by force of gender.[23]

Although this study largely focuses upon the play of feminine humor in nineteenth-century British fiction, the appearance of that humor in the cultural text was equally significant. As Florence Nightingale and Frances Power Cobbe illustrate (in the chapter epigraphs), even tough-minded activists—often historically portrayed as unpleasantly self-righteous or dour—found momentary relief in making fun of the very social conditions that they in other ways labored untiringly to reform. Such mockery satisfied a dual purpose: it acted as psychic balm for the pain associated with chronic feminine constraint and, by disarming its audience, slyly assisted the speaker in voicing her usually suppressed resentment about the gender inequity of both law and custom. Indeed, it may well have been not simply their "inure[ment] to passive submission," as John Stuart Mill memorably argued in presenting an ammendment to the 1867 Reform Bill to extend the vote to women, but their occasional (subversive) indulgence in humorous representation as well that enabled women to bear "grievances" that in other oppressed populations had "provoked revolutions."[24]

Prominent among such grievances were the legal disabilities impressed upon the feminine position. As many recent scholars remind us, the common law in England did not generally recognize a woman as an independent subject.[25] If married, her political and economic rights were supposedly "covered" under those of her husband (*feme couvert*); if single (*feme sole*), her interests were by custom, if not always by law, superintended by her father or family. Of the host of gender discriminatory laws and practices that prevailed in England through the end of the nineteenth century, no two occasioned more outcry than the exclusion of women from the expanding franchise or the inability of married women to own property. As Cobbe observed with a note of amused scorn, for women to be thus legally classed among minors, criminals, and idiots was not simply irrational: it was laughable; and presenting its humor may have helped, if only briefly, to withstand the insult and injury. One would think, Oliphant mused in a similar vein, that men could afford to be generous to women in their desire for more equitable treatment, considering "the strong sense of superiority which exists in the male bosom from the age of two upwards."[26] Yet despite such unassailable self-regard, men continued to refuse women the parliamentary vote until 1918, arguing in one stunningly illogical instance that spinsters ought to be denied because they had failed "to please or attract" mates. Perhaps, Oliphant facetiously suggested, such "men who feel their own notice to be heaven for a woman" might wish to consider the vote as a "trifling compensation" or "poor salve to the mortification of the unmarried" (243). Elizabeth Gaskell, likewise irritated by the gender bias of the law, found a measure of relief in genially mocking it. Citing the dilemma of the Marshalsea turnkey who wanted to secure an inheritance to Little Dorrit but found the legal obstacles too daunting ("'If they wish to come over her, how then can you legally tie it up' &c."?), Gaskell grumbled that the proposed Married Women's Property Act would not likely "do much good" since "a husband can coax, wheedle, beat or tyrannize his wife out of something and no law whatever will help this that I can see." "However," she continued, because "our sex is badly enough used and legislated *against*, . . . I'll sign [a petition in favor of the Act]," playfully added in parenthetical imitation of one of her tyrannized wives: "(Mr Gaskell [now] begs Mr Fox to draw up a bill for the protection of *husbands* against wives who will spend all their earnings)."[27]

Recourse to humor not only gave muted expression to frustration with women's legal "selflessness," but it helped to make other aspects of nineteenth-century femininity—its insistence on marriageability as the primary criterion of female value, for instance—more bearable as well. Although George Eliot (whose heroines are remembered at least as much for their great beauty as for their intelligence) narratively engaged perhaps in wishful thinking, she epistolarily made fun of her own meager physical attractions. Reflecting upon her meeting with Richard Strauss, whose *Das Leben Jesu* she had translated, Eliot reported that "it was rather melancholy. Strauss looks so strange and cast-down, and my deficient German prevented us from learning more of each other than our exterior, which in the case of both would have been better left to imagination." Nor was George Henry Lewes much to look at, she acknowledged, amusingly applying the standards of beauty to which women were implacably held to a member of the master sex: "He is older than I am, not at all full of wealth or beauty but very full indeed of literature and physiology and zoology and other invisible endowments, which happily [as in her case as well proved to] have their market value."[28]

Age, too, was a gendermarked value, generally determining a woman's desirability at least as much as her beauty or wealth. Austen, who for her sister Cassandra's sympathetic amusement frequently cast herself in letters as the victim of specifically feminine fortune (bemoaning the difficulties of a woman traveler or the tedium of social calls), found herself at the age of thirty-eight to have suddenly acquired matronly status—and coped with the shock by making a joke of it: "By the bye, as I must leave off being young, I find many Douceurs in being a sort of Chaperon for I am put on the Sofa near the Fire & can drink as much wine as I like."[29] Harriet Martineau, on the other hand, turned the disability of age itself, together with the duty of moral example, to feminine advantage. "I am told," she remarked, that the campaign for the repeal of the Contagious Diseases Acts "is discreditable work for woman, especially for an *old* woman. But it has always been esteemed our especial function as women, to mount guard over society and social life,—the spring of national existence, and to keep them pure; and who so fit as an old woman?"[30]

Even well-founded fears particular to the female condition could be partially allayed by a timely dose of humor. Virtually all of Austen's letters to Cassandra were written while one of them was visiting at the home of a brother: "visiting" that often entailed household managing during the months surrounding the birth of one of twenty-four nephews and nieces; visiting that, sadly, was more than once prolonged by the death of the newborn's mother. (As Oliphant drily remarked more than half a century later, maternity "perpetually exposed" women of all classes "to dangers as great as those of an army in active service.")[31] When we consider that three of her sisters-in-law died from complications of childbirth, it is small wonder that Austen occasionally used humor to distance herself from the experience, to defend herself from the anxiety it presumably aroused, however shockingly inappropriate—as in her infamous comment about her neighbor's stillbirth—such humor may sometimes seem: "Mrs. Hall, of Sherborne, was brought to bed yesterday of a dead child, some weeks before she expected, owing to a fright. I suppose she happened unawares to look at her husband" (*JAL*, 24).

Together with an alertness to peculiarly feminine social conditions and an inclination to disarming self-deprecation, the most striking common feature of the humor that surfaces in the letters and essays of these nineteenth-century middle-class women is the delight it concocts from the often deadening routines and duties of "women's sphere": observing the intricate workings out of social relations, chronicling the minutiae of domesticity, or otherwise dwelling with fondness upon the culturally trivialized and demeaned. Jane Welsh Carlyle, whose literary reputation is based strictly on her epistolary achievement, habitually related the events of a day at home or an evening out so as to transform even a headache or dull company into an opportunity for amusement. Austen, too, relentlessly mined the diurnal in her efforts to entertain, producing a bit of diversion for family and friends from a weather report, a country ball, or a shopping expedition. (References to her work are exceedingly rare and even then barely noticeable in the sea of gossip.) When the matter itself looked unpromising, rhetorical ingenuity in conveying it could prove effective. Thus, Austen, exploiting apophasis and zeugma, creates not only the following witty nonsense, but an imaginative alternative reading of an otherwise tedious feminine script:

> I am glad you are so well and wish everybody else were equally so. —I will not say that your Mulberry trees are dead, but I am afraid they are not alive. We shall have pease soon—I mean to have them with a couple of Ducks from Wood Barn & Maria Middleton towards the end of next week. (*JAL,* 285)

It is ultimately this embrace of the culturally feminine that distinguishes a strain of humor produced by these women and others like them from more commonly studied varieties. Rather than contesting the contemporary articulation of femininity as dutifully familial, happily self-denying, quietly pleasing, and instinctively maternal, their humor scrupulously reproduces such traits in its own domestic content, demure rhetoric, and most significantly, I think, sympathetic affect. For, contrary to most forms of humor, which demand the strictest emotional distance between the humorist and his victim, the humor of these women consoles the suffering self (or, as we shall see in subsequent chapters, a heroine affectively linked to the narrator), soliciting readerly empathy for her in the process. In thus appropriating the cultural construction of femininity for its own purposes, their humor accomplishes what could not have been achieved by either satiric attack or sober means: it coyly contrives to undermine the authority of that construction even as it faithfully records the conditions, virtues, and behaviors required of life in the feminine position.

PART ONE

Theory and Praxis

ONE

The Poetics of Feminine Humor

She sighed and put a tooth on her under-lip. The gift of humorous fancy is in women fenced round with forbidding placards; they have to choke it; if they perceive a piece of humour, . . . they have to blindfold the mind's eye. They are society's hard-drilled soldiery. Prussians that must both march and think in step. It is for the advantage of the civilized world, if you like, since men have decreed it, or matrons have so read the decree; but . . . haply an uncorrected insurgent of the sex mature[s] here and there.

— George Meredith, *The Egoist* (1879)[1]

Like feminine virility, the notion of feminine humor suggests in the normative discourse of our culture a contradiction in terms. Historically considered a masculine enterprise, humor—either as a general rubric for the amusing or as a subcategory of the same—does not, even in the present theoretically sophisticated climate of literary studies, offer itself up willingly or easily to a feminine reading. But if we can successfully resist the urge to taxonomize humorous practices and attend instead to their discursive gestures and preoccupations—to the repeated occurrence within a text of particular rhetorical tactics, psychological affects, and cultural targets—we may begin to distinguish within humor the subtle, though nonetheless indelible, inscription of the feminine.[2]

The success of such detective work depends in large part on the cooperation of the material. Fortunately, however, if, as G. K. Chesterton once declared, "the novel of the nineteenth century [is] female, as fully as the novel of the eighteenth century [is] male,"[3] then our chance of apprehending feminine humor within its precincts is promising. This chapter investigates two principal areas—rhetoric and affect—where humor exhibits its femininity. In some cases, behaviors culturally attributed to British women of the middle-classes (such as self-denial and submission) become targets of narrative mockery. In others, they constitute features of the rhetoric itself, yielding a humor that is in form quietly pleasing, seemingly passive, and modestly self-effacing. In others still, femininely associated traits like sympathy and maternal feeling contribute both to the affect of humor and to a rationale for its alternative construction. Humor thus saturated in the feminine runs a dual risk: of being ignored, on the one hand, and of being pathologized, on the other, as such femininely gendered forms of expression as hysteria and masochism have notably been. Yet, as the final section of this discussion of a poetics of feminine humor underscores, despite the cultural perversity of hysteria and masochism, they share with my subject a common set of goals and a surprisingly similar grammar. Indeed, in complex if ultimately affectively different ways, all three may be said to speak the same discourse.

HUMOR AND RHETORIC

I am at a loss to understand why people hold Miss Austen's novels at so high a rate, which seem to me vulgar in tone, sterile in artistic invention, imprisoned in the wretched conventions of English society, without genius, wit, or knowledge of the world. Never was life so pinched and narrow. The one problem in the mind of the writer . . . is marriageableness . . . Suicide is more respectable.

—Ralph Waldo Emerson (1861)[4]

To me [her] prose is unreadable . . . Every time I read "Pride and Prejudice" I want to dig her up and hit her over the skull with her own shin-bone . . . It seems a great pity to me that they allowed her to die a natural death!

—Mark Twain (1909; 1898)[5]

Although national bias may well have entered the equation, the dislike Emerson and Twain felt for Austen resulted largely, I suspect, from her highly gendered difference. To the Transcendentalist Emerson, her concerns must have appeared hopelessly material, her subjects tiresomely domestic. When she did not actively offend him with her accounts of social calls and marriage proposals, she simply bored him, one supposes, past tolerance. Twain, proudly the less genteel of the two, presumably found his encounters with Austen even more excruciating. The exquisite delicacy and ladylike discretion of her amusing prose apparently rendered it "unreadable" to his crude, extravagant, magnifying sensibility, which took such obvious delight in phallic inflation.[6]

Appreciating feminine humor depends in great part on the deceptively simple task of locating it. Generally avoiding the popular haunts of the comic, it is seldom found mocking type characters (like the officious, busybody Mrs. Nosebag or the "virago" Mrs. Mucklewrath of *Waverley*) or making fun at the expense of social inferiors (as Scott does in the case of the ploughman Cuddie and his mother, Mause, in *Old Mortality*). Nor does it expend much effort in developing characters whose strongest rationale for narrative existence is their unwitting ability to amuse. *Little Dorrit,* for example (though almost any of Dickens's novels would illustrate the point equally well), is crowded with such "humor characters": the inane Sparkler; the soft-hearted, soft-headed Plornish; and the many Barnacles attached to the Circumlocution Office, to cite only a few. Even Pancks, though an important engine of the plot, is most memorable for his alarming wheezes and whistles, his tugboat tooting of the Benevolent Patriarch—as Flora Casby is for her dizzying, preconscious ramblings.

Feminine humor, rather, tends to hide behind the stereotypes it meticulously reproduces, foregrounding them so as to expose them as risible and, in so doing, to weaken their cultural and psychic authority. The "dutiful daughter"—typified by Fanny Price—is perhaps the most frequent target of this sort of guerilla attack. Austen ever so slyly mocks her—as do Burney and Ferrier, Gaskell and Eliot—whereas Oliphant in *Miss Marjoribanks,* with obvious enjoyment, transforms her very dutifulness into an effective instrument of revenge. Similarly, feminine selflessness is (briefly) appropriated as a tactic of subversion by Edgeworth's Griselda Bolingbroke, while Trollope's Griselda Grantly demonstrates that the perfect realization of the cultural ideal of feminine beauty and comportment is bloodless, automatous, and ultimately chilling. The young Maggie Tulliver delightfully confutes the platitude of female intellectual inferiority, and Lady Juliana in Ferrier's *Marriage* illustrates even more caustically than Maria Bertram the disastrous consequences of an education tailored exclusively to the marriage market.

In thus stealthily assaulting the reigning ideological construction of "woman," feminine humor not only betrays a decided preference for certain narrative and rhetorical tactics but a conspicuous avoidance of others. Ribaldry is as alien to it as it is to other nineteenth-century humorous practices, but so too is comic absurdity whether of the physical variety employed by Thomas Peacock in the first of the following passages, or of the linguistically ludic sort in which Dickens indulges in the second:

> Mr. Flosky, familiar as he was with ghosts, was not prepared for this apparition, and made the best of his way out at the opposite door. Mrs. Hilary and Marionetta followed, screaming. The Honourable Mr. Listless, by two turns of his body, rolled first off the sofa and then under it. The Reverend Mr. Larynx leaped up and fled with so much precipita-

tion, that he overturned the table on the foot of Mr. Glowry. Mr. Glowry roared with pain in the ear of Mr. Toobad. Mr. Toobad's alarm so bewildered his senses that, missing the door, he threw up one of the windows, jumped out in his panic, and plunged over head and ears in the moat.[7]

So grey, so slow, so quiet, so impassionate, so very bumpy in the head, Patriarch was the word for him . . . "Oh! why, with that head, is he not a benefactor to his species! Oh! why, with that head, is he not a father to the orphan and a friend to the friendless!" With that head, however, he remained old Christopher Casby, proclaimed by common report rich in house property; and with that head, he now sat in his silent parlour. Indeed it would be the height of unreason to expect him to be sitting there without that head.[8]

Nor does satire—at least in concentrated form or in prodigious quantities—occur with any regularity. The comprehensive, panoramic cynicism of a *Vanity Fair,* for instance, is too pronounced and transparent, so to speak, for the veiled tactics common to feminine humor to replicate. Even Becky Sharp, perhaps the most famous comic heroine of the nineteenth century, is, despite her sex, a decidedly masculine humorist. Not only is she devoted to ridicule and devoid of sympathy, but her enormously amusing, more than slightly sadistic, mimicry plays in scene after scene to a group of almost exclusively male admirers. Certainly, feminine humor is often satirically as well as ironically inflected (Austen's novels provide ample examples); it refrains, however, from pervasive satiric engagement even of Peacock's relatively good-natured sort. Instead, feminine humor works inconspicuously, as in *Mansfield Park,* to unsay its sober expression, locally undermining the overt ideology of the text, which, reinforced by the plot, favors Sir Thomas's politics and ethics.

The alterations feminine humor makes to narrative conventions also tend to be subtle and at least apparently unthreatening: when it assists in decentering marriage as the authorizing textual principle (as in *Cranford* or Sarah Orne Jewett's *Country of the Pointed Firs*), it does so without openly challenging the authority of culturally dominant oedipal narrative, which almost always culminates in the heroine's erotic and economic transformation from daughter to wife.[9] Moreover, while both genders appropriate and violate narrative *topoi* for comic effect, feminine humorists tend to gravitate toward literary forms generally shunned by their fellows. The nursery rhyme evocation of the opening passage of *Wives and Daughters* proclaims the novel outside the realistic tradition of "serious" fiction, while at the same time insisting upon its literary origins:

To begin with the old rigmarole of childhood. In a country there was a shire, and in that shire there was a town, and in that town there was a house, and in that house there was a room, and in that room there was a bed, and in that bed there lay a little girl; wide awake and longing to get up, but not daring to do so for fear of the unseen power in the next room.[10]

Similarly, fairy tales—which inform the content and closure of most narratives of the period—are openly exploited by writers like Gaskell, Brontë, and Austen for humorous purposes. The general narrative approval of Rochester's prowess in *Jane Eyre* is lampooned by inversion of the damsel-in-distress convention, even as early as chapter 12, wherein Jane rescues her "master" after his fall from a "tall steed": that is, after he's been knocked off his high horse.[11] The Cinderella intertext of *Mansfield Park* and *Persuasion* (both heroines come equipped with the right number of unsympathetic female relations who must be passively thwarted in order for the heroines to marry and thereby be rescued from household unhappiness) mocks the archetype in mimicking it, drawing attention to the factitiousness not only of the model but of the cultural script and its ideal of feminine submission, upon which that model is based. For the reward of femininely virtuous behavior in life is never Prince Charming (not even Edmund or Wentworth can compete), and experience tells us that a middle-class woman's domestic responsibilities—even with the help of servants—are more likely to be increased than relieved by her marriage.

The femininely humorous exploitation of fairy tales works also to revise the family romance that pervades nineteenth-century British narrative. Fairy tales—in which parental figures (fathers primarily) are customarily royal, powerful, and loving, stepmothers cruel and sometimes murderous—make explicit the complex process of parental idealization and devaluation that has come to be a hallmark of that narrative: Dickens, perhaps, provides the richest example. But whereas such "object-splitting" as characterizes the family romance is soberly maintained in *Oliver Twist,* for example, it is mockingly modulated in *Mansfield Park* and Ferrier's *Marriage,* where the fairy-tale origins of the romance are exuberantly pronounced.[12] Furthermore, by insisting on its fantastic origins, the feminine permutation of family romance also hints at the "unnatural" or cultural origins of actual, less idealized family power relations. According to Freud, family romance is founded in nostalgia; it is "an expression of the child's longing for the happy vanished days when *his* father seemed to *him* the noblest and strongest of men and *his* mother the dearest and loveliest of women" (emphasis added). Feminine departures from the form, however, seek not to recapture an imagined golden past but to fantasize a future script in which women are not necessarily doomed either to hopelessly overidealized or disparaged roles. Thus, in *Emma* and *Mansfield Park,* the heroine, although perhaps wishing to marry a younger, spruced-up version of her father, actually marries her *brother*-in-law, whose control over her is decreased by the greater symmetry of their relations to the father.[13] In *Cranford,* Gaskell expunges (masculine) family romance and its limited opportunities for feminine agency by creating a world without parents, men, or active sexual desire (and almost without idealization). Even Eliot, although her alterations in *The Mill on the Floss* ultimately have tragic rather than comic results, seeks to revise the romance rather than simply to reiterate it, narratively belittling the Tullivers through humor yet refusing to provide Maggie with idealized parental substitutes—no matter how much Maggie herself may yearn for them. Such feminine revisions of family romance resemble in purpose and performance feminine revisions not only of "masculine" humor but also of traditional novelistic closure, which, as others have noted, resist, where they do not excise, marriage and regeneration.[14]

This *referential* aspect of feminine humor—its pointed manipulations of well-established literary conventions and narrative strategies—has, in addition, a more specific intertextual component. "Boz" figures as centrally in *Cranford* as Dickens did in its editorial production, and Ruskin's "Lamp of sacrifice," carried by "Woman the Reconciler, . . . Inspirer and Consoler," is mockingly taken up in Margaret Oliphant's *Miss Marjoribanks* (384). The female characters of Emily Eden's *The Semi-Attached Couple* freely advise each other to read "Miss Austen's novels," while one of her protagonists—the witty, langorous Ernest Beaufort—unmistakenly anticipates Lord Goring of Oscar Wilde's *An Ideal Husband* (even as he lends his Christian name to the latter's most famous creation).[15] Moreover, feminine humor engages in onomastic recycling: Austen enlists *Evelina*'s rakish Willoughby as Marianne's callous, untrustworthy suitor in *Sense and Sensibility;* the resignation of a governess called Miss Eyre initiates the narrative action of *Wives and Daughters;* a curate named Wentworth (such is Captain Wentworth's brother in *Persuasion*) is the hero of Oliphant's *The Perpetual Curate;* Maggie and Tom Tulliver are prefigured in Maggie and Edward Browne of Gaskell's *The Moorland Cottage;*[16] and Mrs. Smith in *Persuasion* (who defends gossip on epistemological as well as diversionary grounds) is echoed in Mary Smith, the narrator of *Cranford,* whose narrative—as well as the eponymous community—is based on an economy of associative and speculative exchange. Such allusiveness differs in kind from Peacock's, Thackeray's, Dickens's, and generally from Trollope's (who, though practiced in both feminine and masculine styles, prefers the latter). In feminine humor, the reference itself, founded in playful homage and sympathy of shared purpose, constitutes the joke rather than signaling an opportunity for the aggressive humor of name calling: as it does in *Nightmare Abbey*'s Misters Sackbut (Southey) and Cypress (Byron), Dr. Pessimist Anticant (Carlyle) and Mr. Popular Sentiment (Dickens) of *The Warden,* or the "Count of Pumpernickel" and the like who populate Thackeray's political humor and Dickens's *Sketches by Boz.*

Frequently the relation between feminine humor and narrative structure differs from the norm as well. Whereas the humor in even a strategically complex Dickens novel like *Little Dorrit* tends to operate independently of (or subordinately to) its overarching narrative design, to leave undisturbed the trajectory of its oedipal plot, the humor in *Cranford* essentially informs that novel's different narrative structuring.[17] Its humor, that is, operates through and inheres in its gossip: a form of discourse that, unlike "narrative" or "humor," is culturally identified as feminine. Not only does gossip thematically infiltrate *Cranford,* along with a number of other mostly woman-authored nineteenth-century novels (conversational speculation being the ruling principle in Cranford and *Emma*'s Highbury, as well as a force to be reckoned with in the environs of Middlemarch). But its relational, intimate flow governs the narrative movement of Gaskell's novel as well. Though circulating, like humor, outside the boundaries of official discourse, gossip has constitutive power: it creates an unauthorized but nonetheless authoritative narrative community whose very existence challenges the traditional social order (even the Cadwalladers' gossip in *Middlemarch* unwittingly serves this function).[18]

Syntactically, feminine humor occurs most often undercover: in self-effacing tropes and faint discursive patterns that work to conceal its existence. Unlike masculinized humor, which is normative and can therefore announce its presence with impunity (through hyperbole, for example, as Twain demonstrates in the epigraph), feminine humor invests in forms of representation—such as litotes, apophasis, and meiosis—that permit expression while at the same time guarding against its widespread disclosure. Hence, the humor of *Little Dorrit,* for example, inclines to neologism (the Circumlocution Office), synecdoche (the Bosom), personification ("Society"), allegory (Nobody, Bar, Bishop), metaphor and repetition: the recurring image of the "universal stare," which along with that of the prison (suggesting Bentham's, and now more famously Foucault's, Panopticon), dominates the narrative. The humor of *Cranford*, conversely, works by polysemy (the multiple, ambivalent significance of "Amazons") and by metonymy, metalepsis, and association (the patterns of disfigurement and transvestism that figure so substantially and yet almost invisibly in the humor of *Cranford* are thus cooperatively produced). Feminine humor, indeed, seems positively to resist tropes—like hyperbole and metaphor—that are culturally marked as masculine or to refigure them so as to express gender difference.[19] Apparently for reasons of discretion, it favors italics and dashes over exclamation points to signal its presence, and subjunctive constructions and periphrasis to occlude it: the narrative humor against Sir Thomas Bertram in *Mansfield Park*, for instance, is almost always periphrastically couched. As Nancy Walker and Zita Dresner have noted, the cultural constraints imposed upon the rhetoric of women's humor have often made it seem "more gentle and genteel" than men's, "more interested in sympathy than ridicule." Yet, such rhetoric has also had the persona-protective effect of concealing the aggression behind the humor, "thereby minimizing the risks involved in challenging the status quo."[20] For similar reasons, feminine humor is customarily dispersed throughout a text rather than gathering too forcefully in any one locality. It is as a consequence of working through such quiet, unassuming rhetorical gestures as these (which cumulatively form a palimpsest of sorts) that feminine humor has historically been able to influence the tone of the novels in which it occurs, even while remaining for the most part undetected.

Humor and Affect

Humor is thinking in jest while feeling in earnest.

—George Eliot

. . . the craving one has after the lost mother.

—Elizabeth Gaskell[21]

Although humor comprises, for both genders, a complex set of defensive and aggressive strategies, its defensive function is peculiarly acute for those occupying a culturally feminine position. Circumventing ideological injunctions against the verbalization of female discontent, it provides alternative expression for frustration and resentment, even as it works intrapsychically to defend against cultural expectations of femininity. In so doing, humor revises the standard feminine cultural plot: rather, that is, than silently suffering the melodramatic or tragic fate of the powerless victim, the feminine humorist fictively recasts herself as comic heroine, withstanding life's assaults and occasionally triumphing over them.

To stress the defensive component of feminine humor is not, however, to argue that such humor is devoid of aggression: only that the aggression that generates it is more fully sublimated, or at least more thoroughly disguised, than the hostile impulse sparking (for example) what Freud has termed "tendentious" humor. In *Jokes and Their Relation to the Unconscious* (1905), Freud distinguishes tendentious jokes from "innocent" ones by the degree to which they display the tendency or impulse that motivates them—an impulse that is always either hostile (aggressive usually against a racial or ethnic other) or obscene (aggressive against a sexual—that is, female or feminized—other). Because "innocent" jokes lack obvious hostility and therefore the humorous energy into which that hostility could— through the joking process—be converted, Freud finds them to be less funny than tendentious ones:

> The pleasurable effect of innocent jokes is as a rule a moderate one; a clear sense of satisfaction, a slight smile, is as a rule all it can achieve in its hearers . . . A non-tendentious joke scarcely ever achieves the sudden burst of laughter which makes tendentious ones so irresistible. Since the technique of both can be the same, a suspicion may be aroused in us that tendentious jokes, by virtue of their purpose, must have sources of pleasure at their disposal to which innocent jokes have no access.[22]

In other words, the virile energy of tendentious jokes—which Freud variously describes as satiric, sadistic, aggressive, and aggressively sexual—culturally inscribes them as "masculine" just as the weakness of "innocent" jokes (their relative passivity, the "moderate" pleasure and "slight smile" they evoke) marks them as feminine.[23]

Although Freud never directly makes the connection himself, the aim of innocent ("feminine") jokes is similar to that of the humorous phenomenon he describes in his 1928 paper entitled simply "Humour." There humorous pleasure is attained when a feeling of pain or powerlessness is replaced in its nascent state by a self-consciously assumed, admittedly fantastic, sense of superiority to the cause of distress: "[T]he essence of humour is that one spares oneself the [unpleasant] affects to which the situation would naturally give rise and dismisses the possibility of such expressions of emotion with a jest" (162). (Or, as Kierkegaard tersely put it nearly a century earlier: in humor, "noncompromise with the world" is achieved by "one's not giving two hoots for it" [426].) While the goal, then, of tendentious jokes is the release of aggression against the other, the aim of humor is the avoidance of pain and distress for the self. Yet, such avoidance, however purely defensive it may seem, has in feminine humor a combative component as well, aimed not at the Other but at the Law—the authority of the "situation"—in relation to which one feels childlike and powerless.[24] Rather, that is, than providing momentary release from social inhibitions as tendentious jokes do, feminine humor functions as a sustained, if diffusive, undercover assault upon the authority of the social order itself. Rather than disparaging otherness in an attempt to establish superiority over it, such humor mocks the cultural construction of femininity in order to reduce its psychological power.

More so than tendentious jokes or other male-identified forms of humor (like irony), feminine humor operates as a negotiatory mechanism. It eases the anxiety that arises in the conflict between aggressive urges and behavioral restraints—a conflict that, not surprisingly, centers for many nineteenth-century middle-class women upon the desire for agency in a culture that insists upon female passivity. And it mediates between the wish to avoid pain and the necessity of submitting to social codes—for example, between disagreeable feelings of subservience and the necessary recognition of female political inferiority. Through a change in expression, such humor recasts the psychic impression of external reality—normally authoritative and determinant—as inconsequential or subordinate, thereby lessening its impact: the power of patriarchy is at least psychologically mitigated when it appears as the object of delicate ridicule. Such a "rejection of the claims of reality and the putting through of the pleasure principle" ("Humour," 163) theoretically locate feminine humor on the border of psychopathology; unlike repression and denial, however, which often exceed "the bounds of mental health," feminine humor simultaneously satisfies psychic needs and the cultural demands with which they are continually in conflict. Its logic—being semiotic and linguistically associative (like that of parapraxes and dreams) rather than binary—permits compromises in feeling and thought that are intolerable to ordinary consciousness because they are morally unacceptable or mutually contradictory (mother as the object of both hatred and love, for example). Arguably, feminine humor—fostering harmony in the psychic economy while subtly disquieting the cultural one—represents the most efficient means of satisfying aggression without risking retaliation, affording a temporary escape from the burdens of reality (as opposed to their psychotic rejection) and just enough release of frustration and relaxation of conflict to make possible a more or less "healthy" adjustment to the peculiar constraints of nineteenth-century femininity. For in contrast to satire, the announced aim of which is to alter social conditions, feminine humor quietly enables the subject to survive the circumstances at hand.

By maintaining the tension between the incipient displeasure that initiates its existence and the pleasurable form into which it is subsequently transformed, feminine humor negotiates ambivalence in its affective structure as well as in its content and aesthetic form. Such a thorough-going investment in ambivalence enables it to avoid or to remediate primitive object splitting (a psychic arrangement resulting from the failure to achieve sufficient tolerance of ambivalence in relation to an internalized object such as "mother") by incorporating the split within itself. In this way, the humor of *Cranford*—where the kind, gossipy old women who are the focus of that novel are simultaneously figures both of affection and mockery—contains both the "loved" and "hated," "good" and "bad" mother within its compass.

The relationship that feminine humor bears to internal objects extends beyond remediation to homology. Let us return for a moment to Freud's 1928 discussion of humor. According to Freud, who cites an example of "gallows humor" to illustrate his point, the humorist transforms potential pain into pleasure by adopting an (unrealistic) attitude of superiority to the source of possible suffering. Intrapsychically, such an attitude is accomplished when the ego throws its allegiance to the superego (rather than to the id, as it does in tendentious jokes), which in turn assumes "the role of grown-up" or "father" to the ego's "child" and "smiles at the triviality of interests and sufferings which seem so great to it" (163):

> Genetically the super-ego is the heir to the parental agency. It often keeps the ego in strict dependence and still really treats it as the parents, or the father, once treated the child, in its early years. We obtain a dynamic explanation of the humorous attitude, therefore, if we assume that it consists in the humorist's having withdrawn the psychical accent from his ego and having transposed it on to his super-ego. To the super-ego, thus inflated, the ego can appear tiny and all its interests trivial; and, with this new distribution of energy, it may become an easy matter for the super-ego to suppress the ego's possibilities of reacting. (164)

Astonishingly, the superego—"a severe taskmaster" (166) on other occasions—wears in humor a benevolent aspect: it speaks "kindly words of comfort to the intimidated ego" and enables it "to obtain a small yield of pleasure." Rather than representing the internalization of the Law as it normally does, the superego in humor works to protect the ego from "the provocations of reality" (162) and "the traumas of the external world." Although Freud himself attributes this kindly, protective attitude to the interiorization of the *paternal* principle (the superego treats the ego "as the parents, or *the father*, once treated the child, in its early years" [emphasis added]), others have noted that the more likely parent to be thus credited is the mother.[25] For if the superego, indeed, has "its origin in the *parental* agency" (166; emphasis added), then the component of that agency suppressed by Freud—the nonpunitive, non–Law-affiliated aspect of the internalized parental attitude—must, metaphorically speaking, be a maternal one. In feminine humor, which imitates the psychodynamics of Freud's "gallows humor," this rarely considered maternal principle informing the superego is appealed to, and the paternal or "reality" principle, which usually holds sway, is momentarily denied. Denial of reality occurs in other humorous discourses, of course: in one Twain tall tale, for example, a mine explosion "blew [his brother] into the air and he came down again far away from the place where he had been working" and was consequently docked "a half-day's wages . . . for being 'absent from his place of employment.'"[26] The difference is that humor of this sort requires "an economy of pity" for the suffering of the victim, as Freud notes, rather than, as in feminine humor, a sustained sense of protective sympathy.

The temporary abrogation of the Law of the Father that obtains in feminine humor recalls the preoedipal dynamic.[27] In the configuration of the preoedipal, the child inclines to the maternal object, whose protection and nurturance she seeks—even when she is raging against their threatened loss or fearing possible engulfment. Figuratively at least, the relation between mother and child is symbiotic, governed not by the reality principle or symbolic discourse but by the pleasure principle and maternal empathy: the paternal object is not a competing—and rarely an acknowledged—element of the early psychic picture. In feminine humor, this preoedipal mother-child dyad is invoked when "the provocations of reality" threaten the subject with pain and frustration. Helpless to reduce its own distress, the subject "cries" to the internalized empathic mother, who offers relief by denying the claim of the Real and the power of its provocations. Although the provocations themselves (for example, the inferior legal status of women in nineteenth-century England) cannot in fact be avoided, humor can, by invoking this bond with the archaic mother, circumvent the suffering they would otherwise—under the paternal principle—entail.

Feminine humor, then, may be said to be preoedipal in the way that tendentious jokes—in their aggressive and sexual content and triadic configuration—are oedipal. "Generally speaking, a tendentious joke calls for three people: in addition to the one who makes the joke, there must be a second who is taken as the object of the hostile or sexual aggressiveness, and a third in whom the joke's aim of producing pleasure is fulfilled" (*Jokes,* 100]). The object of aggression—a woman, in Freud's paradigm—need not be present in order to arouse the hostility preliminary to humor; indeed, the presence of her body, while it may arouse aggression, is generally an obstacle to humorous expression. Rather, the humorous exchange occurs between two men—an exchange constituted and maintained by the hostility they share toward the female other: "When the first person finds his libidinal impulse inhibited by the woman, he develops a hostile trend against that second person and calls on the originally interfering third person as his ally." The feminine object, that is—exposed, eroticized, and degraded—functions in sexually aggressive jokes as the commodity necessary for male commerce.[28]

By contrast, bonding occurs in feminine humor, not between humorist and auditor but between humorist and victim, with the auditor participating vicariously in their relationship. In the economy of nineteenth-century domestic fiction, such bonding is performed by the narrator and heroine, who share an empathic (as opposed to identificatory) closeness generally unmatched by the narrator/comic hero relationships found in Scott, Thackeray, or Dickens. This humorous alliance, defensively provoked into being by the frustrations of life under the paternal principle, links humorist and victim within a protective mother-child dyad, characterized by a near merging of identity (the dreamy opening scene of *The Mill on the Floss,* which conflates the identities of heroine and narrator and which precedes the humorous narration of Maggie's childish trials, illustrates this point). To the degree that aggression participates in the dynamic—being not a constitutive factor as it is in oedipal jokes—it is directed outward, against "reality," narratively represented by external and internalized figures of authority and by cultural expectations that threaten the integrity of the preoedipal (mother/child, narrator/heroine) bond. It is by making possible the expression of such aggression while maintaining the love and security of maternal union that feminine humor attains a narcissistic triumph over reality.[29]

The dyadic enclosure of humorist and victim, narrator and heroine (and by analogy, humorous text and reader) functions, in D. W. Winnicott's terminology, as "transitional space": an area of creative play, liminal to both psychic and external reality, where the Law is suspended, anxiety is kept at bay, and desire is safely mediated. Significantly, this psychological manifestation of feminine humor as transitional, intersubjective, and relational corresponds to its formal manifestation as "intercategorical": in both cases, the sharp lines of distinction and separateness that generally characterize (masculine) humor—in the oedipal joking relation, in the binarism of irony, and in its will to individuate into wit, comedy, satire, and so on—are blurred. The particular desire mediated in the safety of feminine humor is the longing for the infantile bond with the mother: a bond that, under the usually operative reality regime, has been displaced or "lost." If, as Winnicott argues, all defenses are "organized in relation to anxiety which [is] derived either from instinct tension or from object loss," then humor (the "highest" form of defense [*Jokes,* 233]) works to recover the loss of the protective, nurturing mother just as jokes work to relieve "instinct tension."[30] By recreating the lost bond in the relation between narrator and heroine, feminine humor defends against the pain and disappointment of the original loss (of the preoedipal mother and of the child's early sense of omnipotence, which she represents) and against feelings of powerlessness, fear, anger, and guilt that generally accompany it. For unlike the hero (and Freud's typical son), whose lost union with the mother is largely compensated by his identification with the father as an active, desiring subject, the heroine—be she a Fanny Price or a Maggie Tulliver—is fated figuratively and often literally to be simply a "motherless" object of either male erotic desire or of male erotic neglect.

From one perspective, this longing for the lost mother constitutes the bedrock of nostalgia. Etymologically derived from *nostos* ("return home"), nostalgia enacts a desire for a return to the motherland—the site of one's origins: in the most literal and most figurative sense, the mother and her womb. In the etiological tale of love told by the *comic* Aristophanes in the *Symposium,* the first humans, severed at the navel shortly after creation from the other with whom they had been joined in spherical unity, spend the rest of life trying to relocate that (m)other: "Love [*eros*] is born into every human being; it calls back the halves of our original nature together; it tries to make one out of two and heal the wound of human nature."[31] This congenital, if not innate, yearning to reunite with the lost mother, or at least to cling to her "inner representation" (which is Winnicott's definition of nostalgia), manifests itself in feminine humor as an urge to recreate the infantile conditions in which that "inner representation" had an unmistakable external potency.[32] Rather than characterizing the longing for an idealized father figure, that is, the nostalgia of feminine humor invokes a space of empathic identification in a time before the onset of the Law: "a transient resurrection," as Eliot describes it in *The Lifted Veil*, "into a happier pre-existence."[33]

This empathic identification—the crux of the preoedipal bond with the mother—is represented both thematically and performatively in the humor of the texts considered in this study. *Cranford* perhaps offers the most immediately persuasive case. Its narrative community is suggestively preoedipal, not only in being an entirely female community formed out of domestic relations and steeped in nostalgia but also in being a community devoid of paternity. Thus, even though the Law maintains a present absence in Cranford (ruling, through the Amazons, *in absentia*), it lacks phallic representation. At the same time, desire for the preoedipal connection with the mother is textually incorporated in the humorously associative episodic structure of the novel, which (as I argue in Chapter 3), working by metonymy and tropic analogy rather than by causal logic, adumbrates a lost maternal presence: a site marked by the merging of words and meanings, presence and absence rather than by the binary divisions of the symbolic order.[34]

Even in novels that maintain the normative structure of oedipal narrative (where the heroine submits to her "lawful" status as wife and mother and, in so doing, her own erasure), humor manipulates that structure so as to disturb its ideological underpinnings. An Austen novel may climax in the prospect of marriage, but it is a climax interrupted or "cut off," as in *Emma*, by the narrator's humorous commentary. Rather than run the risk of further idealizing Emma's acceptance of Mr. Knightley's proposal by dramatizing it, the narrator de-idealizes it, so to speak, by merely referring to it, in terms that are at once teasing and deflating: "What did she say?—Just what she ought, of course. A lady always does."[35] In *Mansfield Park*, too, oedipal closure is undermined: the narrative, in having Fanny marry Edmund, who is structurally her brother and functionally her mother, rewards feminine preoedipal desire rather than the oedipal strain, which would have been the affective motive in her marriage to a father substitute like Henry Crawford. Like Mary Smith and Matty Jenkins of *Cranford* and for a limited time Maggie Tulliver and Dorothea Brooke, Fanny Price is a preoedipal heroine, not only in being relatively exempt from eroticization—the eventual fate of daughters in a masculine, heterosexual culture—but, more crucially, in her relation to the maternal, which is thematically enacted in her affection for Edmund and performatively expressed in her bond with the narrator. Significantly, this empathic narrator-heroine bond ruptures in all the novels considered for only two reasons. First, when the heroine, however momentarily, switches her allegiance from the maternal to the paternal principle (as when Fanny Price and Anne Elliot fall for the cultural construction of feminine desire as "high-wrought" and "eternal"), she becomes the target of humorous aggression rather than the object of humorous protection. And second, when the heroine, thrust into the role of love object, is deprived of her identity as a maternally bonded daughter, she is displaced (as Maggie and Dorothea ultimately are) from the circuit of humor altogether.

Humor not only gives shape to the narrator-heroine bond but collaborates in other textual relationships as well. It links the narrator to witty characters—like Mary Crawford, Mrs. Croft, and *Cranford*'s Peter Jenkyns—whose discourse and perceptions are generally less normative than the heroine's and, in so doing, subtly implicates the narrator in their heterodoxy. It participates, moreover, in a twofold fashion in the experience of the feminine double *(Doppelgänger),* which appears in a number of guises in nineteenth-century texts. Humor may result from the incongruity of the characters doubled (Mrs. Norris's doubling of Fanny, for example, is essentially amusing, not frightening). Or it may be a primary form of the double's expression: as it is in the irrepressible laugh of Mary Crawford (who also doubles Fanny) and, more darkly, in Bertha Rochester's maniacal cackles (which eerily echo Jane's tightly constrained wit), as well as in the lewd, hysterical laughter of the hallucinatory "IT" of Gaskell's "The Poor Clare." In a culture where women are gendered as soberly sentimental, feminine laughter—the antithesis, the repressed aspect of sentimentality—represents in a psychological register the speech of the double, the return, so to speak, of the repressed.

Surviving the Feminine: Humor and Pathology

If corporeal agency is thus powerful in man, its tyrannic influence will more frequently cause the misery of the gentler sex. Woman, with her exalted spirtualism, is more forcibly under the control of matter; her sensations are more vivid and acute, her sympathies more irresistible. She is less under the influence of the brain than the uterine system . . . ; in her, a hysteric predisposition is incessantly predominating from the dawn of puberty.
—J. G. Millingen, M.D., *The Passions; or, Mind and Matter* (1848)[36]

My happiness seemed too infinite to be borne, and I wept, even bitterly I wept, from the excess of joy which overpowered me. In this state of almost painful felicity, I continued, till I was summoned to tea.

—Frances Burney, *Evelina* (1778)

Despite its historically persistent feminine associations, sympathy has been on occasion a contested term in the gendering of discourse. David Hume helped to masculinize it when he declared it primary to his psychology of the senses, and Edmund Burke summarily stripped it of all unmanly connotations when he made it the groundwork for his construction of the Sublime. Even John Ruskin, though ever fearful of sympathy's threat to the rule of intellect, distinguished great poetry from the pathetically fallacious sort by its power to arouse the sympathetic passions.[37] Under such conditions of masculine appropriation, however, sympathy has not always proved immediately recognizable. In *A Philosophical Enquiry into the Origin of our Ideas of the Sublime and Beautiful* (1757), for instance, although sympathy still represents the counterpart to rationality and courts both pleasure and pain, it is far less interested there in condolence than in gazing with "delight" upon the "sublime" spectacle of another's suffering—a spectacle whose sublimity is gauged by its manifestation of "violence," "power," "unity," "strength," "size," and other related phallic attributes.[38] Indeed, rather than conveying maternal tenderness and consolation to the suffering victim, sympathy in the service of the Sublime ("real sympathy," according to Burke)—like the humor of tendentious jokes—provides access to libidinal, even sadistic, pleasure ("[W]e delight in seeing things, which so far from doing, our heartiest [conscious] wishes would be to see redressed" [47]).

When subjected to such gender-change operations as Burke's, sympathy becomes discursively and culturally schizophrenic. For while *masculine* excess of sympathy makes possible the highly desirable experience of sublimity—"the strongest emotion which the mind is capable of feeling" (39), produced in the spectator's dreadful attraction to the scene of another's distress—its *feminine* excess is labeled as either hysteria or masochism: in the former, the subject's spectacle of pain speaks her desire; in the latter, her own suffering yields pleasure. Put another way, to the degree that intense sympathy is normalized as masculine, its feminine manifestations are at risk of being pathologized.[39] Yet, as the final pages of this chapter suggest, culturally abnormal behaviors like hysteria, masochism, and feminine humor—all predicated upon intense sympathy with the victim rather than upon the sublime sight of her suffering—not only exist in large part to resist the pathologizing authority but share a stunningly similar array of tactics in their efforts to do so as well.

* * *

Although one might argue that humor, in negotiating stress rather than repressing it, acts simply as "a kind of inhibition of hysteria," the parallels between these two psychic defenses are multiple and complex enough to warrant some elaboration.[40] Indeed, if, by definition, hysteria is characterized by conversion symptoms (by unconsciously revised tropic representations, physically manifested, of otherwise repressed affect), then humor, curiously, qualifies as a form of hysteria—being, through the smiles and laughter that are part of its end result, the bodily expression in converted form of otherwise unspeakable desire. (For not only clinically hysterical symptoms, but as Darwin reminds us somatic responses like smiles and laughter, tears, blushing, and sexual arousal constitute physiological signs of desire.)[41] In contrast to true hysteria, however, humor functions simultaneously as both symptom and its "cure": it is an affective state, but one that also allows its "strangulated affect to find a way out through speech."[42]

Despite its greater success as a strategy of cultural adaptation, humor nevertheless shares many of its motives and methods with hysteria. Like hysteria, it "originates through the repression of an incompatible idea from a motive of defence" (*SH*, 285) but gives derivative, symptomatic expression to that idea and to the painful feeling it generates. Both are founded upon psychic conflict, and the particular signs they utilize, whether bodily or linguistically configured, represent compromise formations between the opposing affects engaged: between desire and its negation, between conscious intention and the "counter-will" (*SH*, 92), between libidinal drives and internalized cultural expectations of feminine conduct. Both, moreover, express this splitting of consciousness in the dissociation between their initiating affects and their ultimate expression through conversion. As in those hysterical conversions in which desire, defending against discovery, somatically tranforms itself into its negation (so that "psychical excitation" [*SH*, 148] becomes "physical pain"), so in humorous conversion, desire—be it longing for the mother or its frustrated expression as rage against her loss—emerges in altered form as the pleasure of the jest. The jest itself, if not its pleasure, also surfaces rather unexpectedly in hysterical conversion: as Freud has noted, there is something undeniably "comic" (*SH*, 179) about a process in which physical symptoms are linguistically generated, in which paralysis becomes a translation of "such phrases as 'not being able to take a single step forward,' 'not having anything to lean upon'" (*SH,* 176). It could be argued, indeed, that hysteria, in its structure and causes, functions as the inverse—the double—of feminine humor: their semantic interdependence is evident both in the laughter we call "hysterical" and in the freak of temperament we call a "humor," which, after all, was once thought to be simply the *affective* manifestation of a bodily fluid. Though its ultimate form may be pathologic, hysteria, like humor, is essentially a way of articulating desire in a culture that restricts its (especially female) expression.

Hysteria etymologically derives, of course, from *hustera* ("womb"), a linguistic fact that has historically marked it as a female malady and hinted at its putative sexual etiology. But one could argue that such an etymological origin actually locates hysteria in a territory prior to sexual desire, the womb being a space of significant preoedipal preoccupation. Elisabeth von R., a hysterical paralytic, was very much attached to her father, Freud tells us, and overly depressed by his death. Yet "at the same time it kindled a lively desire in her that . . . led her to concentrate her whole affection and care on the mother who was still living" (*SH,* 141). Although Monique David-Menard argues from this that Elisabeth's paralysis figuratively speaks her feelings of "impotence" in the masculine position (since her "illness began when she . . . proposed to replace" her dead father "at her mother's side"),[43] Elisabeth's paralysis might as easily be read as speaking her feelings of "helplessness" in reestablishing the lost maternal bond. For if the infant in Freudian theory is the woman's compensation for her lack of a phallus, the substitute object of her desire, then the hysteric's "inability to afford her mother a substitute for the happiness she had lost" (*SH,* 141) constitutes her inability not to *replace* the paternal phallus but to *be* the infant in the mother-child dyad that was the substitute for the mother's missing phallus in the first place.[44] Although to regain the mother-child bond is as hopeless a project as to find the missing phallus, frustrated desire in Elisabeth's case is further vexed by the role reversal occasioned by her mother's chronic illnesses, wherein she maternally "concentrate[s] her whole affection and care" on her childishly dependent mother. Elisabeth's hysteria, in other words, may be construed as an expression less of phallic than of preoedipal longing, a literalization of the conflict between the desire for maternal union and the conscious rejection of that desire. However oedipally libidinized the hysterical conflict may subsequently be (Elisabeth's extends to the forbidden feelings she has for her brother-in-law), its "essence" is found and "played out in the traumatic relation to the maternal" (David-Menard, 14).

Furthermore, not only the content but the form of hysteria betrays the preoedipal essence of its desire. When Elisabeth's body configures phrases of need and dependency such as "unable to take a single step forward," she speaks a prelinguistic—or in Lacanian terms, presymbolic—discourse ("both hysteria and linguistic usage alike draw their material from a common source" [*SH,* 181]) that in its materiality, its literalization of language, and its reliance upon unconscious, empathic communication invokes (as does feminine humor) the maternal, with its promise of protection from the invasive, painful demands of external reality.

*   *   *

The fact that psychic pain is not only a precondition of humor and hysteria but is experienced through conversion as *pleasure* marks both these phenomena, perhaps surprisingly, as masochistic. Although there is much disagreement about the precise significance and proper application of the term *masochism,* there is, as Arnold Cooper notes, more or less general consensus on the existence of a "primary" or "proto-" masochism that—like primary narcissism—is "a necessary and ubiquitous aspect" of psychic life.[45] Indeed, narcissistic and masochistic drives, according to Eleanor Galenson, are *"prerequisite* for the formation of object relations"[46] and "achieve their particular individual character at preoedipal stages of development" (Cooper, 137). This means that, from the earliest stages, love and aggression are psychically intertwined and together inform the construction both of the self and of parental objects. Consequently, masochism—which in its broadest sense may be construed as the capacity to derive pleasure from pain—constitutes at base an adaptive and defensive strategy essential to normal human development: "the issue of pathology is" strictly "one of quantity" (Cooper, 123).

Yet, despite its developmental importance for both genders, masochism—like hysteria, passivity, and narcissism—has historically been encoded as feminine. Distinguishing between characterological or "moral" masochism (the "'need for punishment'") on the one hand and erotogenic or "perverse" masochism on the other, Freud habitually labels the latter "feminine masochism": an anatomically determined "expression of feminine nature"—though not unseen in men—whereby passivity (putatively instinctual in women) takes on an erotogenic character when aggression is turned inward.[47] In the normative male, aggressive "masculine instinctual impulses" (*CP,* 2:200) are aimed outward where they act directly or in sublimated form upon external objects. In the case of Freud's normative female, however, such aggression as exists (being culturally prohibited access to masculine channels of expression) eventually learns to take "the subject itself for an object" (*CP,* 2:261).

Though he insists upon the fundamentally physiological nature of feminine masochism, Freud also hints at another, more psychologically compelling reason for a feminine masochistic urge.[48] Discussing the centrality to masochism of the fantasy of "'a child being beaten'" (*CP,* 2:172ff)— wherein beating functions both as punishment for the daughter's forbidden incestuous wish to be sexually loved by the father and as "the regressive substitute for it" (184)—Freud notes that, in fact, the "first phase of beating-phantasies among girls . . . belong[s] to a very early period of childhood" (178): a period, that is, before they undergo oedipal sexualization. Although it had not then been theoretically formulated as such, this period is, *ipso facto,* preoedipal: dominated not by the image of the father or the phallic representation of reality but by the mother-child bond and the pleasure principle. Fantasies of being devoured and beaten situate masochism at least initially in this preoedipal period, where the maternal reigns and where neither the threat of castration nor guilt for her incestuous wishes but rather "the fear of losing the mother," as Helene Deutsch maintained, constitutes the primary, preoccupying anxiety (244).[49] It is by means of such fantasies, indeed, that masochism—"the strongest of all forms of love" (269) and the "most powerful factor of femininity" (275)— enacts a "return to an infantile form of existence, . . . a profound union with the mother" (254).

Like feminine humor, then, masochism fleetingly recovers the lost "object world of early childhood": a world "represented by the mother," where the child's "instinctual needs" and desires "have passively received gratification" (Deutsch, 243). Because "the shattering disorganizing anxieties" that emerge when this early union with the mother is threatened are too painful to be easily withstood, the child will "if necessary" sacrifice or distort her "aggressive satisfactions" by redirecting them to the self (Cooper, 127). In thus reoccupying the passive position in relation to an active, powerful mother, the masochist—like the humorist—preserves that preoedipal mother as an object both of love and authority. Indeed, the "obvious interpretation" (*CP,* 2:258) of the content of masochistic fantasies "is that the masochist wants to be treated like a little, helpless, dependent child."[50] Furthermore, because the suffering in both instances is "administered by the loved person" (*CP,* 2:262)—the mother—and "endured" for her sake, both dynamics afford an opportunity for narcissistic satisfaction. In each case, the victim defensively accepts a lesser punishment (suffering at the hand of an idealized maternal imago) to avoid a greater one (suffering at the ungratifying hand of the Real). Consequently, from a theoretical standpoint at least, the feminine masochist/humorist suffers less pain than she would in submitting directly to the demands of experience. For masochism treats such culturally mandated passivity and its attendant frustration as a source of pleasure: like hysteria, it functions as a structually "humorous" attempt to derive pleasure from the pain of the feminine position, thus wringing satisfaction from "necessity." Indeed, by embracing the maternal principle and producing pleasure from the prohibition against female aggression, the masochist turns the very idea of punishment into a joke.[51]

It is this maternal displacement of the father as the figure of authority that ultimately distinguishes masochism from sadism and feminine humor from irony. For unlike sadism and irony, which boast a paternal imprimatur, masochism and humor are founded upon a "contractual partnership between the ego and the oral mother," according to Gilles Deleuze—a contract that requires the ego to "disavow" the mother's lack of power under the Law (to deny, that is, that the maternal phallus is missing) and to exalt "the mother-image [to such a degree that it] serves as a mirror to reflect" the ego "as a narcissistic ideal of omnipotence" (Deleuze, 129–31). Simply put, idealization of the mother-image—not identification with the father (which gives irony its authority and sadism its punitive power)—constitutes the informing principle of both feminine humor and masochism.[52]

Yet, despite their remarkable homological and teleological similarities (the "maintenance of object relations" and "self-esteem enhancement" are, as Helen Meyers notes, primary goals of both),[53] significant variations exist between humor and masochism in emphasis as well as more obviously in affect. Suffering, for example, though a necessary condition for pleasure in both dynamics, has in masochism the value of "an unavoidable guilty ransom" for "undeserved pleasures" (Cooper, 120) while in humor it functions as the raw material necessary for humorous conversion—a medium of exchange (in other figures) rather than a cash payment. The disposition of aggression likewise differs. In masochism, aggressive tendencies are "split off," projected onto the "bad" or phallic mother (where they become suffused with narcissistic value) and then are deflected back upon the self.[54] In humor, however, such aggression turned inward is immediately neutralized by the humorous process, which appropriates the aggressive energy to fuel itself. Similarly, while both offer narcissistic gratification, such gratification in humor comes from the loving mother's defense of the suffering self through empathic identification rather than from the libidinization of the punitive mother. For unlike masochism, humor idealizes not just the mother's power but her nurturing aspects as well. As Lucile Dooley has observed, in humor "the child is treated with tenderness even though punished, and is allowed play and even a disguised aggression" against the "bad" mother and the Law she represents. "The humorous play is a demonstration that the child is really loved both in punishment and *in spite of it*" (emphasis added).[55]

Contrary, then, to Freud's notion of the dominance of the paternal superego in the dynamics of humor, the feminine humorist seeks protection from a magnified preoedipal mother-image, with whom she strikes up a temporary, limited contractual agreement—an agreement to deny reality by returning in fantasy to the mother-child dyad. Although such an agreement permits, indeed demands, that some aggression be defensively expended to annul the presence of the father and his representations (for example, internalized cultural notions of femininity), a return to the preoedipal state requires that—without the superego to direct it effectively outward—aggression for the most part redounds upon the self. No matter what the provocation or target of humor, the feminine humorist is always in some sense its victim, bearing as she does the brunt of her own aggression while seeking comfort and protection from a maternal principle that is in the material world relatively powerless. As Edmund Bergler has succinctly summarized, the humorist is little more than "a frightened, masochistic child."[56]

Yet because humor transforms the pain of frustrated aggression into a source of pleasure, it offers its practitioners a real if momentary triumph over lived experience as well, representing perhaps the most successful strategy culturally available to the feminine position for negotiating frustration. It is considerably less masochistic in fact, if not in theory, than hysteria or masochism *per se* or, indeed, than passively suffering the infliction of phallocratic notions of appropriate feminine behavior. Not only is humor as widely recognized a sign of mental health as hysteria and masochism are symptoms of pathology, but it functions as a preventive cure of sorts to those gendermarked maladies. Wryly enough, while hysteria and masochism have traditionally been considered more or less unavoidable features of the nineteenth-century feminine condition, humor—with which they have so much in common—has remained a barely acknowledged aspect of feminine character or literary production.

TWO

Feminine Difference: Three Paradigms

Hers is not humour of the strongest and vividest kind, which awakens the indirect reminiscence of the Infinite through the disproportion of language and imagery to the finite things which they profess to express. It is not the method of Cervantes, magniloquent on trifles, nor of Swift, trifling away magnificence, both of which methods imply a tacit allusion to a common measure, unseen but felt, which equalizes all finite magnitudes by the overwhelming transcendence of its infinity. Her humour is only partial . . .

—Richard Simpson on Jane Austen (1870)[1]

She sympathises with the sufferers, yet she can scarcely be said to be sorry for them; giving them unconsciously a share in her own sense of the covert fun of a scene, and gentle disdain of the possibility that meanness and folly and stupidity could ever really wound any rational creature. The position of mind is essentially feminine . . . [It is] feminine cynicism . . . It is something altogether different from the rude and brutal male quality that bears the same name.

—Margaret Oliphant on Jane Austen (1870)[2]

In his 1819 essay "On Wit and Humour," William Hazlitt emphasizes two necessary conditions for "the laughable." There must, first, be incongruity: a "contrast between the appearance and the reality" or between "the object" that occasions our laughter and "what is customary or desirable" under the circumstances. And, more tellingly, there must be an absence of sympathy: not only do "we burst into laughter from want of sympathy"; we actually derive "amusement from the very rejection of . . . false claims upon our sympathy." Only those "misfortunes in which we are spectators, not sharers," are capable of evoking our laughter; for when we are the victims of misfortune ourselves, "we feel the pain as well, which more than counterbalances the speculative entertainment."[3]

Unmistakably (and probably unwittingly), both Hazlitt and Simpson (quoted in the epigraph) gender humor as masculine. Both, for instance, presume humor, like irony, to be ontologically grounded in binary distinctions in which one term obviously benefits from the degradation of the other, rather than considering the possibility that "what is customary" or customarily "desirable" might itself be a matter for laughter. Simpson, indeed, not only presumes an Ideal against which the humorous is implicitly registered; he idolizes it as well: "a common measure, unseen but felt, which equalizes all finite magnitudes by the overwhelming transcendence of its infinity." Nor does he fail to notice, with affable condescension, Austen's failure to achieve such lofty realms of comic abstraction. Hazlitt, on the other hand, more keenly concerned with the affective aspects of humor than Simpson, dwells at length upon the necessity of indifference to the suffering of the humorous victim: "In what relates to the laughable, . . . the pain, the shame, the mortification, and utter helplessness of situation, add to the joke, provided they are momentary, or overwhelming only to the imagination of the sufferer" (Hazlitt, 11). Should we, however, identify with the sufferer to the degree that we recognize his situation as potentially dangerous or threatening, then the conditions for humor are violated, and "terror supersedes our disposition to mirth" (3).

From this perspective, humor must entail a clear intellectual contrast between the norm and its violation and an affective distinction between the self and the object of laughter. Aggressive, "strong," and "vivid," *real* humor conforms to a "common measure" that is—by both cultural design and trope—unflinchingly masculine. What is more, humor is (for Hazlitt at least) restricted in practice to male users. Although "women, in general, have a quicker perception of any oddity or singularity of character than men," the "surface of their minds, like that of their bodies," is "soft," and, consequently—having "less muscular strength, less power . . . of reason, passion, and imagination"—they are biologically incapacitated from producing humor of a very high order. For if "the intuitive perception of their minds" makes them "susceptible of immediate impulses," it also, in the end, makes them "less disturbed by any abstruse reasonings on causes or consequences," less intellectual in their comic interests and endeavors (168).

Despite their derogatory inflection, Hazlitt's observations on the character of women's humor accord surprisingly neatly with Oliphant's (quoted in the epigraph). Feminine humor (or, in her terms here, "feminine cynicism") is less concerned with "reason, passion, and imagination" than with sympathy—sympathy being undoubtedly a manifestation of feminine softness and susceptibility, if also, in Hazlitt's view, a theoretical impossibility in the humorous situation. Shunning Simpson's "Infinite" or Ideal against which the follies of the Real are held up to ridicule, Oliphant's feminine humor encourages instead a "gentle disdain of the possibility that meanness and folly and stupidity could ever really wound any rational creature," psychologically denying, that is, the power of the Real to inflict pain. Moreover, rather than resisting what Hazlitt sees as the dangerous urge to identify with the humorous victim, the feminine humorist converts such identification into empathy, maternally seeking to protect the victim from suffering by trying to give "unconsciously a share in her own sense of the covert fun of a scene"—or, if this should fail, at least "a sense that nothing is to be done but to look on, to say perhaps now and then a softening word, to make the best of it practically and theoretically, to smile."[4]

According to her near-contemporaries, then, and despite later claims for placing her in the vanguard of the Great Tradition, Austen trafficks in feminine humor.[5] Even *Pride and Prejudice*—perhaps the least sympathetically humorous of her texts,[6] the one that fits most cozily into the eighteenth-century construction of "wit"—sometimes chafes under the (masculinely) ironic reading customarily imposed upon it. Consider, for instance, its famous opening sentence: "It is a truth universally acknowledged, that a single man in possession of a good fortune, must be in want of a wife."[7] Read ironically (according to a binary system of logic) that statement indicates not that wealthy single men are in want of wives but rather that single women desire wealthy husbands. Were the narrator speaking from a position of disguised authority (the masculine position), one might assume, as Austen critics have traditionally done, that the ironic reading would suffice, that the intention of the statement is to affirm the prevailing cultural attitudes regarding the desire of potential "old maids" to marry rich by stating quite nearly the opposite. In method and purpose, irony here is little less than ridicule, which, as Hazlitt suggests, functions as a coercive instrument of the normative:

> Ridicule is necessarily built on certain supposed facts, whether true or false, and on their inconsistency with certain acknowledged maxims, whether right or wrong. It is, therefore, a fair test, if not of philosophical or abstract truth, at least of what is truth according to public opinion, and is hostile to the common sense of *man*kind. (23; emphasis added)

To see that opening line, however, as evidence of feminine humor—as an utterance by a female narrator (one "soft" and sympathetic and culturally unauthorized to speak) and as a gendermarked subversion of "certain acknowledged maxims" rather than a negatively phrased affirmation of them—yields a quite different reading. In this case, not only does the narrator's scrupulous imitation of the aphoristic style and logic of eighteenth-century discourse mock her model (as some "ironic" readings have noted), but her irony is reduced from a comprehensive vision to a rhetorical device.

That is, the ironic trope—that single women seek rich husbands and are laughable in their quest—is appropriated by a gendermarked tactic of humor that both indicts and disguises its indictment of a culture that "universally" (that is, ideologically) believes that rich men in fact *do* require wives to assure the continuance of their bloodlines, names, and fortunes, the protection of their property (especially their female property), and the stability of the social order (based as it is upon inheritance). Indeed, it *desires* single women to desire rich husbands (and rich husbands to desire wives) in order to secure the perpetuity of its own—largely patriarchal—interests.

* * *

However distinctive in content, rhetoric, and affect, feminine humorous discourse, as I have argued in Chapter 1, baffles easy apprehension: what looks to be simply irony from a critically traditional viewpoint looks from a perspective sensitive to gender identity and social context to subvert customary cultural values, including irony itself.[8] My intention in this chapter is to sketch a set of related paradigms designed to focus and frame this most elusive of subjects. The first of these, which juxtaposes differently gendered humorous passages in Burney's *Evelina,* highlights the maternal aspect of Mrs. Selwyn's humor—humor that, like the narrative humorous discourse in *Mansfield Park* and *Persuasion,* protects the heroine from the aggression of those around her, even while it gently mocks her textual status as an object of romantic interest. The second contrasts the discourse of Trollope's male narrator with that of several of his female characters, pointing to the ways in which the humorous self-representation of a Miss Dunstable or a Lucy Robarts functions as a tactic of resistance to her cultural positioning while it defends her (as it does the narrator of *Cranford*) from attendant frustrations. And the final paradigm—which considers the epistolary and narrative humor of Edith Wharton and Henry James (frequently presumed to be almost symbiotically concordant in their interests and sympathies, as Eliot's narrator claims with regard to Maggie and Tom Tulliver)—charts the aggressive and masochistic tendencies that inform their relationship, paying particular attention to the cultural gendering of those tendencies and to their struggle for textual power. My hope here is to situate humor so as best to foreground its generally obscured feminine difference.

CAPTAIN MIRVAN AND MRS. SELWYN

Madame D'Arblay is, on the other hand, quite of the old school, a mere observer of manners, and also a very woman. It is this last circumstance which forms the peculiarity of her writings, and distinguishes them from those masterpieces which I have before mentioned. She is a quick, lively, and accurate observer of persons and things; but she always looks at them with a consciousness of her sex, and in that point of view in which it is the particular business and interest of women to observe them.

—William Hazlitt on Frances Burney[9]

At first glance, Frances Burney—whose undeserved fate has been for most of the past two centuries to be simply the precursor of Jane Austen—is nowhere less like her successor than in her humor. In *Evelina* particularly, her plot, constructed upon the time-honored principles of English dramatic comedy (gross improbabilities, discovered identities, reunions with long-lost relatives, humor characters, exaggerations of theme and gesture), is more reminiscent of Smollett and Fielding than suggestive of Austen, Gaskell, or Eliot. The sheer force of her comic performance, too, resembles that of her forefathers: nothing in Austen nor in any other nineteenth-century British woman writer comes close to the extravagance or malice of those bawdy, cruel practical jokes of Captain Mirvan's, which readers have often found so unsettling.[10]

Still, if we seriously consider Hazlitt's assessment (while ignoring, if we can, his denigration) of Burney as "a very woman"—if we acknowledge, that is, not only the masculine, violent, or disturbing elements of her humor but also those comparatively less memorable elements peculiar "to the consciousness of her sex"—then we may be able to make space for Burney, beside Austen, in the fore of a feminine humorous tradition.[11] In order to do so, I want to leave aside a great many of the humorous discourses in *Evelina*—the satiric treatment of Madame Duval and the aspiring lower-middle-class Branghtons; the dark comedy of the Vauxhall scenes; the tiny, unconscious ironies of the heroine's letters to her guardian—and concentrate on two: the physical, hostile, misogynistic humor of Captain Mirvan and the verbal, defensive, maternally associated humor of Mrs. Selwyn.[12]

The keenest pleasure and primary textual function of Captain Mirvan—masculinist, chauvinist, francophobe—is to be the scourge of Madame Duval, Evelina's shrewish and vulgar maternal grandmother. The "mischief-loving" (403), "unfeeling" (402) Captain, who terrorizes his wife and daughter with his penchant for insults and elaborate practical jokes, finds in Madame Duval's affectations of French manners and girlish dress the ideal target for his laugh-provoking assaults. The chief of these involves his disguising himself as a highwayman, dragging her from her coach, shaking her violently, and then leaving her bound, disheveled, and hysterical in a foul ditch. The disgrace and physical damage she endures on this occasion not only elicit derision from the male servants—some of whom have collaborated in the joke—and "almost compel" Evelina herself "to laugh" (150), but fail to win her readers' sympathy as well, despite the woman's "extreme agitation, and real suffering" (148).

Mirvan's jokes provide compelling evidence for the theory that (masculine) humor is basically a sublimated form of aggression. Although enmity in this case is barely disguised, Mirvan's humor permits him—and his diegetic and reading audiences—to relieve their hostility toward his victim in a psychically and socially acceptable (if still misogynistic, xenophobic, and abusive) fashion: "instead of pitying her," the men observing Madame Duval's brutalization "could only make a jest of her disasters" (151). The affective bond forged in this instance of humor obviously occurs not between the humorist and victim but between Mirvan and his masculine audience(s) in their shared loathing of Madame Duval. Like the woman in Freud's paradigm of the sexual joke, Madame Duval must be physically vilified before a masculine witness for male bonding to occur and the joke to succeed: "'We shall have rare sport,' said the Captain, 'for do you know the old French-woman is among us? 'Fore George, I have scarce made any use of her yet, by reason I have had nobody with me that could enjoy a joke'" (136). What is at least as significant here as the apparently necessary degradation of the female body is the gender eccentricity of Mirvan's victims: like the explicitly foppish, suggestively homosexual Mr. Lovel, who is brutalized by Mirvan's humor in the final scene of the novel, the brazen, flirtatiously postmenopausal Madame Duval provokes Mirvan's abusive treatment in part for threatening the integrity of the cultural feminine.

Although Mrs. Selwyn, Evelina's temporary guardian and mother substitute, also threatens normative notions of femininity, she escapes the severe punishment of her fellow transgressors. Why this should be so is at the crux of Selwyn's importance to the novel and to its development of a feminine discourse of humor. For even though this blue-stocking is introduced by Evelina in rather contemptuous terms at the end of the second volume, she nonetheless emerges as the heroine's surest source of protection in the remainder of the novel, not only rebuffing Evelina's various unwanted suitors but also playfully encouraging Lord Orville's wooing and working assiduously to obtain Sir John Belmont's paternal recognition of Evelina. Yet many readers consider Mrs. Selwyn to be, if not an object of satire in herself, little more than a confederate of Mirvan's: both, according to Margaret Anne Doody, are "egotists outright" and "uninhibited social aggressors," who "disregard social laws and the comfort of others."[13] Even those who acknowledge her agency on Evelina's behalf consider Selwyn to be irreparably injured by the heroine's initial assessment of her as discomfitingly "masculine":[14]

> "Mrs. Selwyn is very kind and attentive to me. She is extremely clever; her understanding, indeed, may be called *masculine;* but, unfortunately, her manners deserve the same epithet; for, in studying to acquire the knowledge of the other sex, she has lost all the softness of her own. In regard to myself, however, as I have neither courage nor inclination to argue with her, I have never been personally hurt at her want of gentleness; a virtue which, nevertheless, seems so essential a part of the female character, that I find myself more awkward, and less at ease, with a woman who wants it, than I do with a man. She is not a favourite with Mr. Villars, who has often been disgusted at her unmerciful propensity to satire." (268–69)

There are a number of reasons, however, why the textual authority of this description is questionable. First and most obviously, the combined fact of its being Evelina's earliest opinion of Mrs. Selwyn and of *Evelina* being a *Bildungsroman*—which, almost by definition, charts the modification of a heroine's first impressions—should warn the reader to be at the very least suspicious both of Evelina's initial estimation and of her understanding of what is "essential" to "the female character."[15] Second, though her grandfatherly (that is, patriarchal) guardian may often be "disgusted" at Mrs. Selwyn's "unmerciful propensity to satire," he nevertheless quite willingly entrusts his ward to her care—indeed, with less recorded fuss than he exhibits when the thoroughly unsatiric Mrs. Mirvan asks permission to take Evelina away from Berry Hill in the first volume. Third and most significantly, the text—even in this paragraph—works subtly to renovate received notions of masculinity and femininity. That is, Mrs. Selwyn is classified as masculine in Evelina's description, not for staking claim to physical or political power but because her "wit" and "understanding"— being more "'than half her sex put together'" (343)—exceed feminine identification. Evelina apparently does not disapprove of Selwyn's possessing intellectual prowess in itself, only of its being purchased at the cost of "softness"—the *sine qua non* of Hazlitt's unflattering definition of the feminine and what Evelina herself has been taught to see as "essential" to "the female character." Still, Evelina asserts, Mrs. Selwyn is "very kind and attentive," and Evelina herself has "never been personally hurt at her want of gentleness." Moreover, the disgust and uneasiness Selwyn provokes in being resistant to gendering fade in the course of the novel as other features of her behavior that are not *per se* deemed unwomanly come into focus. Through Mrs. Selwyn's agency, the feminine, at closure, is no longer simply a byword for softness but additionally connotes "kind and attentive" maternal protection against those who—like Lords Willoughby and Merton—would "personally hurt" the heroine.

The dominant cultural construction of femininity is undermined on other fronts as well. Mme. Duval's feminine presentation is so grotesquely exaggerated as to threaten the appropriateness of the adjective; Doody, indeed, who notes Mme. Duval's resemblance to stage dames, suggests that she is better understood as a representation of a transvestite than of a woman.[16] Whereas Mrs. Selwyn may thwart masculine ideas of femininity, Mme. Duval's excessive embodiment of such ideas shamelessly burlesques them. The fact, too, that the most damning remarks about Selwyn's unfeminine character are uttered by the disreputable Sir Clement Willoughby throws suspicion upon both their validity and the rigid gendering practices they express. According to Willoughby, Mrs. Selwyn is everywhere "'hated'" for her "'unbounded licence of tongue,'" which "'in a *woman* I think intolerable'": "'she keeps alive a perpetual expectation of satire, that spreads a general uneasiness among all who are in her presence'" (343). Willoughby, however, being something of a reprobate, should—from Evelina's and the reader's perspective—be discomposed at every conceivable opportunity. Thus, while Selwyn's unfeminine behavior may remain diegetically controversial throughout, the textual desirability of its consequences is clear.

Despite the various critical and characterly complaints against her aggressive use of satire, our first direct encounter with Mrs. Selwyn reveals her employing humor in *defense* of the heroine. On their way to the pump room at Bristol Hotwell, Evelina and Mrs. Selwyn are "very much incommoded by three gentlemen, who were sauntering by the side of the Avon, laughing and talking very loud, and lounging so disagreeably that we knew not how to pass them." In an effort to guard Evelina against the "bold" stares and "whispering" of these vaguely sinister libertines, Selwyn launches a barrage of retorts and witty insults that works to fend off the "gentlemen" until she and her charge reach the safety of the pump room (273). In time, Evelina comes actively to seek out Mrs. Selwyn's protection in moments of distress. When Lord Merton late in the novel grabs Evelina's hand and refuses to release it, she begs Mrs. Selwyn to "'speak for me.'" Replying

"'My Lord, . . . in detaining Miss Anville any longer, you only lose time, for we are already as well convinced of your valour and your strength as if you were to hold her an age,'" Mrs. Selwyn humorously impugns her captor's manliness and by so doing secures Evelina's release (313). Indeed, as Susan Staves has noted, Selwyn is more reliably competent than even Lord Orville at protecting Evelina from the brutish, sexually menacing overtures of his fellows.[17]

The particularly maternal associations of Mrs. Selwyn's protection are, moreover, curiously enhanced and complicated by the personal significance that Bristol Hotwell apparently had for Burney herself. Despite its tropic status in the novel as a roiling pit of male sexual aggression,[18] Bristol Hotwell, if Doody is correct, was "privately associated by the author" with the maternal: not merely, that is, the physical cite for the play of feminine humor and its psychodynamic attempt to bond with the archaic mother; nor simply the city where the humorous surrogate mother successfully protects her daughter from the dangers of a masculine-dominated reality; but, specifically, Burney's internalized site of psychic connection with her own lost mother as well.[19]

Although generally engaged in battling discourteous suitors, Mrs. Selwyn's humor, as Lord Orville perceives, is occasionally aimed at flustering Evelina:

> "If you go alone," said he [to Evelina], "Mrs. Selwyn will certainly be offended; but, if you allow me to conduct you, tho' she may give the freer scope to her raillery, she cannot possibly be affronted; and we had much better suffer her *laughter,* than provoke her *satire.*" (382; emphasis added)

Laughter, in this sense, tenderly mocks the victim it otherwise cherishes. Only when Evelina is at last secure (at least in Mrs. Selwyn's mind) of Orville's ardent affection does her surrogate mother indulge in teasing her, and only on the subject that most profoundly threatens the maternal bond: the daughter as erotic object.

> Mrs. Selwyn came to tell me that Lord Orville had been proposing I should take an airing, and persuading her to let him drive us both in his phaeton. She delivered the message with an archness that made me blush, and added, that an airing, in *my Lord Orville's carriage,* could not fail to revive my spirits. There is no possibility of escaping her discernment; she has frequently rallied me upon his Lordship's attention,—and, alas!—upon the pleasure with which I have received it! However, I absolutely refused the offer.

"Well," said she, laughing, "I cannot just now indulge you with any solicitation . . . I would ask you to walk with *me*,—but, since *Lord Orville* is refused, *I* have not the presumption to hope for success."

"Indeed," cried I, "you are mistaken; I will attend *you* with pleasure."

"O rare coquetry!" cried she, "surely it must be inherent in our sex, or it could not have been imbibed at Berry Hill." . . .

She then went down stairs; but presently returning, told me she had acquainted Lord Orville that I did not choose to go out in the phaeton, but preferred a walk, *tête-à-tête* with her, by way of *variety*." (324–25)

Despite her early repugnance to Selwyn's femininely indecorous joking and her latter-day dismay at finding herself the object of raillery, Evelina eventually discovers that Mrs. Selwyn's humor is not only useful in foiling unwanted suitors but "entertain[ing]" (330) in itself and worthy of emulation: she is herself moved on occasion to similar if more restrained shows of wit ("Such a profusion of compliments ensued, that I was obliged to propose dancing, in my own defence" [335]). Evelina's own humorous perspective, that is, grows in the course of the novel through her exposure to Mrs. Selwyn. Lord Orville, too, who is something of a cypher in the first two volumes, develops into a distinctive personality in the third, in part through his appreciation of Selwyn's humor (he is the first to laugh at her remarks). Whereas his fellow Lords are either disconcerted by or dismissive of her humor, Orville happily joins in, even at his own expense: when Mrs. Selwyn playfully accuses him of being "'such a coward as to forbear to frighten women'" by driving his phaeton at moderate speed, Orville, "laughing," replies, "'when a man is in a fright for himself, the ladies cannot but be in security; for you have not had half the apprehension for the safety of your persons, that I have for that of my heart'" (283). Indeed, Mrs. Selwyn functions as a textual litmus test, so to speak, of moral worth: those characters who—like Merton, Willoughby, Lovel, Lady Louisa, and Mrs. Beaumont—fail to recognize or value her humor also fail to win our respect.

The clearest evidence of Mrs. Selwyn's humorous difference occurs in and around the infamous monkey scene at Bath, which in effect closes the narrative. Until then, Captain Mirvan and Mrs. Selwyn never cross paths; hence, it is only in the vignette that immediately precedes the monkey's biting of Lovel's ear (an attack precipitated, if not orchestrated, by Mirvan), in which Lovel is the shared object of their jesting, that the rhetorical and affective distinctions in their humor come sharply into focus. Here we see not only that Mirvan's humor characteristically takes physical form (as in the elaborate practical joke he plays on Madame Duval earlier in the text) but that it thrives upon abusing otherness. As Madame Duval—"old Madame Furbelow" (403)—bears the brunt of Mirvan's misogyny, so the "simpering," effeminate, primping Lovel—who leads "the *ton* in the *beau monde*" (393–94)—falls victim to the captain's homophobia:

> "Secrecy, quoth a!—'Fore George, I wonder you a'n't ashamed to mention such a word, when you talk of telling it to a woman. Though, for the matter of that, I'd as lieve blab it to the whole sex at once, as to go for to tell it to such a thing as you."
> "Such a thing as me, Sir!" said Mr. Lovel, letting fall his knife and fork, and looking very important: "I really have not the honour to understand your expression."
> "It's all one for that," said the Captain; "you may have it explained whenever you like it." (396–97)

Lovel's violation of gender results in his dehumanization: in failing to conform to popular notions of masculine behavior, he forfeits his claim to personhood so far as Mirvan's *ad hominem* humor is concerned, which treats him as insensible to its implied violence (Mirvan variously jokes about beating, ducking, and knocking the teeth out of Lovel). Selwyn's humor, on the other hand, always acknowledges Lovel's human status, indeed, insists upon it, upbraiding him and his fellow *bon vivants* almost exclusively for their insufficiency of "wit" (in both senses of the word, an essentially human attribute). When Mirvan proposes thrashing Lovel for spending "'half an hour thinking what you'd put on'" in the morning, Mrs. Selwyn humorously intercedes on his behalf: "'O pray, Captain, . . . don't be angry with the gentleman for *thinking,* whatever be the cause, for I assure you he makes no common practice of offending in that way'" (394). In direct contrast to Mirvan's crudely humorous sensibility (so crude that he claims to be baffled by the subtlety of grinning),[20] Selwyn's is strictly verbal and highly refined, generally expressed as a series of deflating one-liners that often have the authoritative last word on the absurdity under discussion. Thus, after more than half a page of text devoted to Mirvan's mocking of Lovel for his frequent but inattentive presence at the theatre, where he pays "'five shillings a night to let his friends know he's alive,'" the scene abruptly concludes with Mrs. Selwyn's terse comment: "'And very cheap too . . . if we consider the value of the intelligence'" (392).

Mirvan's and Selwyn's humor differs significantly in its reception as well. Whereas the heroine, as we have seen, eventually learns to imitate her proxy mother's defensive humor in awkward situations, she expresses more than once her revulsion against Mirvan's excessive, sadistic pranks. Even before the rather horrifying consequences of the monkey scene indict Mirvan's methods, Evelina has come to regard his proximity as distasteful and upsetting: "I believe we were all sorry when we saw the Captain return" (399); "even the society of my dear Maria could scarce compensate for the disturbances he excites" (403). Particularly repulsive to Evelina is the phallic quality of his humorous pleasure: he works himself into such a pitch of excitement at the thought of publicly humiliating Lovel by demonstrating his likeness to a dressed monkey that he is "scarce able to contain the fullness of his glee" (399); even after the bloody climax of the incident, "his triumph was intolerable" (403). Nor is his appetite for such humor easily sated. One instance of cruelly humorous gratification simply arouses the desire for more:

> "I'll warrant he won't give an hour to-morrow morning to settling what he shall put on; why his coat," turning to me, "would be a most excellent match for old Madame Furbelow's best Lyons' silk. 'Fore George, I'd desire no better sport, than to have that there old cat here, to go her snacks!" (403)

Mirvan's introduction of the sartorial primate as a dead ringer for Lovel evokes a variety of responses among the party at Bath. Evelina and Maria—in decorously feminine fashion—jump onto the safety of their chairs; Lord Orville chivalrously imposes his body between the beast and Evelina; Lady Louisa screams; and Merton, Coverley, *and Selwyn* all "burst into a loud, immoderate, ungovernable fit of laughter, in which they were joined by the Captain" (400). However, whereas Mirvan's delight actually increases with Lovel's injury ("the unrelenting Captain roared for joy" [401]), Selwyn is rendered silent in the presence of the blood-and-tear-stained victim, sympathy apparently precluding her enjoyment of his suffering. The next (and last) two comments she makes in the text occur only after Lovel's safety has been assured and his equanimity more or less restored. Though mocking Lovel, even these work to reinterpret the significance of the attack so as either to mitigate its pain ("'who knows but it [that is, his slit ear] may acquire you the credit of being an anti-ministerial writer?'" [402]) or to remind him that Mirvan's attack, though partially remediated through humorous revision, cannot be denied altogether. When Lovel tries "pettishly" and "impatiently" to dismiss the attack as "a trifle" so as to avoid the danger of a duel with Mirvan, Mrs. Selwyn gently reinvokes the reality principle: "'A trifle! . . . good Heaven! and have you made this astonishing riot about a *trifle?*" (403).[21]

The name of Selwyn itself encodes at least two references that may bear on our reading of the text. As Gerard Barker has noted, Burney's Selwyn owes much to Mrs. Selwyn of Henry Mackenzie's *The Man of the World* (1773)—rehabilitating her, however, from Mackenzie's blue-stocking termagant to a "sardonic wit" whose exertions on behalf of Evelina "place the character of a learned lady in a more sympathetic perspective."[22] On a more personal note, Selwyn was also the surname of an ardent admirer of Burney's, whose admiration she appears, in some degree, to have returned.[23] Like Bristol Hotwell, then, the very name held resonances for Burney that suggest a deeper authorial investment in Selwyn's perspective than has generally been noticed. Indeed, in *Evelina* (as in *Mansfield Park,* which I shall later discuss in detail), the discourse of the renegade humorous female more fully represents the text than does its heroine's. Unlike Mirvan—whose cruel humor, no matter how well it conforms to established criteria for the comic, is affectively more shocking than amusing—Mrs. Selwyn succeeds in surviving the judgment of the text. In doing so, she makes a compelling case for the understated appeal of a femininely humorous perspective.

THE CASE OF ANTHONY TROLLOPE

He will scarcely rank in the future beside the great novelists of the century. Scott, Balzac, Dickens, George Sand, George Eliot, Charlotte Brontë, Thackeray, Turguenieff, these at least must be put in a first class to which posterity will hesitate to admit him in spite of his range and facility. Neither, we believe, will it admit Miss Austen, great as she is. She and Mr. Trollope, and, perhaps, Mrs. Gaskell, stand at the head of the second order. From their labour has sprung a tribe of novels in which the ways of the English middle class are described with an ease, a humour, and a tenderness of feeling.
— *The (London) Times,* 7 December 1882[24]

More obviously than any other Victorian novelist, Anthony Trollope excited severe gender anxiety in contemporary reviewers. Although George Eliot or Charlotte Brontë may have initially posed a similar threat—being too intellectual, on the one hand, or too "'penetrat[ing] into the "universal" passions and emotions,'" on the other, to be housed comfortably within "the feminine wing" of English society novelists—their placement in a transcendent coterie (composed of both domestic and foreign, male and female writers) provided a solution to their exceptionalism, while still maintaining the biological integrity and hierarchy of gender classifications.[25] Trollope, however, resisted such accommodation. Despite his worship of Thackeray, he was, according to his contemporaries, as incapable of the latter's "satirical narrative" as he was of Dickens's "broad and humorous travestie."[26] Trollope's gifts, rather, lay in a "delicacy of touch," an "aversion to inflicting pain," a "kindliness and good feeling" that, together with a talent for "gossip," made him "as charming a companion" as a reader could wish for.[27]

However effeminizing, this troping of Trollope as a tender, clever wife was apparently less unnerving to reviewers than acknowledging the powerful associations to female sexual reproduction that his voluminous production unavoidably suggested. "'Such fertility is not in nature,'" writes the anonymous critic of the *Saturday Review* disapprovingly—a sentiment that the retentive Henry James (almost gleefully) echoes: "Trollope's fecundity was prodigious," his "fertility was gross, importunate."[28] This excessive literary maternity had its psychological features as well: Trollope, indeed, figures for James as a proto-Lacanian "mirror" into which the reading public "grew very fond of looking" as it learned to recognize itself.[29] Not surprisingly, the frequent allusions to Trollope's ambiguous gender status also rouse a defensive counteremphasis in the critical literature. The reviewer, for example, who found him a charming companion, also insists— rather too often—on Trollope's "masculine" and "manly" appeal, an insistence that, in turn, raises doubt elsewhere about his potency: his style, sneered one critic, "'would be less truly described as limpid than as limp.'" Even James tergiversated, arguing for "a general state of tension" in Trollope's style that, while somewhat crude, prevented it from becoming "flaccid."[30]

Despite the discomfort Trollope's gender bending causes them, virtually all his fellow Victorians dwell on aspects of his work traditionally associated with the feminine. He is repeatedly cited for his lack of imagination and lack of irony, his weakness of plot, his "literalness," and his avoidance of pressing social issues and metaphysical questions. Similarly, his strengths, like those of Hazlitt's typical woman writer, lie in his "portrayal of individual character" and in his clever (if frivolous) rendering of social manners.[31] His humor, too, conforms to Hazlitt's feminine: it "may be called rather a proper appreciation of the paradoxes of social life, than any very original faculty of his own," damned Richard Holt Hutton with severely qualified praise. "Mr. Trollope's humor lay in his keen perception of the oddity of human motives, pursuits, and purposes, and his absolute truthfulness in painting them to the life."[32] Failing equally in idealism, imagination, and originality, Trollope has suffered the literary fate of the feminine as well, having received, until quite recently, little if "any serious or sustained attention."[33]

That Trollope has been collectively, if unconsciously, constructed as feminine and that he has been devalued accordingly is barely arguable: gender binaries, after all, constitute a vertical matrix of value. What is a less settled and more intriguing question is whether that construction is sound—whether it is firmly grounded, so to speak, in textual particulars that are themselves culturally marked as feminine. By investigating the thematic content, the rhetorical devices, and particularly the affective impact of his narrative discourse in some of the Barsetshire novels, I want to consider for the next several pages whether Trollope indeed qualifies as a feminine humorist.[34]

* * *

Although not strictly a woman novelist's novelist (Thackeray, James, and Meredith all write of him with at least qualified admiration), Trollope seems to have been especially appreciated by his female colleagues. Gaskell, for example, who betrays a slight disdain for both Dickens and Thackeray in her letters,[35] writes warmly of the diffuse, prolonged, gossipy pleasure of *Framley Parsonage:* "I wish Mr. Trollope would go on writing Framley Parsonage for ever. I don't see any reason why it should ever come to an end, and every one I know is always dreading the *last number.* I hope he will make the jilting of Griselda a long while a-doing."[36]

At least part of Gaskell's affection for Trollope may have been narcissistic. Not only does *Framley Parsonage* richly resemble *Cranford* in its quasi-nostalgic picture of country life in England of a generation past, in which the threatening encroachment of the city and its associated values may be glimpsed, still safely contained, in the periphery. But Trollope's inattention to the exigencies of plot also recalls Gaskell, as does the apparently desultory structure of his typical narrative. His Barsetshire heroines, too, are familiar, though—with the exception of Lady Lufton, who is a well-heeled Amazon—more reminiscent of Austen than of Gaskell: Mary Thorne, Lucy Robarts, and even Martha Dunstable owe an incalculable debt to Elizabeth Bennett. And like Austen's, his relatively simple plots are conservatively comic: bright, witty female meets eligible, socially superior, usually financially stable, and at least slightly older male with whom (after over-coming cultural obstacles) she joins in more or less traditional marital union.[37]

Although Trollope avoids the feminine exchange and recirculation of character names practiced by Gaskell and Oliphant—preferring allegorical appellations like Dr. Fillgrave and Lord Dumbello or else onomastic crib-bing from real-life friends and foes—his humorous discourse in other ways often precisely imitates the rhetoric of his female fellow novelists. His use of meiosis, litotes, and paradox, for example, can be strikingly Austenian. When Lady De Courcy in *Doctor Thorne,* after obliquely charging Frank Gresham to "marry money," asserts, "'Frank, of course you understand me,'" the narrator meiotically comments: "Frank was obliged to declare, that just at the present moment he did not find his aunt so clear as usual" (119). Likewise, not only the oxymoronic language of the following refer-ence to Augusta De Courcy's loveless betrothal to Mr. Moffat, but the bit-terly amusing sentiment as well, vividly recalls Austen's narrative comment on Maria Bertram's engagement to Mr. Rushworth:

> A cold and chilling time had been named for these hymeneal joys, but one not altogether unsuited to the feelings of the happy pair (*DT,* 280).
>
> In all the important preparations of the mind she was complete; being prepared for matrimony by an [*sic*] hatred of home, restraint, and tranquillity; by the misery of disappointed affection, and contempt of the man she was to marry. The rest might wait. (*MP,* 216)

Trollope's most revealing emulation of feminine models, however, may lie in his alterations. His allusions to the opening lines of *Pride and Preju-dice,* for example—allusions that in their cadences, wittingly or not, ape passages in *Cranford* (see my Chapter 4, pages 140 and 141)—subtly but significantly distort Austen's meanings:

> Ladies think, and I, for one, think that ladies are quite right in so think-ing, that doctors should be married men. (*DT,* 37)
>
> [Mr. Oriel's being "a man of fortune" but "not a marrying man" created] a feeling against him so strong as almost at one time to throw him into serious danger. It was not only that he should be sworn against matrimony in his individual self—he whom fate had made so able to sustain the weight of a wife and family; but what an example was he setting! If other clergymen all around should declare against wives and families, what was to become of the country? What was to be done with the rural districts? The religious observances, as regards women, of a Brigham Young were hardly so bad as this! (*DT,* 419–20)

Despite the almost sheepish self-consciousness of Trollope's reference to Austen (intimated by all those "thinks"), the first quoted passage not only flattens the ironic humor of Austen's famous lines but also explicitly feminizes its subject. Whereas her narration pointedly refrains from attributing investment in "a truth universally acknowledged" exclusively to the likes of Mrs. Bennett, Trollope's figures such an investment as feminine and essentializes it to boot: "Ladies"—not middle-class culture at large—believe that eligible men (or here, simply doctors) should marry. Trollope's narrator, moreover, declares himself masculine in person and perspective by distinguishing himself from the humorous victims of his joke (even if he does so by way of agreeing with their opinion). The second passage—elaborating upon the cultural anxiety generated when a social maxim or universally acknowledged truth is violated—avoids overtly feminizing such anxiety; however, dominated as it is by its *Cranford*ian intertext (which is, in turn, dominated by its Amazonian subject), the passage implicitly treats that anxiety, as well as the business of matrimony itself, as feminine, and being feminine, as a joking matter.[38]

The best evidence for Trollope's case as a feminine humorist ultimately lies not in his narrator's discourse but in the speech and consciousness of a few of his (mostly) female characters.[39] Mary Thorne, Lucy Robarts, and Martha Dunstable all wield what Trollope calls a "soft, kind-hearted, womanly humour" (*SMAA*, 166) to defend themselves against the frustrations of their cultural positioning—positioning that is largely determined, not surprisingly, by their gender and class. Mary Thorne, whose courtship by Squire Gresham's son is jeopardized by her illegitimate and relatively impoverished status, protects herself both from the hostility of Frank's family and the agony of her own doubts (she is a staunch believer in old blood) by turning "every word" her lover speaks "into a joke" (*DT*, 112) and taking refuge "in a low tone of bantering satire" with his relatives (308). Lucy Robarts—whose "ready wit and speaking up, not her beauty" (*FP*, 211), attract Lord Lufton—applies humor as salve to the narcissistic wounds she suffers from his dowager mother's condescension and from her own chagrin at falling in love with a nobleman: "It was evident enough that her misery was real; but yet she spoke of herself and her sufferings with so much irony, with so near an approach to joking, that it was very hard to tell how far she was in earnest" (317).

Less constrained by both her social circumstances and her narrative function, Martha Dunstable jests more prodigiously than either of the others. Unlike Mary or Lucy—who have the narrative luck to be young and beautiful as well as witty—Martha is, frankly, too old and too plain to pass muster as a nineteenth-century romantic heroine; she is accordingly relegated to the subplots, which offer her, in compensation, considerable latitude in her humorous response.[40] Besides her vast fortune as heir to the Oil of Lebanon, her sense of humor is, indeed, her only immediately obvious attraction. She relies on it in answering the impecunious aristocrats who propose to marry her for her money, and, in self-deprecatory fashion, to protect herself from social derision: "[T]he world at large very generally called . . . [Miss Dunstable's residence] Ointment Hall, and Miss Dunstable herself as frequently used that name for it as any other. It was impossible to quiz Miss Dunstable with any success, because she always joined in the joke herself" (343). Humor also allows her to convey thoughts and feelings without risking the responsibility, embarrassment, and possible shame of their direct expression. Chapter 38 of *Framley Parsonage* (entitled "Is There Cause of Just Impediment?") is narratively preoccupied with an interview between Martha Dunstable and Mary Thorne Gresham, in which Mary, through the "uttering of hints in a half-joking way" (450), attempts to ascertain whether Martha would marry her uncle Thorne if asked. Martha's responses are equally coy and humorously noncommittal, yet they reveal even as they conceal what is virtually unspeakable for a woman in her culture: acknowledgment of an active erotic desire. As Martha points out, humor permits one to "'remain perfectly secure in having only hinted'" at one's meaning, while affording great, if fleeting, "'relief'" from the "'terrible curse'" of a social discourse that generally demands that we "'talk sense always'" (452).

Martha's verbal "aptitude for fun" (444) proves to be more than simply disarming: it captivates Dr. Thorne. Their largely unadmitted flirtation consists of a series of bantering engagements in which "abuse from the doctor against the lady's London gaiety" calls forth "raillery from the lady as to the doctor's country habits" (452). From such encounters quickly develops an intimacy so profound as to obviate the need for flattery, romantic indulgence, or formal courtship. Dr. Thorne's letter of proposal is alarmingly blunt, apologizing for being "an old fool; but I try to reconcile myself to that by remembering that you yourself are no longer a girl" (462). Martha, feigning ire at Mary for having divulged to Thorne her partiality, signals her acceptance by declaring, "'Then I suppose I am bound to have him,'" and "dropping the letter on to the floor in mock despair" (464). For Thorne as well as Martha, humor communicates without risk of exposure and defends against the pain of rejection. His humor, too, then, may be called feminine, not only in its method but also in its rhetoric, being "a quiet sarcasm" (*DT,* 59) that often escapes the detection of his fellows: like Martha, he was "inclined to indulge in a sort of quiet raillery, which sometimes was not thoroughly understood. People did not always know whether he was laughing at them or with them" (*DT,* 37).

Curiously, though Thorne seems to find it seductive, Trollope's narrator frets about the sarcastic turn Martha's humor occasionally takes. While the narrator himself satirizes the political situation with confidence and authority, the heroine's "thorough love of ridiculing the world's humbugs" (293) causes him more than mild uneasiness, posing as it does a serious challenge to middle-class notions of femininity:

> Miss Dunstable was by nature kind, generous, and open-hearted; but she . . . was clever also, and could be sarcastic . . . She knew that she was gradually becoming irreverent, scornful, and prone to ridicule; but yet, knowing this and hating it, she hardly knew how to break from it. (222)

Unlike her future husband's similar trait, Martha's sardonic edge requires blunting—an undertaking that tender marital relations will presumably accomplish. Somewhat disappointingly, even though Trollope clearly appreciates feminine touches in a hero like Thorne, a dash of masculinity in his heroine demands expunging.

As Victoria Glendinning argues in her recent biography, Trollope's stories function in some sense as a *working through* of his extratextual life: in fiction, not only could wishes be fulfilled (in creating idealized versions of himself with decidedly different fates), but ambivalences—particularly gender ambivalence—could be safely explored. Yet despite what Christopher Herbert calls the author's "deep intuitive sympathy" for women and emphasis on "comic agility" as "the very basis of female charm," Trollope upholds some decidedly conventional views on feminine decorum, not only in his personal life but in his novels as well.[41] He finds continual amusement, for example, in portraying the husbands of his powerful female matrons as henpecked, notably Bishop Proudie and Squire Gresham (who on first being told that Dr. Thorne had ordered Lady Arabella Gresham "to get out of his house" was stricken with "envy and regret that he could not make the same uncivil request" [*DT,* 360]). And, on occasion, his considerable investment in popular fantasies of romantic love and feminine fidelity can be cringingly embarrassing: to wit, although Mary Thorne exerts "maidenly effort" to resist Frank's loving embraces, in truth "her heart had grown to his. She had acknowledged him to be master of her

spirit; her bosom's lord; the man whom she had been born to worship"
(554). In direct, if coincidental, contrast to Fanny's admonition in *Mansfield Park* that "'it ought not to be set down as certain, that a man must be
acceptable to every woman he may happen to like himself,'"—"'let him
have all the perfections in the world'" (349)—Trollope asserts without the
least apparent trace of irony that Mary must necessarily respond positively
to Frank's affection:

> What could her heart want more, better, more beautiful, more rich than
> such a love as his? Was he not personally all that a girl could like? Were
> not his disposition, mind, character, acquirements, all such as women
> most delight to love? Was it not impossible that Mary should be in-
> different to him? (387)

Not only the content but the rhetoric of Trollope's narrative humor, too,
is often pointedly masculine. Trollope closes *Doctor Thorne* as Austen does
Emma: with the narrator's coy refusal to describe a wedding scene. But
whereas Austen's narration is archly terse on the subject of her heroine's
nuptials, declining even to confirm their occurence (see my Chapter 1,
page 29), Trollope's is swollen, hyperbolic:

> And then Beatrice was wedded and carried off to the Lakes. Mary, as she
> had promised, did stand near her; but not exactly in the gingham frock
> of which she had once spoken. She wore on that occasion—But it will
> be too much, perhaps, to tell the reader what she wore as Beatrice's
> bridesmaid, seeing that a couple of pages, at least, must be devoted to
> her own marriage-dress, and seeing, also, that we have only a few pages
> to finish everything; the list of visitors, the marriage settlements, the
> dress, and all included. (616)
>
> And now I find that I have not one page—not half a page—for the
> wedding-dress. But what matters? Will it not be all found written in the
> columns of the *Morning Post?* (623)

In contrast to its otherwise often feminine effect—its "almost unconscious
relish of comic amusement," as Herbert puts it—Trollope's humorous
discourse here flaunts a "protean limberness and genius for self-
magnification" that is not only more traditionally comic but, for many
readers, at least equally Trollopian.[42]

The affect of his humor is also divided in its loyalties. If the usual comic
victim in Trollope, contrary to convention, seems more friend than foe, it
is a friend whose comic writhings we watch without perturbation.[43] Perhaps the most famous comic scene in any Trollope novel occurs in *Bar-*

chester Towers, when the runaway sofa, accidentally propelled by the incomparable Bertie Stanhope, catches onto Mrs. Proudie's lace train and rips away the backside of her dress. The humor here is physical, almost slapstick, and distances itself completely from the distress of its victim. Indeed, Mrs. Proudie's relative dignity under the circumstances is made to look ridiculous when her wrath is compared to Juno's and her torn regalia parodically treated to a full epic simile ("So, when a granite battery is raised, excellent to the eyes of warfaring men . . ." [99]). Although we may be invited by the narration to anticipate Mrs. Proudie's repeated appearance in the Barsetshire series with comic delight, neither she nor the other determined married women who assert domestic authority (Ladies Arabella and Lufton, for example) are accorded any narrative sympathy in their efforts to enlarge or even maintain their empire of influence. Mrs. Proudie's power struggles with Mrs. Grantly are depicted in the course of the Barsetshire novels as ever more catty, and Trollope's humor increasingly betrays an element of scorn:

> The great disappointment which, as she well knew, the Grantlys had encountered in this matter of the proposed new bishopric had for the moment mollified her. She had been able to talk of poor dear Mrs. Grantly! "She is heart-broken, you know, in this matter, and the repetition of such misfortunes is hard to bear," she had been heard to say, with a complacency which had been quite becoming to her. But now that complacency was at an end . . . Griselda Grantly was engaged to the eldest son of the Marquis of Hartletop! When women are enjoined to forgive their enemies it cannot be intended that such wrongs as these should be included. (*FP* 473–74)

Furthermore, Trollope can treat even acknowledged suffering with rather chilling comic detachment. Lady Arabella is snobbish and spendthrift: faults that are "extremely detrimental to her husband's happiness." Yet, as the narrator admits, no one can accuse her of "being an indifferent mother." When four of her daughters become gravely ill, Lady Arabella ceases to complain about her husband's failures but, instead, "worrie[s] him because Selina coughed, because Helena was hectic, because poor Sophy's spine was weak, and Matilda's appetite was gone" (*DT,* 6):

> Worrying from such causes was pardonable it will be said. So it was; but the manner was hardly pardonable. Selina's cough was certainly not fairly attributable to the old-fashioned furniture in Portman Square; nor would Sophy's spine have been materially benefited by her father having a seat in Parliament; and yet, to have heard Lady Arabella discussing

those matters in family conclave, one would have thought that she would have expected such results.

As it was, her poor weak darlings were carried about from London to Brighton, from Brighton to some German baths, from the German baths back to Torquay, and thence—as regarded the four we have named—to that bourne from whence no further journey could be made under the Lady Arabella's directions. (*DT* 7)

There is something perversely disquieting in our being encouraged to laugh at a character who then suffers such horrifying losses. Rather than offering maternal empathy or protection, Trollope's humor characteristically limits our affective engagement with its victim to a sense of friendliness or goodwill, resulting from a recognition of shared human imperfection. Such friendliness, however, cools to acquaintanceship in the case of his female characters, who, known to the narrator by type rather than personality, appear within their category to be largely interchangeable. Indeed, in Hutton's estimation, Trollope's women are inferior artistic creations precisely because they fail to make "'any profound impression on the feelings and imagination of the narrator.'" [44]

In contrast, then, to the close narrator-heroine bond in Austen or Gaskell, the Trollope narrator's typical relationship with his heroine is less maternal perhaps than avuncular. [45] He can be sensitive to the subtle pressures of the feminine position—

> Men think but little how much of this kind [of sartorial care] is endured that their eyes may be pleased, even though it be but for an hour (*SMAA*, 26)

—or demonstrate an astute awareness of gender difference—

> Lucy was behaving well, and Mark was proud of her. Lucy was behaving with fierce spirit, and Fanny was grieving for her (*FP*, 382)

—but he regularly fails to identify empathically with the heroine's suffering, which feminine humor crucially entails. However sympathetic he may be in principle, Trollope's narrator maintains his polite affective distance.

Such distance is eminently apparent in the narrator-heroine relationship in *The Small House at Allington*. [46] Like Mary and Lucy, Lily Dale is pretty, witty, vibrant, fresh, and young, but her romantic tribulations, unlike theirs, do not comedically resolve themselves in marriage. This plot disparity fundamentally influences her different narrative treatment. Whereas the erotic anxieties of the nuptially bound heroines are textually relieved through humor, Lily's jilting and her efforts to cope in its aftermath are reported—particularly in the chapter entitled "Valentine's Day at Allington"—in excruciatingly sober detail. The narration makes no attempt to ease Lily's mortification or to mediate her self-punishing obsession with the particulars of Crosbie's wedding to Lady Alexandrina De Courcy by making a joke of either her situation or her response to it. Rather than sympathetically identifying with the heroine's suffering as the first step to allaying it, the narrator records Lily's masochistic behavior in this chapter with cool and disapproving detachment. Rather, that is, than facilitating the humorous bonding of the narrator and his heroine, masochism occurs in the text solely as character pathology.

Yet Lily's masochism constitutes more than an individual psychological affliction. It represents both a family tradition—male and female Dales alike are prone to overzealous, self-damaging constancy—and a social ideal of feminine conduct.[47] Her unwavering refusal even to try to overcome her feelings for Crosbie is simply a logical, if extreme, expression of the fidelity and self-abnegation that her culture promulgates as desirably feminine: "The little sacrifices of society are all made by women, as are also the great sacrifices of life. A man who is good for anything is always ready for his duty, and so is a good woman always ready for a sacrifice" (137). Indeed, Lily seems to construe romantic love itself as an exercise in female servility: "It was not only that she would love him, but in her love she would serve him to her utmost" (191).

There is, however, a curious twist to Lily's urge to masochism. On at least three occasions, the narrative hints that Lily has been sexually intimate with Crosbie.[48] From her own cultural viewpoint, the fact of such intimacy eternally binds her to her lover, if only because it morally forbids her to marry another. From a somewhat different textual perspective, however, her refusal to consider a sexual replacement for Crosbie signifies a renewed commitment to sustained maternal connection. For no matter how seductive Crosbie's oedipal attraction is for Lily, it is ultimately less compelling than the preoedipal fascination her mother holds for her. This fascination, indeed, not affection for Crosbie, is what persistently defeats Johnny Eames. Shortly after her betrothal, Lily begins to fret that marriage will necessitate maternal separation: "'Mamma,' she said, 'I hope you and I are not to be divided when I go to live in London . . . I shall want to see you, touch you, and pet you as I do now'" (291). And after Crosbie breaks their engagement, she clings to her mother with infantile ferocity, on the one hand demanding (in a gesture of preoedipal omnipotence) that she be allowed to be "'a tyrant'" over her mother, to make her "'do my bidding in everything'" (631), and on the other desiring that her mother "'beat'" her "'darling, your own darling'" rather than "'pitying'" her (485). Furthermore, her immediate, almost instinctive reaction to Crosbie's abandonment is to turn for love, protection, and consolation to the maternal bond:

> "[Y]ou must be very good to me now; and I must be very good to you. We shall be always together now. I must be your friend and counsellor: and be everything to you, more than ever. I must fall in love with you now." (327)

In effect, Lily partially oedipalizes her attachment to her mother, even as she earlier, in some sense, displaces her preoedipal longing onto Crosbie.[49] His departure from Allington—denoting their first (and, as it turns out, final) parting—precipitates a fit of separation anxiety, in which Lily fears that the very intensity of her love will drive Crosbie away permanently ("'I could not live without you; . . . But I won't bother you; . . . I shall be afraid of writing too much to you, for fear I should tire you'" [164]). The quality of her affection for Crosbie, too, is infantile, so to speak, being imbued with a vigorous orality: "Lily had told him that she would live upon his letters, and it was absolutely necessary that he should furnish her with her first meal" (194); "'[I]f he knew how I hunger and thirst after his love!'" (290).

*   *   *

In the Barsetshire novels at least, maternal bonding can be said to be more often enacted than textualized. For while Lily dramatizes in word and deed her desire for symbiotic union (which Mrs. Dale, given the psychic and physical limitations of life, does her best to fulfill),[50] the narrator's bond with his heroine—friendly and generally supportive, though always so slightly aloof—never achieves the intimacy and durability requisite for sustained feminine humor. Ultimately, Trollope, in both his serious and humorous discourse, is more consciously concerned with the dynamics of class than those of gender. His narrative sympathies are solidly engaged by the Mary Thornes and Lucy Robartses of his world, primarily as a consequence of their being intelligent, witty, and socially respectable. Indeed, the difficulties of being female in a culture that prizes men evoke little response from Trollope unless they are also located in a middle-class subject. The narrator of *The Small House at Allington,* for example, disapproves just as vehemently of Amelia Roper—the daughter of Johnny Eames's landlady who, desperate to break free of the bleak, seedy, pinched life that lies before her, tries to manipulate Johnny into marriage—as he does of the snobbish, often debauched, mercenaries who collectively comprise the aristocratic de Courcy family.[51] Lacking keen feeling for the feminine position, the quintessential Barsetshire narrator is unable to commiserate fully enough with his heroine's frustrations to redeem them through humor. Moreover and perhaps more poignantly, because Trollope's narrative humor fails to register consistent sympathy for its victim—which is the affective hallmark of feminine humor—it is powerless to modify the characterological masochism of a Lily Dale as well.[52]

Sadomasochism and the Humor Relationship: Henry James and Edith Wharton

Perhaps it was our common sense of fun that first brought about our understanding. The real marriage of true minds is for any two people to possess a sense of humour or irony pitched in exactly the same key . . . ; and in that sense Henry James was perhaps the most intimate friend I ever had.

—Edith Wharton, *A Backward Glance*[53]

. . . for a moment they were blent in that closest of unions, the discovery of a common fund of humour.

—Edith Wharton, *The Fruit of the Tree*[54]

Even for avid readers of James and Wharton, the idea that humor should be among the qualities each held dearest in the other elicits amazement. Certainly, the author of *House of Mirth* and *The Custom of the Country* might be expected to treasure the "silver-footed ironies, veiled jokes, and tiptoe malices" that, according to Wharton, threaded James's private conversation; but that she should consider "wide-flashing fun" and "huge cairns of hoarded nonsense" to be among his identifying traits seems ridiculously incongruous with the popular image of the formidable Master (*BG*, 178–79). Similarly, though it is easy enough to recognize, along with James, "needle-point" satire and perhaps "a little purely derisive" irony as characteristic of Wharton, it is much harder to picture her laughing "with the sincerity of complete surrender to every paroxysm that followed a fresh vision of the ludicrous" or rendered "speechless, with shoulders shaking and the tears running down her cheeks, lift[ing] a deprecating hand that bade you spare her another turn of the screw."[55]

Yet to experience "mutual understanding" in moments of humor or to "detect an ally"[56] in ironic comprehension—even when such humor and irony are "pitched," as Wharton claimed, in the very "same key"—does not, of course, mean that both parties occupy an identical position in the psychodynamics of humor. To the contrary, both the triadic configuration of the joke and the dyadic one of feminine humor require a differentiation in the disposition and role of the participants. While it is difficult to be certain, given the lopsidedness of their extant correspondence (he evidently incinerated most of her letters), in the bond of humor that united James and Wharton, it was apparently James who habitually generated the jokes and Wharton who just as habitually received them—functioning not only as the auditor who made his jokes possible but often as the victim of his "malice and merriment" as well (*BG,* 178).

A consideration of the James-Wharton humor relationship is exceptional in the context of this study for at least three reasons. Its subjects (no matter how Europeanized) are Americans in a discussion otherwise preoccupied with English writers; it draws as greatly on biographical data to make its argument as on the internal evidence of the literary texts it examines; and, perhaps most important, at least one of its subjects deviates, subtly but significantly, in fiction and life, from cultural norms of both gender and sexuality. Yet, it is in part due to their singularity that James and Wharton so forcefully demonstrate that humor—however deeply shared, however similar in its rhetorical effects and its targets of derision— is deeply influenced in tone and temperament by its gender positioning. The following discussion—which takes up the last of the paradigms to be explored in this chapter—limns the tensions between masculine and feminine affects in the humor relationship of James and Wharton: a relationship both suggestively symbiotic ("blent in that closest of unions") and hauntingly sadomasochistic. For as Wharton, who frequently addressed her partner in humor as "Dearest Cher Maître," knew, any relationship dominated by a master requires at least the theoretical slavishness of an other.[57]

*   *   *

On 4 October 1907, James wrote to "My dear Edith" requesting a copy of her recent novel, *The Fruit of the Tree.* Having been approached to write an appreciation or "puff" of Wharton by a New York publication (falsely) claiming that Wharton wished the Master to undertake the task, James decided that "the seed having been dropped, by however crooked a *geste,* into my mind, I am conscious of a lively & spontaneous disposition to really dedicate a few lucid remarks to the mystery of your genius."[58] Wharton dutifully petitioned Charles Scribner to send off a copy to James, adding wryly that it "looks to me as if he meant to make mince-meat of me."[59]

Some seven years into their friendship, Wharton had apparently become accustomed to James's finely barbed and generally unsolicited critical assessments. "I always tried to keep my own work out of his way," writes Wharton years later in her autobiography, "and once accused him of ferreting out and reading it just to annoy me—to which charge his sole response was a guilty chuckle." His comments, delivered in a painfully slow and deliberately halting manner that was "full of a terrible benevolence," could be "withering" and "not untinged with malice": when James was once asked by a mutual acquaintance whether he did not think it "remarkable that Mrs. Wharton should have written a story in French for the *Revue?*" he replied, "'Remarkable—most remarkable! An altogether astonishing feat . . . I do congratulate you, my dear, on the way in which you've picked up every old worn-out literary phrase that's been lying about the streets of Paris for the last twenty years, and managed to pack them all into those few pages.'" Such "'dressing-down'" as often as not took place in company under Wharton's own roof, where it was greeted by a collective "shout of laughter" from James's doting, and generally all male, audience of fellow guests (*BG,* 180–84).

James, in the end, never wrote the appreciation of Wharton's work for the New York journal. "I *want* to enthuse over you, I yearn to, quite—but I must wait for the right & bright & honourable occasion for doing so," which the "hole-&-corner publication" did not, in James's estimation, present. Instead, he wrote a short story inspired by the incident, entitled "The Velvet Glove," which he confessed to Wharton "wd. never have been written without you": "the whole thing *reeks* with you."[60] Simply told, the narrative recounts an evening in the life of best-selling author and playwright John Berridge, who, at a reception in his honor (held in Gloriani's studio, of *The Ambassadors* fame), is approached by a wealthy, "dazzling" (240), novel-writing princess (*alias* Amy Evans). Berridge—an amusing, self-deprecatory portrait of James (his wildly popular, if "slightly too fat volume" [241], *The Heart of Gold,* enjoys enormous, wish-fulfilling success in its theatrical adaptation)—is awestruck by the "supremely, divinely Olympian" (240) princess's demeanor: "[S]he might have been . . . Artemis decorated, hung with pearls," with "an impulse just faintly fierce" (244). He at first misinterprets her interest in him as personal: "'You'll come home with me?' gasped John Berridge, while the perspiration on his brow might have been the morning dew on a high lawn of Mount Ida" (253–

54). When he discovers, at the end of a long, nocturnal motor ride through Paris, that she simply wants him to compose an admiring preface for her new work, he is disgusted—as much by "the really affecting folly of her attempt to become a mere magazine mortal" (261) as by her flatly stating her "disconcerting, deplorable, dreadful" (258) motive "with the clearest coolness of her general privilege." "'Princess, I adore you,'" he tells her at parting. "'But I'm ashamed for you . . . You *are* Romance . . . ; so what more do you want? Your Preface—the only one worth speaking of—was written long ages ago by the most beautiful imagination of man . . . You don't need to understand. Don't attempt such base things. Leave those to us. Only live. Only be. *We'll* do the rest'" (263).

Following James's biographer Leon Edel, readers have generally agreed that there is "something deeply mocking and hostile in the tale in spite of its verbal gauze."[61] Not only is the princess described in terms recalling James's epistolary epithets for Wharton (the "Princess Rapprochee," the "all-wondrous Edith," who, "spell-binding" and "iridescent," was "almost too insistently Olympian"); but the working-title of his story, and of the princess's current best-seller, is "The Top of the Tree"—a pun on Wharton's *The Fruit of the Tree,* which James had judged "strangely infirm" in "composition and construction."[62] To be sure, James makes fun of his center of consciousness as well. Yet Berridge endears himself, at least at first, by his bemused, stammering manner, while the "Olympian" princess—who rather than simply "living and breathing her Romance" (252) insists upon "ungrammatically scribbling it"—comes across as silly, shallow, crass. However little resemblance it may in fact bear to Wharton, the likeness is distinctly unflattering. James's parodic rendering of the language of *The Top of the Tree,* while nothing like Wharton's elegant prose, nevertheless suggests both its metaphoric intensity and the plot of her novel:

> It was too much for all the passionate woman in her, and she let herself go, over the flowering land that had been, but was no longer, their love, with an effect of blighting desolation that might have proceeded from one of the more physical, though not more awful, convulsions of nature (249).

The personality of the princess as well—from her "strenuous presence and her earnest pressure" (260) to her enthusiastic motoring through Paris and her desire to charm—unmistakably borrows from Wharton.[63]

Although early in their relationship, Wharton had been "stung," according to biographer R. W. B. Lewis, by James's "devastating criticism" of her work (and had sought on one occasion "to ease her bruised feelings by composing a little parody" of his late style), her response to his caricature of her in "The Velvet Glove" is surprisingly free of resentment.[64] "Read 'The Velvet Glove,'" she wrote to at least two mutual friends, "[a] delightful little story—a motor story!"[65] Even though she denied serving as model for the princess, Wharton did acknowledge the allusions to their relationship and apparently accepted the story as a good (if personally costly) joke.[66] She, too, incorporated her friend in her fiction: as Henry Langhope in *The Fruit of the Tree* and Charles Bowen of *The Custom of the Country*, each intent on *seeing* with "his clear ironical eyes" and "from his own precise angle, the fantastic improbability" of life among the overprivileged.[67] And the sketches of James in her memoir constitute perhaps her funniest piece of writing: here a listener flails "helplessly in the heavy seas of James's parentheses" (178); the Master, "a mountain of misery" in the summer heat, sucks oranges as he mutters to himself "in a sort of low despairing chant" (189) or bewilders an elderly passerby with a request for directions delivered in a seemingly unending "series of explanatory ramifications" (243). But the humor of this portrait offers a sustaining sympathy for its subject (for James's aesthetic, his locutions, his suffering) that is utterly unreciprocated in his portrayal of the Whartonesque princess.

According to Wharton, James's "irresistible tendency to speak the truth" resulted from an "over-scrupulous conscience." "[T]o fib about the art one practises is incredibly painful," and for James, whose punctilious artistic principles had the weight of law, ultimately "impossible" (*BG*, 183, 184). What is remarkable is not only that Wharton was willing to forgive James the infliction of the pain he could not bear himself, but that she experienced even his nastiest remarks as "amusing"; indeed, the more "withering" the comment, the "more amusing [the] experience" (183). She goes so far as to admit a positive *pleasure* in being battered, so to speak, by James's criticism; although "with others . . . he tried to be more merciful," because "he knew I enjoyed our literary rough-and-tumbles," he "scrupled the less to hit straight from the shoulder" (184). Occasional protestations to the contrary, Wharton seems to have sought out the harsh, exacting Master in part because of, not despite, the narcissistic wounds and "painful moment[s]" (180) his "scalpel"-sharp (182) wit administered.

*   *   *

In her 1902 review of Leslie Stephen's *George Eliot*, Wharton expresses irritation with Eliot's public reception on three scores: that critics frequently judged her to be "deformed" or unwomanly simply because she displayed an interest in "biology and metaphysics"; that even appreciative readers did not do "full justice" to her humor, "which has its source" in a "depth of sympathy"; and that those who relished the "'story with a plot'" denigrated her artistry because she valued "the drama of the soul" more than "a succession of outward accidents and mechanical complications."[68] Wharton, in other words, not only defends Eliot's right to explore intellectual territory culturally marked as masculine (for example, science and metaphysics), but also subtly argues that Eliot's (feminine) strengths—her "power of characterisation" (248), her urge to "psychological truth," her sympathetic humor, and her ability to "see" beyond "the incidental, external side of life" (250)—sustain a more highly developed aesthetic than that clung to by most of her male contemporaries.[69] In effect, Wharton simultaneously fashions Eliot as both feminine and protomodern.

Although he probably would have winced at the association, James builds his own highly developed aesthetic upon a number of principles that, like Eliot's, are customarily identified as feminine. Characterization rather than chronicle; psychological exploration rather than sociological investigation; the emphasis on "seeing" life as a fragile, minutely tangled skein of human relations rather than as a socioeconomic construction of pressing political consequence: such attributes as these come increasingly to characterize James's prose and project. Indeed, the rhetoric of the late James might be described as a complex pattern of "feminine" tropes—meiosis, litotes, and periphrasis—woven together with metaphor and reinforced by a staggering number of parentheses. It even betrays a fondness, particularly evident in his letters, for masochistic phrasing: to be "embarrassed . . . fairly to anguish" by a tribute or to be "cut into" by his brother's death, "deep down, even as an absolute mutilation" (but a mutilation that, as Edel notes, nevertheless "gave him a greater sense of power") are typical constructions.[70] His humor, too, is tantalizingly feminine: from its epistolary wittiness and its hint of self-deprecation to what Edel terms "its highly condensed, epigrammatic and also private" quality—so unlike the "broad, visceral, public" humor of that other "American genius," Twain.[71]

Yet even though James, like Trollope, clearly transgresses the bounds of nineteenth-century masculine style and subject, his aesthetic strategies do not precisely register as feminine. There is certainly a slightly hysterical quality about James's rhetoric (his use of periphrasis, for example), but it is a hysteria of expression—an excessive use of figures, a logorrhea—rather than (as in feminine humor) an expression of hysteria, an affective means of giving voice to what would otherwise not be culturally permitted utterance. Seizing upon feminine literary traits like character observation or a taste for gossip, James hyperbolizes them past gender recognition: acute perception of characters and their relations takes on a voyeuristic aspect; scopophilia becomes a fetishized artistic principle. James's late aesthetic, that is, is so exaggeratedly, queerly, feminine as to exceed the category of the feminine itself. Indeed, his over-the-top performance might be better understood as participating in a masculine homoerotic poetics, as Eve Kosofsky Sedgwick has suggested, rather than as a normative representation of feminine characteristics.[72]

Such an alternative framing may be necessary, since sympathy—fundamental to the prevailing concept of the feminine, and to feminine humor specifically—is noticeably absent in James's handling of many of his heroines. Not only the princess of "The Velvet Glove," but Olive Chancellor of the problematic *Bostonians,* and even an early heroine like Daisy Miller are treated with an affective distance that permits acute intellectual interest and sometimes a glint of malice (or sadistic cruelty, in Olive's case), but not narrator-heroine bonding. As a rule, James's narrative humor is tightly controlled and rife with irony. Its victims are easily identifiable, often by apposite names (Henrietta Stackpole, Miss Birdseye, Fanny Assingham), and our response is unfailingly directed; there is, I would venture to say, very little doubt regarding whom we are to laugh at in James (unless it be the prolix narrator of the late novels). Moreover, our laughter comes cheap. Because we are rarely allowed, though sometimes tempted, to identify with the humorous victim, our pleasure costs us virtually nothing in the way of painful empathic bonding.

Writing of James's reaction to a young American companion of his niece Peggy, Edel remarks that "she was like Daisy Miller, a product of the permissive vacuity of a childhood without direction," and that "James had pity" for the "'poor young creature'" (509). Pity, however, in art as in human relations, is a less demanding emotion than sympathy. Daisy evokes from the reader, as she does from Frederick Winterbourne (through whose eyes Daisy is exclusively seen), a sad, perhaps haunting, sense of waste and regret, but she is too affectively remote from the narrator to evoke much pathos. Despite "a sweetness and softness that reverted instinctively to the pardon of offences" and an "apparently inexhaustible good-humor," Daisy fails to charm her readers for the very reason that most provokes the American-European community in Vevey and Rome; her willfulness, that is—however much the sorry result of her upbringing—prevents her from adapting to "the custom of the place" (to do in Rome as the Americans do). And because it is unredeemed by narrative humor, such an otherwise forgivable failing costs her our secret approbation as well.[73]

Curiously, although Daisy is sketched with detail sufficient to emerge as a fully rounded character, Winterbourne—initially and later obstinately—perceives her according to "formula" (11): "'How pretty they are!'" (6), he remarks upon first seeing Daisy; never had he met "a young American girl of so pronounced a type" (11). His subsequent encounters raise for him only one, oft-repeated thought: "She seemed to him . . . an extraordinary mixture of innocence and crudity" (26), "an inscrutable combination of audacity and innocence" (35). Alternately amazed and amused by her, Winterbourne nonetheless resists treating Daisy as anything more than an intriguing intellectual problem: Did her "defiance [come] from the consciousness of innocence, or from her being, essentially, a young person of the reckless class" (47)? And he becomes "vexed with himself" (16) for not being able to figure out "how far her eccentricities were generic, national, and how far they were personal" (48). His emotional distance is, indeed, extraordinary. Although at one moment "touched, shocked, mortified" (18) by a "fancied . . . tremor" (17) in Daisy's voice when she understands she's been snubbed by Winterbourne's aunt, he, at the next, "almost wished that her sense of injury might be such as to make it becoming in him to attempt to reassure and comfort her. He had a pleasant sense that she would be very approachable for consolatory purposes" (18). In the end, he regrets having done her the "injustice" of not recognizing that "'she would have appreciated one's esteem'" (54), yet her death represents for him not a felt loss but foremost an excuse to recur now and again to "the thought of Daisy Miller and her mystifying manners" (54).

The narrator, too, like Winterbourne, is "addicted to observing and analzying" (8) the heroine rather than protecting or bonding with her. His perspective is cool, detached, ironic; his bloodless report of her death, particularly chilling: "[A]s Winterbourne had said, it mattered very little [whether he knew that Daisy was engaged or not]. A week after this the poor girl died" (53). Nothing in the story even modestly approaches sympathetic humor, with the possible exception of Randolph Miller's conversational sallies ("'My father's in a better place than Europe'"; he's "in Schenectady" [9]). There is, to be sure, plenty of satiric irony: Winterbourne, for example, by way of defending the Millers from the charge of social climbing, insists "that they are intellectually incapable" of "the idea of catching a count" (46)—presumably having not yet risen to that level of culture enjoyed by the rest of the expatriate American community where such a custom prevails. As in many of Wharton's novels, the narrator here takes an anthropological view of his fellows and their habits:

> Winterbourne observed to himself that this [Mrs. Miller's] was a very different type of maternity from that of the vigilant matrons who massed themselves in the forefront of social intercourse in the dark old city at the other end of the lake. (21)

But his anthropology bears this significant difference: the aborigines under discussion in "Daisy Miller," unlike Wharton's bitterly described New Yorkers, do not awaken unnerving feelings of self-recognition in the narrator (and, by association, the reader).[74] James's narrator scoffs freely at his victims ("'[I]t is not the custom here,'" Mrs. Walker intones, "with her hands devoutly clasped" [36]), whereas Wharton's derision, as we shall see in *The Custom of the Country*, resembles something closer to self-flagellation.

*   *   *

She uses everything and every one either by the extremity of strain or the extremity of neglect . . . , and passes on to scenes that blanch at her approach.

She rode the whirlwind, she played the storm, she laid waste whatever of the land the other raging elements had spared, she consumed in 15 days what would have served to support an ordinary Christian Community for about ten years. Her powers of devastation are ineffable, her repudiation of repose absolutely tragic, and she was never more brilliant and able and interesting.

—Henry James on Edith Wharton[75]

Begrudgingly or not, most Wharton critics admit a disturbing correspondence between James's descriptions of his devoted, "dearest Edith"—a "Devastating Angel," "beautiful & terrible"; a "Firebird" or an "eagle"—and her creation of Undine Spragg, the terrifyingly destructive, radiantly seductive, man-eating heroine of Wharton's most darkly humorous novel.[76] Certainly, Undine registers at least as forcefully as an "'angel of beautiful ruin,'" whose "Maenad motion" propels one into a "'fatal and prostrating vortex,'" stripping one "'of one's time and domestic economy'" as does Wharton, of whom James here speaks.[77] Even her physical appearance suggests Wharton as viewed from James's specular position: "her black brows, her reddish-tawny hair and the pure red and white of her complexion defied the searching, decomposing radiance: she might have been some fabled creature" aspiring to "Olympian portals" (*Custom*, 21,11). More disturbing than the correspondence itself, however, is the question it raises about Wharton's role in James's extended epistolary joke. Clearly, part of her motive in creating a heroine true to his epithets is to join in and further the fun, to be an active participant or co-conspirator, as it were, in the production of humor rather than simply its victim. But, to fashion out of such epithets one of the most despicable heroines in the literature of the time, and certainly the most unsympathetic heroine of her own canon, suggests an identification with the humorous victim (James's Edith/Undine) that is both painful and self-loathing.[78]

Turning again to Daisy Miller for a moment may help illustrate this point. If, on the one hand, Undine self-consciously recalls Wharton in look and manner, on the other hand she represents a nightmarish (though also cartoonishly indestructible) incarnation of Daisy. Both are adolescently insouciant, incessantly mobile, arrestingly beautiful, and irrepressible in their pursuit of social conquest. Both lack a sense of irony or humor, and both effectively resist all parental attempts at control. But unlike James, who prevents our sympathizing with the childish, self-destructive Daisy by resolutely maintaining his narrative distance, Wharton—who narrates the story in part through Undine's consciousness—forces an identification not only between narrator and heroine but between narrator-heroine and reader as well. The reader, despite great unwillingness, finds herself empathically chained to the soulless, morally repulsive, hideously triumphant Undine.[79]

One way such identification is brought about is through humor. Although something of an *enfant terrible,* Undine is nevertheless accorded maternally humorous treatment in the early pages of the novel:

> Undine's chief delight was to "dress up" in her mother's Sunday skirt and "play lady" before the wardrobe mirror. The taste had outlasted childhood, and she still practised the same secret pantomime, gliding in, settling her skirts, swaying her fan, moving her lips in soundless talk and laughter . . .
>
> Only one fact disturbed her: there was a hint of too much fullness in the curves of her neck and in the spring of her hips. She was tall enough to carry off a little extra weight, but excessive slimness was the fashion, and she shuddered at the thought that she might some day deviate from the perpendicular. (22–23)

Her solipsism evinces a childlike quality that, recalling as it does an earlier age-appropriate narcissism, begs for narrative forbearance: "What was the use of being beautiful and attracting attention if one were perpetually

doomed to relapse again into the obscure mass of the Uninvited?" (50).
Yet we are also alerted early on that Undine's willfulness, long parentally
overindulged, has monstrous potential:

> It was an observation they had made in her earliest youth—Undine
> never wanted anything long, but she wanted it "right off." And until she
> got it the house was uninhabitable.
>   . . . As a child they had admired her assertiveness, had made Apex
> ring with their boasts of it; but it had long since cowed Mrs. Spragg, and
> it was beginning to frighten her husband. (43)

By alternating glimpses of Undine in her mildly entertaining acts of
narcissistic rage with those of Undine the petulant, but not altogether un-
affectionate, recipient of her parents' "humorous fondness" (30), the narration encourages readers to consider its heroine a satiric figure, one whose
actions may be counted on to divert even while her empathic pull is comfortably restrained:

> Pale and listless under the stifling boredom of the Mealey House routine,
> Undine secretly sucked lemons, nibbled slate-pencils and drank pints of
> bitter coffee to aggravate her look of ill-health; and when she learned
> that even Indiana Frusk was to go on a month's visit to Buffalo it needed
> no artificial aids to emphasize the ravages of envy. (53)

However, and significantly, by humorously treating her as a child, the narration also insidiously exacts a sympathetic concern for her welfare, thereby
undermining the affective distance necessary for sustained satire. Thus,
when Undine performs her most reprehensible acts—her cruel callousness
to Ralph or her freezing indifference to her young son, Paul—we are made
not only to recognize her power as more horrifying than that generally
accorded satiric characters, but also to feel vaguely guilty ourselves for having previously been amused by her outrageously self-serving behavior. Indeed, Ralph's suicide is shocking and ghastly in part because it disorders
our understanding of Undine as a satiric heroine, who, however despicable,
is by definition prohibited from inflicting any deeply felt pain. Unlike
Vanity Fair, for example, in which Becky Sharp's villainy amuses until the
end, *The Custom of the Country* switches from social satire to personal tragedy, and so abruptly that, although the narrative of Ralph's breakdown and
death claims our pity and fear, our empathic identification—despite its
ego-dystonic quality—remains with the devastating Undine.[80] Even her
agreeable inversion of Victorian gender conventions (she is selfish, not
selfless; dynamic, not passive; an Angel of Devastation, not an Angel-in-

the-House) does nothing to redeem her, neither winning our forgiveness nor easing our sense of complicity.

This strange, unsettling quality of Wharton's narrative humor—its peculiar marriage of satiric tone and structure with empathic affect—resides largely in its conflation of masculine and feminine effects. In a review essay on contemporary writers, James praises Wharton generally for her "ironic" perception and *The Custom of the Country* in particular for being "consistently, almost scientifically satiric."[81] Here "the light that gathers is a dry light, of great intensity, and the effect, if not rather the very essence of its dryness, is a particular fine asperity." Such asperity, James remarks, accounts for "the dry, or call it perhaps even the hard, intellectual touch in the soft, or call it perhaps even the humid, temperamental air; in other words of the masculine conclusion tending so to crown the feminine observation." A consciousness that would otherwise be softly, weakly, humidly feminine is thus saved by Wharton's masculinity of mind—her cold, detached, "scientifically satiric" intellect— which, as James sees it, crowns or masters her natural interest in detail, character, and relation. The result is a humorous text neither normatively masculine nor feminine but queer: a feature that may account in part not only for Wharton's appeal for James but for her honorary inclusion in the coterie of young, attractive, homoerotic bachelors who surrounded James in his later years.[82]

Moreover, if Wharton's humor is essentially ironic, as James asserts, it is also characteristically self-inflicted: aggression that is normally directed outward in irony and satire is in *The Custom of the Country* turned back upon the narrating self. Unlike Wharton's hero in *The Fruit of the Tree*, who skillfully applies "the antiseptic of an unfailing humour" to "wounds to his self-confidence" (94) and whose emotional detachment proceeds "from the resolve to spare himself pain" (414), the narrative humor of *Custom*, rather than fending off or transforming displeasure, partially internalizes it. However ironically inflected such a comic disposition may be, it is more aptly termed *humor* than *irony*, since it affectively engages with its victim and incompletely prevents the recognition of the disturbing emotion (in this case, hostility toward the heroine-victim) that generates it in the first place. And if humor is generally considered funniest when it most fully co-opts the energy of the motivating distress, then Wharton's humor—in which the distress continues to be experienced through the filter of humor as painful—is not only typically less funny than that of others but masochistic as well. By preserving rather than converting the agony that subtends humorous pleasure, Wharton may be pushing the limits of humor—even of feminine humor—as far as they will go.

In the end, the humorous affect of *The Custom of the Country* might best be described as empathic but without the benevolently maternal aspect that the trope of feminine humor usually entails. The narrator and sympathetic reader experience the humor of the novel not as the kind preoedipal mother's protection against frustrating reality, but rather as (mediated) pain at the hands of her cold, withholding double: Undine is the insensible object of mockery, but the narrator, for whom Undine functions as something like a failed ego ideal, suffers, along with the reader, her humorous debasement.[83] Nonetheless, as in pathological masochism, where the pain of bondage to the cruel mother is preferable to the forfeiture of any psychic maternal connection whatsoever, the masochistic humor of *The Custom of the Country* becomes itself a sought-after literary experience, continually offering a promise of maternal consolation if just as continually disappointing.

"I fear you cannot comprehend my meaning . . . please to attribute your not understanding the sublimity of my sentiments to your own stupidity and dullness of apprehension, and not to my want of meaning—which is only too fine to be clear."—Frances Burney, mocking the authority of the Sublime. (From the Collection of Parham Park, West Sussex, United Kingdom)

"No novel is anything, for the purposes either of comedy or tragedy, unless the reader can sympathize with the characters"; however, "in the love with which" Lily Dale "has been greeted I have hardly joined with much enthusiasm, feeling that she is somewhat of a French prig."—Anthony Trollope. (By courtesy of the National Portrait Gallery, London)

Cher Maître, "the bearded Penseroso of Sargent's delicate drawing, soberly fastidious in dress and manner, cut on the approved pattern of the *homme du monde* of the 'eighties"—Henry James, described by Wharton. (Private collection)

"How can I make myself pretty enough for him to notice me? Well—this time I had a new hat; a *beautiful new hat!* I was almost sure it was becoming, and I felt that if he would only tell me so I might at last pluck up courage to blurt out my admiration for 'Daisy Miller' and 'Portrait of a Lady.' But he noticed neither the hat nor its wearer"—Edith Wharton on James. (By courtesy of the Lilly Library, Indiana University, Bloomington, Indiana)

"By the bye, as I must leave off being young, I find many Douceurs in being a sort of Chaperon for I am put on the Sofa near the Fire & can drink as much wine as I like."—Jane Austen. (By courtesy of the National Portrait Gallery, London)

"And it is true too, for . . . I know the cat that swallowed the lace, that belonged to the lady that sent for the doctor, that gave the emetic &c!!!"—Elizabeth Gaskell. (By courtesy of the National Portrait Gallery, London)

"It was rather melancholy. Strauss looks so strange and cast-down, and my deficient German prevented us from learning more of each other than our exterior, which in the case of both would have been better left to imagination."—George Eliot. (By courtesy of the National Portrait Gallery, London)

LAUGHTER & EXPERIMENT

"We burst into laughter from want of sympathy," writes Hazlitt. Only those "misfortunes in which we are spectators, not sharers," are capable of evoking our laughter; for when we are the victims of misfortune ourselves, "we feel the pain as well, which more than counterbalances the speculative entertainment." Cartoon from *The Passions Humorously Delineated*, by Tim Bobbin (1810). (Reproduced by courtesy of the Director and University Librarian, the John Rylands University Library of Manchester)

Feminine humor, according to Oliphant, is a "laughing assault," a "mocking love" that takes the heroine "to pieces with an affectionate and caressing hand" and lets "us laugh at her . . . tenderly, as we do at the follies of our favourite child." Photograph of Charlotte Yonge and her mother by Lewis Carroll. (Photography Collection, Harry Ransom Humanities Research Center, The University of Texas at Austin)

PART TWO

Readings

THREE

Mansfield Park and *Persuasion:*
Humor as Maternal Aggression

Miss Crawford was glad to find a family of such consequence so very near them, and not at all displeased either at her sister's early care [in choosing a husband for her], or the choice it had fallen on [Tom Bertram]. Matrimony was her object, provided she could marry well, and having seen Mr Bertram in town, she knew that objection could no more be made to his person than to his situation in life. While she treated it as a joke, therefore, she did not forget to think of it seriously.

—*Mansfield Park*[1]

But, fair or not fair, there are unbecoming conjunctions, which reason will patronize in vain,—which taste cannot tolerate,—which ridicule will seize.

—*Persuasion*[2]

For many readers, Jane Austen's novels fall with satisfying symmetry into two distinct camps. There are, on the one hand, the "novels of education" or the "sunny novels":[3] *Pride and Prejudice, Emma,* and *Northanger Abbey.* In these, the narration good-naturedly mocks the heroine for a particular, plot-generating foible (Catherine Morland's ultraliterary reading of the social text, Elizabeth Bennet's rash judgments of character, Emma Woodhouse's overweening self-regard), even as it ridicules a number of her fellow characters for their snobbery or fatuousness. By fully engaging with the comic structure—which bestows marriage as a reward for the heroine's reformation—the narrative humor guarantees that both the narrator's and reader's relation to the heroine is constant, steady, and at a slight psychological distance.

Such, however, is not the case in Austen's "problem" novels. Neither *Sense and Sensibility* nor *Mansfield Park* nor *Persuasion* is, strictly speaking, a comic *Bildungsroman:* although each ends in marriage, none is achieved through the heroine's growing self-knowledge and subsequent regeneration. In fact, Elinor Dashwood, Fanny Price, and Anne Elliot—all dutiful and submissive, if parentally underappreciated, daughters—have no outstanding faults to reform. These narratives, rather, follow the trajectory of their heroines' thwarted desire: their long-suffering devotion to a man beloved from the opening chapters, though not attained by reason of fate and outside interference until closure. Similarly, the narrative humor, rather than reinforcing the chastening authority of the plot as in the "comic" novels, concentrates on the appalling selfishness of subsidiary characters like Mr. and Mrs. John Dashwood, Mrs. Norris, and Sir Walter, leaving the heroine, for the most part, untouched.

Yet, curiously, the narrator's relation to the heroine in the problem novels is at once less distant and less stable than in the others. Even though Elinor, Fanny, and Anne are generally spared direct humorous assault, they are nevertheless sometimes implicated by association, their virtues turning up in other characters as risible vices. Although such humorous treatment does not limit the flow of narrative sympathy to them as it does to Catherine, Emma, and Elizabeth, it disrupts (however momentarily) when it does occur the narrator's otherwise remarkably empathic identification with her heroine.

What has customarily been called Austen's "irony," in other words, critically determines the quality of all her narrator-heroine relationships. Irony—as I have argued in the Preface—is a useful term only insofar as we are scrupulously alert to its internal contradictions and unfortunate imprecision. That said, Austen famously flirts with irony in many forms—structural, ethical, rhetorical—even if she refrains from wholeheartedly embracing any one of its manifestations. What prevents her from being a fully committed ironist—at least in the problem novels—is the affective closeness she sustains between her narrator and heroine, even when the latter is the object of narrative amusement. For regardless of the ontological distinctions among its various forms, all irony presumes a necessary emotional distance between the ironist and the ironized, whether that distance is experienced by the reader abstractly (in the disjunction between the ideal and the real) or immediately (in the disproportionate knowledge of reader and character). It is this affective closeness textualized in the narrator-heroine bond that inscribes Austen's production as feminine humor, no matter (I would argue) how ironically inflected it often may be.[4]

The task of this chapter is twofold. It considers the ways in which the narrative humor of *Mansfield Park* and *Persuasion*, employing at times ironic tactics, expresses "maternal" aggression against a culture that so strenuously restricts a daughter's identity and destiny.[5] By assailing the integrity of otherwise respected representatives of authority (like Sir Thomas and Lady Russell); by mocking in other characters (like Lady Bertram and Sir Walter Elliot) femininely gendered attributes that are highly valued in the heroines; and by countering the cultural ideal of femininity posed by Fanny and Anne with the powerful appeal of other female but less ideally feminine characters (like Mary Crawford and Mrs. Croft), Austen's narrative humor quietly devastates contemporary notions of middle-class femininity. To borrow phrasing from this chapter's epigraphs: her humor, even as it perforce treats its own operation as "a joke," exposes to "ridicule" the "unbecoming conjunction" between female agency and a culture that prohibits its expression. Yet, even though on most occasions the narrator's humor protects the heroine by attacking (stealthily but fiercely) the construction of femininity that constrains her, it also turns upon the heroine whenever she betrays a psychological weakness for one particular feature of that construction: the feminine tendency to overidealize romantic love. At such moments, humor threatens (where it generally sustains) the almost symbiotic bond between narrator and heroine: a bond metonymized by the blurred distinction in these novels between the heroine as a differentiated being and the heroine as an extension of the narrator. For being rendered largely through narrative description and indirect discourse rather than dialogue, neither Fanny Price nor Anne Elliot is as "individuated," for example, as Elizabeth Bennet. Besides, then, identifying instances of outwardly directed maternal aggression, this chapter explores the affectively complicated mother-daughter tensions that inform the humor of Austen's most problematic novels.

The Example of Fanny Price

Mansfield Park is, for many readers, the story of Fanny Price: an "exceedingly timid and shy" (49) young woman, "misunderstood, . . . disregarded, and . . . under-valued" (173), who, by dint of her unwavering virtue, eventually earns both the affectionate respect of her rich adoptive uncle, Sir Thomas Bertram, and the love of his clergyman son, Edmund. Reductive as it is, this account of the plot suggests the qualities most often associated with the novel: its Richardsonian morality, its lack of gaiety, its apparent political and social conservatism.[6] It does not, however, suggest one important, though frequently neglected, aspect of the story that the cover illustration of the 1966 Penguin edition, interestingly enough, does.

The portrait of the Fluyder children, by Sir Thomas Lawrence (1806), shows three small, well-dressed children, presumably siblings: a boy framed by two girls, the younger of whom hangs languidly on his shoulder, while the older watches her from a seated position. The picture seems a curious choice for *Mansfield Park,* there being (in addition to the heroine, whose inclusion in such a family portrait is improbable) *four* Bertram children, all of whom are, even in the opening of the novel, considerably older than the Fluyders.[7] Nor do the relations among the children on the cover as represented by their positioning and expression suggest those of the children within. Yet their presence—which until recently initiated the reading of one of the most popular modern editions of *Mansfield Park*—does serve to remind us that this novel is in large part a story of children and their filial relations: not just of the Bertram children and their collective dread of their father and occasional rebellion against his authority (for example, their staging of "Lovers' Vows"), but especially of Fanny and her protracted prepubescence. Received into the Bertram household at the age of ten (she is the only Austen heroine introduced as a child), Fanny is treated both by the narrator and her fellow characters as little older than that for the greater part of the novel. She is, at eighteen, Sir Thomas's "little Fanny" (194), Edmund's "dear little Fanny" (339), Julia's "child" (128), and the narrator's "My Fanny" (446). Indeed, it is not until Henry is (sexually) attracted in part by her youth—"a youth of mind as lovely as of person" (323)—that "small of her age" (59) Fanny is accorded even adolescent status.[8]

To the extent that *Mansfield Park* is the story of Fanny Price, it is the story of her gradual eroticization as a preoedipal heroine. Prematurely "cut off" from the mother-associated world of Portsmouth when she is suddenly adopted by the Bertrams, Fanny not only comes to idealize that world and the lost connection with her mother that it represents, but also to transfer her emotional investment in Portsmouth to the father-dominated world of Mansfield—a world that she equally idealizes and, notwithstanding the psychic differences it represents, even experiences in somewhat similar ways. That is, because Fanny copes with her early loss of the maternal bond by transforming Edmund into a mother-substitute (as she previously had her brother William), the quality of the attachment she initially feels for Portsmouth is much the same as that which she comes to feel for Mansfield—and to vocalize once her illusions about Portsmouth have been shattered. Rather than the Law of the Father, then, intervening in and disrupting maternal union, Fanny, having transferred her daughterly love to Edmund, becomes intimately attached to—indeed, "nursed-up" on (404)—the paternal principle while avoiding the psychic struggle that the introduction of that principle usually entails. Consequently, and somewhat paradoxically, Fanny's relationship to the Law is largely preoedipal and suggestively masochistic. Despite her eager embrace of paternal authority, preoedipal conflicts of aggression and an ambiguously differentiated identity (represented by her nebulous age and class status and her intellectual oneness with Edmund) dominate her emotional life.

Not surprisingly, Fanny's status as a preoedipal child curtails rather than promotes humorous treatment. Indeed, not only does it evoke from the narrator that claim of proud, protective maternity ("My Fanny") withheld from every other Austen heroine, but it guarantees her a freedom from humor that some have thought not only complete but singular.[9] Yet, however relatively exempt Fanny herself may be, the same cannot be said for the circumstances in which she is plotted. As Tony Tanner among others has noted, Fanny is a direct descendent of Cinderella, who "more sensitive and fine than her lowly origins, is rewarded by winning the handsome prince" (*MP,* 10).[10] The points of comparison are many. She comes equipped with two proud, selfish, pampered stepsisters and a cruel stepmother (in aunt Norris), whose nastiness is hardly less exaggerated than the folklore version; Lady Bertram, indolent and vain, splits the characteristics of the prototype with her sister. Fanny not only performs all sorts of "useful" tasks in the Bertram household, uncomplainingly accepts the verbal abuse of her aunt, sleeps in the attic, and works without benefit of a fire in the old schoolroom, but she is prohibited from attending neighborhood balls as well. Associating the fairy-tale heroine with the textual one throws into high relief the gender and class prejudices that determine the general Mansfield attitude toward Fanny. It also, however, endows Fanny's woeful circumstances with a sense of humorous play, thereby rescuing her narrative from melodrama.

Casting a derisive light on her fellows, moreover, allows humor to shield Fanny textually, if not diegetically, from the pain of their neglect and, in some instances, active cruelty. The insufferable Mrs. Norris, for example, though effective at administering the little miseries of Fanny's life, is too often ridiculed by the narrator to constitute a serious threat to Fanny or to the happiness we anticipate for her as heroine. In this way, the narrative humor protectively encircles the sober handling of the heroine and (to use a favorite term of Austen's) *diverts*—in both senses of the word—our attention away from the serious implications of its own and other utterances: from a recognition that Fanny's character and behavior are marked by her cultural status as a (comparatively) poor woman, or that the treatment she experiences on account of her class difference often simply exaggerates and reinforces the treatment she experiences on account of her gender.[11]

By most male reports in the Mansfield community, Fanny is the ideal woman. Henry Crawford (to give him the benefit of the doubt) loves her for her principle and her silence (298, 302), for "the gentleness, modesty, and sweetness of her character" ("so essential a part of every woman's worth in the judgment of man" [297]).[12] Edmund considers her "the perfect model of a woman" (344), a paragon of self-sacrifice and moral rectitude. And Sir Thomas ultimately finds her to be "indeed the daughter that he wanted," "a prime comfort for himself," and "a great acquisition" (456, 455). In Sir Thomas's opinion, Fanny's "early hardship and discipline, and the consciousness of being born to struggle and endure" have been "advantages" (456), keeping her suitably mindful of her low birth and grateful for his magnanimity, while helping her to attain the selflessness of ideal femininity. Yet, despite Fanny's claim to feminine perfection and despite her personal allegiance to the social code of Mansfield Park ("thoroughly perfect in her eyes" [457]), the very (gendered) values that Fanny struggles to uphold often emerge as objects of mockery in association with other characters.

Gratitude, for instance, when demonstrated by Fanny herself, is generally a desirable trait of character. It counteracts her "habitual dread of her uncle" (193), and it forms the basis of her love for Edmund: "In return for such services" as "assisting the improvement of her mind, and extending its pleasures" Fanny "loved him better than any body in the world except William," her favorite brother (57).[13] In the context of the power relations between the heroine and her fellow characters, however, gratitude wears a slightly sinister mien (it being "much pleasanter to reproach than be grateful" [*JAL*, 74.1]). Fanny, who is repulsed by Henry's selfish, unprincipled behavior, nevertheless softens under the pressure of his persistent courting ("Would he have persevered, and uprightly, Fanny must have been his reward" [451])—partly in gratitude for his considerate blindness to her Portsmouth family's gaucheness and his efforts on behalf of William's advancement, partly as a consequence of emotional blackmail:

> [H]e approached her now with rights that demanded different treatment. She must be courteous, and she must be compassionate. She must have a sensation of being honoured, and whether thinking of herself or her brother, she must have a strong feeling of gratitude. (327)

[Henry was] determined . . . to have the glory, as well as the felicity, of forcing her to love him . . . ; and he had so much delight in the idea of *obliging* her to love him in a very short time, that her not loving him now was scarcely regretted. (325–26; emphasis added)

Gratitude (which along with "grateful" occurs forty-three times in the text) anxiously dominates Fanny's response to Mansfield Park—to Sir Thomas's charity, to Lady Bertram's flattering dependence upon her companionate services, and to Edmund's didactic interest in improving her mind. Having been for the most part emotionally abandoned even at her father's home in Portsmouth,[14] Fanny—whose affections are strong and self-regard weak—quickly learns to meet the slightest show of consideration with sometimes obsequious appreciation. At moments, Fanny sounds uncomfortably like her fellow interloper, Mrs. Norris:

[As they approached Sotherton] even Fanny had something to say in admiration, and might be heard with complacency. Her eye was eagerly taking in every thing within her reach; and after being at some pains to get a view of the house, [she observed] . . . that "it was a sort of building which she could not look at but with respect." (111)

"It may seem impertinent in me to praise, but I must admire the taste Mrs. Grant has shewn in [her shrubbery]." (222)

Not only, then, does gratitude figure as a virtue of Fanny's character, but it functions as a means of her coercion and as a reason for her stunted emotional development as well. Furthermore, in Mrs. Norris's hands, even while it is made to torture Fanny, gratitude also becomes an oblique object of narrative derision:

"Upon my word, Fanny, you are in high luck to meet with such attention and indulgence! You ought to be very much obliged . . . , and you ought to look upon it as something extraordinary: for I hope you are aware that there is no real occasion for your going into company in this sort of way, or ever dining out at all; and it is what you must not depend upon ever being repeated. Nor must you be fancying, that the invitation is meant as any particular compliment to *you;* the compliment is intended to your uncle and aunt, and me. Mrs. Grant thinks it a civility due to *us* to take a little notice of you." (231)

"The nonsense and folly of people's stepping out of their rank and trying to appear above themselves, makes me think it right to give *you* a hint, Fanny . . . Remember, wherever you are, you must be the lowest and the last." (232)

In both of these passages, the joke, which is accentuated by Austen's italics, is purchased entirely at Mrs. Norris's expense; indeed, Mrs. Norris's warnings to Fanny—who is less likely than anyone to take a kindness for granted or to overestimate her worth—properly apply only to herself. Thus, in a darkly humorous way, Fanny functions for her Aunt Norris as a sort of double in reverse, upon whom the latter projects her own social climbing and sycophancy. From Mrs. Norris's perspective, gratitude is merely the proper behavioral attitude of the lowly, extorted by those in power in exchange for their continued charitable support.[15] Such a representation not only drains gratitude of all value but, in being linked to Fanny through its humorous misapplication, throws doubt upon the ethical worth of Fanny's own excessive, if more sincere, thankfulness.

The significance of utility in the novel is similarly vexed by humor. Fanny—whose days are occupied in "carrying messages, and fetching" (56) at Mansfield and in "contributing to . . . [the household] comforts" at Portsmouth—is "very anxious to be useful." She readily complies with requests for assistance from all sides ("the habit of employing her" on "some errand" is common to all but Edmund [168]), and she attends Lady Bertram with daughterly devotion: "The only drawback [to Fanny's visiting her own family in Portsmouth] was the doubt of her Aunt Bertram's being comfortable without her" (365). (Nor, by the way, does Lady Bertram see the point of "Fanny's ever going near a Father and Mother who had done without her so long, while she was so useful to herself.") Usefulness offers Fanny a culturally approved mode of feminine action and a means to domestic acceptance, showing her to be, more than anything else can, a dutiful and grateful girl. Equally important, the "great pleasure" Fanny takes "in feeling her usefulness" (383) hints at its importance as a substitute satisfaction for more directly expressed desire:

> . . . the longing to be useful to those who were wanting her!
> Could she have been at home [that is, Mansfield], she might have been of service to every creature in the house. She felt that she must have been of use to all. To all, she must have saved some trouble . . . She loved to fancy how she could have read to her aunt, how she could have talked to her . . . ; and how many walks up and down stairs she might have saved her, and how many messages she might have carried.
> It astonished her that Tom's sisters could be satisfied with remaining in London at such a time—through an illness. (421–22)

Fanny's infatuation with her own usefulness provokes in this passage a rare instance of the narrator's teasing humor. Although Fanny may "love to fancy" all the minute pleasures of reading, talking, fetching, and carrying for her aunt Bertram, the narrative that records them in deliberately repetitive fashion points to their inadequacy as outlets for female agency.

Most damaging, however, to the textual status of usefulness as a virtue are Mrs. Norris's anxious flurries of manifestly meaningless activity. Almost immediately following Fanny's musing about the peace she derives from being "occasionally useful to all" (186), the narrative turns sharply to Mrs. Norris's diatribe:

> "Come Fanny, . . . you must not be always walking from one room to the other and doing the lookings on, at your ease, in this way,—I want you here. . . . It would be lucky for me if I had nothing but the executive part to do.— *You* are best off, I can tell you; but if nobody did more than *you,* we should not get on very fast." (186)

Mrs. Norris not only falsely accuses Fanny of loafing (and exposes herself to ridicule by introducing a comparison between them), but her own behavior—"trying to be in a bustle without having any thing to bustle about; and labouring to be important where nothing was wanted but tranquillity and silence" (196)—travesties the very idea of a specifically feminine utility, as the heavily ironic humor of the following passage amply confirms:

> Mrs. Norris had been indulging in very dreadful fears, and trying to make Edmund participate [in] them whenever she could get him alone; and as she depended on being the first person made acquainted with any fatal catastrophe, she had already arranged the manner of breaking it to all the others, when Sir Thomas's assurances of . . . being alive and well, made it necessary to lay by her agitation and affectionate preparatory speeches for a while . . . Mrs. Norris in promoting gaieties for her nieces, assisting their toilettes, displaying their accomplishments, and looking about for their future husbands, had so much to do as, in addition to all her own household cares, some interference in those of her sister, and Mrs. Grant's wasteful doings to overlook, left her very little occasion to be occupied even in fears for the absent. (68)

Passive submission—the most obvious of Fanny's feminine virtues— is often found contextually impaled by humor as well. "[S]eeing all the obligation and expediency of submission and forbearance" (390), Fanny demonstrates her "habits of ready submission" (353) in countless examples throughout the novel. Indeed, her quiet resistance to acting in "Lovers' Vows" and to Henry's marriage proposal appears starkly rebellious only against the background of her characteristic passivity, which whether labeled "patience and forbearance" (297), "sweetness of . . . temper" (452), or "diffidence . . . and softness" (326) is particularly prized by the trinity of Mansfield men for whom she represents a financial or emotional investment (Sir Thomas, Edmund, and Henry: father, brother, and would-be husband).[16] Yet, crucial though it may be to Fanny's worth in a patriarchal economy, feminine submission is mockingly discredited almost everywhere else it occurs: be it in the submission to "duty" that misleads Maria to marry Rushworth (72); in the resignation to domestic chaos that constitutes Mrs. Price's "slatternly" housekeeping (383);[17] or especially, and most memorably, in the character of Lady Bertram, whose hyperbolic state of inactivity is the surest source of humor in the novel. Even her children laugh at her indolence:

> "[T]he expectation of his [Sir Thomas's] return must be a very anxious period to my mother, [Tom said to Edmund,] and if we can be the means of amusing that anxiety, and keeping up her spirits for the next few weeks [by mounting a theatrical], I shall think our time very well spent, and so I am sure will he.—It is a very anxious period for her."
>
> As he said this, each looked towards their mother. Lady Bertram, sunk back in one corner of the sofa, the picture of health, wealth, ease, and tranquillity, was just falling into a gentle doze, while Fanny was getting through the few difficulties of her work for her.
>
> Edmund smiled and shook his head.
>
> "By Jove! this won't do"—cried Tom, throwing himself into a chair with a hearty laugh. "To be sure, my dear mother, your anxiety—I was unlucky there." (151)

Lady Bertram—who "might always be considered as only half awake" (340), who speaks "entirely by rote" (209), and who is "a cipher" without her husband (182)—is a paragon of feminine passivity; her only productive activity besides childbearing is letter writing, characterized by a bloated or "amplifying style" (415). Not only are all decisions made for her by her husband (or by her sister, on her husband's behalf), but all her thinking as well: "'I will ask Sir Thomas, as soon as he comes in, whether I can do without'" Fanny for an evening (229). Functioning as little more than a vessel for her husband's various outpourings ("her whole comprehension [was] filled by his narratives" [196]), Lady Bertram is as completely unconscious of her own feelings as of the feelings of others, incapable of calculating her own desire except as a logical probability and in retrospect:

> By not one of the circle was he [Sir Thomas] listened to with such unbroken unalloyed enjoyment as by his wife, who was really extremely happy

to see him, and whose feelings were so warmed by his sudden arrival, as to place her nearer agitation than she had been for the last twenty years . . . It was so agreeable to her to see him again . . . that she began particularly to feel how dreadfully she must have missed him, and how impossible it would have been for her to bear a lengthened absence [N.B.: he'd been absent for two years]. (195)

Although her husband has come to regard at least some aspects of her utter passivity as cloying (it makes her an undesirable partner in Whist, for example [248]), he is far from forswearing the virtue of female submission. Lady Bertram doused with a tonic of usefulness such as invigorates Fanny would presumably suit him quite well. And while Fanny's anxious gratitude and her desire to be useful may forever preserve her from the abyss of inertia into which Lady Bertram has sunk, the parallels between their infantilization, their intellectual dependency, and their sweetness of temper (that is, their passivity—Fanny considers "her aunt as having the sweetest of all sweet tempers" [397]) signal that loss of independent thought, desire, and action threatens Fanny as well.

Henry's astonishing offer of marriage confirms the uneasy feeling spreading in the Bertram household that "little Fanny's" personal attractions may not be so paltry after all ("'Humph,'" sounds Lady Bertram, "looking at her complacently, . . . 'We certainly are a handsome family'" [331]). Whatever nature has bestowed upon Fanny in the way of beauty, however, depends for its visibility upon the privileges of Mansfield Park. A frail child, "with no glow of complexion, nor any other striking beauty" (49), Fanny requires the exercise, fresh air, and relative leisure available at Mansfield in order to bloom; indeed, transplanted, as she temporarily is, into the less hospitable domestic climate of Portsmouth, Fanny begins to wilt. On the day of his return from Antigua, Sir Thomas first notices her improved looks: "[O]n perceiving her, [Sir Thomas] came forward with a kindness which astonished and penetrated her, calling her his dear Fanny, kissing her affectionately, and observing with decided pleasure how much she was grown!" [194]). In this way, Fanny suddenly finds herself entered among the ranks of the "interesting" (219, 278), that is, as an object of erotic attention—a condition that causes her to feel "quite oppressed" (194).

> "Ask your uncle what he thinks, and you will hear compliments enough [said Edmund]; and though they may be chiefly on your person, you must put up with it, and trust to his seeing as much beauty of mind in time."

Such language was so new to Fanny that it quite embarrassed her.

"Your uncle thinks you pretty, dear Fanny—and that is the long and short of the matter . . . ; but the truth is, that your uncle never did admire you till now—and now he does. Your complexion is so improved! and you have gained so much countenance!—and your figure— Nay, Fanny, do not turn away about it—it is but an uncle. If you cannot bear an uncle's admiration what is to become of you? You must really begin to harden yourself to the idea of being worth looking at." (212)

Sir Thomas is the first to eroticize Fanny, with Henry and eventually Edmund merely following suit. His appreciation of her nubile beauty in turn arouses his mercantile interest, which, like his interest in the slave economy of Antigua, he takes pains to protect.[18] Except for her temporary devaluation for refusing to marry Henry, Fanny's "value increase[s]" (219) steadily from the moment of Sir Thomas's return to Mansfield. He gives a ball in order to show Fanny to advantage (285) and shields her from Henry's sight for similar reasons: "[W]hen he looked at his niece, and saw the state of feature and complexion which her crying had brought her into, he thought there might be as much lost as gained by an immediate interview" (320). However dark it may be, by linking Fanny to Lady Bertram through the common attraction they hold for Sir Thomas and through the shared hothouse quality of their beauty (contrast the "remarkably pretty" [74] Mary Crawford, "active and fearless . . . and strongly made" [97]),[19] the narrative humor works to demystify the cultural treatment of daughters as products manufactured and marketed by patriarchy: "[W]ithout attributing all her personal beauty . . . to her transplantation to Mansfield, he was pleased with himself for having supplied every thing else;—education and manners she owed him" (282). In sum, by juxtaposing, commenting upon, or exaggerating in other characters those values (beauty, submission, gratitude, and usefulness) most often praised in Fanny, the humor challenges, if not their ethical worth, than at least their expedience for the dependent females who practice or embody them.

UNDERMINING PATRIARCHY

Although the code of feminine behavior to which Fanny subscribes may be privileged by the plot—in her ultimate triple installation as sister, wife, and daughter at Mansfield Park and by the ousting of those who violate that code (Maria, Mrs. Norris, the Crawfords, and the Grants)—the cultural authority that determines and encourages Fanny's behavior is itself undermined by the narrative humor. To begin with, the humor reveals

proper feminine behavior to be at base an article of purely patriarchal construction. "Loving, guiding, and protecting her, as he had been doing ever
since her being ten years old, her mind in so great a degree formed by his
care" (454), Edmund inculcates in Fanny all his own opinions—including
those of correct moral conduct, which he has inherited directly from his
father. Given the source of her views, it is hardly surprising that Fanny and
Edmund should almost invariably concur. Thus, though Edmund finds
such an occasion of agreement worth noting, the narrator finds it only
worth a witticism: "'I am glad you saw it all as I did,'" he happily remarks,
after examining Fanny on the subject of Mary's unfeminine candor, to
which the narrator dryly retorts, "Having formed her mind and gained her
affections, he had a good chance of her thinking like him" (95).

Yet even though Fanny's opinions are identical to Edmund's, her behavior is restricted by them in ways in which his is not. Edmund, by reason
of his gender, is permitted to share in—and eventually to accede to—his
father's authority (he treats Fanny, for example, "with the kind authority
of a privileged guardian" [351]). Fanny, in contrast, is limited to her reproductive functions—ideological as well as biological—and culturally relegated to the role of mirror.[20] Having learned to distrust her own opinion
whenever it occasionally diverges from Edmund's ("'I ought to believe you
to be right rather than myself'" [61]), Fanny, to our amusement, is taken
aback by her own daring in subscribing to a circulating library and by the
sense of individuated identity such action confers upon her, "amazed at
being any thing *in propria persona*" (390). Most of the time, she simply
reflects Edmund:

> [Fanny:] "When I look out on such a night as this, I feel as if there could
> be neither wickedness nor sorrow in the world; and there certainly would
> be less of both if the sublimity of Nature were more attended to, and
> people were carried more out of themselves by contemplating such a
> scene."
>
> "I like to hear your enthusiasm, Fanny. It is a lovely night, and they
> are much to be pitied who have not been taught to feel in some degree
> as you do . . ."
>
> "*You* taught me to think and feel on the subject, cousin." (139)

Reared to be dutiful and filially respectful by Edmund and motivated
by a childlike earnestness to please,[21] Fanny internalizes the values of
Mansfield Park—"elegance, propriety, regularity, harmony . . . peace and
tranquility" (384)—with a vengeance. She comes (not without cause) to
consider her own father "dirty and gross" (382), her mother "a dawdle"

and "a slattern" (383), and "every body under-bred" in Portsmouth (387). Although Fanny recoils in horror at Edmund's suggestion that she teach Henry those principles Edmund has taught her ("'I would not engage in such a charge,' cried Fanny in a shrinking accent—'in such an office of high responsiblity'" [347]), she nevertheless proves to be their most stalwart defender under pressure. When Edmund fears weakness in moments of crisis—whether on the subject of Mary or on his own participation in the play—it is Fanny to whom he turns for a stronger dose of his own morality. Her tenacity results partially from her devotion to Edmund, partially from "[h]er awe of her uncle, and her dread of taking a liberty" (424), and partially from the personal advantages she sees in obeisance (her "favoured education had fixed in her" not only "juster notions of what was due to every body" but "what would be wisest for herself" [389]). Given that the principles of Mansfield Park are in a general state of decline, being either rejected or ignored by most of its other inhabitants, Fanny's faithfully enacting them works, in effect, to shore up a house crumbling from within. (Such an enactment would soon come to be culturally taken for granted as an edifying display of feminine "influence.")

While Fanny proves to be the dutiful daughter *par excellence*—ideologically compliant but firm in enforcing the social order (even, as in the case of "Lovers' Vows," against her own desire to see a play performed)[22]—her surrogate father, "the master at Mansfield Park" (365), is discovered in the humor to be a tyrannical parent of near-gothic proportions.[23] Emotionally distant and severely authoritarian ("'Advise' was his word, but it was the advice of absolute power" [285]), Sir Thomas rules Mansfield in a spirit of restraint and repression that his children, especially his daughters, find intolerable. "Under his government," it was "all sameness and gloom" (211), and even Fanny feels its oppressiveness: her "relief [at Sir Thomas's going to Antigua], and her consciousness of it, were quite equal to her cousins'" (66). Until his daughters reach marriageable age, Sir Thomas ignores them almost as completely as he does Fanny, delegating the responsibility for their education (an education in "beauty and brilliant acquirements" [68]) to the overly indulgent and fulsome Mrs. Norris. Once they reach nubility, however, his interest noticeably increases—an interest that, as the narrator wryly emphasizes (by means of dashes and rhetorical repetition), is more commercial than affectionate:

> It was an alliance which he could not have relinquished without pain; and thus he reasoned. Mr. Rushworth was young enough to improve;— Mr. Rushworth must and would improve in good society; and if Maria could now speak so securely of her happiness with him, speaking cer-

tainly without the prejudice, the blindness of love, she ought to be believed . . . Such and such-like were the reasonings of Sir Thomas—
happy to escape the embarrassing evils of a rupture, . . . happy to secure
a marriage which would bring him such an addition of respectability and
influence, and very happy to think any thing of his daughter's disposition
that was most favourable for the purpose. (215)

Although piqued by Henry's rejection into her self-destructive insistence
upon marrying the doltish Rushworth, Maria (like Julia after her) marries
largely to "escape" paternal coercion: "She was less and less able to endure
the restraint which her father imposed. The liberty which his absence had
given was now become absolutely necessary" (216).[24] Indeed, the humor
that runs throughout the narrative commentary on Maria's marriage is
strikingly grim, exposing not just Sir Thomas's compelling greed and Maria's callousness ("her feelings . . . were not acute" [215]) but the appalling
baseness of the marriage market and of a feminine education tailored to
meet its interests:

> Maria was more to be pitied than Julia [on the occasion of their
> father's return], for to her the father brought a husband, and the return
> of the friend most solicitous for her happiness, would unite her to the
> lover, on whom she had chosen that happiness should depend. It was a
> gloomy prospect. (134)

> It was a very proper wedding. The bride was elegantly dressed—the two
> bridesmaids were duly inferior—her father gave her away—her mother
> stood with salts in her hand, expecting to be agitated—her aunt tried to
> cry—and the service was impressively read by Dr. Grant. Nothing could
> be objected . . . except that the carriage . . . was the same chaise which
> Mr. Rushworth had used for a twelvemonth before. In every thing else
> the etiquette of the day might stand the strictest investigation. (217)

When Fanny is the object of Sir Thomas's mercantile designs, the narrative humor takes a decidedly less bitter tone, largely because Fanny is less
fatally determined by her education and commodification than are her
cousins. Whatever else she may suffer on account of her inferior class status, Fanny, having "not been brought up to the trade of *coming out*" (273)
is spared both early commercialization and the unwholesome cultivation
of her self-importance. Consequently, unlike her cousins, whose "vanity
was in such good order, that they seemed to be quite free from it" (68),
Fanny is immune to Henry's flattery and flirtation, considering "it all as
nonsense, as mere trifling and gallantry" (304).

Although Sir Thomas only becomes interested in Fanny at a late date,
once he notices her beauty and the attraction she holds for a prospective

buyer as promising as Henry Crawford, he brokers enthusiastically on her behalf. Not only does he arrange for Fanny and Henry to meet on a frequent basis; he engages in merchandising tactics of a rather pointed (if subjunctively expressed) nature:

> In thus sending her away [to bed], Sir Thomas perhaps might not be thinking merely of her health. It might occur to him, that Mr. Crawford had been sitting by her long enough, or he might mean to recommend her as a wife by shewing her persuadableness. (286)

Afraid that Fanny "might not have persuaded herself into receiving [Henry's] addresses properly before the young man's inclination for paying them were over" (352), Sir Thomas even resorts to duplicity. He decides, for the first time in the eight years since she has come to live with him, to return her to Portsmouth for a visit:

> [But] his prime motive in sending her away, had very little to do with the propriety of her seeing her parents again, and nothing at all with any idea of making her happy. He certainly wished her to go willingly, but he as certainly wished her to be heartily sick of home before her visit ended; and that a little abstinence from the elegancies and luxuries of Mansfield Park, would bring her mind into a sober state, and incline her to a juster estimate of the value of that home of greater permanence, and equal comfort, of which she had the offer. (363)

Sir Thomas's plan is, in one sense, so successful that Fanny—"debarred from her usual, regular exercise" (401), "living in incessant noise" (384), and "so little equal" to the inelegant Portsmouth meals—becomes "heartily sick of home" literally as well as figuratively. The "little abstinence" he contrives in order to pressure her into accepting Henry proves, subjunctively speaking, lethal:

> After being nursed up at Mansfield, it was too late in the day to be hardened at Portsmouth; and though Sir Thomas, *had he known all might have thought his niece in the most promising way of being starved,* both mind and body, into a much juster value for Mr. Crawford's good company and good fortune, he *would probably have feared to push his experiment* farther, *lest she might die* under the cure. (404; emphasis added)[25]

Nowhere is Sir Thomas's tyranny so apparent (and so slyly mocked) as in his interview with Fanny shortly after Henry's marriage proposal. Parodying conventions of the gothic novel (which in turn owe much to *Clarissa*), the narrative humor places Fanny alone and "in a good deal of agitation" (312) in the fireless old schoolroom, "when suddenly the sound of a step in regular approach was heard—a heavy step, an unusual step in that part of the house; it was her uncle's; she knew it as well as his voice; she had trembled at it as often, and began to tremble again, at the idea of his coming up to speak to her" (312). Although Sir Thomas intends only to offer congratulations, he delivers two speeches of a far different character. The first is an apology for class prejudice. Noticing the absence of a fire in her room, he first condemns it as an unconscionable oversight; then realizing that it results from the extreme enforcement of his own policies of "distinction" (47), he twists his condemnation (by means of auxiliary repetition)[26] into a paternalistic dictum that actually commands Fanny's gratitude for her treatment as an inferior, while neatly displacing his own guilt in the matter onto Aunt Norris:

> "I am aware that there has been sometimes, in some points, a misplaced distinction; but I think too well of you, Fanny, to suppose you *will* ever harbour resentment on that account . . . You *will* take in the whole of the past, you *will* consider times, persons, and probabilities . . . [;] every advantage of affluence *will* be doubled by the little privations and restrictions that *may* have been imposed. I am sure you *will* not disappoint my opinion of you, by failing at any time to treat your aunt Norris with the respect and attention that are due to her." (314–15; emphasis added)

If Sir Thomas's first speech exposes his class bigotry, his second starkly betrays his gender bias. He finds Fanny's principled refusal to marry Henry so alien to the economy of self-interest he inhabits as to be literally (and comically) incomprehensible: "'I do not catch your meaning'" [315], and "'There is something in this which my comprehension does not reach'" [316]). As a result, he lambastes her for protofeminist behavior:

> "It is of no use, I perceive, to talk to you . . . I will, therefore, only add . . . that you have disappointed every expectation I had formed . . . I had thought you peculiarly free from wilfulness of temper, self-conceit, and every tendency to that independence of spirit, which prevails so much in modern days, even in young women, and which in young women is offensive and disgusting beyond all common offence. But you have now shewn me that you can be wilful and perverse . . . The advantage or disadvantage of your family—of your parents—your brothers and sisters—never seems to have had a moment's share in your thoughts on this occasion. How *they* might be benefited, how *they* must rejoice in such an establishment for you—is nothing to *you*. You think only of yourself." (318)

Although wildly mistargeted and indefensibly harsh, this attack on Fanny for female presumption is mitigated—and the reader's memory of its ferocity consequently dulled—by a sudden narrative reference to Mrs.

Norris, whose name, by this point in the text, is a red flag for mordant humor:

> "There is no occasion for spreading the disappointment; say nothing about it yourself."
>   This was an order to be most joyfully obeyed . . . To be spared from her aunt Norris's interminable reproaches!—he left her in a glow of gratitude. Any thing might be bearable rather than such reproaches. Even to see Mr. Crawford would be less overpowering. (321)

Opportune mocking of Mrs. Norris thus distracts attention from Sir Thomas's bullying of Fanny here (and from his other failings elsewhere).[27] Indeed, far from being the perfect surrogate father (intrapsychically purchased on Fanny's part by devaluing Mr. Price), Sir Thomas resembles his brother-in-law in all but superficials: their rule over their respective households is equally despotic, and their treatment of Fanny similarly dehumanizing. Like her uncle, who first recognizes Fanny only as an erotic object, Fanny's father "scarcely ever noticed her, but to make her the object of a coarse joke" (382).

Such humorous undermining of patriarchal authority occurs not only in the sidelong narrative commentary on Sir Thomas and Edmund, and in the aunts' exaggerated performance of feminine virtues, but also at times in the meticulous textual reproduction of cultural norms and values. Maria, for example, reared in a household where money determines action and alliances, imagines that her most profound daughterly obligation is to marry rich:

> Being now in her twenty-first year, Maria Bertram was beginning to think matrimony a duty; and as a marriage with Mr. Rushworth would give her the enjoyment of a larger income than her father's, as well as ensure her the house in town, which was now a prime object, it became, by the same rule of moral obligation, her evident duty to marry Mr. Rushworth if she could. (72)

Her ethical education having been limited to the feminine arts of attraction, Maria, unsurprisingly, applies commercial logic to her moral conduct. In so doing, she continues a family tradition. Her mother has so completely internalized the ideology of the marriage market ("beauty and wealth were all that excited her respect" [330]) that it warps even her most valued emotional relationships. When Fanny suggests that her aunt would miss her companionship too much to want her to marry, Lady Bertram blithely replies:

"No, my dear, I should not think of missing you, when such an offer as this comes in your way. I could do very well without you, if you were married to a man of such good estate as Mr. Crawford. And you must be aware, Fanny, that it is every young woman's duty to accept such an unexceptionable offer as this."

This was almost the only rule of conduct, the only piece of advice, which Fanny had ever received from her aunt in the course of eight years and a half.—It silenced her. (331)

Even Fanny herself, who has been made "perfect" by her fastidious incarnation of Sir Thomas's beliefs, demonstrates how the reproduction of patriarchy ironically undercuts its own authority. For, notwithstanding her perfection, the heroine of *Mansfield Park* is, as Austen's own mother complained, "insipid" and vaguely tiresome, and as such unlikely to win a mass following to her dutiful way of life.[28] Because she is psychologically underage and vulnerable to indoctrination, we make allowances for "dear little Fanny," generally forgiving—though certainly not forgetting—her dullness.

THE RELIEF OF "THROWING RIDICULE":
MARY CRAWFORD AND THE NARRATOR

Of all the women of *Mansfield Park*, Mary Crawford clearly presents the greatest challenge to phallocratic control. She not only displays a tremendous sexual energy that captivates even an improbable wooer like Edmund Bertram, but she is completely unintimidated by authority, and, next to the narrator, the sharpest wit in the novel. She frankly points out the hypocrisies of others—the lasciviousness of her uncle the admiral and the dangerous flirtation "of those indefatigable rehearsers" (188), Maria Bertram and Henry Crawford—and laughingly demystifies cultural myths of both gender and class. In response to Edmund's query about the size of her naval acquaintance, Mary replies, "'Among Admirals, large enough; but,' with an air of grandeur; 'we know very little of the inferior ranks. Post captains may be very good sort of men, but they do not belong to *us*'" (91). And in response to Fanny's rather pietistic exclamation that "a whole family assembling regularly for the purpose of prayer, is fine!" Mary, "laughing," exposes the paternalistic results such evangelical notions often breed: "It must do the heads of the family a great deal of good to force all the poor housemaids and footmen to leave business and pleasure, and say their prayers here twice a day, while they are inventing excuses themselves for staying away" (115).

She is particularly shrewd on the subject of marriage, avoiding its over-romanticization and accepting the materialism of marital negotiations as *de rigueur* among the leisured middle class: for both sexes, marriage simply boils down to "a manoeuvring business" (79). And while she believes that "every body should marry as soon as they can do it to advantage" (76) and not "throw themselves away," her class allegiance is limited; she is personally "not displeased" with her brother Henry for wishing to marry one who, like Fanny, is "a little beneath him" (296) and even appreciates its symbolic feminist value: "'the glory of fixing one who has been shot at by so many; of having it in one's power to pay off the debts of one's sex!'" (358). Furthermore, Mary is the only character who recognizes how fully Maria has been victimized by her upbringing. While the others view Maria's decision to marry Rushworth with varying degrees of approbation or apprehension, Mary suggests that Maria has little real say in the matter, having been reared from birth by Sir Thomas to be a sacrificial lamb at the altar of Hymen:

> "Don't be affronted," said she laughing; "but it does put me in mind of some of the old heathen heroes, who after performing exploits in a foreign land, offered sacrifices to the gods on their safe return." (135)

Mary's views on daughterly duty are as potentially radical as her views on marriage and class. She holds that financial independence, not marriage, "is the best recipe for happiness I ever heard of" (226), and she betrays a decidedly unfeminine ambition both in becoming "[a]ngry with Edmund for adhering to his own notions and acting on them in defiance of her" (290) and in wistfully longing for a more constructive activity than flirting: "'I often think of Mr. Rushworth's property and independence . . . A *man* might represent the county with such an estate; a *man* might escape a profession and represent the county'" (182; emphasis added). Like Maria's, her sense of duty is unsentimental and self-interested ("'It is every body's duty to do as well for themselves as they can'" [293]); yet unlike Maria's, it is explicitly held and shamelessly masculine.[29]

Precisely because Mary Crawford is not the heroine of *Mansfield Park,* she has narrative permission to scandalize her fellow characters, and often her readers, with relative impunity. Fanny and Edmund may condemn Mary for her weak morality and lack of "feminine loathings" (441), but the narrator shows considerably more mercy. When Fanny thinks Mary undeserving of Edmund and fears that "his worth would finally be wasted on her," the narrator comes to Mary's defense. "[I]mpartiality would not

have denied to Miss Crawford's nature, that participation of the general
nature of women, which would lead her to adopt the opinions of the man
she loved and respected, as her own" (362); in other words, Mary's love for
Edmund would, in the narrator's opinion, lead to her behavioral reformation rather than his vitiation. Moreover, no matter how ethically unsound
it may be, almost everyone finds Mary's witty volubility irresistible. The
reader thanks her for it; Edmund falls in love with her at least partially
because of it; and even the relentlessly somber Fanny has to admit to being
amused: "'I like to hear her talk. She entertains me'" (94); and, wonder of
wonders, "'She made me almost laugh'" (95). Mary's "lively mind" (95)
and "playful manner" (412) are so appealing, in fact, that in order for the
lackluster Fanny to rise to the stature of romantic heroine and for her
moral severity to win our esteem (if not our admiration), Mary must ultimately be exiled from the novel. As D. A. Miller has noted, Mary, whose
language makes up "so much of the text," suddenly "disappears from direct
view" in "the last hundred or so pages of *Mansfield Park*," being "represented only by her letters to Fanny and by Edmund's report of his last
meeting with her."[30] The most damning evidence against Mary, then, consists of interpretive accounts of her speech and letters by Edmund and
Fanny—two of the least impartial of character witnesses. (Were her own
humorous reporting of the facts admitted as testimony, we might, regardless of our better judgment perhaps, acquit her.) Despite her denunciation
by the Mansfield moralists, Mary is allowed to escape the novel not simply
without punishment but with her charm, though somewhat tarnished, still
largely intact. And, thanks to the destabilizing, elusive character of humor,
Mary evades definitive interpretation and labeling as well. Though she cannot possibly be called a heroine, Mary is no villainess either.

Indeed, Mary functions as nothing so much as a narrative analogue to
Fanny. Edmund is simply love-blind in asserting that there is "so much
general resemblance in true generosity and natural delicacy" (270) between
his cousin and his would-be lover. Yet the narrator, too, notes that, although some of the difference between them belongs to "disposition and
habit . . . still more might be imputed to difference of circumstances"
(290); like Fanny, Mary has "really good feelings by which she was almost
purely governed" (170). Hence, examining "some points of interest [upon
which] they were exactly opposed to each other"—namely, their sense of
appropriate feminine conduct—clarifies not only the nature of their
differences, but, more important, how very far our acceptance of Mary
and her ideas actually goes: point for point, we find the witty disruptor of

the patriarchal status quo more sympathetically engaging than its ideal daughter.[31]

Mary's profuse and sometimes brazen talk, for instance, is consistently more agreeable than Fanny's even more profuse feminine silence (arguably, Fanny speaks demonstrably less than any other Austen heroine because she has in Mary a double who speaks so much). Her failure to internalize an upper-middle-class code of feminine conduct exposes Mary to Edmund's charge of unwomanliness (a lack of "feminine loathings"), but it doesn't paralyze her as Fanny's successful internalization does. Indeed, Fanny's strict sense of propriety prohibits her from directly expressing desire of any sort, which, among other things, makes her hostage to Henry's sexual advances.[32] Furthermore, Mary's interpretation of Maria's conduct as mere folly, which so infuriates Edmund, proceeds from a standard of judgment that recognizes no gender distinction in moral culpability: Mary reasonably concludes that Maria, being no more to blame than Henry for their elopement, deserves no severer punishment. Fanny reacts more to Edmund's liking: "[I]f there was a woman of character in existence, who could treat as a trifle this sin of the first magnitude, who could try to gloss it over, and desire to have it unpunished, she could believe Miss Crawford to be the woman!" (429). But the hysterical intensity of her response to the news of Maria's elopement—her "sleepless" "misery," her "feelings of sickness" and "shudderings of horror," her "hot fits of fever" and "cold" (429), as well as her feeling that "the greatest blessing to every one of kindred with Mrs. Rushworth would be instant annihilation" (430)—suggests that such a response owes as much to Fanny's intrapsychic conflicts as to her high-minded morality.[33]

The surest sign of the narrative object-splitting that operates with regard to Mary and Fanny can be found in the presentation of laughter, for in *Mansfield Park,* as in none of Austen's other novels, laughter and cultural authority are internalized as mutually exclusive principles. Nowhere else in Austen, indeed, does a narrator so frequently gesture to a character's suppression of laughter; it rivals similar gesturing to Marianne's violent suppression of speech in *Sense and Sensibility.*[34] Although Fanny comes close at a number of points (she "almost laugh[s]" at Mary [95]; she "could hardly help laughing at" Tom [145]; "in spite of herself, she could not help half a smile, but she said nothing" [340]; "Fanny could not avoid a faint smile, but had nothing to say" [358]), she never actually manages an outright show of amusement.[35] Tellingly, the only (litotically) recorded instance of her having been "not unamused" is when she observes the "selfishness" of her cousins' behavior in squabbling over a play to perform (156). And her only approach to a witticism is a temptation to allude to Dr. Johnson, the most famously moral of wits (385).

Mary, on the other hand, habitually inclines to laughter. In her last dramatized appearance in the novel (as reported by Edmund), she answers his vituperative attack on her for "faults of principle, of blunted delicacy and a corrupted, vitiated mind" (442) with "a sort of laugh" (444), and she exits the scene with "a saucy playful smile" that Edmund interprets as a sexual come-on. In charging Mary with both sexual and gender misconduct (her laughter, to his mind, is not simply femininely indecorous under the circumstances but lewd), Edmund unwittingly associates her with the adulterous Maria. Unlike Maria, however, who is castigated for her crime, Mary finds sanctuary from censure in her doubleness. Not only is she "double" to Fanny (her function as counterheroine, narratologically speaking, precludes her moral condemnation); but because her doubly indecent laughter (sexually suggestive *and* of female origin) proceeds from her (always doubly determined) humor, it evades fixed meaning, and, in so doing, she escapes punishment.

Edmund finds Mary's "habit" of mocking serious principle and her "impudence in wrong" (444) so repugnant that he refuses to admit having ever been in love with her: "[I]t had been the creature of my own imagination, not Miss Crawford, that I had been too apt to dwell on"—an observation that, given Edmund's stuffiness, is quite likely correct. The narrator, however, judges Mary less harshly and far less prejudicially, reproaching not her femininely impertinent laughter but rather her disingenuous "intentions to please" (282) and her near-cynical insouciance (which is most clearly seen in her crass joke about Tom's illness).[36] And yet even these faults are only lightly rebuked in the narrative, largely because Mary is held only limitedly responsible for them. Despite their differences, Mary is, like Fanny, a product of her upbringing, femininely educated (like the Bertram sisters) in "manners" but not in "active principle" (448) and morally abandoned to the "vicious" example of her guardian uncle, the admiral (74). Her impoverished moral education consequently grants her an excuse for speaking indecorously and sometimes insensitively, which in turn permits her—so long as she speaks under cover of laughter—both to disparage patriarchal practices and to challenge, by her own enormous appeal, cultural notions of feminine ideality.

Despite her reserved disapproval of Mary's character, the narrator not only tolerates Mary's laughter but actually participates in it herself. For while she may ultimately judge according to the lights of Fanny's morality, the narrator characteristically responds to the inhabitants of Mansfield with an ironically inflected humor that matches Mary's. For example, when Mary (unlike Fanny, who gravitates to Dr. Johnson) quips on Sir Thomas in a parody inspired by Pope—

> "Blest Knight! whose dictatorial *looks* dispense
> To Children affluence, to Rushworth sense" (182; emphasis added)

—she merely concentrates in two lines the narrative opinion of Sir Thomas's close-fistedness (and of Mr. Rushworth's intelligence) that is dispersed throughout the text in jibes like these:

> [Sir Thomas] would not have wished her [Mary Crawford] to belong to him, though her twenty thousand pounds *had* been forty. (439; emphasis added)

> [Sir Thomas thought Mr. Yates] was not very solid; but there was a hope of his becoming less trifling—of his being at least tolerably domestic and quiet; and, at any rate, there was comfort in finding his estate rather more, and his debts much less, than he had feared. (447)

> [B]y looking . . . most exceedingly pleased with Sir Thomas's good opinion, and saying scarcely any thing, he [Mr. Rushworth] did his best towards preserving that good opinion a little longer. (202)

Similarly, the narrator's assessment of Dr. Grant not only resembles Mary's, but employs the same tone and sometimes the same language:

> [narrator:] It delighted Mrs. Grant to keep them [the Crawfords] both with her, and Dr. Grant was exceedingly well contented to have it so; a talking pretty young woman like Miss Crawford, is always pleasant society to an indolent, stay-at-home man; and Mr. Crawford's being his guest was an excuse for drinking claret every day. (80)

> [Mary:] "And though Dr. Grant is most kind and obliging to me, and though he is really a gentleman, and I dare say a good scholar and clever, and often preaches good sermons, and is very respectable, *I* see him to be an indolent selfish bon vivant who must have his palate consulted in every thing, who will not stir a finger for the convenience of any one, and who, moreover, if the cook makes a blunder, is out of humour with his excellent wife." (137)

> [narrator:] They lived together [Mary and Mrs Grant]; and when Dr. Grant had brought on apoplexy and death, by three great institutionary dinners in one week, they still lived together. (453)

The humor that Mary and the narrator share is as alike in rhetoric as in perspective. Both rely upon wordplay, italics (or emphasis, in Mary's case), litotes, and periphrasis to give their humor form, and both fix upon targets that are consistently, if not exclusively, "feminist": Sir Thomas's oppressively paternalistic treatment of Fanny and his daughters, the debasing practices of the marriage market, or the gender bias of the dominant cultural attitude toward adultery, for example. On the issue of sexual inequality in the punishment of adultery, indeed, not only is the narrator at her most explicitly (proto)feminist, but her moral judgment is notably closer to Mary's than at any other time:

> That punishment, the punishment of disgrace, would in a just measure attend his [Henry's] share of the offence, is, we know, not one of the barriers which society gives to virtue. In this world, the penalty is less equal than could be wished. (452)

The main distinction in their humor lies in their preferences for particular tropes. Mary favors hyperbole (what she calls "'the *never* of conversation'" [120]) and wordplay: her pun on the admiral's intimate acquaintance with "*Rears,* and *Vices*" (91) is the most notorious example. The narrator, on the other hand, inclines to periphrasis and litotes. Periphrasis, by burying the target of her humor (and often the humor itself) in an excess of words, allows the narrator to make her joke subtly and subordinately. Consider the following passage:

> As a general reflection on Fanny, Sir Thomas thought nothing could be more unjust [than Mrs. Norris's complaint of Fanny's having a "little spirit of . . . independence"], *though he had been so lately expressing the same sentiments himself,* and he tried to turn the conversation; tried repeatedly before he could succeed; for Mrs. Norris had not discernment enough to perceive, either now, or at any other time, to what degree he thought well of his niece. (323; emphasis added)

Although easily overlooked in a sentence devoted to Sir Thomas's compensatory appreciation of Fanny, the narrative comment—that "he had been so lately expressing the same sentiments himself"—clearly distinguishes the narrator's opinion of Sir Bertram from Fanny's hopelessly idealized version. For like Mary Crawford, the narrator reminds us that the man who is responsible for Maria's education—and indirectly for her outcome—cannot possibly be, as Fanny describes him, "all that was clever and good" (397). Litotes, on the other hand, which works by negation (and here with intensives), permits the narrator to exercise a linguistic form of denial that, like denial in its psychoanalytic sense, obliquely confirms the validity of what it denies:

> [Sir Thomas was now] at leisure to find the Grants really worth visiting; and though infinitely above scheming or contriving for any the most advantageous matrimonial establishment that could be among the apparent possibilities of any one most dear to him, and disdaining even as a littleness the being quick-sighted on such points, he could not avoid perceiving in a grand and careless way that Mr. Crawford was somewhat distinguishing his niece—nor perhaps refrain (though unconsciously) from giving a more willing assent to invitations on that account.
>
> . . . [He] began to think, that any one in the habit of such idle observations *would have thought* that Mr. Crawford was the admirer of Fanny Price. (247)

As Mary Crawford's humorous remarks scandalize the inhabitants of Mansfield Park, so the narrator's ironic humor dialogically destabilizes (through periphrasis) and "unsays" (through litotes) the dominant, plot-driven discourse of the text, which consistently aligns itself with Fanny's morality. In so doing, the narrative humor constitutes an instance of "feminine lawlessness" (122) as surely as does Mary's more overtly subversive behavior. Furthermore, because laughter—to which the humor gives rise—has its origins and expression in the prelinguistic (or the Lacanian presymbolic), it not only disrupts the symbolic (paternal) discourse of the text but establishes an affective, prediscursive (maternal) connection between narrator and reader as well—a connection that effectively imitates the bond between Austen's narrator and heroine. Most significantly perhaps, the textual blurring of the maternal narrator's humorous perspective with Mary Crawford's implicates Mary in the narrator's protective attitude toward Fanny. Mary's humor, that is, even as it functions as a cover for the narrator's, participates as well in protecting Fanny when it attacks the constructions of femininity that constrain both characters.

Both Mary and the narrator seek to avoid a "too harsh construction" of their "playful manner" (412)—a detection of their "feminine lawlessness"—not only by adopting indirect strategies of humor but sometimes by simply diverting attention from their own humorous utterance. Like the narrator, who draws notice away from her mockery of Sir Thomas by thrusting Mrs. Norris before us, Mary either abruptly "turns the subject" (117, 294) when the point of her remarks becomes too apparent or else insists that she is "merely joking" (135). Unlike the narrator, however, Mary is only partially successful in disguising the tendency of her wit.

Largely because she is more obviously gendermarked than the narrator—because she has a female body and name as well as an identifiable "voice" and a "laugh" (130)—Mary is more often cited and more severely judged for her unfeminine opinions (by readers as well as fellow characters), even when those opinions are virtually identical to those of the narrator.[37]

Finally, humor provides both Mary and the narrator with a linguistic outlet for the frustration that arises when their desires and opinions conflict with internalized cultural definitions of femininity and external demands for conformity. Although in the following passage Mary's access to such an outlet is blocked, the manner by which it is normally achieved throughout the novel is indicated:

> [Mary,] startled from the agreeable fancies she had been previously indulging on the strength of her brother's description, no longer able, in the picture she had been forming of a future Thornton, to shut out the church, sink the clergyman, and see only the respectable, elegant, modernized, and occasional residence of a man of independent fortune—was considering Sir Thomas, with decided ill-will, as the destroyer of all this, and suffering the more from the involuntary forbearance which his character and manner commanded, and from not daring to relieve herself by a single attempt at throwing ridicule on his cause. (256)

By "throwing ridicule" on the patriarchal cause—its customs and hypocrisies, its rigid construction of feminine identity—both Mary and the narrator find temporary relief from the contained aggression (the "involuntary forbearance") they suffer on its account. And by granting them a means of expressing frustration (provoked when Mary's desires are thwarted by her cultural limitations or when the narrator's judgment conflicts with reigning practices of daughterly miseducation), humor not only alleviates that frustration but, indeed, profitably transforms it into both a derivative means of instinctual gratification and—for us as readers—a primary source of literary satisfaction.

Laughable Lovers: Fanny as Romantic Heroine

With the exception of a stray narrative comment or two indicating a fond amusement with Fanny's childish manner (for example, "'Poor William! He has met with great kindness from the chaplain of the Antwerp,' was a tender apostrophe of Fanny's very much to the purpose of her own feelings, if not of the conversation" [137]), we have seen that Fanny herself, though definitely embodying mocked virtues, is almost completely spared humorous treatment. This is largely so because her childishness and overdetermined victimization (economic, emotional, intellectual) call forth the narrator's maternal protection. Yet even Fanny's privileged status has its limits. As long as she remains a purely preoedipal heroine—and thus safely excluded from participation in romantic plots—Fanny is exempt from narrative humor. Once she is eroticized, however—first by her uncle's appreciative ogle, later by Henry's penetrating gaze—Fanny's protective cloak is lifted, and she becomes, like every other Austen heroine in similar circumstances, vulnerable to humorous attack.

Her distress in fending off Henry's unwanted attentions, for example, is narrated with surprising detachment. Intimidated into receiving his declarations of love, Fanny finds herself "angry" and resentful at Henry's "perseverance so selfish and ungenerous," "disgusted" by "his want of delicacy and regard" (327). The narrator, however, though acknowledging the "good truth" of Fanny's ire, makes a joke of the "nervous agitation" it causes her:

> Had her own affections been as free—as perhaps they ought to have been—he never could have engaged them.
>
> So thought Fanny in good truth and sober sadness, as she sat musing over that too great indulgence and luxury of a fire up stairs—wondering at the past and present, wondering at what was yet to come, and in a nervous agitation which made nothing clear to her but the persuasion of her being never under any circumstances able to love Mr. Crawford, and the felicity of having a fire to sit over and think of it. (327)

A similarly unexpected levity marks the narration of Fanny's state the morning of William's departure with Henry to Portsmouth:

> Fanny walked back into the breakfast-room with a very saddened heart to grieve over the melancholy change; and there her uncle kindly left her to cry in peace; conceiving perhaps that the deserted chair of each young man might exercise her tender enthusiasm, and that the remaining cold pork bones and mustard in William's plate, might divide her feelings with the broken egg-shells in Mr. Crawford's. She sat and cried *con amore* as her uncle intended, but it was con amore fraternal and no other. (287)

Unlike the humor that mocks the other characters, the humor here is directed not at Fanny *in propria persona* but at her role in a romance scripted for her by Sir Thomas and Henry. It is Fanny's awkward casting that exposes her to humor, and the degree to which the narrator participates in that casting determines the register of humorous response that Fanny's role as romantic heroine evokes.[38] For instance, Fanny distrusts

Henry's intentions, strenuously resists the domestically popular idea of accepting his proposal, and resents (with astonishing bluntness) being trapped in someone else's love plot: "I *should* have thought," said Fanny . . . , "that every woman must have felt the possibility of a man's not being approved, not being loved by some one of her sex, at least, let him be ever so generally agreeable" (349). Yet even against the evidence of Fanny's protestations, the generally empathic narrator joins ranks (however playfully) with the other characters in considering Fanny as a demure but not unwilling object of romantic regard:

> She could not, though only eighteen, suppose Mr. Crawford's attachment would hold out for ever; she could not but imagine that steady, unceasing discouragement from herself would put an end to it in time. How much time she might, in her own fancy, allot for its dominion, is another concern. It would not be fair to enquire into a young lady's exact estimate of her own perfections. (329–30)

This radical (and coyly humorous) shift in narrative perspective —from Fanny's personal assessment of Henry's fortitude to the narrator's generalizing assertion of the injustice of prying into the thoughts of young ladies— recurs with even greater force at Portsmouth, when the narrator, in a rare moment, openly declares her own textual presence:

> She could not have a doubt of the manner in which Mr. Crawford must be struck [by Mr. Price's deportment]. He must be ashamed and disgusted altogether. He must soon give her up, and cease to have the smallest inclination for the match; and yet, though she had been so much wanting his affection to be cured, this was a sort of cure that would be almost as bad as the complaint; and I believe, there is scarcely a young lady in the united kingdoms, who would not rather put up with the misfortune of being sought by a clever, agreeable man, than have him driven away by the vulgarity of her nearest relations. (394)

The psychological distance that the narrator continually expresses toward Fanny's romantic trials, her tendency to treat them as merely fuel for her humor, reveals itself not only in the humorously axiomatic tone that obtrudes upon the narration of such trials but in the parodic allusion to Clarissa Harlowe that pervades them. Like Clarissa, Fanny is beset by the unwanted attentions of a rakish wooer whom she resists with vigorous passive aggression, who is sexually aroused by her resistance, and whose suit is enthusiastically taken up by her own (surrogate) family, which tries, through various methods of manipulation, to coerce her into acceptance. This comic homage—which at the very least complicates the significance of the novel's oft-noted Richardsonian morality—infuses Fanny's struggles to fend off Henry with referential humor, which in turn exaggerates the humor of such particular diegetic circumstances as the following, where Fanny's fanny, so to speak, is rescued from the perils of Henry's courtship by the saving intervention of a domestic ritual:

> "[W]hen once convinced that my attachment is what I declare it, I know you too well not to entertain the warmest hopes—Yes, dearest, sweetest Fanny—Nay— (seeing her draw back displeased) forgive me. Perhaps I have as yet no right—but by what other name can I call you? Do you suppose you are ever present to my imagination under any other? No, it is "Fanny" that I think of all day, and dream of all night.—You have given the name such reality of sweetness, that nothing else can now be descriptive of you."
>
> Fanny could hardly have kept her seat any longer, or have refrained from at least trying to get away in spite of all the too public opposition she foresaw to it, had it not been for the sound of approaching relief, the very sound which she had been long watching for, and long thinking strangely delayed.
>
> The solemn procession, headed by Baddely, of tea-board, urn and cake-bearers, made its appearance, and delivered her from a grievous imprisonment of body and mind. Mr. Crawford was obliged to move. She was at liberty, she was busy, she was protected. (341)

Nor is the narrator's gentle mocking of Fanny limited to her role as Henry's evasive object of desire. Had such been the case, we might construe that it is Fanny's immunity to Henry's advances that permits the narrator to find humor in her predicament—even though, as the narrator flatly states below, such immunity depends upon her being already smitten with Edmund:

> [A]lthough there doubtless are such unconquerable young ladies of eighteen (or one should not read about them) as are never to be persuaded into love against their judgment by all that talent, manner, attention, and flattery can do, I have no inclination to believe Fanny one of them, or to think that . . . she could have escaped heart-whole from the courtship . . . had not her affection been engaged elsewhere. (241)

The fact is that Fanny is subject to humor whenever she gets in a romantic flutter, regardless of its instigation. Although her secret yearning for Edmund enjoys relative security from attack, the narrator mocks the overwrought nature of Fanny's responses—the "heavenly flight" (269) (and sometimes alliterative excess) into which his "expressions of affection" send her:

[Edmund's note accompanying his gift of a gold chain] was the only thing approaching to a letter which she had ever received from him; she might never receive another; it was impossible that she should receive another so perfectly gratifying in the occasion and the style. Two lines more prized had never fallen from the pen of the most distinguished author—never more completely blessed the researches of the fondest biographer. The enthusiasm of a woman's love is even beyond the biographer's. To her, the hand-writing itself, independent of any thing it may convey, is a blessedness. Never were such characters cut by any other human being, as Edmund's commonest handwriting gave! This specimen, written in haste as it was, had not a *fault;* and there was a *felicity* in the *flow* of the *first four* words, in the arrangement of "My very dear *Fanny,*" which she could have looked at for ever. (271–72; emphasis added)

What the narrator derides here is not the love Fanny bears Edmund but the overidealization (the "enthusiasm") to which she subjects it—an idealization that, like almost every other view she holds, she has learned from Edmund:

[Edmund and Fanny] were also quite agreed in their opinion of the lasting effect, the indelible impression, which such a disappointment [as that of breaking off his courtship of Mary] must make on his mind. Time would undoubtedly abate somewhat of his sufferings, but still it was a sort of thing which he never could get entirely the better of; and as to his ever meeting with any other woman who could—it was too impossible to be named but with indignation. Fanny's friendship was all that he had to cling to. (445)

I purposely abstain from dates on this occasion, that every one may be at liberty to fix their own, aware that the cure of unconquerable passions, and the transfer of unchanging attachments, must vary much as to time in different people. (454)

The narrator of *Mansfield Park*—who refrains from mocking her heroine for her often infuriating passivity, her slavish imitation of Edmund's moral and aesthetic opinions, and her patriarchal zeal on any number of other accounts—refuses to forgive her eager investment in a construction of romantic love that requires not only the destruction of the mother-child bond but the obliteration of a feminine self. "Unconquerable passions" and "unchanging attachments," like those other culturally romanticized values of beauty, dutifulness, and submission, participate in an ideology of gender that circumscribes feminine identity to a would-be object of masculine desire. Not only then does the narrator's maternally aggressive humor attack Sir Thomas, Lady Bertram, and Mrs. Norris for enforcing behaviors

harmful to daughters, but ultimately Fanny herself whenever she subscribes to "the enthusiasm of a woman's love" in full consciousness and, in
the case of her own amorous idealization of Edmund, apparently without
conflict.[39]

Laughable Lovers Again: Anne Elliot's "Eternal Constancy"

Fanny Price and Anne Elliot, despite their political differences (Fanny's
instincts are aristocratic; Anne's, meritocratic),[40] have more in common
perhaps than any other two of Austen's heroines. Both are notably silent:
comparatively little direct discourse is recorded for either of them. Both
are alternately ignored and devalued by their families and equally "hardened to" the domestic "affronts" they suffer [*P,* 34]). And both are pro-
tected from the amorous advances of unwanted suitors by having disposed
of their affection elsewhere (*P,* 192). Moreover, the narrative humor—diverting attention away from its subtler and more ambivalent treatment of
the heroines—assails other members of their families for remarkably similar reasons. Like Lady Bertram, Sir Walter is ridiculed for his parasitical
passivity (being "a foolish, spendthrift baronet," with little "principle or
sense" [*P,* 248]) and for his superlative, effeminized vanity—memorably
evinced in his extreme fondness for mirrors and his unsolicited beauty tips
("'I should recommend Gowland [Lotion], the constant use of Gowland,
during the spring months'" [*P,* 146]). Elizabeth Elliot's grand-scale snobbery, while it reflects her father's, also recalls and exaggerates the class prejudices of the Bertrams; and Mary Elliot Musgrove, although considerably
less loathesome than Mrs. Norris, shares the latter's false "sense of being so
very useful" (*P,* 130).

The most significant similarity between these heroines is their overidealization of romantic love (perhaps because their experience of the familial
variety is so very unsatisfying). The narrative humor that targets the heroine of *Persuasion* for her faith in "unconquerable passions" and "unchanging attachments," however, achieves a sharper tone than can be found any-
where in Austen's earlier novel. In the following passage (which occurs
shortly after Captain Wentworth, piqued by Mr. William Elliot's attentions to Anne in Bath, betrays that he is still "jealous of her affection"
[190]), the narrator's humor takes a swift and scornful turn:

> She [Anne] felt a great deal of good will towards him [Mr. Elliot]. In
> spite of the mischief of his attentions, she owed him gratitude and re-
> gard, perhaps compassion. She could not help thinking . . . of the right

he seemed to have to interest her, by every thing in situation, by his own sentiments, by his early prepossession. It was altogether very extraordinary.—Flattering, but painful. There was much to regret. How she might have felt, had there been no Captain Wentworth in the case, was not worth enquiry; for there was a Captain Wentworth: and be the conclusion of the present suspense good or bad, her affection would be his for ever. Their union, she believed, could not divide her more from other men, than their final separation.

Prettier musings of high-wrought love and eternal constancy, could never have passed along the streets of Bath, than Anne was sporting with from Camden-place to Westgate-buildings. It was almost enough to spread purification and perfume all the way. (192)

As a rule, the narrative humor of *Persuasion* not only consistently defends the heroine from her family but, in contrast to that of *Mansfield Park*, faithfully supports her perceptions and judgments as well: for unlike Fanny who idealizes the Bertrams, Anne is excruciatingly conscious of her relatives' shortcomings. Thus, when the narrator derides Anne, as she does here, for sanctifying what is little more than her fated loyalty to Wentworth (in the years prior to Wentworth's reappearance, no one more qualified than Charles Musgrove shows an interest in her), the resulting contrast in narrative tone and perspective is startling. Even though the narrator resumes her customary sympathy in the sentence immediately following this passage, her sarcastic reference to Anne's glorification of female constancy ("It was almost enough to spread purification and perfume all the way") disrupts the text, disturbing the overt impression of intimate narrator-heroine identification traditionally held by Austen critics as well as undermining the apparent plot endorsement of Anne's fidelity to Wentworth.[41]

Nor is this incident of narrative derision singular. Once Anne is eroticized by William Elliot's gaze in Lyme, instances of narrative mockery dramatically increase. Witnessing that gaze, Wentworth, who has till then successfully resisted a rekindling of his passion for Anne, is stirred: "It was evident that the gentleman . . . admired her exceedingly. Captain Wentworth looked round at her instantly in a way which shewed his noticing of it" (104). And once Wentworth is roused, Anne's status changes. No longer simply a "nobody" (5) with whom the narrator is in full, almost invariant sympathy, she becomes the contested object of masculine desire, the prized heroine of a conventional love plot. As a result, the "agitation, pain, pleasure, a something between delight and misery" (175) she feels in Bath in Wentworth's actual or anticipated presence are treated dismissively as the common lot of a heroine in love, and the insouciant imprecision with which the narrator refers to such anxiety (not even caring to name the "something"—the everything—"between delight and misery" which her heroine undergoes) indicates her amused indifference. Though Anne's glimpse of Wentworth from the window of Molland's shop may send her into flurried state of indecision, her shuttling back and forth from the doorway first to get a better look and then to avoid detection (175) is presented as muted high comedy. The narrator similarly mocks Anne's love-blindedness in mistaking Lady Russell's interest in "some window-curtains" (179) for an irresistible attraction to the image of Wentworth strolling down Pulteney Street. And she laughs at Anne's (short-lived) euphoria upon determining that, to judge from his behavior at the concert, Wentworth "must love her" (186):

> Anne's mind was in a most favourable state for the entertainment of the evening [that is, at least one Italian love song]: it was just occupation enough: she had feelings for the tender, spirits for the gay, attention for the scientific, and patience for the wearisome; and had never liked a concert better, at least during the first act.

Although Anne herself is embarrassed and faintly amused by her foolishly romantic behavior (she "sighed and blushed and smiled" [179] upon discovering the real object of Lady Russell's fascination in Pulteney Street), her humorous self-deprecation falls considerably short of the narrator's perspective. Anne may compare herself to Burney's "Miss Larolles, the inimitable Miss Larolles" (189), when she connives for an aisle seat so as better to encounter Wentworth, but the narrator makes the more biting allusion in associating Anne—in her devotion to her man—with Matthew Prior's ridiculously slavish Emma (116).[42] Moreover, the humor that initiates closure (which, with its capitalizations, underlining, and dash, is more robust in the manuscript than in most published editions) casts the heroine at such a remove from the narrator as to rupture whatever vestigial bonds of intimate narrator-heroine identification still remain at that point between them. Although increased narrative distance at closure is typical of Austen, there is clearly a difference in stance between a narrating "I" who claims possession of the heroine ("My Fanny") and one who, by depersonalizing the heroine, reifies her into "*an* Anne Elliot" (emphasis added):

> Who can be in doubt of what followed? When any two Young People take it into their heads to marry, they are *pretty* sure by persever-

ance to carry their point,—be they ever so poor, or ever so imprudent, or ever so little likely to be necessary to each other's ultimate comfort. This may be bad morality to conclude with, but I believe it to be truth; and if such parties succeed, how should a Captain Wentworth and an Anne Elliot, with the advantage of maturity of mind, consciousness of right, and one independent fortune between them, fail of bearing down every opposition? (MS; cf. *P,* 248)[43]

According to the narrative humor, "high-wrought love and eternal constancy" are not simply culturally overvalued but ludicrous and, like the incense ("purification and perfume") to which it allusively compares them, potentially nauseating ideals. Anne, who has dutifully maintained these ideals, is rewarded in the denouement with a marriage that promises to be all that a heroine with a "severe degree of self denial" (13) could ever want from life. The narrator, however, is less easily satisfied than her heroine, attacking in her humor an ideology of love that insidiously debilitates already socially curtailed powers of female agency.

This is not, of course, to suggest that the narrator is opposed to the marriage of Wentworth and Anne. They have equal understanding, shared sensibilities, and financial solvency: for Austen, three prerequisites to a good marriage. They do not, however, have equal authority or opportunity. Having been persuaded at nineteen against her wishes, will, and better judgment to break her initial engagement to Wentworth, Anne forfeits what appears to be her single chance for culturally significant action: that is, to marry, and so to be inscribed for that action into "the book of books" (7)—the Baronetage of her father rather than the Bible of the Father, though these haut-patriarchal texts bear similar symbolic weight. Prohibited from even exerting influence at home ("her word had no weight" [5]) and therefore excluded not only from public activity but from "woman's sphere" as well, Anne remains in stasis until the return of Wentworth eight years later. In the interim, he goes to sea and succeeds in "distinguish[ing] himself" (29) and in amassing a "handsome fortune" (30); she, on the other hand, apparently succeeds only in internalizing a middle-class formulation of romantic love:

> How eloquent could Anne Elliot have been,—how eloquent, at least, were her wishes on the side of early warm attachment, and a cheerful confidence in futurity, against that over-anxious caution which seems to insult exertion and distrust Providence!—She had been forced into prudence in her youth, she learned romance as she grew older—the natural sequel of an unnatural beginning. (30)

> With the exception, perhaps, of Admiral and Mrs. Croft, who seemed
> particularly attached and happy, (Anne could allow no other exception
> even among the married couples) there could have been no two hearts
> so open, no tastes so similar, no feelings so in unison, no countenances
> so beloved. (64)

All textual evidence points to the depth of her regard, and there is no doubt
that the loss of Wentworth has caused her great unhappiness. The fact
remains, however, that Anne, having no emotional outlet, no activity in
which to apply her "strength, zeal, and thought" (111), has turned her
energy inward, not simply mourning her loss but dwelling in her maturity
"unnaturally" (morbidly) on a romanticized version of its memory.

Consider the following passage, which occurs shortly after a conversation in which the name of Wentworth is first mentioned in the novel and
its possible significance for Anne suggested:

> [Anne] left the room, to seek the comfort of cool air for her flushed
> cheeks; and as she walked along a favourite grove, said, with a gentle
> sigh, "a few months more, and *he,* perhaps, may be walking here."
>
> Chapter IV.
>
>   *He* was not Mr. Wentworth, the former curate of Monkford, how-
> ever suspicious appearances may be, but a captain Frederick Wentworth,
> his brother, who . . . had come into Somersetshire, in the summer of
> 1806 . . . He was, at that time, a remarkably fine young man, with a
> great deal of intelligence, spirit and brilliancy; and Anne an extremely
> pretty girl, with gentleness, modesty, taste, and feeling.—Half the sum
> of attraction on either side, might have been enough, for he had nothing
> to do, and she had hardly any body to love; but the encounter of such
> lavish recommendations could not fail . . . It would be difficult to say
> which had seen the highest perfection in the other, or which had been
> the happiest; she, in receiving his declarations and proposals, or he in
> having them accepted. (25–26)

However amicable, the humor here is directed at Anne: in the repetition
and accentuation of "he," in the narrative aside of "however suspicious
appearances may be," in the inflated reference to their character traits as
"such lavish recommendations," and in the distance in tone assumed by
the narrator after the dash. Worth noting is the almost inconspicuous contrast the narrator makes between Anne and Wentworth: "for he had nothing to do, and she had hardly any body to love." In a less gendered world,
an alternative, parallel construction, such as "neither of them had anything

else to do," would presumably have sufficed to bring about the same consequence of mutual attraction. The implication here, however, is that a heroine never has anything to do: men do, women love. Although Anne is
thoroughly capable of independent, efficacious action ("'no one . . . so capable as Anne!'" [114]), her opportunities for such are severely restricted by
both her cultural and domestic situations. Like Fanny Price, she must wait
patiently at home for the infrequent chance to "be allowed to be of any
use" (*P,* 33), to demonstrate "all her wonted ways of attention and assistance" (221).

Yet Anne, like Fanny, takes comfort in "utility" (58): it provides her
with a culturally acceptable means of sublimating desire (she craves "the
satisfaction of knowing herself extremely useful" [121]) and of winning
the gratitude and "real affection" (220) of those she serves—so long as they
are not members of her own family.[44] Once she is stationed among the
residents of Uppercross, Anne finds ample if compromised opportunity
for employment:

> She was intreated to give them as much of her time as possible, . . . and
> on Charles's leaving them together was *listening* to Mrs. Musgrove's his-
> tory of Louisa, and to Henrietta's of herself, *giving opinions* on business,
> and *recommendations* to shops; with intervals of *every help* which Mary
> required, from *altering* her *ribbon* to *settling* her *accounts,* from *finding*
> her *keys,* and *assorting* her *trinkets,* to *trying to convince* her that she was
> not ill used by anybody; which Mary, . . . could not but have her mo-
> ments of imagining. (220–21; emphasis added)

Next to facilitating the actions of others, Anne's most often solicited activity at Uppercross is mediation. Continually drafted to play "umpire" (77)
in Musgrove family squabbles, she finds herself equally "appealed to by
both parties" (43) to exert her influence with the other. (Three uninter-
rupted pages of text are devoted to detailing her acts of persuasion [43–
47].) Persuasion, then, not only gives the novel its title and instigates its
plot but declares itself as a form of gendermarked usefulness (Lady Russell
is the only other character noted for persuasion) and as a twofold feminine
duty.[45] On the one hand, women are called upon to influence the behavior
of others; on the other, they are duty bound to be paragons of persuasibility
themselves. As Anne tells Wentworth in justification of her earlier refusal
to marry him, "'When I yielded [to Lady Russell's persuasion], I thought
it was to duty'" (244), having felt a daughterly obligation to submit to the
authority of one who claimed "mother's rights" (27), no matter how much

her own feelings in the instance differed or how wrong that parental advice turned out to be. For, "'if I mistake not,'" Anne notes with a trace of sarcasm, "'a strong sense of duty is no bad part of a woman's portion'" (246).

Although Anne is "glad to have any thing marked out as a duty" (33), regardless of its gender-typed status, the narrative goes some way to deconstruct persuasibility and usefulness as specifically feminine character traits. Anne, for instance, in rejecting Wentworth, submits not to the authority of her patriarchal papa but to the wishes of her surrogate mother, conceiving it "possible to withstand her father's ill-will" (27) but not the loss of maternal affection or the thought that "such steadiness of opinion, and such tenderness of manner" (27) as Lady Russell's could advise her unwisely. The following passage, however, with its excess of intensifiers, casts into doubt the purity of Lady Russell's motives:

> She could only resolve to avoid such self-delusion [that is, expecting sympathy] in future, and think with *heightened* gratitude of the *extraordinary* blessing of having one *such truly sympathizing* friend as Lady Russell. (42; emphasis added)

Had Anne known what the narrator here implies (that Lady Russell's sympathy is not as complete as Anne has supposed), she would have married Wentworth despite all protest to the contrary. Furthermore, Anne's persuasibility, even operating under a delusion as she may be, is limited. While she sees it her duty at eighteen to yield "on the side of safety" (244) to the wishes of her guardians, she considers the claims of parental authority to be insignificant at the age of twenty-seven; indeed, the only duty Anne distinguishes the second time around is the duty *not* to yield to paternal persuasion to marry William Elliot.

Similarly, the narrative distinguishes between usefulness as a debilitating feminine condition (a state of perpetual physical and emotional availability) and usefulness as a "de-gendered" response to the distress of others. Like Edmund before him, Wentworth breaks down gender barriers in nursing the afflicted: as "Edmund was all in all" (*MP,* 419) to Tom in his near-fatal illness, so Wentworth saves Benwick from dying of grief, according to Captain Harville (108), whose own utility is noteworthy.[46] Moreover, Anne's command at the scene of Louisa Musgrove's fall at Lyme, being in direct response, as well as in contrast, to Wentworth's utter uselessness on that occasion ("'Is there no one to help me?'" he cried "in a tone of despair" [110]) proves an example of reverse-role assistance and the turning point in their relationship: "the scenes on the Cobb . . . fixed her superiority" in Wentworth's mind (242).

The episode of Louisa's accident (her false step on the Cobb, which in knocking her senseless knocks some sense—and a fondness for poetry—into her [167]) illustrates how limited as a rule are Anne's opportunities to exercise her native authority. She accedes, in this instance, to a position of responsibility solely through general default. The only one to retain sense amid a mass exhibition of hysteria, Anne "suggest[s]" and "prompt[s]" plans of action, one of which consists in sending Captain Benwick for a surgeon. "Every one capable of thinking felt the advantage of the idea," remarks the narrator, reminding us that there are "two dead young ladies" (111) on the scene who are literally insensible (if not literally dead) and insinuating that the mental activity of the rest is questionable, thereby highlighting the fact that Anne, with "steadiness of principle" (242) and "the resolution of a collected mind," is the only one intellectually in evidence, if still prohibited by reason of gender from forthrightly directing the situation.[47]

The undercurrents of this narrative complaint—that gender bias prevents a daughter's talents from being adequately recognized or expressed—can be found earlier in the description of Dick Musgrove. A singular example of exceedingly black humor in Austen's writing, the following passage when correlated with that describing Anne's behavior above seems less like an uncontrolled authorial outburst (as it has seemed to some) than a purposive contrast:[48]

> The real circumstances of this pathetic piece of family history were, that the Musgroves had had the ill fortune of a very troublesome, hopeless son; and the good fortune to lose him before he reached his twentieth year; that he had been sent to sea, because he was stupid and unmanageable on shore; that he had been very little cared for at any time by his family, though quite as much as he deserved; seldom heard of, and scarcely at all regretted, when the intelligence of his death abroad had worked its way to Uppercross, two years before.
>
> He had, in fact, though his sisters were now doing all they could for him, by calling him "poor Richard," been nothing better than a thick-headed, unfeeling, unprofitable Dick Musgrove, who had never done anything to entitle himself to more than the abbreviation of his name, living or dead. (50–51)

Being male, Dick Musgrove (whose first name suggestively rhymes with the first syllable of the adjective here that modifies him: thick = Dick) has the opportunity for profitable, productive, self-determined action that Anne, being female, is denied. Arguably, it is precisely his foolish squandering of that opportunity that brings down upon him a degree of narrative contempt, not only exceeding his apparent deserts but unmatched elsewhere in the humor of the novel.

As Anne herself suggests in the famous passage on women's constancy, cultural restraints on female activity precipitate the overvaluation of romantic love:

> "We certainly do not forget you, so soon as you forget us. It is, perhaps, our fate rather than our merit. We cannot help ourselves. We live at home, quiet, confined, and our feelings prey upon us. You [that is, men] are forced on exertion. You have always a profession, pursuits, business of some sort or other, to take you back into the world immediately, and continual occupation and change soon weaken impressions." (232)

As the narrator in *Mansfield Park* notes, "There is nothing like employment, active, indispensable employment, for relieving sorrow" (431). But loving "when existence or when hope is gone" (235) has been as eagerly prescribed to daughters as subscribed to by them. Anne's declaration is followed by Captain Harville's claim that men are biologically more constant in their love than women ("as our bodies are stronger, so are our feelings" [233]), and by his invocation of masculinely penned literature as authoritative proof of women's underachievement in eternal constancy. Although Anne on this occasion is placed in the uncomfortable position of defending women's right to an attribute that she herself is not proud of possessing ("'[I]t is not an enviable one, you need not covet it'" [235]), the narrative humor intervenes elsewhere on her behalf to show both the fraudulence of Harville's claim and the debilitating effects of the supposed virtue.

In the following passage, Captain Benwick, once devoted to Harville's now deceased sister, Fanny, is here currently devoted, with the aid of Scott and Byron, to an aggravation of his feelings for her:

> [Benwick] showed himself so intimately acquainted with all the tenderest songs of the one poet, and all the impassioned descriptions of hopeless agony of the other; he repeated, with such tremulous feeling, the various lines which imaged a broken heart, or a mind destroyed by wretchedness, that she [Anne] ventured to hope he did not always read only poetry; and . . . to recommend a larger allowance of prose in his daily study (100–101).

Using Benwick as an analogue, the narrator humorously intimates the effect that the literary discourse of romantic love—and the exaltation of psychological turmoil it inspires—has had upon Anne without jeopardizing either our trust in the sincerity of her feeling for Wentworth or our own affection for her character. Arguably, Benwick's portrayal of "high-wrought love" could only achieve its intended effect with a man as a model. A female Benwick might evoke our annoyance, but it is doubtful that such a creation would so provoke a contrast between love and masochistic self-indulgence. (In like fashion, Sir Walter's "feminine" vanity ridicules the cultural idealization of female beauty more devastatingly than Lady Bertram's possibly can.)

Yet Anne's enthusiasm for romance is only somewhat less exaggerated than Benwick's. She considers it her "right" (101), earned by her longer experience in melancholic suffering, to advise him to read palliatively in "the works of our best moralists," and, like him, she fancies herself permanently bound to her former fiancé, despite their estrangement ("Their union, she believed, could not divide her more from other men, than their final separation" [192]). Furthermore, while Anne's wistful comparison of her own plight with Benwick's (97) contains an important cultural truth— that youth and beauty, essential for women to be objects of high-wrought love, make them ineligible for such in a very brief time—her self-pity in the context of the narrative humor and plot resolution mocks her ("I cannot believe his prospects so blighted forever. He is younger than I am; . . . younger as a man. He will rally again, and be happy'" [97]).

Although the novel ends with textual testimony to the rewards of eternal constancy, the two facts—that Anne has been constant in love and that love, in the form of the long-anticipated Elliot-Wentworth marriage, is ultimately satisfied—are not necessarily causally related. Whatever else, the nuptial ending is a foregone conclusion: a recapitulation of the traditional feminine plot, in which marriage is not only the "happiest" fate (given the alternatives) for a middle- or upper-class heroine but, in a text as culturally and conventionally mimetic as Austen's, virtually the only means of closure. Anne's fate is specifically feminine: she will either be married or she won't. In either case, as Anne is painfully aware, an offer of marriage is hers to ratify or refuse but not to initiate: "Had he wished ever to see her again, . . . he would have done what she could not but believe that in his place she should have done long ago, when events had been early giving him the independence which alone had been wanting" (58).

The constraints Anne suffers may be culturally imposed, but the narrative subtly argues that her own propensity for sentimentalizing romance simply worsens her predicament. Mrs. Smith—crippled, impoverished, widowed, childless—evinces, much to "Anne's astonishment" (153), "something more" (154) than a "submissive spirit" and "a strong understanding": "here was that elasticity of mind, that disposition to be comforted, that power of turning readily from evil to good, and of finding employment which carried her out of herself." Mrs. Smith, in other words and in contrast to Anne, works hard to wrest "enjoyment" from the material conditions of "depression." She befriends Nurse Rooke,[49] who not only teaches her how to knit (and thereby enables her to earn money) but who, more important, provides her with "gossip" (155). Like humor, gossip circulates indirectly and often by exaggeration and distortion, and though subject as a consequence of its medium to inaccuracies, it remains essentially reliable, as Mrs. Smith declares: its authority (like that of humor) lies in its savvy interpretation ("the little rubbish it collects in the turnings, is easily moved away" [204–5]). Operating outside the laws governing authoritative discourses—and therefore free from the restrictions normally imposed upon female speech—gossip provides not only "entertaining and profitable" knowledge about "one's species" and its "newest modes of being trifling and silly" (155), but also temporary relief from the customary feminine condition of verbal frustration. Mrs. Smith, despite being more physically and financially confined than Anne, thrives nonetheless on free unfettered talk, while Anne exacerbates her suffering in (and by her) silence.[50]

With "vigour of form" and "no doubts of what to do" (48), Sophia Wentworth Croft also actively resists the idea of femininity as beautiful, subservient, and persuasible. Rather than pining away at home, Mrs. Croft spends "almost as much time at sea as her husband" and shows an unfeminine indifference to the facial weatherbeating she receives in consequence. And though clearly not on the naval payroll herself, her activity is never construed as subordinate; rather, "Mrs. Croft seemed to go shares with him in every thing" (168). In fact, if "their style of driving" (92) is indeed "no bad representation of the general guidance of their affairs," then Mrs. Croft, "by coolly giving the reins a better direction," reveals herself to be the authority (the "driving" force) in their marriage. She rails upon her brother's "'superfine, extraordinary sort of gallantry'" (69) in declaring women unseaworthy: "'I hate to hear you talking so, . . . as if women were all fine ladies, instead of rational creatures'" (70). And she dismisses—with dispatch and sisterly condescension—his defense of his position on grounds of chivalry ("'My dear Frederick, you are talking quite idly" [69];

"'All idle refinement!'"). Furthermore, even though (or perhaps because) she is blessed in being "particularly attached [to] and happy" (63) with a husband appreciative of her talents ("'My wife should have the credit'" [127]), Mrs. Croft denounces the cultural consecration of "high-wrought love and eternal constancy," considering even long engagements to be "'unsafe and unwise'" (231), and at least as emotionally destructive to women as "the wearing, anxious, youth-killing dependence" (27) of financial insecurity that Lady Russell fears.

Yet precisely because Mrs. Croft ("as intelligent and keen as any of the officers around her" [168]) provides an example of successful self-fashioning, she is relegated to secondary status in the narrative. Just as reference to Mrs. Norris distracts attention from the humorously deprecating treatment of Sir Thomas, so narrative approval of Mrs. Croft is diluted by the "amusement" (92) caused by her driving skills and by her husband's characteristic use of a naval vernacular. The one joke made (partially) at Mrs. Croft's expense, moreover, comes on the heels of her most blatantly progressive statement (that is, that women are "rational creatures"), thereby diverting notice from the potentially radical nature of her sentiments:

> "I have crossed the Atlantic four times, and have been once to the East Indies, and back again; and only once, besides being in different places about home—Cork, and Lisbon, and Gibraltar. But I never went beyond the Streights—and never was in the West Indies. We do not call Bermuda or Bahama, you know, the West Indies."
>
> Mrs. Musgrove had not a word to say in dissent; she could not accuse herself of having ever called them any thing in the course of her life. (70)

However mild, the undercutting of Mrs. Croft is narratologically imperative, *Persuasion* being not the story of an enterprising middle-aged woman with exceptional opportunities and "no distrust of herself" (48) but rather of a more representative, far less confident unmarried daughter who suffers severely from internalized prohibitions against female speech and agency. "'The only time that I ever really suffered in body or mind, the only time that I ever fancied myself unwell, or had any ideas of danger, was the winter I passed by myself,'" asserts Mrs. Croft. "'I lived in perpetual fright at that time, and had all manner of imaginary complaints from not knowing what to do with myself, or when I should hear from him next'" (71). Having no children—the traditional culturally approved outlet for a married woman's "interest, amusement, and wholesome exertion" (43)—Mrs. Croft packs herself up and sets sail with her husband, leaving her hypochondria on shore. But "pensive" (123) and "silent" Anne, without the independence that Mrs. Croft's marriage affords her, has no equivalent corrective for her emotional turmoil—either in the aftermath of her broken engagement (when Wentworth "wanted to be doing something" and did [65]) or in the midst of their renewed relationship (when, as Wentworth acknowledges, "'*I* could at least put myself in the way of happiness, *I* could exert myself, *I* could do something'" and does [243; emphasis added]). Consequently, her suppressed energies express themselves in displaced and aberrant form—in the "shudderings" (66) and "fatigues" (227) she experiences when forced to endure Wentworth's company without the freedom to speak her desire, and even occasionally in psychosomatic paralysis: "[H]er own emotions still kept her fixed. She had much to recover from, before she could move" (89); "She was in the carriage, and felt that he had placed her there, that his will and his hands had done it" (91).

Nor does Anne's knowledge of Wentworth's renewed interest relieve her hysterical symptoms. She suffers painful, crippling "agitation" in her love for Wentworth (the word recurs at least a half-dozen times: 80, 89, 184, 189, 229, 238) regardless of whether she knows that love to be requited. The overwhelming anxiety she initially feels in Wentworth's presence simply gives way with time and knowledge to an "overpowering happiness" (238) that is no less debilitating. Indeed, "high-wrought felicity"—the reward of high-wrought love fulfilled—proves to be so intolerable that Anne is "obliged to find an alloy in some momentary apprehensions of its being impossible to last" (245).

The final "joke" of the novel (and of nineteenth-century middle-class feminine life) is that not even marriage—with its promise of connubial bliss and exertion, sex and children—is likely either to offer sufficient means of sublimating the energy that confined results in extreme agitation or to compensate adequately for the lack of such means. Although as Mrs. Wentworth, Anne has "the full worth of . . . Captain Wentworth's affection," she continues in her married state to be "tenderness itself" (unlike her "weather-beaten" sister-in-law, she never develops a tough skin) and "must pay the tax of quick alarm" for the glory of "being a sailor's wife" (252). The psychological dangers of romantic overidealization—its "agitation" and "quick alarm"—are apparently as persistent as the ideological ones. Or so the narrative implies in the canceled penultimate chapter. The following passage occurs in that chapter after Wentworth's proposal has been made and accepted:

> She was almost bewildered—almost too happy in looking back. It was
> necessary to sit up half the night, and lie awake the remainder, to com-
> prehend with composure her present state, and pay for the overplus of
> bliss by headache and fatigue. (263)

More telling even than the content of this passage is its lack of humorous
intonation. Compare the foregoing to the following, which in the revised
narrative precedes Wentworth's proposal, though after Anne is convinced
of his continuing affection:

> She had only to submit, sit down, be outwardly composed, and feel her-
> self plunged at once in all the agitations which she had merely laid her
> account of tasting a little before the morning closed. There was no delay,
> no waste of time. She was deep in the happiness of such misery, or the
> misery of such happiness, instantly. (229)

The second-quoted passage is obviously a reworking of the first: "Deep in
the happiness of such misery, or the misery of such happiness" replaces
"pay for the overplus of bliss by headache and fatigue," retaining the intent
of the canceled phrasing but increasing (through the oxymoron and the
chiasmus) its humorous inflection. By mocking Anne's heightened emotional state, the narrator not only reveals the pernicious psychological
effects that the "superlatives & rapture" of romantic love (*JAL,* 74.1) have
had upon her heroine; she also creates an outlet for expressing her own
frustration with gendered constraints upon female speech and agency—
constraints that are capable of distorting an occasion of happiness into a
source of misery and misery into a masochistic pleasure. Like Mary Crawford, who in the epigraph of this chapter, does "not forget to think . . .
seriously" of what she "treat[s] . . . as a joke" (*MP,* 75), the narrator of
Persuasion, even while she makes fun of her heroine's idealization of romantic love and converts her masochism into our humorous enjoyment, does
not in the end forget to acknowledge the self-annihilating consequences of
such culturally promoted feminine behaviors.

*   *   *

For many of her readers, Austen advocates a conservative ideology of political and social virtue, a world in which the "Tory who believes in King,
country and a responsible and influential clergy is right."[51] For others (particularly recent and often feminist ones), she is a "progressive," sometimes
even a "radical," who subverts her own plots—their inevitable marital clo-

sure and timeworn feminine scripts—and problematizes moral categories and values (for example, "sense" and "sensibility"). Indeed, as Rachel Brownstein has noted, "[I]n the struggle for power between politically radical and conservative critics," Austen "has for years been claimed by both parties."[52]

Reading Austen through the perspective of her narrative humor—interrogating the discourse of her laughter rather than the putatively ironic structure of her comprehension—offers a way to accommodate these conflicting views. While such a reading leaves untouched Austen's own private political opinions (she was familially, and apparently emotionally, tied to Toryism), it discloses the ways in which the ideological values commonly associated with political conservatism are undercut even as they are upheld in her fiction: by mocking figures of established social authority; by parodying in other characters those values idealized in and by the heroines; and by associating the narrator with views held by such subversively appealing challengers to femininity as Mary Crawford, often through their shared production of humor. Austen's narrative humor, in other words, encodes a cultural critique that challenges the significance of the overt conservatism of the text. A reading of this critique in *Mansfield Park,* for example, discovers not an "under-valued" (173) young woman, who by dint of her unwavering virtue earns the respect of her guardian and the love of his clergyman son, but rather an emotionally, financially, and intellectually dependent daughter, who, in an effort to win affection and approval from the "masters" to whom she is bound, meticulously inculcates behaviors and opinions marketed as properly feminine. Embedded as it is in the narrative humor, such a critique permits critics like Lionel Trilling to retain their reading of *Mansfield Park* as a triumph of Fanny's "Christian" values, yet prohibits their doing so with the complete acquiescence of the text.[53] Similarly, although reading *Persuasion* through its humor neither negates its autumnal aura nor diminishes Anne's stature as the most mature and least flawed of Austen's heroines, it both accounts for narrative outbursts of vexation that ring discordant with such an aura and exhibits (with rather new force in her fiction) Austen's impatience with conventional femininity. By permitting an outlet for frustration and ambivalence, the narrative humor enables Austen, that is, not only to tolerate the cultural constraints suffered by even relatively leisured middle-class daughters, but also to textualize aggression against those constraints without incurring censure and frequently (as in the case of the traditionalists) without even incurring notice.

F O U R

Cranford: Humor as Daughterly Defense

"She has married for an establishment, that's it. I suppose she takes the surgery with it," said Miss Pole, with a little dry laugh at her own joke. But, like many people who think they have made a severe and sarcastic speech, which yet is clever of its kind, she began to relax in her grimness from the moment when she made this allusion to the surgery.

— Cranford[1]

In 1865, nearly fourteen years after the first installment of *Cranford* (1851–53) had appeared in *Household Words,* John Ruskin wrote to Elizabeth Gaskell expressing his fondness for her novel. Gaskell responded with warm thanks, related an additional anecdote about "'Cranford,'" apologized for doing so ("See what you have drawn down upon yourself, by gratifying me so much!"), and swore to the veracity of the book: "And it is true too, for I have seen the cow that wore the grey flannel jacket—and I know the cat that swallowed the lace, that belonged to the lady that sent for the doctor, that gave the emetic &c!!!" (*EGL,* 747).

Where Gaskell claims to have seen such strange sights was Knutsford ("her 'Cranford,'" as her son-in-law observed),[2] a Cheshire village some twenty miles south of Manchester, wherein she had spent her childhood and to which she frequently returned both in life and in fiction. Firmly, if not altogether comfortably, situated as an adult in industrial Manchester, held there by her duties as wife to a Unitarian minister and mother to four daughters, Gaskell found in her imaginative and bodily escapes to Cranford/Knutsford temporary relief from the grimness of her urban surroundings. What is more, she found a different sort of literary inspiration from that which prompted *Mary Barton* and her other "social problem" novels: not the unswerving consciousness of social wrong, but childhood memories of village life in England a generation earlier pervade *Cranford* and her other "Knutsford stories."[3]

The youthful quality of those memories can be seen even in Gaskell's response to Ruskin quoted above. The nursery rhyme cadence—the

House-That-Jack-Built construction of her reference to "Cranford"—is amusing in its strung-together form, in its evocation of a childish mode of perception and utterance. Although long since displaced in importance by adult thought processes (such as the logic of causation), the repetitive, associational mode of perception and formulation operative in the nursery rhyme remains familiar and appealing, both in the psychological distance it offers to the reader and writer who have mastered and surpassed it and in the humor that results when that distance is momentarily abridged. Indeed, the humor of Gaskell's response to Ruskin depends upon the reader's recognition of its juvenility.

Such a childish perspective similarly informs both the narrative and the humor of *Cranford*. The familiar yet peculiar world of the novel—its nostalgic, utopian community—is fashioned not merely upon childhood memories but upon those memories viewed from a psychological distance. When that distance is both confidently achieved and temporarily suspended, humor occurs. The eccentricities of the Cranford inhabitants, for example, recalled from the safety of an adult perspective but recorded with the immediacy of a child's, become a laughing matter. So too, in a subtler way, does the episodic narrative structure of *Cranford*, which, built upon association and repetition, harks back to nursery rhyme convention.

Although reported from a child's viewpoint, the humor of *Cranford* is far from innocent. *Cranford* is neither a simple celebration of a pastoral childhood nor an elegy to a bygone way of life. It is, rather, a wryly amused and amusing tale of an eccentric community told from the viewpoint of a younger, marginal participant. Marginality, no matter how eccentric the cultural community may be, entails isolation and estrangement, provoking frustration and often bitterness in those relegated to its territory. As Miss Pole illustrates in the epigraph to this chapter, however, one may sidestep pain and frustration by making a "joke" of its provocation. In this way, the humor of *Cranford* permits the narrative "to relax," to avoid "grimness," while at the same time expressing the pain of its narrator's daughterly perspective—a perspective marginal not only in relation to the narrative community but to nineteenth-century culture at large. It is this narrative perspective and the humor to which it gives rise that I wish to disclose in my discussion of *Cranford*.

Locating the Narrator

> In the first place, Cranford is in possession of the Amazons; all the hold-
> ers of houses, above a certain rent, are women. If a married couple come
> to settle in the town, somehow the gentleman disappears; he is either
> fairly frightened to death by being the only man in the Cranford evening
> parties, or he is accounted for by being with his regiment, his ship, or
> closely engaged in business all the week in the great neighbouring com-
> mercial town of Drumble, distant only twenty miles on a railroad. In
> short, whatever does become of the gentlemen, they are not at Cranford.
> What could they do if they were there? The surgeon has his round of
> thirty miles, and sleeps at Cranford; but every man cannot be a surgeon.
> For keeping the trim gardens full of choice flowers without a weed to
> speck them; for frightening away little boys who look wistfully at the said
> flowers through the railings; for rushing out at the geese that occasionally
> venture into the gardens if the gates are left open; for deciding all ques-
> tions of literature and politics without troubling themselves with unnec-
> essary reasons or arguments; for obtaining clear and correct knowledge
> of everybody's affairs in the parish; for keeping their neat maid-servants
> in admirable order; for kindness (somewhat dictatorial) to the poor, and
> real tender good offices to each other whenever they are in distress, the
> ladies of Cranford are quite sufficient. "A man," as one of them observed
> to me once, "is so in the way in the house!" Although the ladies of Cran-
> ford know all each other's proceedings, they are exceedingly indifferent
> to each other's opinions. Indeed, as each has her own individuality, not
> to say eccentricity, pretty strongly developed, nothing is so easy as verbal
> retaliation; but somehow good-will reigns among them to a consider-
> able degree.(39–40)

Arguably, the most salient characteristic of this opening passage of the
novel is its good-natured humor, its *charm* as critics have generally termed
it,[4] a quality of style that materially contributes to the representation of
the "good-will" that "reigns" in the town of Cranford. Such charm, however, while undeniably genial is also disarming: it allows the text to put
forward, under the guise of humor, a number of curious facts. "Cranford
is in possession of the Amazons; all the holders of houses, above a certain
rent, are women." Although many have taken this statement to mean that
the Amazons, the upper-middle-class female householders of Cranford,
form an oligarchy of sorts (which, indeed, they do), the sentence itself, at
least initially, states something quite different.[5] The Amazons may in fact
be "in possession of" Cranford, but the sentence reads: "Cranford is in
possession of the Amazons"—as though they were a captive population, a
historical artifact, or a tourist attraction. To be sure, the subsequent com-

ment that "all the holders of houses, above a certain rent, are women" goes far to reinforce a reading of Amazonian possession; yet the fact remains that the authority of the Amazons, even as it is asserted, is likewise undercut.

This mitigation of the Cranford women's authority becomes more striking when we recall that in the 1830s and 1840s (the years in which *Cranford* takes place), as well as in the years of its initial publication (1851–53), female holders of houses were necessarily single women or childless widows, since it was not until the passage of the Married Women's Property Acts of 1870 and 1882 that married women were permitted under common law to own property.[6] Consequently, the women householders who rule Cranford do so not by virtue of character, or even by virtue of class, but by virtue (or default) of marital status. Though the narrator implies that some of the Cranford women are de facto householders—their husbands being soldiers, sailors, or businessmen elsewhere employed—in fact, all the householding women "of a certain rent" that we hear about in Cranford have neither husbands nor children.

Furthermore, although the ladies of Cranford are termed *Amazons,* their arena of action is domestic, not martial. Cranford is "women's sphere" become hegemonic. There is no masculine activity here, nothing for men to do (with the exception of the surgeon) but to be "'*so* in the way in the house!'" Indeed, the narrator—playfully inverting the popular Victorian notion of a spinster as a "redundant woman"—informs us that the single "ladies of Cranford are quite sufficient"; it is the men who are unnecessary.[7] Yet, despite their sufficiency and the august origins of their name, these women are described in terms less befitting a troop of Amazons than a bevy of hens: their fighting consists of only "an occasional little quarrel, spirited out in a few peppery words and angry jerks of the head," and their conversation constitutes a "clacking noise" (95). Their sole weapon appears to be "verbal retaliation," and their primary source of power to lie in frightening males of all ages: they frighten little boys away from their gardens and frighten gentlemen "to death." Like the phallic mother (psychologically endowed by the infant with omnipotence despite her relative lack of power in the Real), these latter-day Amazons are *perceived* as frightening, though their power is largely limited to that perception; they are in fact— or at least rendered in humor—quite harmless.

Before considering how the humorously ambivalent description of the Amazons in this first passage fits into an overall textual strategy of humor,

I want to look at two consecutive paragraphs immediately following the opening passage:

> Their dress is very independent of fashion; as they observe, "what does it signify how we dress here at Cranford, where everybody knows us?" And if they go from home, their reason is equally cogent: "What does it signify how we dress here, where nobody knows us?" The materials of their clothes are, in general, good and plain, and most of them are nearly as scrupulous as Miss Tyler, of cleanly memory; but I will answer for it, the last gigot, the last tight and scanty petticoat in wear in England, was seen in Cranford—and seen without a smile. (40)

A gigot (a leg-o-mutton sleeve), gathered wide at the shoulder, tapering down from the elbow to the wrist, exaggerates to an almost absurd degree the Amazon's biceps muscle, while her "tight and scanty petticoat" de-emphasizes her female figure. On the other hand, the vast layers of petticoats fashionable elsewhere in England during the narrative time of *Cranford* (as well as the crinoline or hooped skirt which superseded them during the time of *Cranford*'s serial publication) not only exaggerate the hips and buttocks (while at the same time disguising them) but immobilize the wearer by their sheer weight and awkwardness, thus rendering her weak, powerless, and—as the following paragraph associatively suggests—vulnerable to attack: turning her, metonymically at least, into "a stick in petticoats."

> I can testify to a magnificent family red silk umbrella, under which a gentle little spinster, left alone of many brothers and sisters, used to patter to church on rainy days. Have you any silk umbrellas in London? We had a tradition of the first that had ever been seen in Cranford; and the little boys mobbed it, and called it "a stick in petticoats." It might have been the very red silk one I have described, held by a strong father over a troop of little ones; the poor little lady—the survivor of all—could scarcely carry it. (40)

Petticoats are the associative link between this paragraph and the paragraph directly preceding it, constituting an obvious tropic reference to women. The stick—a standard symbol of authority (and slang for a curveless woman)—is here (ef)feminized, dressed in petticoats, and rendered vulnerable to physical and verbal attacks by little boys. Although the umbrella had once been wielded by a "strong father," it has devolved upon a "poor little lady" who has come into possession of it solely by virtue of her longevity (she is "the survivor of all"); thus, as with the other little ladies of

Cranford, authority has settled accidentally into the hands of a woman who can "scarcely carry it." Furthermore, authority in the hands of a woman is hardly recognizable as authority (hidden as it is among petticoats) and is so weakened, so emasculated, as to be derisible both to the little boys and to the narrator who tells this anecdote.

Considering that Cranford is generally acknowledged to be a "charming" novel, chronicling the domestic adventures of a handful of loyal, kindhearted, often generous women, we might well ask what purpose all this aggressive humor serves. Beyond the convention of the "mock heroic," what accounts for the textual impulse to make fun of the very women whom the novel celebrates?[8] Any investigation of this issue must necessarily consider the generative source of the humor (that is, the narrator); but in most discussions of the novel, Mary Smith the narrator is curiously overlooked. Her neglect by readers until very recently, indeed, rivals the neglect that Mary Smith the character habitually experiences at the hands of the Amazons.[9]

That there is so little direct textual information about Mary Smith complicates the problem of distinguishing her voice not only from Gaskell's—with which it is too often conflated—but also from its apparent function as communal chorus (she frequently expresses herself with the pronoun *we*).[10] Although the reader may surmise that the narrator is female from, among other cultural cues, the fact that she lives as an intimate member in the households of the women she visits, the narrator never explicitly discloses her gender until she reveals her name in the last twenty-eight pages of the novel. Similarly, she suppresses her age, though by tracing dates and following a handful of numerical clues, we can ascertain that she is 12–15 years of age in the first two chapters, reaching no more than twenty-three by the book's end.[11]

This lack of marking—the indeterminate age, the withheld name, and the long-unconfirmed gender of the narrator—is in distinct contrast to the representation of the narrating figure in another quasi-autobiographical novel of the period. In *David Copperfield,* not only are the narrator's sex, name, and age clearly stated (the latter two in all their multiplicity), but the narrator himself is the eponymous hero, the subject of more than 900 pages of text. His is a long tale of self-development, chronicling family (and other early and lasting) relationships and only those events and influences significant to his own interpretation of that development.[12] Furthermore, while David Copperfield stands squarely in the center of his story—as both hero and determining conciousness—Mary Smith exists only tenuously in the margins of hers, despite their common age and class: (middle-class) subjectivity is here, as it generally is elsewhere, figured masculine. Popular nineteenth-century notions of male selfhood and female selflessness, that is, find metonymic expression in these narratives as presence of the male speaking subject and absence of the female. In *Cranford,* the near invisibility of the narrator results in the almost complete erasure of the *character* Mary Smith—whose name is so undifferentiated, identityless, one wonders why Gaskell bothered to name her at all unless to underscore the point.

Indeed, except for the rare occasions when the narrator refers to herself as *I* (and thereby fleetingly and ambivalently attains the status of a character), the Cranfordian *we* dominates the text.[13] Even though the "I" is linguistically included in that "we," because the narrator's self-references usually distinguish her from the group, her personal inclusion is at least qualified, and probably suspect. Whereas the Amazons are rural, middle-aged, reserved in speech and behavior, and, though impoverished, of the gentry class, the narrator is urbanized, young, "indiscreet and incautious" (163), and solidly, thrivingly middle-class (her father is a "capital man of business" [195] in Drumble). In fact, aside from gender and approximate social status, the narrator and the Amazons have little in common. Such being the case, the use of "we" is curious if not perplexing. As in the well-to-do narrator's comment "that we were, all of us, people of very moderate means" (42), the "we" at times signals the narrator's lack of actual or willing participation in the pronoun, rather than the expected reverse. This ambivalent participation in the "we" often merely acknowledges the narrator's polite bowing to Cranfordian ways when in Cranford (for example, wearing calashes or scattering paper to protect a rug) rather than indicating her own habits or personal preferences. Alternatively, the "we" sometimes signifies the narrator's positive exclusion from the opinions and action narrated; she is, according to Matty, "a stranger in the town" (136). Since her status as character is dependent upon her affiliation with the Amazons, when the narrator's own unasked opinion runs counter or askew to theirs, it is expressed not by direct contradiction but by silence, by a quiescent acceptance of the reigning opinion. The result is a rather coy form of humor:

> We were thankful, as Miss Pole ["a stick in petticoats"] desired us to be, that we had never been married; but I think, of the two we were even more thankful that the robbers had left Cranford; at least I judge so from a speech of Miss Matty's that evening, as we sat over the fire, in which

she . . . said, that she did not think she should dare to be always warning
young people against matrimony, as Miss Pole did continually . . . (157)

By a contrary logic, "we" here means "they," the Amazons, and specifically
Matty. Although the narrator may, like Matty, applaud spinsterhood and
fear robbers, her own youth places her among the young people warned
against matrimony rather than with those who warn or who refrain from
warning. Furthermore, whatever thanks she might feel in her own right
for her single status or for a robber-free Cranford is displaced by her perception of what Matty feels and thinks: she judges that "we" think husbands are less odious than robbers "from a speech of Miss Matty's."

The humor that arises from this sudden though subtle exposure of the
disparity between Matty and the narrator where no disparity was contextually anticipated both disguises and underlines that the narrator, in relation
to the Amazons, lacks authority, influence, even an opinion. Her presence
is manifested here as "I" and thus distinguished from Matty's, but only to
report Matty's thought, not to express her own. Although in the absence
of a stated alternative opinion, the narrator's opinion might be assumed to
bear some similarity to that articulated by "we," the humor makes clear
that the self-inclusion of the narrator with the Amazons indicates at most
a partial, mocking identification—an identification of the powerless with
the perceived source of authority. Even while acknowledging the absurdity
of such an identification (the narrator clearly has more authority with her
audience than do the Amazons), the humor forces from the reader the
recognition that the Amazons and their eccentric notions hold sway in
Cranford and that the narrator-as-character is under their dominion.[14]

The difficulty in locating the narrator as a distinctive character lies not
only in her linguistic evasiveness—her ambiguous "we," her selfless "I"—
but in her disembodied state: since the narrator remains unnamed until
the last pages of the book, there is—narratively speaking—literally no
identifiable body in which to place her. This being the case, the occasion
of her naming is itself significant. Shortly following word of Miss Matty's
bank failure, the narrator is singled out for the first time to attend a colloquy of the Cranford ladies. After she confirms for them Matty's financial
ruin, Miss Pole speaks to her about their collective intention of providing
Matty with an income:

"Miss Smith," she continued, addressing me (familiarly known as
"Mary" to all the company assembled, but this was a state occasion), . . .
"our object in requesting you to meet us this morning, is, that believing

you are the daughter—that your father is, in fact, her confidential adviser in all pecuniary matters, we imagined that, by consulting with him,
you might devise some mode in which our contribution could be made
to appear the legal due which Miss Matilda Jenkyns ought to receive
from—. Probably, your father, knowing her investments, can fill up the
blank." (191–92)

Although "familiarly known as 'Mary,'" the narrator is first named by her
patronym—an appropriate address not only because the occasion is a formal one but because she owes her presence in the colloquy to her father.
By including her in their meeting, the Cranford ladies acknowledge for the
first time Mary's maturity; and by calling her by name, they both confer
upon her a legible identity and affirm her existence as a quasi-participant
in Cranford society. Both of these marks of recognition, however, are dependent upon her status as her father's daughter: Mary Smith by any other
name would not be in attendance. The Amazons want neither her mone-
tary contribution (though Mary's father is financially better able than they
to provide one) nor her personal advice. Rather, Mary is solicited solely for
her daughterly access to the authority of Mr. Smith, Miss Matty's "confidential adviser in all pecuniary matters."

Well before she is called upon, by name, to make herself useful in this
affair of Matty's, the essentially functional nature of Mary's relationship to
the Amazons has manifested itself in a number of textual details. For example, although the guest of honor at the card party that produces the
famous Johnson versus Dickens dispute (Deborah and Captain Brown
championing the merits of "the Great doctor" and "Boz" respectively),
Mary is rather unceremoniously ordered by her hostess to "fetch . . . Ras-
selas" (47). She is frequently imposed upon to assist in household tasks
and to execute shopping errands in Drumble on behalf of the Amazons;
furthermore, when, on one such errand, Mary fails to procure for Matty a
desired sea-green turban, Matty makes no attempt to disguise her disappointment from her guest. Apart from her regular annual visits, Mary's
trips to Cranford are inevitably made in response to an Amazonian sum-
mons or need, whether to deliver a purchase, to conduct a business task
(settling Matty's tea accounts and correspondence on a quarterly basis), or
to perform a delicate personal service (preparing Matty for the birth of her
servant Martha's baby). Once in Cranford, Mary functions as a generally
helpful—and silent— companion to the older women she visits.

Indeed, Mary Smith exists for the Amazons less as an individual, less as
a mature young woman with a selfhood of her own, than as simply a type.[15]

Being deprived by fate, and Gaskell, of daughters of their own, they cast Mary in the role of surrogate: a dutiful nineteenth-century daughter, always "prepared to comfort and cosset" (79), and, being single, useful in caring for and assisting elder family members, particularly Miss Matty (in whose house the narrator maintains a room for her "use in case of Miss Matty's illness" [200]), but also Miss Pole and, before them, Miss Deborah Jenkyns.

As contemporary accounts of the period make clear, limited extrafamilial activity and the Victorian ethos of self-sacrificing duty combined to exert great pressure on young middle-class women to devote themselves to the care and needs of other (especially male) family members.[16] In the case of a woman who married, this single-minded devotion would ideally be transferred to her own husband and children (resulting in her apotheosis as the "Angel in the House"). In the case of a spinster, however, such devotion toward her parents and in some cases siblings and elderly kin was expected to continue as long as the need existed: as long, that is, as the needy party survived. This cultural insistence on the selflessness of the unmarried daughter surfaces in *Cranford* not only in the treatment of Mary Smith (both as elusive narrator and as subordinated character) but also in the youthful history of Deborah Jenkyns and in the story of Jessie and Mary Brown. Like Milton's daughters, Deborah, when her father's "eyes failed him, . . . read book after book, and wrote, and copied and was always at his service" (102), despite the fact that her self-sacrifice goes largely unappreciated ("she was quite put in a corner" by her father when her brother Peter came to visit [103]). The narrative of the Brown family demonstrates a similar familial devotion: Mary Brown, whose "mother's death left her the young anxious *[female]* head of the family, of whom only Miss Jessie survived," is patiently nursed until the end of her long, ultimately fatal illness by that sister, who refuses to marry her lover so long as Mary or their father requires care (58).[17]

As these textual daughters illustrate, the ethic of doing for others may lead to doing without a self. Deborah's devotion to her father reduces her to the role of handmaiden during his lifetime and to that of replica thereafter, and Mary Brown ceases to be herself when she takes on the role of mother (only on her deathbed are her voice "and her face, too," restored to "just what they had been formerly," that is, before her mother's death [58]). Jessie, too, is limited to her function as a sororal nurse and filial homemaker until she is freed from such by the annihilation of her family. As for Mary Smith, the self's obliteration by its function as devoted daughter is less visible and less complete than for these other daughters, partially because she is, as a character and as we have already seen, less in evidence than they. However, although neither the narrator nor her history is ever explicitly under discussion, her voice permeates the text. Consequently, any struggle between self-denial and desire that she experiences will be most audible in her language: her discourse, that is, rather than her story comprises the site of conflict. This being the case, not only her humor but other linguistic acts as well, such as the complex trope of the "eyes" in the following confession of her secret fear, provide ground for disclosing the aggression and frustration aroused by such conflict:

> Having braved the dangers of Darkness-lane, and thus having a little stock of reputation for courage to fall back upon; and also, I dare say, desirious [*sic*] of proving ourselves superior to men (*videlicet* Mr. Hoggins) in the article of candour, we began to relate our individual fears, and the private precautions we each of us took. I owned that my pet apprehension was eyes—eyes looking at me, and watching me, glittering out from some dull flat wooden surface; and that if I dared to go up to my looking-glass when I was panic stricken, I should certainly turn it round, with its back towards me, for fear of seeing eyes behind me looking out of the darkness. (147)

The passage begins with two jokes: the ancient Amazonian reputation for courage has been falsely appropriated by the Cranford variety, since the dangers the Amazons have braved in Darkness-lane are strictly chimerical; and their poor regard for male candor is erroneously based on a collective refusal to believe that Hoggins, in denying being robbed, is in fact being candid. Yet, despite the introductory jokes and the tone that they establish for the reading of the rest of the paragraph, the topic of discussion— Mary's fear of eyes—is in itself far from humorous. "Seeing eyes behind me looking out of the darkness" is a manifestation of the double *(Doppelganger)*—an uncanny experience founded on an unconscious recognition of oneself in the form of an Other: a self-recognition that is textually reinforced here by the implication, strong until the very last line of the passage, that the eyes that Mary fears are actually her own in reflection, "glittering out from some dull flat wooden surface" or observed in "my looking-glass." Psychoanalytic theory suggests that the double gives form to an early phase of narcissistic rage that, having become unacceptable to the maturing self, has long since been mastered (that is, repressed).[18] Accordingly, the appearance of the double in Mary's mirror represents a return of that primary anger, split off and rejected by the self as something alien to it and projected outward, onto the other. At least part of what Mary fears, then, in the other's eyes (the other's "I") is her own aggression.[19]

Through synecdoche and homonym (an I for an eye) and inversion (one I for an Other), Mary's fear of eyes becomes as well a fear of herself. Her terror at being observed by eyes whose very presence, if not explicit intention, is felt to be aggressive calls into question the aggressive nature of her own observing: indiscretion, she tells us, is her "bugbear fault" (163). Characterologically, her cognizance of her aggression gives rise to anxiety (she becomes "panic stricken"); narratologically, it results in humor, which contains and neutralizes that self-terrorizing aggression. Although the mechanics by which aggression becomes humor are far from explicit in this passage, recourse to another, quite different Gaskell story of a double may shed glancing light on this transformative process.

"The Poor Clare" (1856) tells a story of sin, retribution, and redemption.[20] Bridget, a "wild and passionate" (334) woman, rumored by her neighbors to be a witch, curses a stranger named Gisborne who has wantonly killed her late beloved daughter's dog. In doing so, she also unwittingly curses her only grandchild, Lucy (of whose existence she is unaware), causing an evil "Double" (361) of Lucy to spring into existence. This double, who roams the vicinity "always about some mischievous or detestable [that is, lascivious] work," impersonates the "pure" Lucy so successfully that even Gisborne, her father (though his cruelty is responsible for the double), comes quickly to shun his own daughter's presence as hateful by association.

Banished from her father's house with her faithful nurse, Lucy is spotted by the unnamed male narrator of the story, who falls in love with her "pale, quiet, resigned look of intense suffering" (352). Soon, however, he encounters her double: first as "a peal of ringing laughter . . . verging on boisterousness" (358); later, as an image lurking behind her, "a ghastly resemblance, complete in likeness, so far as form and feature and minutest touch of dress could go, but with a loathsome demon soul looking out of the grey eyes, that were in turns mocking and voluptuous" (362). Like the narrator of *Cranford,* this narrator is frightened by "eyes"; like Mary Smith, Lucy can only see those eyes in reflection:

> "I looked up in terror. In the great mirror opposite I saw myself, and right behind, another wicked, fearful self, so like me that my soul seemed to quiver within me, as though not knowing to which similitude of body it belonged." (361)

The intensity of conflict between these selves—the "pure," "resigned" self that goes by the name of Lucy and the "wicked, fearful self" called simply "IT" (363)—begets profound psychic confusion. Caught between internalized injunctions to female chastity and passivity and the inexorable force of desire (the primal "IT") seeking an outlet for expression, Lucy's "soul," like the ego to which it corresponds, is terrifyingly uncertain where identity lies.[21]

Lucy's father's murder of the dog and, more important, his sin against Lucy's mother (his "terrible deceit upon her" [366] led to her suicide) are responsible for Lucy's affliction; but because her grandmother has inadvertently called the double into existence, only she can remove it. Reversing the curse, which has resulted from a murderous wish ("my wishes are terrible—their power goes beyond my thought" [348]), requires more than Bridget's wishful thinking to remove, however. Lucy can only be delivered from her double through her *grandmother's* forgiveness of her *father's* sins, forgiveness that is partially enacted by Bridget's penitential service in the cloistered religious order of the Poor Clares (hence, the title of the story).

If, as Lucy's nurse declares, this story shows how "'the sins of the fathers shall be visited upon the children'" (363), it is evident that in this case the only children who suffer are daughters. Lucy not only acts as scapegoat for her father's crimes but is exiled from society altogether, because the mark of the punishment she endures—a splitting of the (female) self into angel and demon—violates, even while it enforces, the Law of the Father.[22] If patriarchal law demands control of female sexuality and speech, then Lucy, in splitting in two, both capitulates to that demand and thwarts it. Like her mother, Mary, another daughter, who suffers death for transgressing the law in birthing her (presumably) illegitimate child, Lucy forfeits paternal recognition for exposing, in the form of IT/Id, how female sexuality and speech (that is, the IT's boisterous laugh) exceed and outwit phallocratic control, despite heavy psychic and cultural prohibitions against their expression.

Even Bridget ultimately suffers a daughter's fate. Because her uncontrolled speech has released her granddaughter's "demon," she too is implicated in "the sins of the fathers." Unlike Gisborne, however, she alone bears the burden of atonement, which requires both that she enter a *silent* sisterhood and that she forgive the father's sins against herself, her daughter, and her granddaughter. The Law of the Father, then, requires not only the (grand)mother's complicity for its enforcement but her acceptance of wrongs perpetrated in the name of that Law upon her and her gender. In order to rid Lucy of her "demon," Bridget must sacrifice her own "passionate anger," "masterful spirit, and vehement force of will" (338). In submitting to the "laws" of the Poor Clares, she relinquishes not only her sexuality and speech but, indeed, her selfhood: Bridget becomes Sister Magdalen. It is by the example of her own self-abnegation that the mother shows her daughters the way to compliance, duty, and selflessness, to becoming the saintly sister—or the domestic angel—who both forgives and enforces the law against her.

Although differing in strength, the doubles in "The Poor Clare" and *Cranford* are similar in kind. Lucy's IT may be explicitly more sexual than that of Mary Smith, but aggression is common to both. Moreover, at least one mode by which that aggression is expressed is the same: laughter— whether in the mocking eyes and gestures of Lucy's double or in the narrative humor of *Cranford*—is the speech of the double, an expression of repressed aggression and a response to cultural oppression.[23] Thus, unlike Lucy's double, Mary Smith's is actually twofold: represented not only by the eyes in the mirror but, second, by her narrative humor. Maintaining the angelic Lucy and the compliant, dutiful Mary Smith requires a repression of primary aggression, which in turn engenders the demonic double and the frightening mirrored eyes. Arguably, the double is less powerful for Mary Smith simply because the aggression it represents finds partial relief and release in the narrative humor.

In other words, humor in *Cranford* arises in part from the narrative sublimation of Mary Smith's aggression—aggression provoked by the conflict between self-denial and desire, between the internalized cultural demand to submit oneself to the role of daughter and a psychological resistance to that demand. The role of daughter is particularly oppressive in the nineteenth century, but in *Cranford* where parent figures are at best inadequate (like Miss Matty), at worst neglectful and disabling (like Mr. Smith or Deborah Jenkyns), that oppressiveness is aggravated by a sense of loss— the daughter's loss of nurturing—entailed in her becoming a parent *to* the parent, an affectionate caretaker of her needy surrogate mothers. Humor operates in *Cranford,* then, not only to give derivative expression to the anger at parent figures who prevent rather than assist the narrator to authority and selfhood, but to defend as well against the pain invoked by the loss of adequate parenting. Abounding with images of disfigurement and gender ambiguity, which I shall later discuss, the humor tactically protects and retaliates against parental authority—authority judged by the humor to be arbitrary, tyrannical, and ultimately destructive of female selfhood.

AMAZONS AND PATRIARCHS

A masculine woman must naturally be an unamiable creature. . . . An Amazon never fails to be forbidding.

—Dr. Fordyce, *Sermons to Young Women* (1796)[24]

Even though parents in *Cranford* are the targets of humorous aggression, they are also clearly figures of narrative affection. The Amazons, no matter how narrow-minded and silly they may at times be, remain fundamentally endearing old women. Moreover, some of these parents are, to borrow D. W. Winnicott's term, *good enough,* if not exemplary—the deceased Mrs. Jenkyns and Captain Brown, for instance (although it should be noted that in their capacity as "good" parents, such characters are treated with poignancy and pathos, never with humor). Yet, because humor has its very origins in ambivalence, constituting itself in the contained irresolution of contrary feelings and impulses, it represents its objects as both "good" *and* "bad," gratifying *and* frustrating. It maintains ambivalence, even while it masks and relieves the anxiety that ambivalence provokes. In this way, the Amazons are narratively experienced as a source both of (humorous) satisfaction and (unconscious) resentment.

In relation to the young Mary Smith, the Amazons are ostensibly figures of maternal authority. Their maternity, however, is not nurturing—they are, as the etymology of their name indicates, "without a breast"—and as we saw even in the opening pages of the novel, their authority is so restricted as to be a source of laughter. Furthermore, their authority is wholly circumstantial: gentlemen who enter Cranford society, namely Captain Brown and Peter Jenkyns, sooner or later assume its leadership. Largely derived as it is from their adherence to a "strict code of gentility" (109), Amazonian authority amounts to little more than the enforcement of class snobbery, a slavish devotion to rules, empty rituals, and archaic forms (Dr. Johnson, for example, is their stylistic model).[25] And, although their "strict code of gentility" is traceable to Rector Jenkyns (noted for "laying down the law" [101]), and thus bears the mark of cultural approval, its application is limited to the body (bodies) of upper-middle-class Cranford

women, narrowly defining and harshly governing their (female) behavior.
In this way, the "good-will" (40) that "reigns" in Cranford also reins in its
female population:

> Then there were rules and regulations for visiting and calls; and they
> were announced to any young people, who might be staying in the town,
> with all the solemnity with which the old Manx laws were read once a
> year on the Tinwald Mount.
>   . . . "I dare say your mama has told you, my dear, never to let more
> than three days elapse between receiving a call and returning it; and also,
> that you are never to stay longer than a quarter of an hour."
>   "But am I to look at my watch? How am I to find out when a quar-
> ter of an hour has passed?"
>   "You must keep thinking about the time, my dear, and not allow
> yourself to forget it in conversation."
>   As everybody had this rule in their minds, whether they received or
> paid a call, of course no absorbing subject was ever spoken about. We
> kept ourselves to short sentences of small talk, and were punctual to our
> time. (40–41)[26]

The most authentic (though ultimately self-destructive) authority these
women possess lies in silence. Their discourse is restricted by their "gentility" in its content and duration, but they transform this disability into a
meager sort of power. They refuse not only to speak on certain subjects
but to acknowledge their existence altogether:

> We none of us spoke of money, because that subject savoured of com-
> merce and trade, and though some might be poor, we were all aristo-
> cratic. The Cranfordians had that *esprit de corps* which made them over-
> look all deficiencies in success when some among them tried to conceal
> their poverty. When Mrs. Forrester, for instance, gave a party in her
> baby-house of a dwelling, and the little maiden disturbed the ladies on
> the sofa by a request that she might get the tea-tray out from underneath,
> every one took this novel proceeding as the most natural thing in the
> world; and talked about household forms and ceremonies, as if we all
> believed that our hostess had a regular servants' hall, second table, with
> housekeeper and steward, instead of the one little charity-school maiden,
> whose short ruddy arms could never have been strong enough to carry
> the tray up-stairs, if she had not been assisted in private by her mistress,
> who now sat in state, pretending not to know what cakes were sent up,
> though she knew, and we knew, and she knew that we knew, and we
> knew that she knew we knew, she had been busy all the morning making
> tea-bread and sponge cakes. (41)[27]

Generally such behavior can be accounted for and dismissed simply as eccentricity: Cranford is, after all, a town with "eccentricity, pretty strongly developed"—as the name of Cranford's prototype, Knutsford, pointedly suggests.[28] But continually denying external reality as the Amazons do can have its more serious consequences. Miss Matty, culturally schooled in suppression, has hardly more knowledge of the world in her late fifties than would a small child (her brother refers to her always as his "little girl"). And in at least one case—where Matty, totally oblivious to her maid-servant Martha's pregnancy and subsequent delivery, is only made to understand the fact by being presented with a "bundle of flannel" containing the fait accompli—that innocence borders uncomfortably on psychosis.

Where silent disavowal fails to ward off the stark character of reality, however, euphemism generally succeeds. "Elegant economy" is the Cranfordians' description of the penury they suffer from having to eke out a passably gracious existence from diminutive incomes, which they are prevented by gender and class from increasing through professional employment. Even while their description of their finances cheats the socioeconomic truth of the situation—that these women are hounded by worries of insolvency—it also disarms the pain of poverty, by making money seem ungenteel. Thus, Captain Brown, whose incursion into Cranford society occupies the greater part of the first two chapters of the novel, is rightly perceived by the Amazons as dangerous, not merely because he is "other" but because he boldly flouts, however unwittingly, the silence and euphemism upon which their "strict code of gentility" and "elegant economy" are based:

> I never shall forget the dismay felt when a certain Captain Brown came to live at Cranford, and openly spoke about his being poor—not in a whisper to an intimate friend, the doors and windows being previously closed; but, in the public street! in a loud military voice! alleging his poverty as a reason for not taking a particular house. The ladies of Cranford were already rather moaning over the invasion of their territories by a man . . . [I]f, in addition to his masculine gender, and his connexion with the obnoxious railroad, he was so brazen as to talk of being poor— why! then, indeed, he must be sent to Coventry. (42)

Eventually, however, the Amazons not only succumb to the masculine appeal of the invader; they elevate him to "an extraordinary place as authority among" them (43):

I am sure he was startled one day, when he found his advice so highly esteemed, as to make some counsel which he had given in jest, to be taken in sober, serious earnest. It was on this subject; an old lady had an Alderney cow, which she looked upon as a daughter . . . The whole town knew and kindly regarded Miss Betty Barker's Alderney; therefore great was their sympathy and regret when, in an unguarded moment, the poor cow tumbled into a lime-pit. She moaned so loudly that she was soon heard, and rescued; but meanwhile the poor beast had lost most of her hair and came out looking naked, cold, and miserable, in bare skin . . . Miss Betty Barker absolutely cried with sorrow and dismay; and it was said she thought of trying a bath of oil. This . . . proposal, if ever it was made, was knocked on the head by Captain Brown's decided "Get her a flannel waistcoat and flannel drawers, ma'am, if you wish to keep her alive. But my advice is, kill the poor creature at once."

Miss Betty Barker dried her eyes and thanked the captain heartily; she set to work, and by-and-by all the town turned out to see the Alderney meekly going to pasture, clad in dark grey flannel. (43–44)

Here jesting—which is trivial, whimsical, disruptive of sober discourse and, as such, an affront to the Law—attains a position of absolute authority. Analogically, such a heightened position raises the status of the jest throughout, lending authority to the humor of the narrative voice (as well as to Peter Jenkyns's pranks) and underscoring the serious implications of humor. Part of the joke about Betty Barker's cow is that she is a natural nurturer turned into an object of superfluous care by an unnurturing (breastless) mother. Similarly, the surrogate mothers of Cranford, in being breastless Amazons, have reversed the natural order, demanding care and nurturing from children who have been deprived of the same. With the possible exception of the late Mrs. Jenkyns, whose mothering Matty recalls in an affecting anecdote, the women "above a certain rent" in Cranford are anything but adequately maternal: Matty Jenkyns is a perpetual child; Deborah Jenkyns is a version of her tyrannical father (a phallic mother); and Betty Barker and the widow Mrs. Jamieson are hysterically, hyperbolically maternal only to their pets. The only one among them who does become a mother (and, following her father's example, an apparently successful one) is Captain Brown's daughter, Jessie; she, however, must escape Cranford before doing so.[29]

Despite their very real charity toward each other and others (nursing Signor Brunoni through his illness, for example), not even their solicitude is exempt from humor. Intent upon showing her gratitude to the Cranford ladies (particularly Mrs. Jamieson) for condescending to be entertained by a former shopkeeper, Betty Barker heaps her serving board high with delicacies ordinarily prohibited—because prohibitively expensive—at Cranford tea parties. "However, Mrs. Jamieson was kindly indulgent to Miss Barker's want of knowledge of the customs of high life; and, to spare her feelings, ate three large pieces of seed-cake, with a placid, ruminating expression of countenance, not unlike a cow's" (111). Besides mocking Mrs. Jamieson, this descriptive linking of Betty's imperiously lethargic guest with her own fashionably clad Alderney calls into question the value of Betty's solicitude. Her anxious attention to Mrs. Jamieson not only mimics her "maternal" concern for her bovine "daughter," but, in doing so, is itself exposed as laughable and, like her mothering of the cow, misplaced.

A more appropriate candidate for maternal concern is Mary Smith. However, though Mary is considered by the Amazons to be a child, not just in her youth but years into her adulthood, she enjoys few of the benefits of such consideration while enduring its disadvantages.[30] Excluded from active participation in Amazonian exploits primarily on account of her exaggerated child status (she is past nineteen years of age when she is obliged to look at picture books of sorts as the others play cards at Betty's tea party [112]), Mary is also excluded from the considerate attentions that the Amazons, under normal circumstances, show only to each other. Mary is regarded as a child, in other words, simply to be dismissed as such and ignored. In a community where affection is reserved for pets and petty aristocrats, Mary's lifelong designation as a mere child secures her chronic neglect.

The Amazons are subjected to humor, then, not only for their general lack of authority and maternity but for their particular failure to guide and nurture their surrogate daughter to adulthood.[31] Futhermore, and somewhat curiously, given that female sexual repression is a commonplace of Victorianism, their more or less communal denial of sexuality is attacked with particularly disparaging humor. Preconscious sexuality lurks everywhere in Cranford, cropping up most dramatically in the ladies' response to the "Grand Turk," the turbanned Signor Brunoni, alias Sam Brown. If Captain Brown was regarded by the Amazons as "other" for his blunt masculinity, this "foreign" Brown is doubly "other" for his exotically sexual and suggestively racial difference. (This difference is increased by association with another turbanned foreigner, the Hindu servant who accompanies Matty's Anglo-Indian cousin on his visit to Cranford and who reminds Matty of Blue Beard.) The ladies are "awestruck" by Brunoni's conjuring powers, which affect them as both "wonderful" and uncomfortably "strange," even slightly demonic (Miss Matty wants to know whether "this wonderful man is sanctioned by the Church" [136]). Playing upon the inveterate masculine fear of female sexuality as treacherous and sinful, the humor here inverts and travesties the traditional male/female binary: the exotic foreign male becomes the dangerously sexual other of the Amazons. Because his occupation is to make things disappear, but certainly also because his presence is suggestively illicit (according to Mrs. Forrester, "going to see that conjuror was rather too much like a forbidden thing" [140]), Signor Brunoni is suspected of having committed a chimerical rash of robberies in Cranford. Although disturbed, the ladies are also clearly excited by the possibility of such violation: they take to inspecting "kitchens and cellars every night" (138), to rolling a ball under a bed in order to detect a hiding male figure, and to installing a man's hat in the foyer—precautions suggesting that the tantalizing threat of theft has, at least in part, a displaced sexual component.

Although the Amazonian response to the presence of Brunoni is so exaggerated as to be ludicrous, the repression of female sexuality, which generates that response, is as symptomatic of their culture as of their individual psychology. Because neither physical nor emotional adulthood can be gained without access to sexuality, the Amazons' failure to achieve sexual awareness signals not only their failure to achieve adulthood but a failure of nineteenth-century middle-class culture, which idealizes both feminine sexual and worldly innocence. In the context of *Cranford,* the Amazons' exaggerated adherence to this ideal (like their adherence to such other ideals of Victorian ladyhood as "a strict code of gentility" and "elegant economy") prevents them from achieving emotional and intellectual maturity themselves and thus from assisting the narrator to such. The narrator, that is, aggressively mocks the Amazonian fear of sexuality because, in effect, it blocks her own access to adulthood.

Repression is so strong in Matty's "mysterious dread of men and matrimony" (64) as to warrant special attention. Indeed, her responses suggest those of Freud's classic hysterics. She suffers "a long, long illness, . . . following the dismissal of the suit of Mr. Holbrook" (81), a yeoman for whom she cared in her youth but refused to marry out of deference to her father's and sister's class snobbery. Many years later, she develops a chronic tremble—the sign of her "effort at concealment" (81)—upon first hearing of the death of this former lover, who had recently renewed their acquaintance, and she takes to wearing widows' caps (though she does not acknowledge them as such). She shuns candlelight, at least partially to conceal her facial expressions and feelings: "'[P]ut out the candle, my dear; I can talk better in the dark'" (101). And she is almost phobic about the violation of her bedroom: "[S]he piqued herself on the precise neatness of all her chamber arrangements, and used to look uneasily at me, when I lighted a bed candle to go to another room for anything" (85). Moreover, she successfully denies, as we have seen, both the sexual act and its outcome in the form of Martha's pregnancy, and although apparently subjected to the sights and sounds of Fanny's lover in the kitchen, only suspects Martha's predecessor of "many flirtations": a real male hiding in her house makes less impression on her imagination than the phantom robber. The fact, too, that "Fanny had to leave" (65) Matty's employment hints further at the extent of Fanny's sexual conduct and Matty's insufficient attention to it.

Matty is frightened by virtually all men, from her father on down, in almost every capacity: she is afraid, for example, of selling tea to male customers. For an agreeable, docile woman, "meek and undecided to a fault" (67), she is peculiarly rigid in her insistence that her maidservants have no "followers" and is (not without reason in Fanny's case) constantly suspicious of them. She softens, however, on this point after Holbrook dies, from rather mysterious causes. According to Miss Pole, "That journey to Paris was quite too much for him. His housekeeper says he has hardly ever been round his fields since; but just sits with his hands on his knees in the counting-house, not reading or anything, but only saying, what a wonderful city Paris was! Paris has much to answer for, if it's killed my cousin Thomas" (80). Mr. Holbrook, a yeoman of great appetites—for poetry, travel, food—must be killed off, once familial opposition to marriage with Matty has been removed, since marriage with the zestless Matty is, narratively speaking, out of the question. Earlier in the text, Matty's scanty appetite is compared to Aminé's, the enchantress in the *Arabian Nights* who eats only a few grains of rice at mealtime with her husband, having previously feasted on disinterred corpses with a female Ghoul. This horrifying—yet humorously macabre—association of the sweet, shy, man-fearing spinster with the seductive man-eater suggests that cultural denial of female sexual desire results in the insatiable carnal appetite—filthy, cannibalistic, and concupiscent—that is manifested by Aminé and transculturally feared in "woman." Significantly, Aminé's hunger can be indulged only outside her husband's presence—only, that is, outside the bounds of the Law. Within those bounds of conscious and cultural reality, Aminé—and Matty—are forbidden from exhibiting appetite/desire both by the Law itself and by its successful internalization. Analogically, Matty is an abstemious enchantress, a seductress unconscious of her own desire, and, as such, an impossible match for the enchanted Holbrook, who apparently dies from overindulgence.

Despite (or perhaps because of) her exceptionally severe androphobia, Matty is often considered to be the most representative of the Cranford ladies.[32] Yet although undoubtedly the most memorable, Matty is in some ways the least Amazonian of her cohorts. She is not merely more timid and more easily befuddled than the others (excepting perhaps Mrs. Forrester) but more childish as well—in her knowledge of the world, in her relations to others, in her latent sexuality. Matty "never could believe that the earth was moving constantly, and . . . would not believe it if she could, it made her feel so tired and dizzy whenever she thought about it" (127). Servants and tradesmen spot her gullibility at a glance; some (like Fanny or the coalman who delivered her an underweight order) take advantage of her innocence, while others (like Martha, whose "tone to Miss Matty was . . . that . . . usually kept sacred for little children" [186]) work to protect her from the demands of the Real. In general, "People would have felt as much ashamed of presuming on her good faith as they would have done on that of a child" (201).

Matty's childishness is nowhere more apparent than in her relationship to Deborah. Both during Deborah's lifetime and beyond (even more strictly when beyond), Matty unquestioningly follows her older sister's precise rules of decorum, largely out of inflated admiration for Deborah's intelligence and intimidation by her rather irascible authority. Although Matty's innocence guarantees her simple-minded goodness, her moral understanding is merely a weakened, passively accepted version of Deborah's: apart from Deborah's dictates, her test for determining right conduct is that it be sufficiently disagreeable ("I only hope it is not improper; so many pleasant things are!" [75]). Matty's fear of her sister's displeasure extends, in fact, even to the expression of her private thoughts:

> Miss Matilda Jenkyns (who did not mind being called Miss Matty, when Miss Jenkyns was not by) wrote nice, kind, rambling letters; now and then venturing into an opinion of her own; but suddenly pulling herself up, and either begging me not to name what she had said, as Deborah thought differently, and *she* knew; or else putting in a postscript to the effect that, since writing the above, she had been talking over the subject with Deborah, and was quite convinced that, &c.—(here, probably followed a recantation of every opinion she had given in the letter). (51)

While the bond between an elder and younger sister may suggest that of mother and daughter—where what was lost or idealized in the past maternal relationship might be recapitulated, reconstructed, in the sisterly one—Deborah and Matty's bond, in fact, resembles nothing less. Indeed, the sentimental portrait of sacrificing maternity, at least as stereotypical in mid-nineteenth century literature as that of authoritarian paternity, is altogether missing in the narrative present of *Cranford* (though we catch glimpses of it in the subsidiary tales of Mrs. Brunoni's trek across India and of Mrs. Jenkyns's reaction to Peter's exile from Cranford). Their relationship, rather, parodies as it replicates the authoritarian/subservient relations inscribed in literary and legal fiction as those between master and servant, father and daughter. Tellingly, it also recalls the relations between the domineering Rector Jenkyns and his submissive, naive wife, thus underscoring the paternalism of Victorian marriage relations. And, finally, Deborah and Matty's relationship serves as a model for the Amazons' bearing toward Mary Smith, whose first tie in Cranford is to the patriarchal Deborah (doubly patriarchal in being the advisee and representative of Mary's own father), to whose household and supervision she is annually committed until that lady's death.

To a large extent, standard nineteenth-century daughter-rearing practices are responsible for Matty's infantilization. Deprived of sufficient intellectual and vocational education, Matty is culturally compelled, as were her real world counterparts, to a lifelong dependence upon family: legal, financial, and emotional. In some cases, like that of Mary Smith, the protection that such dependence requires is paid for in service, in caring for the domestic needs of other family members.[33] In other cases, however, such as Matty's (and that of Dickens's Dora Spenlow), infantilization by culture and family is so complete and debilitating as to render these childwomen "fragile," "feeble and languid" (212), useless in caring for others and in desperate need of care themselves.

Yet, somewhat paradoxically, Matty, besides being the most childish of the Amazons, is also by far the most maternal. Her fondness for little children (and theirs for her), her stated regret at not having been a mother, and her recurring dream of a baby girl of her own ("very noiseless and still, . . . she comes to me when she is very sorry or very glad, and I have wakened with the clasp of her dear little arms round my neck" [158–59]) comprise some of the most touching moments in the novel. Unlike her cronies who make babies of their pets, Matty is metaphorically as well as literally childless. Miss Barker has her cow, Mrs. Jamieson her dog, and (in "The Cage at Cranford")[34] Miss Pole her cockatoo; but, except for her phantom baby (and at the end of the novel, Martha's real one), Matty has no substitute object for her motherly affection. She is, perhaps as a consequence of this lack, the most directly caring of the Amazons, anxious about the feelings of others and the harmony of the community, a purveyor "of peace and kindliness." Presumably, it is this aspect of Matty's character that wins for her Mary Smith's own love and loyalty ("We all love Miss Matty, and I somehow think we are all of us better when she is near us" [218]). Unfortunately, however, because Matty is herself a child, her ability, if not her desire, to nurture and care is limited.

On the other hand, having identified Matty as a child allows the narrator to then identify *with* her as such. Mary, from her earliest days in Cranford, has been "a favourite" of Matty's (66), and "dear Miss Matty" (218) is clearly favored by the narrator. Their mutual regard is encouraged by their shared status as children, which places them together in submission to Deborah's authority and its legacy. From this position of subordination, they share as well a humorous perspective, even though Matty's humor is sporadic and altogether unwitting. Matty, for instance, in leaving a copy of *A Christmas Carol* on the dying Deborah's nightstand, which Flora Gordon then looks at on the sly while reading aloud to Deborah from the *Rambler,* subversively, though not deliberately, undercuts her sister's authority as the narrative commentary intentionally does throughout. Similarly, Matty's remark on her father's Napoleonic War sermons ("'I remember my father rather thought he should be asked to print this last set; but the parish had, perhaps, had enough of them with hearing'" [91]) innocently conveys the public's opinion of the reverend's pomposity—an opinion heartily endorsed by the narrator ("[H]e could hardly write a letter to his wife without cropping out into Latin" [88]).

The jokes that result from Matty's ingenuous responses to her situation as well as those that are narratively made about her naivete link her to the novel's two other children and jokesters, Mary Smith and Peter Jenkyns. Yet, because Mary and Peter are conscious wits as Matty is not, their humor elevates them vis-à-vis Matty, granting them an interpretive authority inaccessible to her. As in Freud's 1928 formulation of humor, where the subject "acquire[s] his superiority by assuming the role of the grown-up . . . and reducing the other" to the role of child, the stance and strain of their attitude toward Matty is kindly parental, preserving her innocence and protecting her from frustration "as an adult does toward a child" ("Humour," 163). Matty, by the end of the novel, bears much the same relationship to Mary as to Peter: his "little girl" is her "dear Miss Matty," placidly accepting her position as dependent child to both her younger brother and to her fondly anxious surrogate daughter. Although there are indications from the beginning that Mary functions more as caretaker than as fellow child to Matty (Matty "begged me to stay and 'settle her' with the new maid" [65]; "I made her empty her decanters, and bring up two fresh bottles of wine" [68]), it is only through the course of the novel and largely through the narrator's increasingly protective humor that the relationship between Mary and Matty is transformed from that of surrogate siblings to that of parent and child.

For all the humor that is directed at the Amazons, and no matter how much these surrogate mothers are reduced in stature as a result, the patriarchs of Cranford hardly fare much better. Gentlemen may be looked to as figures of authority by the Amazons, but masculine authority in general is far from idealized by the narrative. Mr. Jenkyns is exposed as self-important and insensitive, given to poetic seizures rather than practical advice (his wife notes, "'Hebrew verses sent me by my honoured husband. I thowt to have had a letter about killing the pig, but must wait'" [88]); and he is at least indirectly culpable for the snobbery that afflicts Cranford society. Holbrook, too, though a welcome antidote to the magniloquent Mr. Jenkyns and his regime, is too "uncouth" and "eccentric" to qualify as an alternative moral authority. A "Don Quixote-looking old man" (70) who "despise[s] every refinement which had not its root deep in humanity" (69) and who takes "ever-increasing delight in the daily and yearly change of season and beauty" (73), Holbrook is yet shown on occasion to be a little insensitive and self-important himself:

> He walked before me . . . and . . . quoted poetry to himself; saying it out loud in a grand sonorous voice, with just the emphasis that true feeling and appreciation give. We came upon an old cedar-tree, which stood at one end of the house:—
>
> The cedar spreads his dark-green layers of shade.
>
> "Capital term—'layers!' Wonderful man!" I did not know whether he was speaking to me or not; but I put in an assenting "wonderful," although I knew nothing about it; just because I was tired of being forgotten, and of being consequently silent.
>
> He turned sharp around. "Ay! you may say 'wonderful.' . . . Now, what colour are ashbuds in March?"
>
> Is the man going mad? thought I. He is very like Don Quixote.
>
> "What colour are they, I say?" repeated he, vehemently.
>
> "I am sure I don't know, sir," said I, with the meekness of ignorance.
>
> "I knew you didn't." (76)

Holbrook's snappishness here toward the young Mary Smith anticipates that shown by her father on the occasion of Matty's bankruptcy. Unlike Holbrook, however, who later confesses to having not known himself the color of ashbuds in March, Mr. Smith, in his sole appearance in the novel, evinces an impatience toward his daughter unbroken by any such candid admission:

> Miss Matty and I sat assenting to accounts, and schemes, and reports, and documents, of which I do not believe we either of us understood a word; for my father was clear-headed and decisive, and a capital man of business, and if we made the slightest inquiry, or expressed the slightest want of comprehension, he had a sharp way of saying, "Eh? eh? it's as clear as daylight. What's your objection?" And as we had not comprehended anything of what he had proposed, we found it rather difficult to shape our objections; in fact, we never were sure if we had any. So, presently Miss Matty got into a nervously acquiescent state, and said "Yes," and "Certainly," at every pause, where required or not: but when I once joined in as chorus to a "Decidedly," pronounced by Miss Matty in a tremblingly dubious tone, my father fired round at me and asked me "What there was to decide?" And I am sure, to this day, I have never known. But, in justice to him, I must say, he had come over from Drumble to help Miss Matty when he could ill spare the time, and when his own affairs were in a very anxious state. (195–96)

The motive for humor in this passage (and one of its targets) is Mr. Smith's business-like abruptness, but the victim of that abruptness is his child. Although the narrative humor deflects the pain caused by his peremptory treatment, Mary (and, to some degree, that other child, Matty) is nevertheless obliged to suffer her father's bad temper. Generally considered, when she is considered at all, to be an ignorant girl incapable or unworthy of an opinion, Mary accepts both her father's and Holbrook's treatment with no more resistance or retaliation than is contained in her sharply amusing record of their bossiness and in a few mildly sarcastic observations:

> I then alluded to my idea that she [Matty] might add to her small income by selling tea; and, to my surprise . . . , my father grasped at it with all the energy of a tradesman . . . I evidently rose in his estimation for having made this bright suggestion. (197)

> But I was right. I think that must be an hereditary quality, for my father says he is scarcely ever wrong. (204)

Although Mr. Smith's appearance in the novel is fleeting and his speech severely limited, Mary's references to him—how she sews his shirts; how she "was summoned home by my father's illness" to care for him [128]; how, according to her father, she "was not to think of leaving Miss Matty while [she] could be of any use" (172)—show him to treat her as little more than an emissary, whose physical presence is generally less useful to him in proximity than it is deployed on a mission to the Cranford ladies ("Miss Matilda begged me to stay . . . ; to which I consented, after I had heard from my father that he did not want me at home" [65]).

There is, besides Peter, only one male character to escape Cranford narratively unscathed. Captain Brown, like Peter, who in some ways figures as his replacement,[35] has an active sense of humor (he "joked quite in the way of a tame man" [43]) and a penchant for performing small kindnesses toward family, friends, and (in Brown's case) the poor. Often described as "manly" when he shows tenderness or sheds tears, Captain Brown is noted for "attend[ing] to every one's wants . . . and so much as if it were a matter of course for the strong to attend the weak, that he was a true man throughout" (46). Consequently, he emerges as the most maternal of Cranfordian parents, in relation to both his own daughters and the community at large. Even though billed as a conquering invader and a troublemaker (to wit, his challenge to Deborah's authority and composure in favoring Dickens over her beloved Samuel Johnson), Captain Brown, like Peter, attains not only honorary membership in the Amazonian community (and admission to their card parties) but a position of leadership as well. His opinions, indeed, so threaten Deborah's rule that his death is narratively required to halt the ascendancy of his influence.

THE DUTIFUL DAUGHTER IN DRAG: MARY SMITH AND PETER JENKYNS

Unlike Captain Brown, the advent of Peter Jenkyns brings "Peace to Cranford," as the title of the novel's last chapter indicates. Returning from his self-imposed exile in India in order to care for his sister Matty, Peter quickly becomes the leading authority in Cranford, a position left effectively vacant since Deborah's death many years before. While some readers consider that Peter, in mediating Amazonian disputes, functions not in his own right but merely as Matty's representative (and thus that Matty is the real authority in Cranford), few if any have considered the ways in which Peter functions as Mary Smith's representative, a figure for the narrator.[36] Peter, for example, owes his *deus ex machina* reappearance in the novel to Mary; her letter, her authorship, calls him back into the world of Cranford. Furthermore, even though Peter is male and older than Mary and, upon his return to Cranford, more worldly and exotic than she, he shares with her a childhood spent under patriarchal and Amazonian rule as well as a humorous perspective shaped by that circumstance. The textual representation of feminine selflessness calls for the erasure of Mary Smith as both narrator and character, but Peter Jenkyns, whose history complements hers, is sufficiently able by virtue of the visibility of his gender to represent them both.

As the youngest of the Jenkyns children and the only boy, Peter bears the weight of paternal expectations. Sent "to win honours at Shrewsbury school, and carry them thick to Cambridge, and after that" to settle into a clerical living provided by his aristocratic godfather, "Poor Peter" distinguishes himself only in "the art of practical joking" and is consequently forced to return to Cranford, where he studies under his disappointed father's tutelage (93). Although "like dear Captain Brown in always being ready to help any old person or a child" (94), Peter nevertheless "seemed to think the Cranford people might be joked about, and made fun of" (93), that "the old ladies in the town wanted something to talk about." His joking becomes ever bolder, extending eventually to his father, whom he fools "by dressing himself up as a lady that was passing through the town and wished to see the Rector of Cranford, 'who had published that admirable Assize Sermon.'" Although Peter is "awfully frightened" (94) by his success at mocking his father with impunity, having done so once only increases his desire for more, and he attempts an even more blatant attack on paternal authority. One day Peter dresses himself in Deborah's clothes and parades around the rectory gardens in view of a group of avid watchers, cuddling a pillow and cooing at it as though it were an infant. Discovered by his father, who flogs him in front of the gathered crowd, Peter flees home and joins the navy, subsequently rising to the level of lieutenant. Although he once visits Cranford on leave, Peter remains abroad, eventually taking up residence and making his fortune in India. Only some forty years later, upon receiving Mary Smith's letter informing him of Matty's lonely situation, does he return to Cranford permanently.

Peter's fate bears little resemblance to Mary Smith's. While Peter suffers overbearing paternal and communal attention, Mary suffers comparable neglect. Although both are reared according to "the strict code of gentility" that obtains in Cranford, Peter is able (like Austen's Captain Wentworth) to escape its purview by going to sea and earning fame and fortune; Mary, however, like Anne Elliot, must submit to the domestic regime. While Peter is able to establish independence and authority outside of Cranford— first as a naval lieutenant, later as the Aga Jenkyns—and then to transport it back into the community intact, Mary remains forever a child in the eyes of the Amazons and subject to a code of conduct that circumscribes, when it does not simply ignore, her existence.

Yet in spite of their dissimilar destinies, the child Peter—in his character and responses—anticipates Mary. Both children challenge the authority of their fathers and of "the old ladies in Cranford" by mocking them: Peter, through gross physical parody; Mary, through cautious verbal humor. When, late in the novel, the fastidiously circumspect Mary remarks that "indiscretion" is her "bugbear fault" (163), she is suggesting that the young Peter's lack of restraint—his "animal nature" (92)—is not foreign to her own character but simply better checked, contained *by* and *in* the rebellious countermeanings of her humor. However compliant Mary appears, her spirit of "indiscretion" links her to Peter and to his active insurrection, his wildest pranks. Conversely, putting on drag transforms Peter into a female jokester. Both figures gain force in their association. Mary as narrator appropriates Peter's jokes and profits by them in the retelling; and Peter enacts more than oedipal resentment in dressing as a woman to deride his father. In literalizing his identification with the feminine and devalued, he defies not just his father and family structure but a cultural ideology that forbids such identification. For if the mere presence of an effeminized phallus (the ridiculed "stick in petticoats" in the opening pages of *Cranford*) threatens the integrity of the binary order, then Peter's becoming "a stick in petticoats" makes his defiance all the more devastating. Furthermore, as Peter appears unexpectedly before the townspeople of Cranford with a "baby" in his arms, so Mary appears unexpectedly before the leading lady of Cranford with a baby (Martha's) in hers. That Mary, although under very different circumstances, performs the identical scene of mock mothering for which Peter is flogged implicates her in *his* act of rebellion even while her own act remains feminine, normative, unexceptional. In this way, through their reflexive association, Mary the narrator's quiet little jokes about her father's temper or the Amazons' code of gentility participate on the sly in Peter's glaring affronts to his father and to the social order (note: Peter's "baby," being Deborah's, is perforce illegitimate), while Mary the character slips the responsibility—and the flogging—for such trespass.[37]

Humor serves Mary and Peter not only as a means of assault against patriarchal authority but also as a defense against the conscious knowledge of that assault. Since the mechanics of humor allow one to vent hostility while remaining blissfully unconscious of its motivation and significance—and therefore not responsible as such for the reception of one's jokes—Peter can understand his cross-dressing as simply a public service, as providing "the old ladies in town" with "something to talk about" (94), rather than as an act of subversion. Although even Matty interprets his transvestism as intended "to plague Deborah" because she "vexed him," Peter himself "never thought" of his prank "as affecting her" (95). Moreover, because humor appropriates aggressive energy, constituting itself in the conversion of that energy, it defends against the pain that frustrated aggression usually provokes: it allows both Mary and the young Peter to give voice to their alienation from parental authority and affection while avoiding the evocation of loss usually associated with such an admission. Following the cue of their environment, Peter and Mary cast themselves in their jokes as children (ergo innocent) vis-à-vis withholding (ergo guilty) parental figures. In doing so, they effectively protect themselves from the wrath of the authority—external and internalized—that they undermine. It is only when Peter's "boy's trick" (96) fails, when it exceeds the indulgence allowed both to children and to dissension couched in humor, that he is punished for insubordination. Furthermore, it is only when his humor *does* fail to protect him, only when his behavior is perceived as a threat to authority (as Mary's never is), that he is accorded adult status. For unlike Mary who remains a child throughout, Peter achieves manhood with his flogging: "Peter came in, looking as haughty as any man—indeed, looking like a man, not like a boy" (96).

Peter's jokes, however, do not cease with the onset of adulthood. His wildly exaggerated accounts of his adventures in India (he "told more wonderful stories than Sinbad the Sailor") are, like his youthful pranks, extravagant, ostentatious, phallic: "[I]f we swallowed an anecdote of tolerable magnitude one week, we had the dose considerably increased the next" (211). Indeed, Peter so imposes upon the credulity of the Amazons that he convinces Mrs. Jamieson (who "required strong stimulants to excite her out of her apathy") that he once "shot a cherubim" (217). Mary's jokes, on the other hand, are generally so suppressed as to be barely noticeable. Even those that tend most toward ridicule are muted in effect, at least partially because the audience for them (unlike the audience for Peter's jokes) is limited to the reader. This is true of the jokes perpetrated by both Mary the narrator and Mary the character. When Betty Barker violates the Amazonian rule of elegant economy by serving her guests adequate portions of more than meagre fare, the character makes the joke, but silently; the reading audience hears it only by secondary narrative report: "Another tray!

'Oh gentility!' *thought* I, 'can you endure this last shock?' For Miss Barker had ordered (nay, I doubt not, prepared . . .) all sorts of good things for supper" (113; emphasis added).

Regardless of their differences in form, audience, and intention, however, the jokes fashioned by Peter and Mary (as character) share the fate of being habitually misunderstood by the Amazons. Like Captain Brown's advice regarding Betty Barker's cow, Peter's tall tales are taken as truth, while Mary's jokes are taken as simply lapses in feminine decorum:

> I had once said, on receiving a present of an elaborate pair [of garters], that I should feel quite tempted to drop one of them in the street, in order to have it admired; but I found this little joke (and it was a very little one) was such a distress to her [Matty's] sense of propriety, and was taken with such anxious, earnest alarm, lest the temptation might some day prove too strong for me, that I quite regretted having ventured upon it. (185)

> In joke I prophesied one day that this [quarrel between Mrs. Jamieson and Lady Glenmire Hoggins] would only last until Mrs. Jamieson or Mr. Mulliner were ill, in which case they would only be too glad to be friends with Mr. Hoggins [the doctor]; but Miss Matty did not like me looking forward to anything like illness in so light a manner. (214)

Although Mary's sense of humor separates her from the Amazons, it enables her to read Peter correctly. When the town suspects Peter of amorous designs on Mrs. Jamieson, Mary is assured upon overhearing his cherubim-shooting tale that the town's suspicions are as false as his story. Not only does she decipher Peter's meaning (in killing the cupid-like cherubim he intends to kill the rumor of romance between himself and Mrs. Jamieson), but by virtue of the "twinkle" (217) that Peter extends to her, she participates in the enjoyment of his joke as well. Like the relationship between the narrator and reader of humor, the alliance between Mary and Peter hinges upon their shared intellectual and affective understanding of humorous intention.

Narrative Structure, Humorous Tropes, and Cultural Text

Even more crucial to the pervasive humor of *Cranford* than the memorable contributions of its joking characters are the *narrator's* jokes—as distinct from those attributed to the thought or speech of the *character* Mary. While there is no significant discontinuity between the identity of Mary the narrator and Mary the character (that is, Mary when she plays a role in the narrative action), there is a distinction between the narrator's jokes, whose reception is restricted to the reading audience, and Mary Smith's jokes, whose audience potentially includes the other characters. Some of the narrative jokes are aggressive—targeting the pretension of Deborah's Johnsonian letter writing, for instance (when "Miss Jenkyns was evidently very much alarmed . . . the first part of her letters was often written in pretty intelligible English" [90–91]). But most are defensive, transforming potential hurt or pathos into more tolerable affect. Deborah's at first funny indignation at Captain Brown's preference for Dickens threatens to turn sour until the narrative humor (at the semi-colon) intervenes:

> He [Captain Brown] endeavoured to make peace with Miss Jenkyns soon after the memorable dispute I have named, by a present of a wooden fire-shovel (his own making), having heard her say how much the grating of an iron one annoyed her. She received the present with cool gratitude, and thanked him formally. When he was gone, she bade me put it away in the lumber-room; feeling, probably, that no present from a man who preferred Mr. Boz to Dr. Johnson could be less jarring than an iron fire-shovel. (50)

Distracting attention away from Deborah's mean-spiritedness by alluding to the primal comedy of the Boz-Johnson feud, the humor cuts short our growing irritation with Deborah's dismissive treatment of Brown and offers laughter as a substitute response. Similarly, the following passage, which nearly succumbs to sentimentality, is rescued by reference to Deborah's voodoo incantations:

> I had often occasion to notice the use that was made of fragments and small opportunities in Cranford; the rose-leaves that were gathered ere they fell, to make into a pot-pourri for some one who had no garden; the little bundles of lavender-flowers sent to strew the drawers of some town-dweller or to burn in the chamber of some invalid. Things that many would despise, and actions which it seemed scarcely worth while to perform, were all attended to in Cranford. Miss Jenkyns stuck an apple full of cloves, to be heated and smell pleasantly in Miss Brown's room; and as she put in each clove, she uttered a Johnsonian sentence. Indeed, she never could think of the Browns without talking Johnson; and, as they were seldom absent from her thoughts just then, I heard many a rolling three-piled sentence. (54–55)

Even the narrator's joke about the inconvenience of Matty's "candle economy" stands as an attempt at defense. Her complaint of having missed the opportunity to "scorch" herself strives in its hyperbole to reduce her actual annoyance:

> I had been very much tired of my compulsory "blind man's holiday," especially as Miss Matty had fallen asleep, and I did not like to stir the fire, and run the risk of awakening her; so I could not even sit on the rug, and scorch myself with sewing by fire-light, according to my usual custom. (84)

By curtailing the rise of emotions (such as anger and annoyance) that threaten to betray bitterness or those (such as pathos) that threaten to belie it, humor enables the narrator to attain detachment from the events narrated and to divert attention away from their "seriousness," while peripherally gesturing to the source of resentment that provokes its own existence. Deborah's coldness, the Amazons' clubbiness, Matty's indifference to her visitors' needs: all are irritating in a general sense, but particularly so to the narrator as character who, surrogate daughter to the Cranford ladies, suffers them on a daily and intimate basis.

The persona-protective quality of the narrator's humor extends even to the linguistic fabric of the novel, to the tropes, signs, grammar, and other discursive elements that comprise its means of circulation. However, being widely dispersed throughout the text and thus conspicuous and accessible only in an accumulative act of reading, this humorous rhetoric is both subtler and more subversive than the jokes generated or related by the narrator. Whereas the narrative humor is more or less "conscious" in its conception and reception (the narrator and reader share an acute sense of its presence and some immediate, if general, understanding of its significance), the discursive humor is "unconscious." Like dreams, it constitutes itself in repetition and association, giving rise to clusters of words—such as the repetition and associations of "petticoat" in the first few paragraphs of the novel—that together create a pattern of subtextual significance.

Foremost among these linguistic clusters is that of (castrating) disfigurement. The Amazons are missing a breast, and Captain Brown is run over by a (phallic) train. Both the postman and the tailor are lame, and Peter, sitting cross-legged, is compared to the tailor—as (indirectly) are the other Indian exotics who occasionally surface in Cranford. Matty notes in a letter that "a little child's arm" was once eaten by one of "Wombwell's lions" in Cranford (128), and the narrator reports that Matty and Mary "fell to upon the pudding" called a "lion *couchant*" (187). It is Matty also who is prevented from "disfigur[ing] herself with a turban" (129), while the

Rector Jenkyns "disfigured his shirt-frill" with a "strange uncouth brooch" (195). This disfiguring brooch, moreover, links the fathers of *Cranford:* it is passed from Matty's father to Mary's father (via their daughters) and includes, by association, the "uncouth" (75) Holbrook in its passage. The Amazons, who brandish an "array of brooches" on state occasions (one evening the narrator counts "seven brooches . . . on Miss Pole's dress" alone [120]), are also implicated as castrating or phallic mothers.

Cross-dressing likewise forms a knot of association. Deborah wears a helmet; the Rector Jenkyns wears a frill; the umbrella "stick" wears a petticoat. Peter dresses up as a girl, and Betty Barker's daughter / cow—in grey flannel waistcoat and drawers—dresses androgynously. The Alderney cow, furthermore, in receiving nurturance rather than giving it, suggests some fellow beasts: the "ruminating" Mrs. Jamieson and her dog, Carlo, who guzzles cream ("which should have been ours") while her guests get only milk (124); the milk-greedy cat who swallowed in its haste Mrs. Forrester's soaking lace; and the lions—Wombwell's and *couchant*—devouring and devoured.

These knots of association, formed by the accretion of discrete humorous moments, participate both aggressively and defensively in the subtextual significance of the novel. Hence, the fathers and Amazons are *aggressively* maimed, while the "little child's arm" (metonymically, the narrator's instrument of inscription) is wounded in defensive, guilty self-punishment for its aggression—as is the audaciously derisive Peter, who carries the mark of his castration in his exoticism, his "difference." Although the fear of castration may signal an oedipal component to the trope of disfigurement, the pervasive images of sexual ambiguity and devouring suggest that the objects of humorous aggression—the withholding parents of *Cranford*—are in fact primarily preoedipal, sexually undifferentiated, figures. Their withholding inspires both rage—evinced in a desire to bite, to devour (as in Matty's and Mary's devouring of the lion *couchant* and the animal pseudochildren's voracious guzzling)—and a sense of loss and frustration: that "which should have been ours" (nurturance) is withheld (the surrogate mothers of Cranford are breastless). And yet, the preoedipal alternative to withholding, the overwhelming presence of the mother figure, inspires its own fears: the fear of engulfment, of nonindividuation, of the mirrored eyes / I's, of being devoured—of *Womb* / *well*'s lion.

Not only these knots of signifying tropes but the narrative structure itself—its ordering of event and commentary—gives form to the ambivalent responses provoked by the objects of humor.[38] Like the "charm" of the

Pickwick Papers, an episodic narrative saturated with comic humor and interpolated with stories of patricide (in which the children are always abused and the fathers always wicked), the "charm" of *Cranford* depends in part on the repression of aggression in the text at large and on its limited expression both in humor and in tales of violence: "the horrid stories of robbery and murder," "rummaged up, out of the recesses of their memory" (141) by Matty and Miss Pole; the "headless lady" of Darkness-lane, "wringing her hands as in deep grief" (150); "The Panic" aroused by the robber scare; the little boys' treatment of "the stick in petticoat."[39] These tales, like the instances of humor, serve not only as outlets of aggression at the "bad" parents who withhold nurturance and guidance but as defenses against the frustration and guilt aroused by such aggression. Confined to a joke or a ghost story, aggression cannot harm the "good" parents cherished by the narrative proper.

Conveniently, the narrator herself confirms the ambivalence embedded in the narrative structure and tropes. A third of the way into the novel, at the beginning of the chapter entitled "Old Letters," the narrator comments on the idiosyncratic nature of hoarding: "[A]lmost every one has his own individual small economies—careful habits of saving fractions of pennies in some peculiar direction—any disturbance of which annoys him more than spending shillings or pounds on some real extravagance" (83). Such small economies function psychologically as a way to cope with anxiety, by defining a delimited area of often compulsive control, distinct from, though linked associatively with, the actual source of overwhelming anxiety.

> I am not above owning that I have this human weakness myself. String is my foible. My pockets get full of little hanks of it, picked up and twisted together, ready for uses that never come. I am seriously annoyed if any one cuts the string of a parcel, instead of patiently and faithfully undoing it fold by fold. How people can bring themselves to use India-rubber rings, which are a sort of deification of string, as lightly as they do, I cannot imagine. To me an India-rubber ring is a precious treasure. I have one which is not new; one that I picked up off the floor, nearly six years ago. I have really tried to use it; but my heart failed me, and I could not commit the extravagance. (83)

String, according to Winnicott, symbolically functions "as an extension of all other techniques of communication." On the one hand, string communicates—connects—by joining or securing one thing to another, by holding together "unintegrated material" (*PR,* 22). Thus, an obsession with string clinically suggests "a fear of separation": an attempt to tie or secure the self to its source of nurturance (to recreate the umbilical cord) and to deny separation by reenacting oneness (*PR*, 20). On the other hand, string communicates—expresses, informs—by symbolizing in its visible presence the desire of the self for bonding. In this way, an obsession with string is textually linked, so to speak, to other manifestations or "techniques of communication"—such as letters (in the sense both of correspondence ["Old Letters"] and of marks of inscription)—that forge a connection by their visible, doubly literal presence and that offer themselves as substitute satisfactions for the loss of oneness.

The narrative of *Cranford, strung* and *knotted* together by the association and repetition of trope and event, loosely *tied* by episodic moments rather than driven by inexorable plot, thus stands as an attempt to connect with the lost source of nurturance, the preoedipal mother (who, despite a number of Amazonian surrogates, is clearly absent in this text). Put another way, in being preoedipal (rather than oedipal), associative (rather than causal), gyno- (rather than phallo-) centric, the narrative denies the authority of the Law that has superseded the mother's presence: it enacts this denial in its encoded discourse of loss, anger, and ambivalence; in its narrative structure; and even to some degree in its thematic content (in its emphasis on mother/daughter, Amazon/narrator activities and its lack of nuptial closure).[40]

Although a fetish for string may be understood as a means to communicate, to compensate for loss, and to negotiate frustration, understanding why the narrator's heart should fail her when she tries to use an India-rubber ring requires a shift of focus from subtext to cultural text. According to Winnicott, when string represents a denial of separation, aggression is its hallmark. String serves, then, not only as a means to express the lost connection with the mother but also to retaliate against the person or thing held responsible for the loss. In Winnicott's case, a boy obsessed with string ties a string "round his sister's neck (the sister whose birth provided the first separation of this boy from his mother)" (*PR*, 20). In Gaskell's case, a narrator obsessed with string strings together a text that in its form and substance defies the paternal principle, which has replaced the mother's presence and which dictates (among other things) how texts should be written.[41] Hence, the aggressive use of string in *Cranford* constitutes a narrative attack on authority—authority that is extratextually located in the person of Dickens.

For if string is metonymy for Gaskell's narrative technique, and is, as

J. Hillis Miller has suggested, in contrast to what one might call the rubberband, full-circle narrative of Dickens, then the female narrator's preference for string represents not only a defense against loss and anxiety but also a jibing at the authority of the prime male practitioner of "rubberband narrative" and of the society that privileges it.[42] Having picked up a rubberband "nearly six years ago" (and *Mary Barton,* begun nearly six years earlier, is a rubberband narrative), the narrator tells us that she "could not commit the extravagance," could not be so imprudent, so unrestrained, as to use it. Although her excuses for not using a rubberband are overvaluation ("a precious treasure") and lack of courage (her "heart failed" her), "extravagance" suggests that there is something improvident, even morally wrong, about availing herself of "India-rubber rings, which are a sort of a *deification* of string": which represent, in other words, that which surpasses string, an embodiment of the Father, an exaltation of his Law (emphasis added). Prudence and self-interest lie, rather, in string itself: in the narrative tie to the preoedipal mother.

Gaskell's undercutting of Dickens and masculine authority is not limited to her narrator's suspicion of his "rubberband" model of narrative (a suspicion, incidentally, that would become identified with Modernism). Dickens himself is specifically lampooned at a number of points in the text. Captain Brown is not only killed for reading the *Pickwick Papers* (which as Nina Auerbach points out are the memoirs of a misogynist club, in direct contrast to the Amazonian community of *Cranford*), but he is killed in the same manner as Dickens's Carker, who met his demise three years earlier in *Dombey and Son.*[43] *Dombey*'s Captain Cuttle, captured and dragged to the altar by his landlady, resurfaces in *Cranford* in the form of Mr. Jenkyns's successor, the Rector Hayter (Hater? Hate Her?), who flees at the slightest opportunity from the allegedly marriage-minded Amazons ("He would rush into a shop, or dive into an entry, sooner than encounter any of the Cranford ladies in the street" [136]). Moreover, in the famous contest between Dr. Johnson and Boz, the stylistic and moral authority of the eighteenth century, in Cranford at least, triumphs over his nineteenth-century literary successor. Although Johnson's victory is certainly hollow (jokes about Johnsonian style are a staple of the novel's humor), Dickens's defeat is no less of one for that. Johnson may not be an appropriate model for writing daughters, but neither, the text implies, is Dickens.

Gaskell's digs at Dickens—impugning his authority as a literary model, parodying his plot device for getting rid of Carker, murdering him by association when she has Captain Brown killed for reading the *Pickwick Pa-*

pers—are astonishing in themselves, but particularly so when we remember that *Cranford* was originally published in Charles Dickens's *Household Words:* where contributions were published without bylines and the name "Charles Dickens" appeared, as a running title, on every page. Besides being flattered by Gaskell's lionizing him as a literary authority, Dickens, it seems, also sensed the disquieting possibility that the lion *couchant* was being stealthily, if playfully, attacked. In his capacity as editor, he removed all references to himself in *Cranford,* substituting them with those to his contemporary Thomas Hood, who also published his own monthly periodical and whose work sometimes recalled Dickens's early comic writing (though he is best remembered for the sentimental sobriety of "The Song of the Shirt"). Gaskell furiously objected to the substitution and attempted (unsuccessfully) to withdraw *Cranford* from *Household Words* altogether.[44]

Dickens's substitution thwarted Gaskell on two fronts. It weakened the aesthetic integrity of the installment: Hood, unlike Dickens—who set the trend for nineteenth-century literary values much as Johnson had more consciously defined those of the previous century—was clearly no match for the "Great Doctor." And it constituted a blatant affront to Gaskell's authorship—an affront that was hardly mitigated by the hyperbole and vague condescension of his apology.[45] Although as editor and publisher, Dickens was clearly entitled to make changes where he saw fit, his rather too comfortably assuming the role of mentor to Gaskell (of Father to daughter, or to use his own analogy of Sultan to "Scheherazade") roused her resentment—resentment, however, which Gaskell, like Mary Smith in relation to Amazonian authority, allowed expression only in humor.[46] In the first book edition of *Cranford,* Gaskell was able to reinstate Boz, but there without the contextual frame of her anonymous article appearing underneath the rubric "Charles Dickens"—of her voice being subsumed by and thereby subversively ventriloquizing that of the Father—some of the complexity of her humorous treatment of Dickens and of the cultural authority he represented was inevitably lost.

* * *

Unlike Dickens, whose keen social perception rarely strikes his readers as incompatible with his comic sense, Gaskell sometimes poses an interpretive problem for those who see the bleak determinism of her "social problem" novels as ideologically at odds with the appealing nostalgia of her "Knutsford" stories.[47] Attempting to reconcile this apparent discrepancy of vision, Margaret Ganz argues that Gaskell's work is united on the ground of conflict: the "clash of the claims of emotion and the demands of convention" marks both Gaskell's "humorous vision of reality" and her "serious handling of social problems." Indeed, Gaskell's "humorous works" (foremost among which is *Cranford*) offered her nothing less than "artistic liberation": "they enabled her to relieve a private dilemma by projecting it in such comic terms as would suggest that it was both universal and not necessarily dismaying."[48]

No matter how "private" Gaskell's own conflict between "emotion and the demands of convention" might have been (and no matter how personal the provocation for Gaskell's humorous assault on Dickens), the conflict as it is particularized in *Cranford*—the daughter's urge for selfhood struggling against internalized demands for female selflessness—was common to legions of other nineteenth-century middle-class daughters. Although denied overt expression in a culture that dismissed female perspectives generally, such daughterly conflict yet finds voice in the humor of *Cranford*: not only in Gaskell's battle of authorship with Dickens but in the challenge her young female narrator's viewpoint presents to parental authority and in the preoedipal ambivalence embedded in the tropic and narrative structures of the text. Humor, that is, gives the daughter's anger derivative utterance even as it defends against both the guilt provoked by that anger and the pain engendered by cultural and familial neglect. In so doing, it may be said to function less as a reaction to anxiety and conflict than as a means of their transformation: rather than simply warding off the pain of daughterly frustration, the humor of *Cranford* converts it into a positive source of both psychological and aesthetic enjoyment. As Anne Thackeray Ritchie pointed out, the humor of *Cranford* allows "oddities" to be "tolerated, nay, greatly loved for the sake of the individuals."[49]

Not only for the reader but for the author as well, those "oddities" proved "greatly loved." As Gaskell remarks in her letter to Ruskin (written only months before her death in 1865): "It is the only one of my own books that I can read again;—but whenever I am ailing or ill, I take 'Cranford' and—I was going to say, *enjoy* it! (but that would not be pretty!) laugh over it afresh! And it is true too, for I have seen the cow that wore the grey flannel jacket—and I know the cat that swallowed the lace . . ." (*EGL*, 747).

FIVE

The Mill on the Floss:
Humor as Maternal Protection

But in art and literature, which imply the action of the entire being, in which every fibre of the nature is engaged, in which every peculiar modification of the individual makes itself felt, woman has something specific to contribute. Under every imaginable social condition, she will necessarily have a class of sensations and emotions—the maternal ones—which must remain unknown to man; and the fact of her comparative physical weakness, which, however it may have been exaggerated by a vicious civilization, can never be cancelled, introduces a distinctively feminine condition into the wondrous chemistry of the affections and sentiments, which inevitably gives rise to distinctive forms and combinations. A certain amount of psychological difference between man and woman necessarily arises out of the difference of sex.

—George Eliot, "Woman in France: Madame de Sable" (1854)[1]

A cluster of great names, both living and dead, rush to our memories in evidence that women can produce novels not only fine, but among the very finest;—novels, too, that have a precious speciality, lying quite apart from masculine aptitudes and experience . . . [Fiction] may take any form, and yet be beautiful; we have only to pour in the right elements—genuine observation, humour, and passion.

—George Eliot, "Silly Novels by Lady Novelists" (1856)[2]

Humor is of earlier growth than Wit, and it is in accordance with this earlier growth that it has more affinity with the poetic tendencies, while Wit is more nearly allied to the ratiocinative intellect . . . Humor is chiefly representative and descriptive; it is diffuse, and flows along without any other law than its own fantastic will . . . Wit is brief and sudden, and sharply defined as a crystal.

—George Eliot, "German Wit: Heinrich Heine"(1856)[3]

In her 1856 *Westminster Review* essay entitled "German Wit: Heinrich Heine," George Eliot isolates three distinct, if sometimes overlapping, species of the genus humor. The least literate and cultivated of these she labels "barbaric" humor, which finds its fun in "the ludicrous" (67), its "flavor" in "triumphant egoism or intolerance," and its origins in "the cruel mockery of a savage at the writhings of a suffering enemy" (68). The second type she identifies as wit, which is so thoroughly grounded in the rational faculty that only its "ingenuity, condensation, and instantaneousness" (67) distinguish it as a separate phenomenon. Wit, in fact, is little more than "reasoning raised to a higher power." Last, there is what she calls "sympathetic" humor—a refined, "higher form" of humor, which "in proportion as it associates itself with the sympathetic emotions," with the "sympathetic presentation of incongruous elements in human nature and life," frequently attains the status of "poetry."

What is more significant even than the similarity Eliot's distinctions bear to Freud's later ones—his "gallows humor" and her "sympathetic humor" are nearly identical in affect; his tendentious jokes are an amalgam of her "barbaric humor" and "wit"—is the subtly gendered quality of those distinctions. Both barbaric humor and wit are troped by Eliot here as masculine strategies. Although her interest in discussing barbaric humor quickly wanes (being "taken too little account of in sober moments" [65] to have any claim to being "Art"), wit gradually comes in the course of her essay to display some of the former's features: both, for example, exhibit hostility toward the Other ("coarse and cruel wit abounds" [68]). Consequently, wit is figured masculine not only in being closely "allied to the ratiocinative intellect" (66) and in being (like the phallus) "sharply defined," but also because it is a "powerful," "direct and irresistible force" that "takes us by violence quite independently of our predominant mental disposition" (68).[4] Wit, indeed, emerges at one point as the patriarchal weapon par excellence, wielded by Father Zeus—"who holds in his mighty hand the most scorching lightnings of satire"—while sympathetic humor, on the other hand, appears as the gift of a fairy godmother "who touches leaden folly with the magic wand of . . . fancy, and transmutes it into the fine gold of art—who sheds . . . [a] sunny smile on human tears" (73). In Eliot's description, such humor is not simply feminine but preoedipally maternal. "Poetic" (69) and imaginative, it is "of earlier growth than Wit," and thus prior to reason and the Law. And although it is drawn from "situations and characteristics" (and is thus more material than intellectual), it has "no limits imposed on it by its *mater*ial, no law but its own ex*uber*ance" (my emphasis: Lat. *mater* = mother; *uber* = breast). It is, rather, "diffuse" (66), flowing, and unbounded.

Perhaps surprisingly, instead of positing masculine, Father-associated wit as the culturally superior product, Eliot privileges humor for its maternal aspects. Being essentially divorced from sympathy with its victim, wit fails to achieve the moral stature of humor, which in "its later development" (67) acquires its very character from the "sympathetic emotions." While wit takes unconscious pleasure from inflicting pain, humor symbiotically participates in the suffering of its object. It rules neither by "violence" nor "shock" (68) but "approaches us . . . deliberately and leaves us masters of ourselves." Although wit and humor rarely exist independently, but rather "like other species . . . overlap and blend with each other" and are mutually benefited by their intercourse, humor—even when it is ideally "checked by wit" (69)—confidently emerges in Eliot's schema as the morally dominant partner, whose sympathy is not only tropically associated with the preoedipal experience of the maternal (exuberant, diffuse, unbounded) but derives affectively from it as well.

Eliot's assertions that "maternal" feelings are exclusive to women and that great woman-authored novels have "a precious speciality, lying quite apart from masculine aptitudes and experience" (quoted in the epigraphs to this chapter) lead us to infer, moreover, that "chastened delicate humor" (73) may be not only figuratively maternal but, for Eliot, the chief aim and measure of female writing as well. In "The Natural History of German Life: Riehl," she faults Dickens for the psychological shallowness of his characters, for his lack of sympathy with "their conceptions of life, and their emotions" (185). Although she admits his comic appeal, she devalues its attachment to "idiom and manners" and other "external traits" (184). Humor, like other aspects of art, ought to be employed, Eliot argues, as "a mode of amplifying experience and extending our contact with our fellow-men beyond the bounds of our personal lot" (184)—an amplification and extension that is possible only through *sympathetic* bonding. Because women have "sensations and emotions" that are "maternal" and that therefore (according to Eliot) "must remain unknown to men," they are, she suggests, uniquely endowed with the capacity to bring sympathy together with humor, to offer emotional understanding and protection rather than hostility to the humorous victim.

Eliot's own humor—as well as the "realism" of her fiction generally—is founded on this strategy of psychological "maternalism," a sympathy for the ordinary and familiar that (at least theoretically) shuns sentimentality and other forms of idealized expression.[5] Nowhere, perhaps, is the maternal aspect of her humor more clearly seen than in *The Mill on the Floss*. Intricately bound up with the linguistic unconscious or what Eliot calls "the subtle ramifications of historical language" ("Riehl," 209), humor here enacts a bond of sympathetic understanding, uniting the narrator as mother to the heroine as child. Because Maggie Tulliver is a girl, moreover, the narrator's humor works not just to defend her maternally from psychic pain by transforming her frustrations and losses, her disagreeable "situations and characteristics" into a source of amusement, but to articulate what is at least initially the female narrator's pleasurable ache of identification with her as a fellow daughter under patriarchy.[6] Through such complex identifications within the humorous dynamic, the narrator indirectly offers succor to Maggie, while at the same time, in her symbiotic relation to Maggie as victim, she appeals to the powerful, archaic mother of humor to forestall the Real and its "lawful" authority.

So long as Maggie remains a child, the narrator's frequent early humorous interventions on her behalf work to mitigate, if not Maggie's actual suffering, then at least the reader's perception of it. Once Maggie becomes eroticized, however, and thereby relocated within the oedipal order, the relationship between narrator and heroine is thoroughly transformed. In *Mansfield Park* and *Persuasion,* the heroine's eroticization (as we saw in Chapter 3) provokes the maternal narrator to turn her humorous aggression, in part, upon the heroine herself. In *The Mill on the Floss,* by contrast, Maggie's eroticization prompts the narrator to abandon both humor and eventually the maternal role altogether and to take up an identification with Maggie and her suffering so profound and intense as to border on the pathological. The narrator, that is, who in humor is able to offer her heroine momentary relief from pain, is outside of it helpless to provide more than suffering empathy. Consequently, Maggie's tendency to masochism, effectively checked or countered in the early chapters by humor, overwhelms the later ones, eventually acquiring affective control of the text and dictating her tragic outcome. Yet, like the narrative humor, Maggie's masochism, too, enacts a search for the preoedipal mother. The significant difference, as I hope will become evident, is that whereas humor is fleetingly successful in that search, masochism discovers only the continual pain of maternal loss.[7]

PARENTAL FAILURES

> Mrs. Tulliver was what is called a good-tempered person—never cried, when she was a baby, on any slighter ground than hunger and pins; and from the cradle upwards had been healthy, fair, plump and dull-witted; in short, the flower of her family for beauty and amiability. But milk and mildness are not the best things for keeping, and when they turn only a little sour, they may disagree with young stomachs seriously. I have often wondered whether those early Madonnas of Raphael, with the blond

faces and somewhat stupid expression, kept their placidity undisturbed when their strong-limbed, strong-willed boys got a little too old to do without clothing. I think they must have been given to feeble remonstrance, getting more and more peevish as it became more and more ineffectual.[8]

By middle-class Victorian standards, Bessy Tulliver has all the apparent qualifications of an exceptional wife and mother. Not only is she pretty and passive, but she manages her home with an industry, economy, and attention that even Sarah Stickney Ellis and Isabella Beeton would be forced to approve. In expression ("somewhat stupid") and appearance ("fair" and "plump"), she resembles a Raphaelite Madonna, with its promise of patient tolerance and "placidity undisturbed." Yet as the foregoing passage suggests, the popular Victorian *mythos* of mother as Madonna (which covertly prizes "dull-wittedness" as highly as "beauty and amiability") is founded upon a falsehood. Although "milk and mildness" may suffice nicely for infants, older children—who, "strong-limbed" and "strong-willed," must learn to control their aggression as they come increasingly under governance of the reality principle—require intelligent guidance and, above all, sympathetic understanding to thrive.

Despite her domestic allegiance and household expertise, Mrs. Tulliver is too much of a child herself to function adequately as a mother—especially to Maggie. "The objects among which her mind had moved complacently" and "which had made the world quite comprehensible to her for a quarter of a century" (276) are not internalized figures of affection and authority but literal objects: the loss of her china and linens following her husband's bankruptcy causes her greater outward grief than any subsequent trauma, including his death. Indeed, Mrs. Tulliver only becomes "fond" of her daughter when, after their financial reverses, Maggie is "the only bit of furniture now on which she could bestow her anxiety and pride" (294). So thoroughly attached is she to the literal and identified with the animal (she is narratively referred to as a "sheep" [42], a "waterfowl" [55], and a "patriarchal goldfish" [72]) that she is apparently incapable of analogical thinking. When Mr. Tulliver, accusing her of habitually seeing a minor problem as insurmountable, suggests, "'You'd want me not to hire a good waggoner, 'cause he'd got a mole on his face,'" his wife "in mild surprise" responds, "'[W]hen did I iver make objections to a man because he'd got a mole on his face?'" (10). Such incapacity for analogy exemplifies her more profound failure at association of other kinds. Because Maggie is physically and temperamentally different (Maggie's "'brown skin as makes her look like a mullater'" and her propensity for reverie '"niver run i' my family, thank God'" [13]), Mrs. Tulliver finds it impossible to identify with her, which in turn severely compromises her maternal love:

> "Lucy Deane's such a good child—you may set her on a stool, and there she'll sit for an hour together, and never offer to get off. I can't help loving the child as if she was my own; and I'm sure she's more like my child than sister Deane's." (43)

> Mrs. Tulliver had to look on with a silent pang while Lucy's blond curls were adjusted. It was quite unaccountable that Mrs. Deane, the thinnest and sallowest of all the Miss Dodsons, should have had this child, who might have been taken for Mrs. Tulliver's any day. And Maggie always looked twice as dark as usual when she was by the side of Lucy. (60–61)

Essentially kind-hearted if dull-witted, Mrs. Tulliver tries her best to mother Maggie as she herself has been mothered. But her Dodson style of child-rearing—which threatens Maggie with loss of love for naughtiness (27) and considers her daughter's behavior foremost as a potential blot upon the family honor ('"Folks 'ull think it's a judgment on me as I've got such a child—they'll think I've done summat wicked'" [28])—simply aggravates her feelings of estrangement from Maggie.

Mr. Tulliver, on the other hand, is curiously close to his daughter, "the thought of Maggie" being "very near to him" (81). He regards her intelligence, of which he is vocally proud, as patrilineally derived, taking obvious pleasure not only in her public displays of "quickness" but in her clever thwartings of Dodson respectability; he laughs, for example, with much enjoyment" (68) when Maggie cuts off her hair in defiance of her maternal aunts.[9] Associated in his mind with his younger sister, Gritty, Maggie evokes in her father a nostalgic longing for his own idealized childhood relations, which in turn increases his "love and anxiety for 'the little wench'" (84). He provides refuge to Maggie in distress ('"Come, come, my wench,' said her father soothingly, putting his arm round her, '. . . father'll take your part'" [68]), shields her from Mrs. Tulliver's nagging demands that she behave in a properly feminine fashion, and acts as a highly partial advocate in her relationship to her self-righteous and punitively retributive brother, Tom ("[H]is perspicacity or his fatherly fondness for Maggie . . . [made] him suspect that the lad had been hard upon 'the little un,' else she would never have left his side. 'And be good to her, do you hear? Else I'll let you know better'" [38]).

Mr. Tulliver's "maternal" sympathy for Maggie, however, stops short of identification. His very first comment about her reveals the unbridgeable gap her femaleness poses for him:

> "It seems a bit of a pity, though," said Mr. Tulliver, "as the lad should take after the mother's side istead o' the little wench . . . : she's twice as 'cute as Tom. Too 'cute for a woman, I'm afraid," continued Mr. Tulliver, turning his head dubiously first on one side and then on the other. "It's no mischief much while she's a little un, but an over-'cute woman's no better nor a long-tailed sheep—she'll fetch none the bigger price for that." (12)

Uncritically accepting cultural notions of female inferiority (he "felt very much as if the air had been cleared of obtrusive flies now that the women were out of the room" [74]), Mr. Tulliver—despite his pleasure in Maggie's intelligence—not only considers it a liability in the marriage market but apparently disapproves of it as a gender violation: "'[A] woman's no business wi' being so clever; it'll turn to trouble'" (17). Maggie's gender thus prevents him from bonding with her sufficiently well to allow him to serve as a substitute maternal object (as Silas Marner serves for Eppie), while his failure to represent the Law (dramatized most forcefully by the loss of his legal suit against Pivart) interferes with her recognition of his paternal authority.

In like manner, the narrator's phonetic rendering of Tulliver's speech, the repeated observation of his finding the world and its ways "uncommon puzzling" (11), and the frequent emphasis upon his temperamental outbursts, childish gestures, and unsophisticated thought processes (of which the following passages are only the earliest of many examples), all serve to weaken his paternal stature:

> Mr. Tulliver paused a minute or two, and dived with both hands into his breeches pockets as if he hoped to find some suggestion there. Apparently he was not disappointed, for he presently said, "I know what I'll do—I'll talk it over wi' Riley." (11)

> If Mr. Tulliver had been a susceptible man in his conjugal relation, he might have supposed that she [his wife] drew out the key [to the cabinet containing burial linens] to aid her imagination in anticipating the moment when he would be in a state to justify the production of the best Holland sheets. Happily he was not so; he was only susceptible in respect to his right to water-power. (11)

By humorously regarding her parents as children, the narrative diminishes—on the level of text, if not plot—both their power over Maggie and the psychic significance of their parental failings (they "who were so unlike what she would have them be" [287]). For when parents are perceived as children, their inadequacies may be more easily forgiven as well as endured. In noteworthy contrast to the typical family romance, however, where parents are belittled or killed off only to be replaced by idealized surrogates, *The Mill on the Floss* resolutely leaves Maggie emotionally orphaned and estranged (despite her own vigorous efforts to construct a sustaining fantasy life around Walter Scott).[10]

Her aunts and uncles—quarrelsome, ignorant, and obstinate—are even less suitable parental figures for her than the Tullivers. Mr. Glegg, both the Deanes, and Mr. Pullet are all cut down by the humor in importance and character to a few mildly disparaging clauses:

> Mr. Glegg, who was fond of his jest; and, having retired from business, felt that it was not only allowable but becoming in him to take a playful view of things. (70)

> "The clergymen have highish notions, in general," said Mr. Deane, taking snuff vigorously, as he always did when wishing to maintain a neutral position. (70)

> "I can give no account of it, I'm sure," said Mrs. Deane, closing her lips very tightly again. Mrs. Deane was not a woman to take part in a scene where missiles were flying. (72)

> [T]he idea that a clergyman could be a schoolmaster was too remote from Mr. Pullet's experience to be readily conceivable. I know it is difficult for people in these instructed times to believe in uncle Pullet's ignorance; but let them reflect on the remarkable results of a great natural faculty under favouring circumstances. And uncle Pullet had a great natural faculty for ignorance. (70)

Although somewhat more fully addressed by the narrative, Mrs. Pullet's character, like that of the other Dodsons and their spouses, is essentially an elaboration of a temperamental "humor." Her "melancholy air" (89) and morbid interests (she takes keen pleasure in reporting the graphic details of Mrs. Sutton's gout, for example) emerge as her identifying traits:

> It was not everybody who could afford to cry so much about their neighbours who had left them nothing; but Mrs. Pullet had married a gentleman farmer, and had leisure and money to carry her crying and everything else to the highest pitch of respectability. (58)[11]

In contrast, Mrs. Glegg, although as easily caricatured as her sisters, signifies more than her own parsimony. Like Deborah Jenkyns in relation to the Amazons of *Cranford,* Jane Glegg is the acknowledged head of the

Dodson clan. Her rule comprises the strict enforcement of family customs and attitudes, which, even in their narrative rendering, are so remarkably Amazonian as to warrant quoting at some length:[12]

> There were particular ways of doing everything in that family: particular ways of bleaching the linen, of making the cowslip wine, curing the hams, and keeping the bottled gooseberries; so that no daughter of that house could be indifferent to the privilege of having been born a Dodson, rather than a Gibson or a Watson. Funerals were always conducted with peculiar propriety . . . When one of the family was in trouble or sickness, all the rest went to visit the unfortunate member, usually at the same time . . . In short, there was in this family a peculiar tradition as to what was the right thing in household managment and social demeanour . . . And it is remarkable that while no individual Dodson was satisfied with any other individual Dodson, each was satisfied, not only with him or her self, but with the Dodsons collectively. (43–44)

Although Mrs. Glegg is not constrained by need to "elegant economy," her principles of food and fashion nonetheless follow the Amazonian model. "One would need to be learned in the fashions of those times to know how far in the rear of them Mrs. Glegg's slate-coloured silk-gown must have been" (54); "it was not her way to wear her new things out before her old ones" (53). Extravagant meals are likewise judged to be in bad taste: "'I hope you've not gone and got a great dinner for us—going to expense for your sisters, as 'ud sooner eat a crust o' dry bread nor help to ruin you . . . A boiled joint . . . and a plain pudding, with a spoonful o' sugar, and no spice, 'ud be far more becoming'" (55). As the most concentrated form of Dodsonianism, Mrs. Glegg represents not just her own family but the cultural authority of the narrative world. Although she refuses on principle to join the rest of the community in ostracizing Maggie after her "elopement" with Stephen Guest, Aunt Glegg generally speaks for "public opinion," which, especially on issues of female behavior, "is always of the feminine gender—not the world, but the world's wife" (490). The world's wife is a representative of patriarchy, enforcing codes and values dictated by the "man of maxims" ("the popular representative of minds that are guided in their moral judgment solely by general rules . . . without . . . a wide fellow-feeling with all that is human" [498]).[13] Being female, however, and thus at least symbolically linked to motherhood, she exerts her influence as much by withholding nurturance as by threat of castration:

> "And his sister, too," continued Mrs. Glegg, looking severely at Maggie, . . . "she must make up her mind to be humble and work; for there'll

be no servants to wait on her any more—she must remember that. She must do the work o' the house, and she must respect and love her aunts as have done so much for her, and saved their money to leave to their nepheys and nieces." (212)

Despite promising appearances, Aunt Moss also ultimately fails Maggie as a surrogate mother, though, curiously, as a result of excessive rather than deficient maternity. A female version of Maggie's father—"patient" and "loving-hearted" (79), "with affection enough in her not only for her own husband and abundant children, but for any number of collateral relations" (156)—she has for Maggie the added identificatory advantage of being extremely fraternally attached. Furthermore and most crucially, she offers refuge from the demands of the Real: "[H]er aunt Moss's . . . was her Alsatia, where she was out of reach of law" (80). Being worn down, however, by poverty and the pressing needs of her own children, Aunt Moss is able to offer her niece only occasional, fleeting sanctuary and sporadic affection instead of the sustained emotional and intellectual understanding that Maggie craves.

It is Tom in whom Maggie is most emotionally invested. Yet being the ultimate "man of maxims," he is as unfit as her Aunt Glegg to be the object of Maggie's maternal transference. Although the narrator claims that "there were tender fibres in the lad that had been used to answer to Maggie's fondling; so that he [occasionally] behaved with a weakness quite inconsistent with his resolution to punish her as much as she deserved" (39), by the time we are introduced to Tom he is only rarely susceptible to Maggie's affection, usually finding her caresses "uncalled-for" and "inexplicable" (93). Like his mother in looks and intelligence (he "was an excellent bovine lad" [176]), Tom also resembles her in his inability both to analogize (witness his lion-fighting discussion with Maggie [34]) and to sympathize with his sister's temperament ("'I like Lucy better than you: I wish Lucy was my sister'" [86]). Yet, unlike Mrs. Tulliver, whose gender and childishness assure her subjection to patriarchal rule, Tom eagerly affiliates himself with its authority. Not only does he maintain a "contemptuous conception" (100) of women and advocate their political marginality ("'[Y]ou should leave it to me to take care of my mother and you, and not put yourself forward . . . I can judge better than you can'" [234]); but his unanalogical thinking is so intractably binary as to make him "prone to see an opposition between statements that were really quite accordant" (50). His behavior, too, betrays a zeal for law enforcement. Although "well-meaning" (166) and disliking "anything sneaking" (175), he is neither "disinclined to a little strategem in a worthy cause" nor likely "to inquire subtly into his own motives . . . ; he was quite sure that his own motives as well as actions were good, else he would have had nothing to do with them" (344). He sports "a disposition to exert control over others" (456), a "profound contempt" (99) for the imagination (he likes only "fighting stories" [165]), and "a slight air of patronage" (238)—intending, for example, "always to take care of" Maggie, to "make her his housekeeper, and punish her when she did wrong" (40).

Being "a Rhadamanthine personage" with "more than the usual share of boy's justice in him" (52), however, Tom betrays in his "desire for mastery" (92) over such "inferior animals" as "small sisters" more than the usual share of sadistic pleasure. Indeed, "an inferior . . . had necessarily a fatal fascination for Tom" (48). He is "fond of . . . throwing stones" (88) at animals, of torturing worms "(it was Tom's private opinion ["that worms couldn't feel" and] that it didn't much matter if they did)" (39), and of "having dear old Maggie to dispute with and crow over" (146). By identifying himself as simply an upholder of the social order, Tom is able not only to give his "desire to punish" (101) the imprimatur of "high moral sanction" (159)—though he himself "had no idea" that such a desire "might be called" justice (101)—but also to indulge his sadistic urges, "to hurt culprits as much as they deserve to be hurt," yet to be "troubled with no doubts concerning the exact amount of their deserts" (53).

Present from the earliest pages of the novel, Tom's punitive tendencies are (at least initially) humorously reported and thereby softened. When Maggie accidentally knocks down his painstakingly constructed house of cards, Tom in unconscious retaliation shoots peas at "a superannuated blue-bottle which was exposing its imbecility to the spring sunshine, clearly against the views of Nature, who had provided Tom and the peas for the speedy destruction of this weak individual" (87). Likewise, Tom's intention "to punish" Maggie, "and that business having been performed," to occupy "himself with other matters, like a practical person" (37) is less off-putting and, indeed, wryly amusing when we know the referent to be only thirteen years old. In contrast to the adults of the story, who are treated by the humor as children, the child Tom is humorously portrayed as an adult. Such a portrayal not only emphasizes Tom's native affinity for the Law but undercuts Lawful authority by having a child as its chief representative. Furthermore, humor permits the narrator to express her ambivalence about Tom (who however Draconian is still ostensibly a protagonist) in a less guarded fashion than she would otherwise be able to do. Thus, under cover of an extended humorous attack on Mr. Stelling's pedagogical techniques lies a narrative jest about Tom's unimpressive intellect: "Tom was gradually allowed to shuffle through his lessons with less rigour, and having Philip to help him, he was able to make some show of having applied his mind in a confused and blundering way, without being cross-examined into a betrayal that his mind had been entirely neutral in the matter" (170).

Despite his putative hero status and the oft-repeated epithet of "poor Tom," narrative sympathy for Tom is sparse and where it does occur almost always clausally undercut. Faint praise and the insinuation that even such qualities as Tom's pity and "manliness" (or masculine virtue) are treacherously paternalistic contaminate, for example, the following mildly flattering remarks:

> If Tom had had a worse disposition, he would certainly have hated the little cherub Laura, but he was too kind-hearted a lad for that—there was too much in him of the fibre that turns to true manliness, and to protecting pity for the weak. (143)

> Surely there was some tenderness and bravery mingled with the worldliness and self-assertion. (293)

Nor, apparently, can Tom's primary affection for Maggie, which is narratively insisted upon at several points in the text, be represented without compromising qualification:

> In his secret heart he yearned to have Maggie with him . . . though . . . he always represented it as a great favour on his part to let Maggie trot by his side. (144)

Similarly, after perhaps the longest sustained account of Tom's virtues—in which his perseverence and business acumen are cited as responsible for the early payment of his father's debts and his own brighter prospects— the narrator asks, "Did he not deserve it [that is, his better fortune]?" and sabotages the implied praise with the barbed comment, "He was quite sure that he did" (325).

Significantly, the least adulterated sympathy narratively extended to Tom occurs at Mr. Stelling's school where, judged by standards that find him "uncouth and stupid" and thus lacking, he not only suffers from the pain of inadequacy but "became more like a girl than he had ever been in his life before." In this symbolically castrated state, Tom, with his "girl's susceptibility," is treated even in the humor of the early King Lorton scenes (such as when he prays for divine help in mastering Latin "supines of the third conjugation") with a generosity that is usually reserved for Maggie (141). For though humor may be said to "mother" Tom, to protect him from harsher, nonhumorous narrative judgments, his faults are not as a rule excused by the humor, as are Maggie's, but remain open to disparagement. Moreover, Tom's own utter humorlessness—except in the suffering inflicted upon others ("[H]e couldn't help feeling it was rather good fun: Maggie would look so queer" with her hair cut off [64])—both confounds his understanding and prevents him from experiencing the bonding function of humor. Tom can only gather, for instance, that in choosing to decline roast beef rather than "the Latin for it" he "had in some mysterious way refused beef, and, in fact, made himself appear 'a silly'"—a condition of estrangement that "for the first time in his life" causes him "a painful sense that he was all wrong somehow" (136).

Preoedipal Longing and the Objects of Displaced Desire

Such rare moments of vulnerability as Tom betrays constitute the sole evidence for his narratively idealized childhood relationship with Maggie. A "little tremor in Tom's voice" may still elicit near the end of the novel "Maggie's ready affection . . . with as sudden a glow as when they were children, and bit their cake together as a sacrament of conciliation," but otherwise the two are affectively at odds (394). Tom continually claims paternalistic authority over his sister ("'[Y]ou might have sense enough to see that a brother, who goes out into the world and mixes with men, necessarily knows better what is right and respectable for his sister than she can know herself'" [392–93]), while Maggie rarely tires in her campaign to turn Tom into a maternal object, looking to him for unconditional love ("'I wouldn't mind what you did—I'd forgive you and love you'" [36]) and for symbiotic sympathy ("[I]f he had been crying on the floor, Maggie would have cried too" [66]). Yet despite his psychic primacy for Maggie ("'[T]he first thing I ever remember in my life is standing with Tom by the side of the Floss, while he held my hand: everything before that is dark to me'" [307]), Tom nevertheless often crops up even in her mind in the paternal position: "Her brother was the human being of whom she had been most afraid, from her childhood upwards: afraid with that fear which springs in us when we love one who is inexorable, unbending, unmodifiable" (483). Put in slightly different terms, the intense, suprafilial bond that ties Maggie to Tom results in large measure from her having, as it were, "maternalized" the Law, having, that is, taken as her object of "perpetual yearning"—which "had its root deeper than all change" (454)—one who "subdues every counteracting impulse," whose character is "strong by its very negations" (310). Arguably, the most striking evidence of Maggie's having thus internalized such a punitive maternal object lies in her mothering of her doll: "a Fetish which she punished for all her misfortunes" and with which she "soothed herself by alternately grinding and beating" its head, "sobbing all the while with a passion that expelled every other form of consciousness" (28).

Maggie's desire for a nurturing, empathic mother (who would love "well enough to bear with me, and forgive me everything" [328]) thus remains unsatisfied and, in so remaining, generates the plot.[14] Although sometimes almost explicitly articulated (for example, "she had to endure this wide hopeless yearning for that something, whatever it was, that was greatest and best on this earth" [288]), her longing for maternal union is more often detectable in her responses to forms and objects associationally linked to the preoedipal. Music, for instance—in reaction to which "her eyes dilated and brightened into that wide-open, childish expression of wondering delight, which always came back to her in her happiest moments" (416)—recalls for Maggie the bliss and satiety of breastfeeding:

> "I think I should have no other mortal wants, if I could always have plenty of music. It seems to infuse strength into my limbs, and ideas into my brain. Life seems to go on without effort, when I am filled with music." (386)

It evokes, as well, a mourning for such loss ("'I never felt that I had enough music'") and a "longing" in "her young limbs" (328). Significantly, Maggie's own maternal acts—such as her "nursing" of her bedridden, half-demented (and therefore increasingly childlike) father day after day—sharpen rather than quench her desire for the mother, her nostalgia for the womb:

> Maggie . . . , looking from the bed where her father lay, was a creature full of eager, passionate longings for all that was beautiful and glad; thirsty for all knowledge; with an ear straining after dreamy music that died away and would not come near to her; with a blind, *unconscious yearning* for something that would . . . give her soul a *sense of home*." (235; emphasis added)

Books, similarly, both stimulate Maggie's "hungry nature" (385) and offer a temporary haven from the Real. Being, however, patriarchal texts (whether the historical romances of Walter Scott or *The Eton Latin Grammar*), they require imaginative reconstruction in order to provide her with even momentary relief. Only by stitching the "vague, mingled images of all the poetry and romance she had ever read" together with those "woven in her dreamy reveries" (385) and those spun "when she fashioned the world afresh in her own thoughts" (235) does Maggie evoke the "half-remote presence of a world of love and beauty and delight" (385), full of "fondness" and "indulgence" (235). Such an imaginative preoedipal "re-fashioning" (48) of things ("[T]his was the form in which she took her opium," her escape from the Real) makes it possible for her to be tolerant of the *Grammar*'s "astronomer who hated women generally" (150) and to ignore the often oppressively prescriptive gender-typing of Scott (although *The Pirate* stumps her: "'I could never make a happy ending out of that beginning'" [306]).[15] It even allows her—by displacing Lucy—to resituate herself as the object of her mother's affection:

> She was fond of fancying a world where the people never got any larger than children of their own age, and she made the queen of it just like Lucy, with a little crown on her head, and a little sceptre in her hand . . . only the queen was Maggie herself in Lucy's form. (61; textual ellipsis)

The river, too, complexly recalls the maternal. From the first page of the novel, where it is personified as a "living companion" with the "low placid voice . . . of one who is deaf and loving" (7), the river—particularly the tributary Ripple, with its "curtain of sound, shutting one out from the world beyond" (8)], and its offspring, the Round Pool—invokes a sense of protection, otherworldliness, and dreaminess that link it tropically to the preoedipal. This is true for the narrator as well as for Maggie, whose attraction to the river is both powerful (mere proximity can send her into "dreamy reverie" and "fits of absence" [464]) and constant (the first and last textual references to Maggie, among many others, place her in its thrall).[16] The "dreamy deafness" (8) of the river expresses and at least figuratively elicits the "dreaming" of the narrator with which the novel begins (thus adumbrating their symbiotic bond), even as it foreshadows the "dream-like" (517) last chapter and Maggie's state of mind therein; for although the flooding river may objectively be complicitous in her death, it subjectively brings her "an undefined sense of reconcilement" (518) and of "strong resurgent love." In the first and final chapters as well, "the threads of ordinary association"—that is, the logic of the paternal principle—are "broken" (517) and replaced by a rendering of temporally ambiguous, fragmented, interior consciousness that is stylistically distinct from the "realism" of the rest of the novel.[17] Furthermore, in the form of the Lady of St. Ogg—an incarnation of the "Blessed Virgin" as "a woman with a child in her arms" and "a worn and withered look" who "mourn[ed]" and "craved to be rowed across the river" (116)—the river is associated not only with overwhelming desire but with the Mother, who, contrary to her normal function as handmaid of the Father, here explicitly privileges desire over the Law:

> "Ogg the son of Beorl, thou art blessed in that thou didst not question and wrangle with the heart's need, but wast smitten with pity, and didst straightway relieve the same." (117)

Although desire for the mother cannot, of course, be directly satisfied in the Real (which is perhaps why the river is as insistently inscribed as "deaf" as it is "loving" and "dreamy"), the ending of the novel demonstrates that at least the literary equivalent of the Real—the aesthetic laws of probability and verisimilitude—can be thwarted. Not only is the Law, in the form of normative plotting and plausible consequences, drowned, so to speak, by the overflow of unbounded desire symbolized by the river, but the enactment of Maggie's longing for maternal union—in her and Tom's "mutely gazing at each other" (521) and in their "embrace never to be parted"—constitutes a more threatening and scandalous violation than does her elopement with Stephen.[18] For despite the quasi-orgasmic imagery of their embrace, what Maggie recovers in her final, fatal bonding with Tom are the "deep, underlying, unshakable memories of early union" (518) and the "sweet monotony" (41) of *symbiosis*: "'In their death they were not divided'" (522).

Appearances to the contrary, even Maggie's emotional susceptibility to Stephen is largely grounded in preoedipal desire. Rather than being attracted by his masculine difference, Maggie falls for Stephen's "firm tender care" (464) and the possibility he offers for infantile dependence: "there was an unspeakable charm in being told what to do, and having everything decided for her" (467); his "stronger presence . . . seemed to bear her along without any act of her own will" (464). Similarly, his "admiring eyes always awaiting her" (401)—however erotically intended—speak to a primary narcissistic need in Maggie, to her "keen" and hitherto unfed "appetite for homage": "she was no longer an unheeded person, liable to be hid, from whom attention was continually claimed, and on whom no one felt bound to confer any" (419). The powerful appeal of the boat excursion itself, the consequences of which are so disastrous for Maggie, lies predominantly in its illusory recapitulation of a symbiotic environment. The "delicious dreaminess of gliding on the river" (401) lulls the "entirely passive" (469) Maggie into a "strange, dreamy, absent" (465) state of consciousness characterized by "delicious visions melting and fading" (470). (The reiteration of "delicious" emphasizes the particularly oral satisfaction of this generally sensuous experience.) Such a state of consciousness, moreover, induces a feeling of symbiosis ("the sweet solitude of a twofold consciousness that was mingled into one by that grave untiring gaze" [464]) and privileges preverbal communication: "Some low, subdued, languid exclamation of love came from Stephen from time to time . . . : otherwise, they spoke no word; for what could words have been but an inlet to thought? and thought did not belong to that enchanted haze in which they were enveloped."[19]

Although apparently gratified in fleeting fashion with Stephen upon the river and perhaps ultimately fulfilled in her death with Tom, Maggie's desire for the maternal finds its most consistent—if derivative and inevitably frustrated—satisfaction in her own recuperative attempts at mothering. This is particularly clear with regard to Mr. Tulliver, whose stroke forces him into a condition of "heart-cutting childish dependence" (235) upon Maggie: "he took passively everything that was given to him, and seemed to have a sort of infantine satisfaction in Maggie's near presence—such satisfaction as a baby has when it is returned to the nurse's lap" (200). In part because he represents her earliest and most sustained encounter with maternal affection (his "dear, time-worn face . . . had been present with her through long years, as the sign of her deepest love" [358]), Maggie, in ministering with "little caresses" (279) to her father's infantile needs, not only inversely recapitulates the maternal bond but herself obtains a measure of maternal sustenance in the exchange: "her loving remembrance of his tenderness was a force within her that would enable her to do or bear anything for his sake" (205). Likewise, Mrs. Tulliver's increased infantilization following the shock of bankruptcy offers Maggie the opportunity to become a mother to her mother and, in so doing, consciously to experience her own maternal love for the first time: "amidst this helpless imbecility there was a touching trait of humble self-devoting maternity, which made Maggie feel tenderly towards her poor mother amidst all the little wearing griefs caused by her mental feebleness" (277). Such encounters with the maternal, however, are necessarily limited and ephemeral, serving largely to underscore the irrevocable loss of the early mother-child bond. Hence,

although enjoying "sweet rest" (485) in the motherly "embrace" Mrs. Tulliver offers her when she accompanies her daughter in banishment from
the Mill, Maggie comes to realize that the constant "companionship of her
mother's narrow griefs" (235) cannot satisfy her yearning for the archaic
mother, and she eventually convinces Mrs. Tulliver to return to Tom.[20]

Maggie's fondness for Philip participates in this twofold sense of the
maternal as well. His "entreating voice" (326) and bodily pain call forth her
"pity and womanly devotedness" and "tranquil, tender affection" (41)—as,
indeed, do Stephen's "vexed complaining look" and "beseeching discontent" (407)—while at the same time she turns to him, with a "childlike
affectionate smile" (443), for tenderness and nurture: "how she looked forward to . . . the affectionate admiring looks that would meet her; . . . to
the certainty that Philip would care to hear everything she said, which no
one else cared for!" (325). More than any other character, Philip offers
Maggie the doting attention, the "tender, demonstrative love" (286), she
desires; he is "the only person who had ever seemed to love her devotedly,
as she had always longed to be loved" (382). Yet, at least partly because she
identifies with the deformed and devalued Philip so strongly, he fails her
as a mother substitute. "Brought . . . up like a girl" (421), with nerves "as
sensitive as a woman's" (426), and with feelings played upon only by "the
power of love" (174) or the "common current of suffering" (181), Philip
functions more powerfully as a figure for Maggie (and to some degree, for
the narrator) than as an object of love. It is for this reason that Maggie,
despite her sympathy for his pain and person, ultimately feels "relief" when
Tom, by forcing their "separation," breaks up her ego-threatening identification with Philip:

> Her heart bled for Philip: she went on recalling the insults that had been
> flung at him with so vivid a conception of what he had felt under them,
> that it was almost like a sharp bodily pain to her, making her beat the
> floor with her foot, and tighten her fingers on her palm.
>   And yet, how was it that she was now and then conscious of a cer-
> tain dim background of relief in the forced separation from Philip?
> (348)[21]

NARRATIVE MOTHERING

Mothering depends largely upon empathy, which requires, in the maternal
situation, the mother's fundamental identification with her child. Such
identification, however, is also necessarily limited, since not only insufficient but excessive identification interferes with active empathy. In order

for maternal empathy to be successful as such, it must allow for the child's difference and separateness as well as for similarity and symbiosis; it should invoke a desire to protect as well as to commiserate.[22] Unlike the diegetic characters in *The Mill on the Floss,* whose collective failure to function adequately as a maternal object for Maggie results largely from under- or overidentification, the narrator extends to Maggie an empathic understanding that, though grounded in a sense of sameness, nevertheless recognizes—at least initially—psychic distinction and separate need.

Such a delicately negotiated relation of empathic identification is emblematized in the opening chapter. The narrator begins by describing, in the immediacy of the present tense, the Floss and the Mill as a memory scene, initially unoccupied by any human presence or activity besides the narrator herself engaged in an act of remembering: "I remember those large dripping willows. I remember the stone bridge" (7). As I have already mentioned in discussing the narrative's maternal gendering of the river, this scene is tropically dominated by the preoedipal. The "great curtain of sound, shutting one out from the world beyond" (8), protects the narrator in womb-like fashion not just from the demands of reality, but from social interaction (a man with his horses is observed but not addressed), and thus, symbolically, from the triadic (oedipal) construction of the Real. It evokes, moreover, in grateful response for its soothing presence, the narrator's loyalty and love: "I am in love with moistness" (that is, with the wetness of the river and, associatively, that of the womb). Even the "little girl"—who is seen "standing . . . at the edge of the water ever since I paused on the bridge" and is likewise mesmerized by its presence—remains outside "the dreamy deafness" of the narrator/river (child/mother) bond. This unnamed little girl, however, whose actions imitate the narrator's, is more than just similarly "rapt" in her own preoccupying relation to the river. She is, as we learn from the last passage of this chapter with its abrupt shift in spatial and temporal consciousness, a dream image produced by and referent to the narrator herself:

> It is time, too, for me to leave off resting my arms on the cold stone of this bridge. . . . .
>
> Ah, my arms are really benumbed. I have been pressing my elbows on the arms of my chair, and dreaming that I was standing on the bridge in front of Dorlcote Mill, as it looked one February afternoon many years ago. Before I dozed off, I was going to tell you what Mr. and Mrs. Tulliver were talking about, as they sat by the bright fire in the left hand parlour, on that very afternoon I have been dreaming of. (8–9)

The narrator and little girl are thus at least momentarily conflatable: their initially similar but fundamentally distinct identities merge in the indeterminate, suggestively preconscious gap (discursively represented in the extended ellipsis) that immediately precedes the awakened state of the final paragraph. Significantly, almost immediately after we recognize this psychological nexus, so to speak, of the narrator and the girl, we become acquainted with the existence of Maggie—a little girl whom we not only retrospectively identify as the child standing on the riverbank but who herself remains unnamed for several pages following her introduction into the narrative (being initially referred to simply as "the little wench").

The empathic complexity of the narrator-heroine bond, established in this framing first chapter, is perhaps most strongly evident in the narrator's sallies on behalf of Maggie's character and behavior. Explicitly inserting herself into the text or otherwise interrupting the diegesis, the narrative "I" rushes to Maggie's defense on a number of quite different accounts. She begs forgiveness for Maggie's general carelessness and disregard of property by claiming greater knowledge of her motives than we as readers could otherwise determine ("She really did not mean to" knock down Tom's house of cards [86]; "I must urge in excuse" for Maggie's deliberately ruining her bonnet "that Tom had laughed at her" in it [60]). Even when Maggie's motives are clearly rather mixed—as when, despite her conscious intention to inform Tom by degrees of the consequences of their father's failed lawsuit, she blurts them out in a fit of pique—the narrator strives to protect her by disguising those motives from Maggie herself. Rather, that is, than starkly stating Maggie's anger at Tom's misreading "her agitated face" as "part of her girlish way of taking things," the narrator tells us only that Maggie "said loudly and rapidly, as if the words would burst from her, 'O Tom, he will lose the mill and the land, and everything; he will have nothing left'" (188), and thus she successfully prevents our seriously faulting her heroine for callousness and withdrawing our sympathy.

By arguing its probable transience, the narrator excuses Maggie's rebelliousness ("[T]he dark-eyed, demonstrative, rebellious girl may after all turn out to be a passive being compared with this pink-and-white bit of masculinity with the indeterminate features" [33]); and by pleading Maggie's irrepressible nature and innocence of feminine wiles, she exonerates her from charges of coquetry: "The words might have been those of a coquette, but the full bright glance Maggie turned on Philip was not . . . She really did hope he liked her face as it was now, but it was simply the rising again of her innate delight in admiration and love" (300–301). Such "innate delight," the narrator implies, is not only distinct from but more ac-ceptable than vanity, being simply the healthy expression of a gratified pri-mary narcissism rather than its pathological distortion. (Even "her vanity" is less distasteful than others', constituting as it does not a "form of mere coquetry and device" but "the poetry of ambition" [401]). The narrator similarly defends Maggie's apparent flirtatiousness with Philip, insisting that, however misleading her behavior might be to an infatuated young suitor, hers is nothing more than "sweet, simple, girlish tenderness" (334) and "half-penitent dependent affection" (414) arising naturally from "the recollection of that childish time" (335) they shared together.[23] Indeed, despite their obvious consequence of encouraging Philip's hopes, her ac-tions, we are told, are governed by a noble desire to spare pain and should therefore be lightly judged: "Maggie, in her impulsiveness, wanted Philip to know at once the position they must hold towards each other; but she checked herself. The things that had happened since he had spoken of his love for her were so painful that she shrank from being the first to allude to them" (412). By continually calling our attention to Maggie's childish-ness, the narrator asks us not only to forgive her heroine's blunders of judg-ment and failures of empathy but to relieve her from the full responsibility for her conduct as well. This plea for special treatment is particularly no-ticeable with regard to her romantic deportment. For in contrast to Ste-phen—who, educated and experienced, "wilfully abstained from self-questioning, and would not admit to himself that he felt an influence [in Maggie's near presence] which was to have any determining effect" upon him—Maggie is narratively absolved from wrongdoing by virtue of her sexual ignorance: "Maggie only felt that life was revealing something quite new to her; and she was absorbed in the direct, immediate experience, without any energy left for taking account of it and reasoning about it" (403).

Yet, even as she argues for Maggie's innocence, the narrator wants ac-knowledgment of her heroine's erotic appeal as well. Long protectively par-tisan about Maggie's looks ("a connoisseur might have seen 'points' in her which had a higher promise for maturity than Lucy's natty completeness" [61]), she takes maternal pride in Maggie's success with the male popula-tion of St. Ogg's and in her being "an object of some envy" (400) among the young women. Indeed, much of what little humor remains in the novel after Maggie's entry into physiological (as distinct from psychological) adulthood—an event that is overshadowed in the narrative by the cotem-

poraneous incident of Mr. Tulliver's bankruptcy—is found in the narrator's gloating reports of the catty female reaction to Maggie's powers of attraction:

> The Miss Guests, who associated chiefly on terms of condescension with
> the families of St. Ogg's, and were the glass of fashion there, took some
> exception to Maggie's manners . . . [B]ut it is a fact capable of an amiable
> interpretation that ladies are not the worse disposed towards a new ac-
> quaintance of their own sex because she has points of inferiority. And
> Maggie was so entirely without those pretty airs of coquetry which have
> the traditional reputation of driving gentlemen to despair, that she won
> some feminine pity for being so ineffective in spite of her beauty. (400)

Curiously, no matter how strongly Maggie's adult sexuality is hinted at and
apparently approved, there is a concommitant narrative impulse to urge its
fundamentally childish nature. Thus, even on those occasions when Maggie's desire, despite all attempts to render it otherwise, seems undeniably
mature, the narrator resorts to humor (through punctuation) to deflect its
heat and minimize its acknowledged impact: "Such things, uttered in low
broken tones by the one voice that has first stirred the fibre of young passion, have only a feeble effect—on experienced minds at a distance from
them" (469).

While repeated narrative emphasis on Maggie's youthfulness prevents
readers from judging her too harshly, the narrator's humorous rendering
of Maggie's often dreadful childhood experience protects her on the level
of text, if not plot, from the full pain of that experience. In describing her
childish "anguish" with a seriousness usually reserved "for what we are fond
of calling antithetically the real troubles of mature life" (65), the narrator
not only exploits the humor arising from the discrepancy between style
and content, but elevates Maggie above her circumstances, thus mitigating
their power to hurt. When Maggie runs away to the gypsies, our fear of
her being in real danger is greatly relieved by her being humorously cast as
superior in position and power to the threats of her new environment:

> [T]he scene was really very pretty and comfortable, Maggie thought,
> only she hoped they would soon set out the tea-cups. Everything would
> be quite charming when she had taught the gypsies to use a washing-
> basin, and to feel an interest in books. (108)

Maggie's condition as humorous victim, indeed, serves in large part to in-
oculate her against becoming a victim of the Real:

> She thought anything was better than going with one of the dreadful
> men alone: it would be more cheerful to be murdered by a larger party.
> (113)

Granting Maggie grown-up status in the humor distinguishes her from
the adult characters of the novel, who are humorously treated as children,
yet it also accentuates her vulnerability.[24] This is especially so when Maggie's adult stature occasionally takes on heroic proportions. The vehemence
of her restrained fury at being scorned and abandoned by Tom in favor of
Lucy suggests Medea, while specifically associating her with the Gorgon
("Maggie lingered at a distance, looking like a small Medusa with her
snakes cropped" [98]). Elsewhere, the imposed inactivity of her feminine
life recalls the fate of Hecuba, who watched "the world's combat from afar,
filling [her] long, empty days with memories and fears" as Hector
"quench[ed] memory in the stronger light of purpose" or "in the hurrying
ardour of action" (308–9). And her "despair" at having shorn her hair in a
fit of spite directly alludes to Ajax's slaying of the innocent flocks (65–66).
Yet unlike the mythic Greeks to whom she is compared, Maggie is only
capable of eliciting our (humorous) pity. Although she may demonstrate
rage and grief in adult measure, her inability as a child to make reasoned
choices prevents her actions (according to Aristotle) from achieving the
"magnitude" necessary for genuine tragedy:

> There were passions at war in Maggie at that moment to have made a
> tragedy, if tragedies were made by passion only; but the essential [*ti meg-
> ethos* or certain magnitude] which was present in the passion was want-
> ing to the action. (101)

From a Victorian cultural perspective, Maggie's failure of magnitude is the
consequence not simply of her youth but of her gender as well. For as a
daughter ideologically constrained by her nineteenth-century middle-class
upbringing, she lacks the power requisite for either tragic action or heroic
standing. Unlike her brother—who identifies with any number of legendary warriors who "laid about them with heavy strokes" (166)—Maggie is
forced by the scarcity of imitable female models (literary and otherwise)
into imagining an epic heroine who embodies her own sisterly status under
patriarchy: "She wanted to know if Philoctetes had a sister, and why she
didn't go with him on the desert island and take care of him" (182).[25]

Functionally distinct from the fondly humorous treatment of Maggie's
character are the few but persistent narrative jokes that are made at the
expense of the plot. In this case, humor is achieved when empathic engage-

ment is so attenuated and distanced as to disappear almost entirely. When the narrator comments that "Maggie's destiny" was "to reveal itself like the course of an unmapped river" (402), or has Mrs. Tulliver exclaim on more than one occasion that she fears her children will "'be brought in dead and drowned some day'" (13, 103), the aptness of the simile or of the observation produces (upon a re-reading of the novel) a moment of irony-infected humorous satisfaction that is simultaneously dependent upon our intellectual recognition and our almost perfect emotional denial of the narrative reality. The result is that in such instances the humor rather than simply easing the discomfort that Maggie's situation causes affectively removes the reader (and, to as great an extent as possible, Maggie herself) from the narrative situation entirely. Thus, the concretizing of a metaphor—Maggie "being led down the garden" path [464] by Stephen to the boat ride that is to be her undoing, for example—or a metanarrative jest (such as Maggie proving herself innocent precisely because, like the women tried for witchcraft in her copy of Defoe's *History of the Devil,* she drowns when submerged in water) amuses to the degree that it ignores narrative consequences.[26] Even the notoriously bleak, anti-fairy-tale ending—utilizing catachrestic constructions like the "fatal fellowship" of the lethal machinery or the orgasmic "embrace" in which Maggie and Tom experience "again in one supreme moment" their memory of childish union (521)—offers, in this way, its bit of odd, even macabre, amusement. For, if Hazlitt is right in contending that the ludicrous arises from the improbable (in contrast to realism, which arises from the plausible), then the highly unlikely aquatic closure may be said to share in some sense at least the *structure* of humor if never actually its affect.[27]

RECAPITULATING THE MATERNAL BOND

Watch your own speech, and notice how it is guided by your less conscious purposes. (459)

The mother-child bond that characterizes the narrator's relationship to Maggie crucially depends upon humorous discourse for its very existence. Indeed, although it occasionally achieves nonhumorous articulation as a chronic longing—a "peremptory hunger of the soul" for "satisfaction" (276)—only in moments of humor does this textualized yearning for maternal union attain compensatory gratification. Through humor, the narrator is able to offer Maggie sympathetic understanding and a salve to her suffering while simultaneously deeply identifying with her as a fellow victim. Such a narrative relationship is both functionally and figuratively maternal and claims for itself the right to protect Maggie from the threats of her environment, even if it ultimately lacks the power to do so.[28] For "maternal" humor can only stave off the reality principle fleetingly: because it spares the narrator (and by association, the reader) an equal share in Maggie's agony only at the price of symbiotic separation, such humor can neither, in the end, prevent Maggie's distress as a victim of the Real nor the narrator's pain of inevitable loss. It is perhaps this sense of ineluctable pain incorporated into even the humorous moments of the novel that contributes most to its tragi-comic tone.[29]

In one sense, *The Mill on the Floss* is the story of Maggie's desire for *nostos*: a rendering of her longing not for a return to an idealized past but rather for a bond that, except in faint, associative traces, is hopelessly lost even to memory. Despite the narrator's (either ironic or denial-heavy) comment that with Mr. Tulliver's bankruptcy "the golden gates of their childhood had for ever closed behind" (186) Maggie and Tom, the narrative itself presents quite compelling evidence that Maggie's childhood has from the outset been far from Edenic.[30] Nevertheless, her *longing* for a childhood within the golden gates—that is, a longing for Eden (or its psychological equivalent, the womb)—constitutes the motivating force and determining characteristic of her postinfantile, post-Edenic existence.[31] This longing expresses itself most substantively in her attachment to certain fondly recalled images or objects—objects that by a process of internalization and association collectively suggest the primary maternal bond. Home, for instance, signifies for Maggie neither a select group of long-known and loved individuals nor a specific geographical location; on the contrary, the thought of St. Ogg's reliably depresses Maggie and elicits bitter humor from the narrator. Rather, "'home'" comprises those "dear familiar objects" (389) that, filtered through the transforming power of memory and displacement, have attained almost primary psychic status:

> There is no sense of ease like the ease we felt in those scenes where we were born, where objects became dear to us before we had known the labour of choice, and where the outer world seemed only an extension of our personality: we accepted and loved it as we accepted our own sense of existence and our limbs. (151)[32]

> [A]ll long-known objects, even a mere window fastening or a particular door-latch, have sounds which are a sort of recognized voice to us—a

voice that will thrill and awaken, when it has been used to touch deep-
lying fibres. (221)

As the narrator remarks, "[S]uch things as these are the mother tongue of
our imagination, the language that is laden with all the subtle inextricable
associations the fleeting hours of our childhood left behind them" (41–42).
Put rather less poetically, the maternal bond—being prelinguistic—resists
representation in the (Lacanian) symbolic order. Though repeatedly alluding to infantile experience and its related affects goes some way to "objecti-
fying" lost maternal union, because such union is both "maternal" and
"lost," its existence can only be fathomed through "subtle inextricable" association rather than direct discourse, and its presence limned as an absence:

> We have all of us sobbed so piteously . . . when we lost sight of our
> mother or nurse in some strange place; but we can no longer recall the
> poignancy of that moment and weep over it . . . Every one of those keen
> moments has left its trace, and lives in us still. (65–66)

In its efforts to suggest the unrepresentable, the narration frequently and
not surprisingly enlists the aid of tropes, which by definition figure their
subjects indirectly. Perhaps the most effective of these for the purposes of
invoking what is prelinguistic is implied or implicit metaphor. Here a tis-
sue of linguistic association is generated by a recurrent primary image
which, appropriately enough, is itself absent (the allusive description of the
river as a preoedipal mother is an example).[33] Though carefully wrought,
the narratorial use of metaphor is not wholly unconflicted. In a strategically complicated passage, the narrator calls on Aristotle—"the greatest ancient" and undisputed patriarch of poetics—to join her in lamenting "that
intelligence so rarely shows itself in speech without metaphor,—that we
can so seldom declare what a thing is except by saying it is something
else" (140). Although the narrator's comment may be largely self-mocking
(given her own heavy commerce in tropes), it is nonetheless true that figurative communication is the only sort possible in our fallen condition; in
the Real, there is no literal identity or even direct correspondence between
a word and its referent (words are "mere words, which must remain weaker
than the impressions left by the old experience" [254]). Consequently,
however facetiously intended, the narrator's lament for the loss of a literal
language reads metonymically as a lament for the loss of literal (umbilical)
connection with the archaic mother. Moreover and on a different front, the

narrator's disclosure that we generally speak metaphorically poses a serious challenge to our faith in the "truth-value" of discourse—no matter how authoritative or official it might be—and thus, by implication, in paternal authority itself.

Occurring just a few pages after this indictment of metaphor is the famous Latin Grammar scene, in which Maggie is set straight by Mr. Stelling about the cultural opinion of the female intellect. As Mary Jacobus has discussed in detail, this scene—which demonstrates the indeterminacy of words ("almost every word" signifies "several things" [145]) and thus the doubtful universality of maxims—is rich in evidence for the case against phallocentric discourse.[34] What I would like to point to is how this scene both metonymically intimates the maternal bond and, through humor, momentarily recapitulates it.

Ignoring the syntactical rules (which are, like the Euclidean theorems that elude her, masculinely marked in the passage), Maggie opts instead for the (feminine) examples, going "very deep[ly]" into the "absorbing" and "mysterious" fragments of this dead language that gives such "boundless scope to her imagination" (147); indeed, at one point she becomes "quite lost in the 'thick grove penetrable by no star'" (148). "The most fragmentary examples were her favourites," arguably because without "context—like strange horns of beasts, and leaves of unknown plants" (147)—they are the most material and least subject to the laws of linguistic order. Similar to the "tunes" she elsewhere repeats "again and again until she had found out a way of producing them so as to make them a more pregnant, passionate language to her" (401), these "mysterious sentences . . . were all the more fascinating because they were in a peculiar tongue of their own" (147): Latin and music, in other words, both speak a lost maternal language.

Occasionally rising from the depths to the surface level of linguistic meaning, Maggie encounters "the astronomer who hated women generally"—a sentiment that "caused her so much puzzling speculation that she one day asked Mr. Stelling if all astronomers hated women" (150). Although Stelling (who apparently in name as well as deed is implicitly misogynist [*stella* = star]) is greatly amused by Maggie's unconscious humor, he nevertheless declares her intellect to be "quick and shallow" and unable to penetrate ("to go far into anything") by reason of her gender.[35] Maggie suffers so dreadfully under this (phallic) judgment that she is left speechless as well as depressed. The narrator, however, comes to her aid with a bit of humor, which though it cannot diegetically dispel Maggie's misery at the thought of her "dreadful destiny" (151) anymore than it can prevent that daughterly destiny itself, *is* able to offer Maggie sympathy in her victimization. Ridiculing Mr. Stelling's patriarchal assessment of Maggie in simply repeating it, the narrative humor protects Maggie by discrediting the source of her pain while it quietly retaliates against Tom (both by depriving him of Maggie's ready affection and by attacking him in his most vulnerable area) for having brought Mr. Stelling's judgment down upon her:

> But when this small apparatus of shallow quickness was fetched away . . . , and the study was once more quite lonely for Tom, he missed her grievously. He had really . . . got through his lessons better, since she had been there; and she had asked Mr. Stelling so many questions about the Roman empire . . . that Tom had actually come to a dim understanding of the fact that there had once been people upon the earth who were so fortunate as to know Latin without learning it through the medium of the Eton Grammar. (151)

Like the Latin grammar episode, though without its humor, the repeated image of "a firm arm" also arouses tropic associations of the lost mother. First introduced as Stephen's most seductive appendage ("There is something strangely winning to most women in that offer of the firm arm"), by the end of the description this arm is at least as evocative of primary maternal union as of its sexual substitute. It is not the "physical" arm itself that is "wanted" (either in the sense of being desired or lacked), the narrator assures us. Rather, "the sense of help—the presence of a strength that is outside them and yet theirs—meets a continual want" or perpetual longing of the feminine "imagination" (408). This sense of the arm as an allusive synecdoche for the archaic mother is strongly reinforced later when Stephen is moved to passionate display at the sight of Maggie's reaching for a rose:

> Who has not felt the beauty of a woman's arm?—the unspeakable suggestions of tenderness that lie in the dimpled elbow, and all the varied gently-lessening curves down to the delicate wrist, with its tiniest, almost imperceptible nicks in the firm softness. A woman's arm touched the soul of a great sculptor two thousand years ago, so that he wrought an image of it for the Parthenon which moves us still as it clasps lovingly the time-worn marble of a headless trunk. Maggie's was such an arm as that. (441)

Although cited by some critics to verify the masculinity of the narrator and his (hetero)sexual desire (and presumably those of the implied reader as well), it should be noted that this passage waxes rhapsodic on the appeal of the *maternal* arm: from the beginnings of conscious (and Western cultural) time, the "loving" arm that "moves us" is Demeter's, clasping her daughter, Persephone. Not only is the feminine arm, then, inextricably situated in *the* prototype of the mother-daughter relation; but described as it is in suggestively phallic terms ("the varied gently-lessening curves down to the delicate wrist," the "almost imperceptible nicks in the firm softness"), it suggests the maternal phallus as well—a phallus that, like Persephone's head, is in reality missing. Although perhaps consciously justifying Stephen's erotic desire, the passage silently speaks to the longing for and imaginative force of the archaic maternal imago, in which both the mother's nurturance and her (benign) power are held together intact.

* * *

Commenting in a letter to her publisher, William Blackwood, on the stylistic development of *The Mill on the Floss,* Eliot remarks that "the comedy inevitably diminishes as the lives of Tom and Maggie advance" (*GEL,* 3:262). That the humor wanes is obvious to any attentive reader: why it should *inevitably* diminish is altogether another question. For Eliot, apparently, adult hardship and suffering fiercely resist humorous representation; yet, as the narrator of *Mill* insists, the trials of childhood are at least as painful as the adult variety: "Surely if we could recall that early bitterness, and the dim guesses, the strangely perspectiveless conception of life that gave the bitterness its intensity, we should not pooh-pooh the griefs of our children" (66). The difference lies perhaps in the perceived capacity of humor to protect its victim. If, indeed, feminine humor recapitulates early mother-child union—wherein the humorist occupies the maternal position, offering relief from reality to the victim as child—then it may very well be narratively easier to effect that bond when the victim is *literally* (so to speak) a child in the Real of the text. When Maggie crosses the threshold from child to adult sexuality (a passage concomitant, as noted earlier, with her father's bankruptcy), she enters, by reason of her nubility, irrevocably into the patriarchal order. In so doing, she ceases to be a maternal daughter, and the humorous empathic bond between narrator and heroine is, as a result, psychologically severed. In terms of narrative dynamics, such an affective rupture suggests that the narrator's identification with Maggie as a fellow oedipal daughter overwhelms her maternal capacity, resulting in her abandoning the role of humorous mother. Consequently, even though Maggie's longing for the lost mother remains vital until her death, its representation, from Book Three on, is almost completely solemn. The one brief, but recurring, exception addresses her capacity as romantic object.

Although far less energetically than Austen's narrators under similar circumstances, the narrator here—in mocking the self-deceptions and behavioral inconsistencies of the courting male—indirectly makes fun of Maggie as well (see 381–82, 405, 409). Stephen surely bears the brunt of the rather cutting jocularity in these passages;[36] but Maggie, too, if only by association is implicated—an implication that, although it severely strains the narrator-heroine bond in its own right, nonetheless offers in the midst of Maggie's emotional turmoil the (ultimately false) hope of comic redemption.

The narrator's sudden renunciation of the humorous maternal attitude toward Maggie sharply recalls the even more precipitous humorous renunciation of Dorothea by the narrator of *Middlemarch*. *Middlemarch* is altogether more richly veined with humor than *The Mill on the Floss:* besides the Fred and Mary subplot and the caustically amusing treatment of Rosamond and Casaubon, there are a chorus of characters—including Mr. Brooke, the Chettams and the Cadwalladers—whose primary narrative function is to alleviate the urgent pathos of the Dorothea and Lydgate stories. Yet, the playful narrative mocking of Dorothea's "childlike ideas" (4) and of her rather exasperating self-seriousness (or lack of self-"irony"), which characterizes the tone of the first chapter and is detectable throughout her brief courtship, evaporates with her engagement to Causabon even more quickly than does the humorous treatment of Maggie. Like Maggie (though perhaps a less fond object of maternal care), Dorothea is daughter to the mother-in-humor so long as she remains primarily outside the sexual register. Her foibles, in this case, are a source of fond amusement, and her yearning for a vocation (which is at heart simply a more sublimated version of Maggie's "nameless yearning" for lost maternal union) escapes painful representation. Once she becomes, through eroticization, a full-fledged patriarchal daughter, however, Dorothea loses her humorous maternal protection: her desire—for activity, agency, affection—is then increasingly thwarted (at least until her marriage to Ladislaw) and becomes in consequence an incessant font of frustration and misery.[37]

Dorothea's hasty banishment from the economy of humor helps to clarify Maggie's less obvious break with the humorous mother. Although Maggie remains "childlike" far longer than Dorothea, like her sister heroine and for similar reasons, she eventually finds herself stranded in a paternal universe without the psychic safeguard of her narrative mother's reality-denying humor. Her unsatisfied longing for affection and acceptance, her fits of frustration and depression—which under the earlier dispensation could be soothed, countered, moderated, or laughed off—are henceforth represented as unrelievedly painful and dangerously self-destructive. Internalized and cathected (if not in fact eroticized), her frustrated desire becomes a source perhaps not of perverse pleasure in itself but of recurring opportunity for the peculiar pleasures of self-sacrifice. Although the humorous narrator-heroine bond *affectively* dissolves at the moment when Maggie becomes fully subject to the paternal principle, the bond itself survives in transmogrified *structural* form in this inclination to masochism. As I have argued in Chapter 1, humor and masochism, despite their very different consequences, both claim the common goal of union with the lost mother. I would now like to consider not only how Maggie's *self-sacrificing* behavior constitutes an attempt to enact that union by abolishing differentiation from the archaic mother (through the abolition of a separate self), but how such an attempt actually participates in and elaborates upon the dynamics of humor.

Bonds of Suffering and the Ties That Bind

Etiologically and functionally, humor and masochism are remarkably similar strategies. Both possess the logic-defeating capacity to experience pain as a source of pleasure, and both utilize this capacity to preserve self-esteem. Moreover, the circumstances that activate these narcissistic defenses are virtually identical. The childish ego, helpless to vent its rage on the object or representative of authority that thwarts its desires and that it blames for its suffering (figured either by the father or, especially in the case of masochism, by the phallic mother), turns its rage upon itself. It is at this juncture, however—with regard to the ultimate disposition of fury—that humor and masochism dynamically part company.

Frustration of desire inevitably results from the invasion of the Real into the fantasmatic symbiotic union of benevolent mother and omnipotent child. Humor, however, miraculously avoids this frustration by simply denying the presence of the unwanted intruder. In this way, the all-powerful, benevolent maternal imago of humor retains its strength, rather than being displaced or overwhelmed by the Law and its objects, and redirects the child's now internalized aggression outward once again in the form of a jest. In so doing, humor maintains the illusion of omnipotence associated with the infant's symbiotic relation to the archaic mother. Described another way, the experiences of reality cause the maternal object to split into preoedipal and oedipally derived images. Humor gives fantasied control over that part of the maternal that is affiliated with the Real and is perceived to be cruel and withholding (the phallic mother), while it momentarily satisfies the desire for the mother's loving, protective care. In humor, pain is a precondition for pleasure, but only insofar as it calls forth the care of the benevolent mother in defense against it. By protecting the infant from pain (or, more accurately, from its undisguised perception), the mother reaffirms her love for the infant, whose self-esteem is thereby restored. In humor, then, embracing the loving mother who turns pain into pleasure—rather than the pain itself—is the repeatedly sought-after experience.

In contrast, the "bad" or phallic mother dominates in masochism. Displacing the "good" mother from her active role in the psychic scene, the phallic mother becomes the object both of authority and entreaty. While the narcissistic blow that reality delivers to one's infantile sense of omnipotence is the same as in humor, the insupportable feeling of helplessness and the self-directed aggression such a blow causes are left uncountered in masochism by the efforts of the benevolent, humorous mother. In order, therefore, to retain a sense of control and to rescue self-esteem, the infantile self learns to interpret the blow of reality as a caress; that is, she comes to take the punitive (oedipally affiliated) mother as a (preoedipal) love object and to consider her own suffering as necessary to maintain maternal connection. Pain in this way becomes ego-syntonic, desirable not only as currency to buy the withholding mother's love but as a means of restoring a sense of power to the self (since—although no longer able to call forth the protection of the kind, indulgent mother—the child *is* still capable of provoking the phallic mother's rejection). By associating the desired mother with pain, the masochist in effect libidinizes suffering, thus creating the urge to repeat the experience of maternal rejection, which, in its very familiarity, offers pleasure.

Up until Book 3, the narrator of *The Mill on the Floss* performatively functions in her humor as a benevolent mother to Maggie. For the duration of the humorous moment, this mother both validates and soothes her heroine's feelings of being misunderstood and emotionally abused by affectively depriving those who frustrate her of their power to hurt. Once the narrator abandons her role as humorous mother, however, Maggie's rage at the injuries she suffers at the hands of Tom, Mrs. Tulliver, and various other members of the Dodson clan is no longer capable of deflection and comes consequently and increasingly to be turned upon herself. Her masochistic tendencies, which before were negotiated and partially alleviated by humor, now come to dominate her behavior. Although Maggie continues throughout the novel to seek relief for her suffering from the benevolent mother, her attempts to reach that mother are henceforth blocked by the latter's punishing double, represented by the withholding love objects she has internalized (most notably, Tom).

Under the aegis of humor, Maggie's behavior is narratively revealed to be rebellious but, at the same time, comfortably childish and only mildly unsettling to domestic order. Without the cover of humor, however, her rebellious rage as she reaches adolescence becomes too culturally threatening to be given direct narrative expression or blessing. Maggie herself is aware of this stricture against the female vocalization of discontent and, like many another dutiful daughter, struggles to extinguish her desire for agency as well as her anger at its frustration. Happening upon Thomas à Kempis's *The Imitation of Christ* in a vulnerable moment, Maggie for a time enthusiastically embraces his example of self-renunciation. His quietly persistent exhortations to resign oneself to the will of God—sympathetically intoned in sentences of similar length and character—fill "her mind with a continual stream of rhythmic memories" (293) and "a strain of solemn music" (289) that stylistically suggests the condoling monotony of the maternal. His advice, too, is for the most part congenial, making a virtue of the seemingly necessary and unalterable deprivations of her life: "take delight in being unknown and unregarded"; "It is good . . . that men think ill of us and misjudge us, even when we do and mean well."[38] Moreover, the emphasis à Kempis places on self-renunciation (be "dead to self and free from inner conflict" [à Kempis, 38], "'pluck up and destroy that hidden inordinate inclination to self'" [289]) appeals strongly to Maggie's urge to masochism. Selflessness represents not only the path to the kingdom of heaven—to a state of "complete security" and "perfect peace," where one "may be dissolved" in "the blessing of original happiness" (à Kempis, 39–40) or, in psychological terms, the womb—but also a rejection of individuation and (paternal) agency in favor of nondifferentiation and passivity. Such a rejection, while it may promise bliss in heaven or in the womb, entails in the bodily world a program of narcissistic suffering in which pleasure and pain are psychically conflated: "Consider yourself unworthy of God's comfort, but rather deserving of much suffering" (à Kempis, 54); "'Forsake thyself, resign thyself, and thou shalt enjoy much inward peace'" (290). Eventually, Maggie realizes that the "quiet ecstasy" (471) she seeks in self-mortification eludes her and that renunciation in practice is little more than unrelieved pain ("she saw it face to face now . . .

and saw that the thorns were for ever pressing on its brow" [471]). Rather than affording refuge from the frustrations of reality, à Kempis's theory of resignation demands submission to the Law of the Father in imitation of Christ: "[N]owhere will you find rest except in humble obedience under the rule of a superior" (à Kempis, 36). Thus, Maggie discovers, despite a common route of self-sacrifice, perfect surrender to the will of a paternal God and primary union with the maternal imago are quite different propositions. Thomas à Kempis turns out to be not a guide to the archaic mother but just another "man of maxims."

Interestingly enough, although Maggie is never able to read it (having been written after her fictive death and not translated by her author into English until 1854), Ludwig Feuerbach's *The Essence of Christianity* comes closer than à Kempis's book to providing a spiritual map to the lost maternal.[39] According to Feuerbach, the "essence" of Christianity is not self-sacrifice to the will of an omnipotent, Law-giving God but the bonds of human fellowship that are created when one empathically enters into the suffering of others. Although for Feuerbach, as for à Kempis, "the Christian religion is the religion of suffering" (*EC,* 62), his understanding of the significance of that suffering crucially differs.[40] Rather than buying admission into the heavenly kingdom, suffering in Feuerbach constitutes both the *process* through which God is experienced and the foundation of all love: "Love is God himself, and apart from it there is no God"; "Christ, as the consciousness of love, is the consciousness of the species" (*EC,* 48, 269; emphasis added). In such a schema, Christ's importance lies less in his role as dutiful son than in his narcissistic affirmation of the self: "That which exists . . . loves itself, and loves itself justly." Feeling that is "not depreciated and repressed . . . can mirror and reflect itself, . . . can project its own image as God. God is the mirror of man" (*EC,* 63).

What Feuerbach does, in effect, is to replace the Will of the Father with a principle of human love and relatedness that elaborates upon the infant's umbilical connection to the mother. In so doing, religious longing becomes merely alternative phrasing for the unsatisfiable desire for a return to primary maternal union:

> [T]he Son is the yearning after the Mother . . . It is true that the Son, as a natural man, dwells only temporarily in the shrine of this [female] body, but the impressions which he here receives are inextinguishable; the Mother is never out of the mind and heart of the Son . . . [W]e find in God the beating of a mother's heart. The highest and deepest love is the mother's love. (*EC,* 72)

Not only are Feuerbach's bonds of suffering fellowship symbiotically described:

> In feeling man is related to his fellow man as to himself; he is alive to sorrows, the joys of another as his own. Thus only by communication does man rise above merely egoistic sensation into feeling. (*EC,* 283)

But they are forged out of a capacity for masochism traceable in origin to the mother-child bond. For if maternal love, being "the highest and deepest" love is equivalent to Christ ("the consciousness of love"), who is in turn equivalent to suffering ("God as Christ [crucified] is the sum of all human misery"; "to suffer for others is divine" [*EC,* 59, 60]), then maternal love may itself be most definitively experienced as empathic participation in the child's suffering ("Love attests itself by suffering" [*EC,* 59]). At the very least, the maternal bond requires the mother's willing identification with the child as a passive, dependent being. By this light, one's primary masochistic tendencies are seen to be symbiotically derived and to enable one to enter into affectionate sympathy with the pain of others. In thus transfiguring pain into an occasion for loving communion, Feuerbach's bonds of suffering (in contrast to more extreme masochistic behaviors) resemble the process of humorous conversion, which similarly converts pain into sympathetic affect.

Eliot's idealization in *The Mill on the Floss* of an ethic of "wide fellow-feeling with all that is human" (498) is based on this Feuerbachian-derived notion of maternal empathic suffering: "that simple, primitive love, which knits us to the beings who have been nearest to us, in their times of helplessness or of anguish"; that "gift of sorrow," which elevates "the bare offices of humanity . . . into a bond of loving fellowship" (200, 191). In contradistinction to the inadequate man of maxims, who lives according to "formulas" and "general rules" and other manifestations of the Law, which "repress all the divine promptings and inspirations that spring from growing insight and sympathy" (498), the empathically suffering mother offers a new model of nonreligious moral behavior while reinforcing the nineteenth-century cultural demand for female selflessness (and curiously anticipating some recent views on the gendered ethics of behavior).[41] Relatedness rather than autonomy; narcissistic gratification through self-sacrifice rather than through self-aggrandizement: maternal masochistic bonding makes a virtue out of the unavoidable pain of human existence.

So deeply inherent is it in this life of ours that men have to suffer for each other's sins, so inevitably diffusive is human suffering, that even justice makes its victims, and we can conceive no retribution that does not spread beyond its mark in pulsations of unmerited pain. (243)

Maggie develops her capacity for masochistic bonding far beyond the level necessary for human fellowship, however. While she remains prepubescent, her repetitive attempts at seeking out the familiar pain of maternal rejection (generally through Tom's agency) are presented and defended against in humor: "Maggie, gifted with that superior power of misery which distinguishes the human being, and places him at a proud distance from the most melancholy chimpanzee, sat still on her bough, and gave herself up to the keen sense of unmerited reproach" (46–47). But as she grows older, and her relationship to the narrator less humorously filial, her masochistic tendencies become increasingly well-defined. By the time she finishes with Thomas à Kempis, Maggie has so internalized the cultural ethic of feminine selflessness that "affection" has become equivalent to "self-sacrifice" (469). Yet, curiously, Maggie is more or less content in her program of renunciation so long as the maternal object she is intent on pleasing is overwhelmingly punitive—so long, that is, as she can count on maternal connection to be unwaveringly, but controllably, painful.[42] Only when the *benign* mother is psychically resuscitated—first, through the eagerly bestowed affection of Philip; later, through Stephen's pressing ardor—does Maggie once again become conflicted and distressed. After "years of contented renunciation, she had slipped back into desire and longing" (374). Soon life seems to Maggie little more than a heightened state of consciousness in which "every sensitive fibre in her were too entirely preoccupied by pain ever to vibrate again to another influence" (492)—a state, however, in which she feels such pain to be "not . . . bitter" but "welcome" (440).

It is the eagerness with which Maggie greets opportunities of pain that marks her disposition as masochistic rather than simply unselfish. Even as a young child Maggie searches out occasions for self-denial, not in order to spare another's deprivation but to garner acknowledgment of—and possible affection in return for—her own sacrifice ("I fear she cared less that Tom should enjoy the utmost possible amount of puff, than that he should be pleased with her for giving him the best bit" [45]). She pursues renunciation over resignation for similar reasons, preferring the "joy" of "subduing" her "own will" (327) to what Philip calls "'the willing endurance of a pain that is not allayed'" (328). Precisely because it provides secret access to forbidden pleasure—by libidinizing pain Maggie is able to gain access to the (rejecting) mother and thus to outwit the Law—guilty suffering becomes a highly valued commodity:

> In her deep humiliation under the retrospect of her own weakness—in her anguish at the injury she had inflicted—she almost desired to endure the severity of Tom's reproof, to submit in patient silence to that harsh disapproving judgment against which she had so often rebelled . . . She craved . . . being in the presence of those whose looks and words would be a reflection of her own conscience. (483–84)

So thoroughly inextricable, indeed, are pleasure and pain for Maggie that even her longed-for reunion with Tom (a "maternal" reunion enacted in an amniotic-like medium only upon pain of death) begins with a mutual "mute gaze," evoking "a long deep sob of that mysterious wondrous happiness that is one with pain" (520). It is no wonder, then, that Maggie, despite her better judgment, should fall for Stephen, whose love is rich in possibilities for anguish (as are Lucy's, Philip's, Tom's) and whose own suffering Maggie finds most excruciating of all to endure. It was "easier even to turn away from his look of tenderness than from this look of angry misery, that seemed to place her in selfish isolation from him" (466); "The worst bitterness of parting—the thought that urged the sharpest inward cry for help, was the pain it must give to him" (471).

Perhaps Maggie's most masochistically telling gesture is her effort to bond maternally with the person she most deeply fears. She clearly recognizes Tom's sadism:

> "But you have always enjoyed punishing me—you have always been hard and cruel to me: even when I was a little girl, and always loved you better than any one else in the world, you would let me go crying to bed without forgiving me. You have no pity: you have no sense of your own imperfection and your own sins." (347)

Yet she nonetheless persists in clinging to him as a maternal object, surrendering herself willingly to his abusive treatment: "[H]er mind ceased to contend against what she felt to be cruel and unreasonable, and in her self-blame she justified her brother" (343). Not only does Maggie eagerly overidentify with Philip as Tom's victim (see the passage quoted above on p. 181, where Maggie seems to take vicarious pleasure in the verbal abuse Tom heaps upon Philip, luxuriating in the almost "sharp bodily pain" it causes). But, on occasion, she even does her best to turn the kindly, often motherly, Philip into a persecutor as well ("'Yes, Philip,' she said, with her childish contrition when he used to chide her, 'you are right, I know. I do always think too much of my own feelings . . . I had need have you always to find fault with me'" [413]).

This persistent conflation on Maggie's part of the maternal and phallic principles functions as a counterstrategy to differentiation. When Maggie rhetorically asks, "If the past is not to bind us, where can duty lie?" she consciously refers to her moral responsibility to consider Lucy and Philip's feelings. Yet, the past as Maggie unconsciously conceives of it is, throughout the novel, illusory and elusive, a maternally edenic sanctuary from the demands and strictures of her present-day reality. Duty, conversely, is firmly associated in the collective consciousness with the Law or reality, not with the pleasure principle. To locate duty in the past, then, as Maggie does, constitutes an attempt to do away with difference—to eliminate the distinction between past and present, pleasure and pain, maternal and paternal—in order to recover the archaic mother in the midst of the Real. Rather than seeing painful duty as allied with the phallic principle, Maggie treats it as maternally affiliated and derives pleasure from its very harshness. Self-sacrifice, likewise, becomes a way to achieve the undifferentiation characteristic of the mother-child dyad, and extreme passivity a means not only to placate authority but also—by renouncing all claim to active, *paternal* power—to connect with the omnipotent mother.[43]

Not only is Maggie's masochism given free play once the mediating, protective influence of the humorous mother disappears from the novel, but hysteria, too, makes a brief but memorable appearance. As many readers have suggested, the flood that inundates St. Ogg's metaphorizes Maggie's dammed-up desire ultimately overrunning its repressively narrow channels of expression.[44] Such a physical (if textual) abreaction of desire is both fundamentally hysterical—hysteria being understood at least in the nineteenth century as the somatic manifestation of repressed desire—and specifically preoedipal, provoked in part (as we saw to be the case with the somatic symptoms of Freud's classic hysteric, Elisabeth von R.) by the unbearable conflict between the unconscious longing for the lost mother and its realistic denial. In this reading, the flood functions as a final, desperate effort to destroy reality—and realism—by the overflow of primal forces associated with the archaic mother, who in such guise is able to reassert her power. Characterologically, hysteria appears as well in Maggie's fits of uncontrollable sobbing and in her quasi-paralytic attacks (feeling as though she is borne "along without any act of her own will," for example), which come into being only after Stephen has revived in her the "remnants of the repressed affectionate bond."[45] Surely Maggie's feelings for Stephen are also oedipally libidinized, yet both the desire that underlies them and the symbolization they utilize (paroxysms of crying and her paralytic illustrations of dependency and helplessness) link them strongly to issues of early infantile development.

Although the narrator—despite both her humorously maternal and, later, sororal identification with Maggie—betrays no sign of sympathetic hysteria or masochism, her creator did. In the three years following the completion of the novel, Eliot reportedly suffered one of her worst periods of symptomatic depression, complaining of migraine-type headaches, general feebleness, heavy hands, weak eyes, and other debilitating bodily expressions of psychic conflict. According to George Lewes, Eliot identified, indeed, so strongly with Maggie that in the final days of composition her eyes became "redder and *swollener* every morning as she live[d] through her tragic story" (*GEL*, 3:269).[46] What is particularly striking about this comment is the curious double significance of the phrase "her tragic story." Eliot's severe somatic reaction intimates that this story was not simply hers by reason of composition but constituted a rewriting of an earlier, more personal one. While the autobiographical elements of the novel have received a great deal of critical attention, almost completely overlooked has been the opportunity the act of writing offered Eliot not just (through the narrator's agency) to identify with her heroine (explaining Maggie's behavior so as to exculpate her and win her readers' affection), but indeed to function as her *mother* (providing her with the empathic understanding, protection, and unwavering love that she otherwise lacks)—and thus to recapitulate her *own* maternal union in the act of narratively recuperating Maggie's. Although the double identification required to achieve the recapitulation of such union may not be exclusive to humorous discourse, it is perhaps most easily performed therein, where the boundaries between humorist and victim (mother and daughter, narrator and Maggie) are fluid and shifting.

More remarkable, ultimately, than Eliot's "hysterical" identification with Maggie is her exalting the masochistic energy that fuels it. Both as narrator of *The Mill on the Floss* and as essayist in the *Westminster Review*, Eliot accepts the cultural gendermarking of masochism as feminine; but contrary to her culture, she consciously privileges it:

Of those two young hearts Tom's suffered the most unmixed pain, for Maggie, with all her keen susceptibility, yet felt as if the sorrow made larger room for her love to flow in, and gave breathing-space to her passionate nature. No true boy feels that: he would rather go and slay the Nemean lion, or perform any round of heroic labours, than endure perpetual appeals to his pity. (259)

[K]een sympathy with human misery . . . makes a woman prefer to suffer for the term of her own life, rather than run the risk of causing misery to an indefinite number of other human beings.[47]

Indeed, in *The Lifted Veil*—which she interrupted "her tragic story" to write—Eliot goes so far as to have her narrator partially define femininity itself by its capacity for suffering: a woman is "a woman born of woman, with memories of childhood, capable of pain, needing to be fondled."[48] By thus insisting upon both the femininity and virtue of sympathetic suffering, Eliot transforms a female liability into a cultural asset. And by locating that suffering within the context not just of femininity but of the early mother-daughter bond in particular ("a woman born of woman, with memories of childhood, . . . needing to be fondled"), she "maternalizes" it as well. In so doing, Eliot indirectly establishes the groundwork for a humor that (as we saw in the chapter epigraphs) she theorizes as specifically, psychologically feminine: a humor founded upon affectionate protection, sympathetic suffering, and the momentary recapitulation of the mother-infant bond.

Feminine Humor in the Twentieth Century

I remember at that time I went to the hairdresser's . . . The child, whose hair was about to be cut for the first time, screamed with terror and clung to her mother. The hairdresser stood by gravely, comb in hand: he recognized that this was a serious moment. The mother, blushing, tried to comfort the child who had suddenly plunged into despair; all around the shop women smiled in sympathy. What impressed me, and what I particularly remember, was the child's passionate attempt to re-enter her mother, the arms locked around the woman's neck, the terrified cries of unending love . . . I had tears in my eyes, witnessing that bond, seeing that closeness, of which only a sorrowful memory remained in my own life . . . One grows up, one becomes civilized, one learns one's manners, and consequently can no longer manage these two functions—sorrow and anger—adequately. Attempts to recapture that primal spontaneity are doomed . . . And so feelings are kept inside . . . but this proves hard, sometimes.

—Anita Brookner, *Brief Lives* (1990)[1]

To conclude a study of feminine humor with Eliot's abandonment or perversion of that discourse is, I confess, to be a little misleading. It may imply that women writing after Eliot not only generally capitulated to prescriptive femininity, but forfeited humor as a tactic of rebellious accommodation as well. At the very least it insinuates that humor—however successful it had been throughout the first part of the nineteenth century in negotiating the frustrations of feminine life—was no longer adequate to the task in late-Victorian culture, where earnestness (as Wilde was soon to point out) had for both genders become almost sacralized. Nor, I'm afraid, does my earlier discussion of Wharton's humor provide compelling evidence for the continued vitality of the feminine variety. Writing more than fifty years after Eliot, Wharton practices a humor so allusively self-deprecatory as to be barely experienced as amusing—a humor in which painful identification overwhelms at moments every other competing affect.

If feminine humor became more or less reclusive in England for many decades, it was in part because, beginning around the turn of the century, social, political, and aesthetic changes conspired to make other types of humor available for female use. Fin de siècle culture, women's suffrage, the Great War, and Modernism—in both its particular and general sense—expanded the definition of femininity sufficiently to accommodate a wider spectrum of acceptable behaviors, duties, and virtues: intelligence, for example, after the founding of Girton and Newnham Colleges, was no longer the feminine impediment it had been for Maggie Tulliver. Racy jokes, satire, black comedy, and burlesque became increasingly popular, and women who utilized such forms were generally perceived to be funnier than their nineteenth-century predecessors. Stella Gibbons's grand spoof of the English rural novel, Molly Keane's bleak and vengeful comedy, Muriel Spark's corrosively witty satires, Iris Murdoch's comic absurdity, and Fay Weldon's and Angela Carter's macabre humor are, for the most part, virulent, aggressive, and *other*-directed rather than soft, passive, and internalized. Broadly speaking, as the humor produced by women has become more diverse, more "masculinized," in its strategies, targets, and affects, it has also become less *feminine* according to the prevailing nineteenth-century connotation of that term.

But feminine humor is not only a product of nineteenth-century historical contingencies: it is part of that century's legacy to our own. As Mary Poovey has noted, despite enormous cultural and legal changes over the last two hundred years, "many of the same values and inhibitions persist, sedimented deep in the layers of our culture and our consciousness." Whatever the difference in material conditions, the "psychological experience of many women" still resembles to a significant degree that of the writers I have examined here.[2] It is hardly surprising, then, that appropriations of masculine tropes like hyperbole and extended metaphor tend to supplement rather than supplant traditionally feminine ones, even in Spark or Weldon. Periphrasis may have been largely abandoned, but indirection, litotes, and meiosis—if Barbara Pym, Anita Brookner, and Penelope Fitzgerald are any evidence—continue unabated. Indeed, the peculiarly anachronistic quality of their work, I would argue, results less from their putative imitation of Austen than from their participation in a discourse of humor shared by a number of (mostly female) nineteenth-century novelists.

Curiously, and despite its largely Victorian sensibility, feminine humor demonstrates in these late twentieth-century writers a degree of visibility never before achieved. Pym's fiction, in particular, offers perhaps the most extensive example of such humor at work in either century. Her heroines—acutely self-conscious but otherwise psychologically undifferentiated from the narrator—are by and large, from novel to novel, disorient-ingly interchangeable: capable, underappreciated, quietly lonely Anne Elliot types, whose amorous expectations, never very great, are sadly di-minished by the time we meet them. With few exceptions, they wander about in the confines of an almost static romantic plot—but a romantic plot gone awry, in which persevering love is not inevitably fulfilled but rather frustrated, misallied, disillusioned, or rejected. Yet, even against the loss of conventional comic closure, the most memorable feature of Pym's stories is surely their "odd, oblique, elegant humor."[3]

Such humor springs, in part, from the abundant, affectionate reference to nineteenth-century women writers and their creations. Prudence Bates of *Jane and Prudence,* for example, apophatically associates herself with "poor silly Miss Bates": "if she resembled any character in fiction, it was certainly not Miss Bates. And yet how could Miss Trapnell and Miss Clothier call her anything else?" And Jane Eyre ("who must have given hope to so many plain women who tell their stories in the first person") blithely haunts more than one Pym novel.[4] Like her namesake, Catherine Oliphant of *Less than Angels* churns out articles for women's magazines to support herself and her sometime boyfriend (who, like so many of Marga-ret O's dependents, eventually dies on her), while Mildred Lathbury of the euphemistically entitled *Excellent Women* is only one of many examples of the eponymous, Fanny Price–inspired species: aging young churchwomen who dutifully apply themselves to charitable causes of both a personal and impersonal nature, less from a positive desire to be useful than to combat a feeling of uselessness or redundancy.

Such allusions generate a richly complicated humorous connection to literary foremothers—a connection augmented not only by an affinity for self-denying rhetoric and a shared thematic concern with peculiarly femi-nine frustrations but also by similar affective goals. Humor, that is, still crucially informs the narrator-heroine bond, offering at least a sense of commiseration, if no longer reassurance and comfort, to the discontented heroine. "Dr. Weiss, at forty, knew that her life had been ruined by litera-ture," states the first line of Brookner's *The Debut.*[5] Escaping from parents far more infantile than the Tullivers, more distant than the Amazons, and more demanding than the Bertrams (her mother doesn't simply loll on the sofa; she refuses to leave her bed), Ruth Weiss loses herself in nineteenth-century novels, where she discovers a modicum of emotional security. Yet even though "she ponder[s] the careers of Anna Karenina and Emma Bo-vary" (7), and, at forty, is the author of the cautionary *Women in Balzac's*

Novels, she nevertheless finds, when she turns her own "life into literature" (8), that the heroine she most imitates is Little Dorrit (7). Less willingly dutiful, Ruth is every bit as self-effacing as Amy (she dresses so as to disappear); and perhaps because more consciously resentful, she is also more fatalistically submissive:

> "I don't like the idea of your going away, Ruth [her father said]. Don't like it at all . . . You have a duty to your mother, you know." Then he left, in a hurry to get to Harrods to oversee his purchases and perhaps buy himself a towelling bathrobe.
>
> This was the first Ruth had heard of her duty, which she had imagined was confined to the characters of Balzac. She had a duty to them, certainly, and the British Council, no less, had recognized it. Her father could not really imagine that she would be of any use here?
>
> In the days that followed, it became quite clear that he did. (96–97)

Understatement is here honed to an almost lethal sharpness, and its cut is felt to be largely self-inflicted. Though perhaps equally painful, such humor differs qualitatively from Wharton's masochistic practice: rather than actively soliciting punishment, Brookner's humor tries unsuccessfully to shield the heroine from the blows of reality. The effect is less of perverse pleasure in self-deprecation than a cosmic sense of absurdity, less of bonding with a punitive mother than a recognition of the consoling mother's utter inaccessibility. The dynamic structure of feminine humor is retained; yearning for the lost mother can still be heard murmuring. But even momentary solace has become hyperattenuated, or exhausted, as it is in the epigraph. For despite the classically comic arrangement of the beauty parlor scene in *Brief Lives,* the acuity of loss precludes the narrative hope of a maternally humorous embrace. "Sorrow and anger"—once the very fuel of humorous sublimation—are here "no longer manage[able]."

In the globalizing middle-class culture of the late twentieth century—a culture based economically and psychologically on the gratification of self-interest—it is extremely difficult for feminine virtues like self-sacrifice and eager sympathy not to appear contextually absurd. As the narrator of Fitzgerald's *The Bookshop* remarks of her widowed heroine, Florence Green, "She had a kind heart, though that is not of much use when it comes to the matter of self-preservation."[6] The "insignificant," indeterminately middle-aged Mrs. Green wonders "whether she hadn't a duty to make it clear to herself, and probably to others, that she existed in her own right" (7). This "want[ing] to be doing something" (*Persuasion,* 65), to be "any thing *in propria persona*" (*Mansfield Park,* 390), leads her to establish a

bookshop in her Suffolk village, notwithstanding the profound indifference of the local population (which only converts at moments into active
hostility) and the express disapproval of the malignant Mrs. Gamart, the
self-appointed "world's wife" (*Mill on the Floss,* 490) of Hardborough,
whose "strict code of gentility" (*Cranford,* 109) is "'rather upset by the
sudden transformation of our Old House into a shop'" (26). Despite her
"ready sympathy" (14), her strong passive resistance ("her courage . . . was
the determination to survive" [88]), and her active self-denial (she lives, in
elegantly economic fashion, on tea, herring, and biscuits), Mrs. Green is
ultimately vanquished by the combined forces of nature, culture, and the
supernatural: by the book-hating damp of East Anglia, the treachery of
Mrs. Gamart, and the demoralizing attacks of a poltergeist, whose actions
(like Mrs. Gamart's) are sudden, unjust, and unpredictable and whose "fu-
rious physical frustration" (17) intimates similar, though untapped, re-
serves of her own. The last line of the novel ends with the now penniless
Mrs. Green taking permanent leave of Hardborough, "her head bowed in
shame, because the town in which she had lived for nearly ten years had
not wanted a bookshop" (123).

Remarkably, despite the profound sadness of this closing image—and
without either romance or a comic resolution to offset the tragic trajectory
of the plot—the narrative nevertheless manages not only to maintain our
amused empathic engagement with Florence and her travails but to leave
us with a sense of humorous satisfaction. Steering clear of both sentimentality and cynicism, feminine humor in the late twentieth century shows
its postmodernity in being heavily intermingled with self-irony—with the
sense that its very identity lies in its ineffectualness. Penetrating the humor,
such irony dissolves faith in maternal consolation, but it leaves the empathic bond intact. Even in the face of such loss, however, the affective
result is neither self-loathing nor despair. For although poignantly acknowledging the unreachability of the mother, feminine humor still offers
comfort—as all these novels from both centuries attest—in the very process of trying.

Notes

PREFACE

1. Among the first to have noted the inadequacies of traditional comic taxonomies to describe women's humor is Judith Wilt, "The Laughter of Maidens, the Cackle of Matriarchs: Notes on the Collision between Comedy and Feminism," in *Gender and Literary Voice,* Women & Literature, n. s., vol. 1, ed. Janet Todd (New York: Holmes and Meier, 1980), 173–96, who suggests "matriarchal cackle" and "maiden laughter" as two possible ways to think about women's humor.

Recently, women's use of humor has become the focus of a number of critical studies. Prominent among these are Nancy Walker, *A Very Serious Thing: Women's Humor and American Culture* (Minneapolis: University of Minnesota Press, 1988); Regina Barreca, ed., *Last Laughs: Perspectives on Women and Comedy* (New York: Gordon and Breach, 1988); Regina Barreca, ed., *New Perspectives on Women and Comedy* (New York: Gordon and Breach, 1992); and Regina Barreca, *Untamed and Unabashed: Essays on Women and Humor in British Literature* (Detroit: Wayne State University Press, 1994). To the degree that she considers the same material as I do (Austen and Eliot, in particular), Barreca has, not surprisingly, made similar observations to my own: for example, that women's humor is trivialized when it is noticed at all, that it is related to gossip, that it makes use of "feminine attributes." Our work differs significantly, however, in two fundamental ways. Barreca looks at "women's humor" in all its complexity (that is, what I might call its masculine as well as feminine varieties), rather than at a strain of humor that has been culturally marked feminine, regardless of the sex of the practitioner. And, in contrast to my interest in the gendered implications of sympathy in humor, what most intrigues Barreca about her subject is its anger: "Women's writing of comedy is characterized by its thinly disguised rage" (*Untamed and Unabashed,* 21).

2. Anne Brontë, *The Tenant of Wildfell Hall* (Harmondsworth: Penguin, 1979), 183.

3. Margaret Homans, to whose example this study is greatly indebted, argues in *Bearing the Word: Language and Female Experience in Nineteenth-Century Women's Writing* (Chicago: University of Chicago Press, 1986) that there exists "a daughter's language" detectable but rarely noted in the work of Gaskell, Eliot, and Charlotte and Emily Brontë that is based not on the absence of the mother (as discourse generally is) but "as far as possible" on her "continued presence" (16). In *The Proper Lady and the Woman Writer: Ideology as Style in the Works of Mary Wollstonecraft, Mary Shelley, and Jane Austen* (Chicago: University of Chicago Press, 1984), Mary Poovey discovers that the cultivation of propriety in these women's texts, far from prohibiting the expression of desire as has generally been assumed, "effectively facilitated" it by disguising "impermissible emotions" and "making their expression indirect" (xvi). Other noteworthy contributions to our understanding of the muted and indirect ways in which female or feminine "difference" makes itself felt in women's writing include Judith Kegan Gardiner, "On Female Identity and Writing by Women," *Critical Inquiry* 8, no. 2 (1981): 347–61; Patricia Yeager, "Toward a Female Sublime," in *Gender &*

Theory: Dialogues on Feminist Criticism, ed. Linda Kauffman (Oxford: Basil Blackwell, 1989), 191–212; Robyn R. Warhol, *Gendered Interventions: Narrative Discourse in the Victorian Novel* (New Brunswick: Rutgers University Press, 1989); and Barbara Claire Freeman, *The Feminine Sublime: Gender and Excess in Women's Fiction* (Berkeley: University of California Press, 1995).

Mahadev Apte suggests, in *Humor and Laughter: An Anthropological Approach* (Ithaca: Cornell University Press, 1985), that women's humor has transculturally received little recognition or attention, in part because of "attempts to force women's verbal creations into preexisting categories and genres developed from men's expressive culture" (74).

4. There has been much theoretical conjecturing on the topic of humor. Regenia Gagnier ("Between Women: A Cross-Class Analysis of Status and Anarchic Humor," in *Last Laughs,* 135–48) admirably reviews and synthesizes these theories into three main groups: humor as incongruity (for example, Kant), humor as disparagement (for example, Hobbes), and humor as release (for example, Freud). One could also effectively group such theories according to discipline: humor as adaptive function, in which laughter is considered beneficial to health and a corrective to sympathetic investment in the disagreeable spectacles confronting humanity (biological theory—Darwin and Spencer); humor as a triumph over other people or circumstances (social theory—Cicero, Hobbes, Bergson); humor as an economy in feeling, thought, or inhibition (psychological theory—Freud); and humor as a bisociational perception of incongruity in which two ill-suited ideas or situations are nevertheless associated, such as treating children as though they were adults or small things in terms of great ones (cognitive theory—Kant, Schopenhauer, Raskin). Incongruity, indeed, may be the common element of all theories of humor. The incongruity or "disproportion" in the spectacle that Aristotle and Kant in different ways found to be the source of the comic becomes in Freud the incongruity within the spectator, the conflict in feeling that demands "release." Disparagement theory, too, utilizes incongruity: what is perceived as incongruous, nonnormative, evokes feelings of disparagement in the humorist.

For extensive reviews of the literature on humor theory, see Paul E. McGhee and Jeffrey H. Goldstein, eds., *Handbook of Humor Research,* 2 vols. (New York: Springer-Verlag, 1983); and Edmund Bergler, *Laughter and the Sense of Humor* (New York: Intercontinental Medical Book, 1956). In *Trollope and Comic Pleasure* (Chicago: University of Chicago Press, 1987), Christopher Herbert helpfully summarizes several studies of humor theory of the past two centuries.

5. Bruce Robbins, *The Servant's Hand: English Fiction from Below* (Durham: Duke University Press, 1993), 13.

6. Apte writes in *Humor and Laughter* that, cross-culturally, "women's humor reflects the existing inequality between the sexes not so much in its substance as in the constraints imposed on its occurrence, on the techniques used, on the social settings in which it occurs, and on the kind of audience that appreciates it" (69).

7. In *English Humour* (New York: Stein and Day, 1976), J. B. Priestley hesitantly suggests that the term *feminine humor* might be employed to describe the "plentiful supply of light satirical wit, much candid sharp humor, and fine eyes lighting up with laughter" (115) that characterize the novels of nineteenth-century women (his primary examples are *Pride and Prejudice* and *Cranford*). I find a number of the particulars he cites pertinent: "Most women novelists . . . use humour briefly then pass on to more serious matters" (116); it is quite different from humor "that is aggressive, coarse in grain, predominantly masculine" (128);

it leaves us "with our sympathies broadened instead of being further constricted" (129); it is a "very gentle humour" (122), a *tender humor,*" and "while it is essentially feminine in spirit, any man not armoured in *machismo,* too stiffly male, might create it" (129).

8. See Michel de Certeau, *The Practice of Everyday Life* (Berkeley: University of California Press, 1984), for a discussion of "creative consumption" as a tactic for subverting the conventions, laws, and other products of the dominant culture. For Certeau, "difference" lies in "tactics" of consumption rather than in "strategies" of production.

Both in its form and in the politics of its reception, feminine humor qualifies as a type of minority humor. Like the humor produced by various ethnic groups, feminine humor is "coded" for a specific marginalized audience, which is assumed to share the writer's familiarity with her topic (subjection to the stereotypes of the dominant culture, for example) as well as the resentment that topic arouses in her. However amusing such humor may be to those outside the targeted audience, its experiential specificity guarantees that it will be found funny (and stealthily tendentious) primarily by those whose own cultural experience is similar to that of the writer. Like other forms of minority humor, feminine humor represents a political and psychological tactic for managing the anger and frustration arising from the experience of being culturally other.

9. Quoted in Paul Lauter, ed., *Theories of Comedy* (New York: Anchor Doubleday, 1964), 253.

10. Barreca contends in *Last Laughs* that traditional definitions of comedy "as celebration of fertility and regeneration . . . as happy ending, joyous celebration, and re-establishment of order" (8) are inadequate in assessing women's comic productions: for Barreca, "the pleasure [of women's comedy] derives not from the perpetuation of the familiar but from its destruction" (16).

In "An Essay on Comedy" (1877; rpt. Wylie Sypher, ed., *Comedy* [Baltimore: Johns Hopkins University Press, 1980]), George Meredith, enjoining women to take up comedy as an instrument to combat both men and folly, discourages them from humor, which betrays "pity" (42). If, however, comedy is scarcely to be found in "a state of marked social inequality of the sexes" (3), as Meredith rued, then humor may, in fact, be the most effective weapon available.

Two years after the publication of his "Essay," Meredith's *The Egoist* appeared, in which he practices his theory of comedy as a chastening agent. In essence, a (verbose) stage comedy in novel form rather than a novel in which narration alleviates the dangers of plot, *The Egoist,* despite its incontrovertibly feminist sympathies, avoids "feminine" humor: rather, our amusement derives, in traditionally comic fashion, from the discomfort administered to the insufferable title character and to the restoration of social harmony.

11. Freud perhaps most fully established humor as a subspecies of the comic, distinguishable, particularly in affect, from wit and comedy. See Sigmund Freud, *Jokes and Their Relation to the Unconscious* (New York: Norton, 1960); and "Humour" (1928) in vol. 5 (215–21) of *Collected Papers,* vols. 1–5 (New York: Basic Books, 1959). Further references to this edition are noted by volume and page number (thus, *CP,* 5:215–21).

12. For a detailed analysis of Hegelian irony, see Søren Kierkegaard, *The Concept of Irony* (Princeton: Princeton University Press, 1989). For other, related discussions, see Wayne C. Booth, *A Rhetoric of Irony* (Chicago: University of Chicago Press, 1974); Gary J. Handwerk, *Irony and Ethics in Narrative* (New Haven: Yale University Press, 1985); and Candace Lang, *Irony/Humor: Critical Paradigms* (Baltimore: Johns Hopkins University Press, 1988).

In his classic study, "Laughter," reprinted in Sypher's *Comedy* (61–190), Henri Bergson makes the following useful distinction between irony and humor: "Sometimes we state what ought to be done, and pretend to believe that this is just what is actually being done; then we have irony. Sometimes, on the contrary, we describe with scrupulous minuteness what is being done, and pretend to believe that this is just what ought to be done; such is often the method of humor. Humor, thus, is the counterpart of irony" (143).

13. As Gilles Deleuze points out in *Masochism: Coldness and Cruelty* (New York: Zone, 1989), unlike irony, which tries to supersede the Law by appealing to a "transcendent higher principle," humor undermines the authority of the Law by conscientiously observing its "very letter" (88). Bergler, *Laughter,* corroborates: "Instead of an outright contradiction," humor "feint[s] with a seeming confirmation, but the confirmation so over-extends the original statement that it collapses of its own weight" (123). See also Richard Terdiman, "Counter-Humorists: Strategies of Ideological Critique in Marx and Flaubert," *Diacritics* 9 (1979): 18–32, who makes much the same argument.

14. The maternal represents such a major component of the feminine that Janine Chasseguet-Smirgel, in *Sexuality and Mind: The Role of the Father and the Mother in the Psyche* (New York: New York University Press, 1986), declares it to be the defining characteristic: the two terms of the fundamental bisexuality of the human being are "maternity on the one hand and the legislatory character of the paternal phallus on the other" (42). See also Jane Silverman Van Buren, *The Modernist Madonna: Semiotics of the Maternal Metaphor* (Bloomington: Indiana University Press, 1989), who proposes the term *maternal metaphor* to describe the basic counterimpulse in phallocentric culture: "The maternal metaphor acts as a semiotic instrument to invoke the unrepresentable and absent aspects excluded from the mainstream of 'father'-dominated culture" (14).

15. See Mikhail Bakhtin, *The Dialogic Imagination* (Austin: University of Texas Press, 1981), whose model for dialogism is "humorous" Socratic irony and for whom humor is "a comical operation of dismemberment" (241).

16. Kierkegaard, *The Concept of Irony,* 426.

17. As Kate Flint reminds us in *The Woman Reader, 1837–1914* (Oxford: Clarendon Press, 1993), gender cannot in the material world be isolated: "[E]ach woman [and presumably man] reader is constituted by a complicated set of material, ideological, and psychoanalytic forces" (42) that potentially locates her in many communities of interest. Indeed, the range, complexity, and varying strength of affiliations that comprise the identity of any particular individual prevents meaningful classification of the sort that "identity politics" encourages.

INTRODUCTION

1. The choice of any two years or events to delimit the greater nineteenth century is necessarily somewhat arbitrary. Although 1778 may seem a bit early as a starting date, it has the advantage of being the year that saw both the death of Jean-Jacques Rousseau (whose not altogether original ideas about femininity were already having such pervasive and pernicious influence throughout middle-class culture in Europe) and the publication of Frances Burney's *Evelina* (whose character Mrs. Selwyn inaugurates a discourse humorous enough to sabotage gender constructions and feminine enough to pass surveillance). The "Victorian age," as R. K. Webb reminds us, "had been an unconscionable time a-dying"

(*Modern England: From the Eighteenth Century to the Present,* 2d ed. [New York: Harper and Row, 1980], 481), taking its last gasp on the eve of the Great War. The year 1913, then, does double-duty as both the last full year of the sociopolitical nineteenth century and the publication date of Edith Wharton's *The Custom of the Country,* whose tightly controlled, furtively self-punishing humor pushes the feminine strain to the edge of recognition.

2. Florence Nightingale, *Cassandra: An Essay* (New York: Feminist Press, 1979), 54, 53.

3. Frances Power Cobbe, "Criminals, Idiots, Women, And Minors," in *"Criminals, Idiots, Women, & Minors": Nineteenth-Century Writing by Women on Women,* ed. Susan Hamilton (Peterborough, Ontario: Broadview Press, 1995), 110.

4. Margaret Oliphant, *The Literary History of England; in the End of the Eighteenth and Beginning of the Nineteenth Century,* 3 vols. (London: MacMillan, 1882), 3:206. Subsequent page references to this volume of *The Literary History* appear parenthetically in the text.

5. Recent important studies on the gendering of culture in the late eighteenth and nineteenth centuries include Leonore Davidoff and Catherine Hall, *Family Fortunes: Men and Women of the English Middle Class, 1789–1850* (Chicago: University of Chicago Press, 1987); Nancy Armstrong, *Desire and Domestic Fiction: A Political History of the Novel* (New York: Oxford University Press, 1987); Mary Poovey, *Uneven Developments: The Ideological Work of Gender in Mid-Victorian England* (Chicago: University of Chicago Press, 1988); Elizabeth Langland, *Nobody's Angels: Middle-Class Women and Domestic Ideology* (Ithaca: Cornell University Press, 1995); and Claudia L. Johnson, *Equivocal Beings: Politics, Gender, and Sentimentality in the 1790s: Wollstonecraft, Radcliffe, Burney, Austen* (Chicago: University of Chicago Press, 1995). In *Art of Darkness: A Poetics of Gothic* (Chicago: University of Chicago Press, 1995), Anne Williams notes that Aristotle's "ten pairs of opposites," headed up by "male" and "female," not only constitute "some of the most ancient categories of otherness in Western culture" but are "broadly consistent" with nineteenth-century binaries as well (18).

6. Thus, Flint, *The Woman Reader,* 55, summarizes Lewes's position in his article "The Heart and the Brain," *Fortnightly Review* 1 (1865): 66–74.

7. In a note to his poem *The Dunciad,* Alexander Pope calls Eliza Haywood "scandalous" and maliciously depicts her with "Two babes of love close clinging to her waist" (li. 158): rpt. William K. Wimsatt, Jr., ed., *Alexander Pope: Selected Poetry & Prose* (New York: Holt, Rinehart and Winston, 1967), 400. For the eighteenth-century critical response to the "female wits," I am greatly indebted to Catherine Gallagher, "Who Was That Masked Woman? The Prostitute and the Playwright in the Comedies of Aphra Behn," in *Last Laughs: Perspectives on Women and Comedy,* ed. Regina Barreca (New York: Gordon and Breach, 1988), 23–42; and to Janet Todd, "Life after Sex: The Fictional Autobiography of Delarivier Manley," in *Last Laughs,* 43–55.

Although, as Todd points out, women have been satirized for unfeminine behavior since Juvenal—thereby marking satire not only masculine but, at root, so to speak, misogynistic—humorous women of the late seventeenth and early eighteenth centuries, like Behn, Manley, and Haywood, came in for special attack. Citing the Gould poem, Gallagher argues that "the equation of poetess and 'punk' (in the slang of the day) was inescapable in the Restoration. A woman writer could either deny it in the content and form of her publications, as did Catherine Trotter, or she could embrace it, as did Aphra Behn. But she could not entirely avoid it" (27).

8. For a discussion of Burke's influence on the gender codifying of behavior, particularly of sentimentality, see Johnson, *Equivocal Beings.*

9. Virginia Woolf, *A Room of One's Own* (New York: Harcourt, Brace and World, 1929), 67.

10. Richardson, though not frequently an agent of humor, was famously its object—at least in part because of the gender threat he presented. According to John Forster, Fielding "sate [*sic*] down to revenge himself on Richardson's emasculated fiction," its "want of all manly passion," by producing *Shamela,* which turned the "wit" of *Pamela* "'the seamy side without'" (quoted in Geoffrey Tillotson and Donald Hawes, eds., *Thackeray: The Critical Heritage* [London: Routledge and Kegan Paul, 1968], 53).

11. Scott's remark on Edgeworth comes from his "General Preface," in *Waverley* (1814; New York: Dent, 1969), 9; his appreciation of Ferrier is noted by Oliphant, *Literary History,* 245, 248; and his by now well-known tribute to Austen is extracted from his journal entry of 14 March 1826 and is reprinted in B. C. Southam, ed., *Jane Austen: The Critical Heritage,* vol. 1 (London: Routledge and Kegan Paul, 1968), 106.

William Hazlitt, though relatively silent on Austen's merits, concurred in "The English Novelists," in *Lectures on the English Poets, and the English Comic Writers,* ed. William Carew Hazlitt (London: George Bell and Sons, 1984), with Scott's assessment of his own aesthetic as lacking in (feminine) sympathy: "[T]he author himself never appears to take part with his characters, to prompt our affection to the good, or sharpen our antipathy to the bad" (174).

12. W. L. Courtney, *The Feminine Note in Fiction* (London: Chapman and Hall, 1904), x. Courtney is careful to note that such "scenes of domestic life, humorously treated" "rarely" participate in "the masculine humour" (xxviii) that we generally associate with the term.

The implicit gendering of literary forms has been recognized by any number of other critics besides Courtney, either as the subject of their work or simply in passing. Marilyn Butler, for example, in her discussion of Maria Edgeworth in *Jane Austen and the War of Ideas* (Oxford: Clarendon Press, 1975; reissued with a new introduction in paperback, 1987), describes "the 'feminine' novel" as a "domestic comedy, centring on a heroine, in which the critical action is an inward progress towards judgement" (145).

13. Marilyn Butler, *Maria Edgeworth: A Literary Biography* (Oxford: Clarendon Press, 1972), 282. According to Elizabeth Harden, *Maria Edgeworth* (Boston: Twayne, 1984), Edgeworth was encouraged to dramatize the essay by her Aunt Sneyd, who thought it too entertaining not to be given wider play (47).

14. Maria Edgeworth, *The Modern Griselda,* in *Tales and Novels,* vol. 10 (New York: Harper and Bros., 1859), 215. Subsequent page references to this edition appear parenthetically in the text.

15. Margaret Oliphant, *Miss Marjoribanks* (1866; rpt. New York: Viking Penguin, 1989), 26.

16. Edgeworth's Bolingbroke also mischievously glances at the latter-day Henry Bolingbroke (1678–1751), who, like Edgeworth's father, was an advocate of Rousseau and his championship of natural man, as well as being Burke's object of satiric attack in "A Vindication of Natural Society" (1756).

17. Butler, *Maria Edgeworth,* 320; Harden, *Maria Edgeworth,* 49, 48.

18. Butler, *Maria Edgeworth,* 321.

19. Sophy is, of course, the ideal young woman, counterpart and eventually betrothed of the eponymous hero, of Rousseau's conduct-bookish pseudonovel *Emile: or, On Education.*

For examples of the prodigious recent scholarship on conduct literature of the seventeenth through nineteenth centuries, see Armstrong, *Desire and Domestic Fiction,* and Poovey, *Proper Lady.* Johnson in *Equivocal Beings* intelligently argues that Burke, not Rousseau, was the more infamous promulgator of femininity in British culture and at least as much a target of attack in Wollstonecraft's *A Vindication of the Rights of Women* as Rousseau. Regardless of who started it, however, as Armstrong notes, there came in short work to be a single feminine ideal for all classes: the domestic woman (61).

20. The translation is from *Emile: or, On Education,* ed. Allan Bloom (New York: Basic Books, 1979), 363, of the following: "Tout ce qui caracterise le sexe doit être respecte comme etabli par elle [la nature]." Bloom's faithful translation of this line makes clear Rousseau's implied distinction between what is (cultural) and what ought to be (natural), even if Rousseau collapses the distinction so far as women are concerned. The edition of *Emile* otherwise cited—Jean-Jacques Rousseau, *Emile,* trans. Barbara Foxley (London: Dent, 1974)—fails in its rendering of this line ("The native characters of sex should be respected as nature's handiwork" [326]) to register the nature/culture demarcation of Rousseau's original. See Jean-Jacques Rousseau, *Emile, ou de l'Education* (Paris: Carnier-Flammarion, 1966), 473.

21. Quotations taken from *Emile* (London: Dent, 1974), 321–73. Subsequent page references appear parenthetically in the text. Anne Crippen Ruderman, in *The Pleasures of Virtue: Political Thought in the Novels of Jane Austen* (Lanham, MD: Rowman and Littlefield, 1995), argues for "Austen's sympathy with Rousseau" (141) on the gendering of virtues.

22. "Professions for Women," *Death of the Moth and Other Essays* (New York: Harcourt Brace Jovanovich, 1942), 235–42, 236–37. The figure of the Angel in the House first appears, of course, in Coventry Patmore's poems by that title: *The Angel in the House: Book 1 ("The Betrothal," 1854) and Book 2 ("The Espousals," 1856).* See *The Poems of Coventry Patmore,* ed. Frederick Page (London: Oxford University Press, 1949).

Rousseau's description in *Emile* of the ideal wife's behavior at a dinner party (346) uncannily anticipates Mrs. Ramsay and the *Boeuf en Daube* scene in *To the Lighthouse* (New York: Harcourt, Brace and World, 1927).

23. Rousseau's description of feminine wit forcefully suggests Certeau's formulation of the power of resistance residing in what he calls "tactics of consumption": "the ingenious ways in which the weak make use of the strong" (*Practice of Everyday Life,* xvii).

24. Quoted by Lee Holcombe, "Victorian Wives and Property: Reform of the Married Women's Property Law, 1857–1882," in *A Widening Sphere: Changing Roles of Victorian Women,* ed. Martha Vicinus (Bloomington: Indiana University Press, 1977), 13.

25. There were, of course, notable exceptions, such as full responsibility for capital crimes like murder and treason. For recent lucid discussion of some of the most controversial laws affecting women, see Holcombe "Victorian Wives and Property"; Poovey, *Uneven Developments;* Mary Lyndon Shanley, *Feminism, Marriage and the Law in Victorian England, 1850–1895* (Princeton: Princeton University Press, 1989); Susan Staves, *Married Women's Separate Property in England, 1660–1833* (Cambridge, MA: Harvard University Press, 1990). See also Barbara Leigh Smith Bodichon, *A Brief Summary, in Plain Language of the Most Important Laws of England Concerning Women, Together with a Few Observations,* 3d rev. ed. (Lon-

don: Trubner and Co., 1869); Caroline Norton, *English Laws for Women in the Nineteenth Century* (London: privately printed, 1854); John J. S. Wharton, *An Exposition of the Laws Relating to the Women of England: Showing Their Rights, Remedies, and Responsibilities, in Every Position of Life* (London: Longman, Brown, Green and Longmans, 1853); and Erna Reiss, *The Rights and Duties of Englishwomen; A Study in Law and Public Opinion* (Manchester: Shervatt and Hughes, 1934).

26. Oliphant, "The Grievances of Women," 241.

27. Letter to Eliza (Tottie) Fox, daughter of William Fox, MP (rpt. *The Letters of Mrs. Gaskell,* ed. J. A. V. Chapple and Arthur Pollard [Manchester: Manchester University Press, 1966]), 379. Subsequent page references to this edition are parenthetically noted within the text.

28. *The George Eliot Letters,* ed. Gordon Haight (New Haven: Yale University Press, 1954), vols. 1–9, 2:171, 333. Subsequent page references to this edition are parenthetically noted within the text.

29. *Jane Austen's Letters to Her Sister Cassandra and Others,* ed. R. W. Chapman, 2d ed. (London: Oxford Univeristy Press, 1952), 370. Subsequent page references to this edition appear in the text. For a discussion of Austen's negotiating cultural gendering through a dual policy of accommodation and resistance, see Deborah Kaplan, *Jane Austen among Women* (Baltimore: Johns Hopkins University Press, 1992).

30. Martineau, *Autobiography* (quoted in Gayle Graham Yates, ed., *Harriet Martineau on Women* [New Brunswick: Rutgers University Press, 1985]), 241–42.

31. Oliphant, "The Grievances of Women," 238.

CHAPTER ONE

1. Meredith, *The Egoist* (1879; rpt. Harmondsworth: Penguin, 1968), 117.

2. Problematically, much of the scholarly work on humor has stressed taxonomy. Not only are the classifications thus generated idiosyncratic as well as inevitably overlapping, but as Victor Raskin in *Semantic Mechanisms of Humor* (Boston: D. Reidel, 1985) points out, humor is "indiscriminately" used in most humor discussions to refer to the "subject matter, the intention, the technique" (29). Apte proposes analyzing the phenomenon of "humor" not according to predetermined categories and attributes but "in terms of such components as time and place, formal and semantic properties . . . , participants' identities (sex, age, social status, role, and so forth), motives and expectations . . . , and cultural values" (20). Following Apte, I concentrate on "the formal and substantive aspects of humor, its sociocultural foundations and determinants," and "its functions" (*Humor and Laughter,* 21).

3. G. K. Chesterton, from *The Victorian Age in Literature* (1913; rpt. *Jane Austen: The Critical Heritage,* vol. 2: *1870–1940,* ed. B. C. Southam [London: Routledge and Kegan Paul, 1987]), 239.

4. From the *Journals of Ralph Waldo Emerson: 1856–1863* (1913; ed. E. W. Emerson and W. E. Forbes; rpt. Southam, *Jane Austen: Critical Heritage,* 1:28). Emerson's particular disregard for Austen may be traceable in part to his larger disdain of humor: "Reason does not jest, and men of reason do not. A prophet in whom the moral sentiment predominates, or a philosopher in whom the love of truth predominates—these do not joke . . . Beware

of jokes ... True wit never made us laugh" (quoted in George Vasey, *The Philosophy of Laughter and Smiling,* 2d ed. [London: J. Burns, 1877], 177).

5. Reprinted in *Jane Austen: Critical Heritage,* 2:232.

6. A typical example of Twain's phallically inflated humor is given in my Chap. 1, 26. Christopher Herbert in *Anthony Trollope and Comic Pleasure* defines comedy in terms so strikingly phallic as to discourage female usage: "protean limberness and genius for self-magnification" are the "sign[s] of comedy" (29); the "heartbeat and the *idée fixe* of the comic" is a "fantasy of multiplied, of virtually boundless, pleasure, in which imagery of protean limberness is fused with the idea of voluptuous gratification" (13). True comedy, moreover, exhibits "a basic element of cruelty" (24) and a penchant for exaggeration.

7. Thomas Love Peacock, *Nightmare Abbey* (1818; rpt. Harmondsworth: Penguin, 1969), 110–11.

8. Charles Dickens, *Little Dorrit* (1857; rpt. Harmondsworth: Penguin, 1967), 187.

9. The disposal of the heroine in marriage, however, comprises just about her only contribution to oedipal narrative. As Laura Mulvey points out in "The Oedipus Myth: Beyond the Riddles of the Sphinx," in *Visual and Other Pleasures* (Bloomington: Indiana University Press, 1989), 175–201, "the feminine"—whether wife, daughter, or mother—is remarkably "marginal" even to the Oedipus myth itself. The major preoccupations of oedipal narrative are rather the personal history of the hero (the search for his "true" origins), his accession to his "true" father's cultural power, and his marriage to a mother substitute (the biological mother often having been narratively killed off before the hero's story begins). It seems to me more than simply fortuitous that oedipal narrative should have reached the pinnacle of its popularity in the age of Darwin and Freud, for both of whom the determination of origins was so pressing a concern.

10. Elizabeth Gaskell, *Wives and Daughters* (1864–66; rpt. Harmondsworth: Penguin, 1969), 35.

11. Charlotte Brontë, *Jane Eyre* (1847; rpt. New York: Norton, 1970), 98.

12. In "Family Romances," *CP,* 5:74–78, Freud asserts that fairy tales are the prototype and often the instigator of family romance. Hence, feminine modifications of the conventional romance are particularly important to the expression of female desire, since, according to Freud, such fantasies provide about the only preconscious outlet available for its expression: in women "erotic wishes dominate the phantasies" to the exclusion of ambitious ones ("The Relation of the Poet to Daydreaming," *CP,* 4:176–77).

13. See Marianne Hirsch's "Female Family Romances and 'The Old Dream of Symmetry,'" *Literature and Psychology* 23, no. 4 (1986): 37–47, for an extended and absorbing account of feminine difference in the structure and signification of family romance.

14. See Nancy K. Miller's "Emphasis Added: Plots and Plausibilities in Women's Fiction, *PMLA* 96 (1981) 36–48, on the relation between female desire and closure in *The Mill on the Floss.* D. A. Miller, in *Narrative and Its Discontents: Problems of Closure in the Traditional Novel* (Princeton: Princeton University Press, 1981), without making a feminist argument, gestures more or less to the same phenomenon. Barreca *(Last Laughs)* notes the resistance to closure specifically in women's comedy.

15. See Emily Eden, *The Semi-Attached Couple* (1860; rpt. Boston: Houghton Mifflin, 1947). The resemblance Eden's Ernest bears to Wilde's drollishly effete Goring is, I suspect, too strong to have been merely coincidental. Not only does Eden's character amuse his fellows with his witty nonsense and his artful laziness ("'[S]he seems to me as good a little

creature as ever breathed; pretty and ladylike, and so serviceable; never mind what trouble she takes for other people. I think she will suit me exactly; we shall be very happy together'" [244]), but his betrothal to the "little creature" takes place in the same location (the conservatory) and under circumstances of plot almost identical to those Wilde later constructs.

16. George Meredith also allusively employs Willoughby, decidedly less rakish but more ludicrously self-centered, as the title character of *The Egoist.* His Laetitia Dale—whose idolization of Willoughby initially surpasses even that of Lily Dale for the priggish Crosbie— pointedly recalls Trollope's heroine.

Eliot herself denied any direct association between her characters and Gaskell's, though a number of readers, including Swinburne, believed her to have been remiss in not acknowledging the striking connection. See Gordon S. Haight, *George Eliot: A Biography* (Oxford: Oxford University Press, 1968), 525. For a discussion of Eliot's other borrowings or "fugitive" references to other women's texts, see Gillian Beer, "Marian Evans: Reading Women Writers," in *George Eliot* (Bloomington: Indiana University Press, 1986).

17. In *Reading for the Plot: Design and Intention in Narrative* (New York: Knopf, 1984), Peter Brooks argues that narrative is fueled by a male textual erotics: see especially chap. 2 ("Narrative Desire," 37–61) and chap. 4 ("Freud's Masterplot," 90–112). Susan Winnett in "Coming Unstrung: Women, Men, Narrative, and Principles of Pleasure" (*PMLA* 105, no. 3 [May 1990]: 505–18) appropriately and convincingly takes him to task for his blindness to gender difference.

18. For discussion of gossip as a narrative principle, see Patricia Meyer Spacks, *Gossip* (Chicago: University of Chicago Press, 1985), who associates gossip with joking and play and considers it an expression of both "aggression and intimacy" (64).

19. Homans and Barreca have both pointed to such feminine refigurings of metaphor. See Homans, *Bearing the Word;* and Barreca, *Last Laughs* (243–56). The latter considers metaphoric reliteralization as a "female" comic device; a Muriel Spark character, for example, is described as "not all there," then fades away literally as well as figuratively.

20. Nancy Walker and Zita Dresner, eds., *Redressing the Balance: American Women's Literary Humor from Colonial Times to the 1980s* (Jackson: University of Mississippi Press, 1988), xxi.

Apte notes that cross-culturally "women's humor generally lacks the aggressive and hostile quality of men's," stressing in so doing that "prevalent cultural values and the resultant constraints" determine the production and reception of women's humor (*Humor and Laughter,* 70).

21. *EGL,* 797.

22. Freud, *Jokes,* 96.

23. In "Gender Differences in Humor Appreciation" (*Humor* 1, no. 3 (1988): 231–43), researchers Norbert Mundorf et al. found that, in accord with previous studies, women find absurdity funnier than they do sexual or hostile humor. When the victim of the humor is a man, however, this study also found that women show a significant preference for hostile over sexual humor (a preference that is absent when the victim is female). See also Louise Omwake, "A Study of Sense of Humor: Its Relation to Sex, Age and Personal Characteristics," *Journal of Applied Psychology* 21 (1937): 688–704; and Frank J. Prerost, "Reduction of Aggression as a Function of Related Content of Humor," *Psychological Reports* 38 (1976): 771–77.

In "What Is Funny to Whom? The Role of Gender" (*Journal of Communication* 26

[1976]: 164–72), Joanne R. Cantor concludes from her experimental study not only that female respondents find jokes with female victims to be "funnier" than those with male victims but that female respondents identify with the disparager—whether male or female—when the victim is female: the implication being not that women are self-loathing but that the role of victim is culturally marked as feminine.

24. Discussing the "four types" of comic hero, Hans Robert Jauss in "On Why the Comic Hero Amuses" (*Aesthetic Experience and Literary Hermeneutics,* trans. Michael Shaw [Minneapolis: University of Minnesota Press, 1982], 189–20) distinguishes two—the unheroic hero and the humoristic hero—who together bear more than a passing resemblance to my formulation of the feminine humorist. At once performing the functions of "relief, protest, and solidarization" (193), Jauss's unheroic hero "attack[s] the validity of ideal . . . social norms," while his humoristic hero, like Freud's, enacts a "triumph of consciousness over the demands and the harshness of reality" (195).

25. See, for example, Alfred Winterstein, "Beitrage zum Problem des Humors" (cited in Lucile Dooley, "A Note on Humor," *Psychoanalytic Review* 21 [1934]: 49–58), 50; and Gilles Deleuze, *Masochism.* Martin Grotjahn, in *Beyond Laughter* (New York: McGraw-Hill, 1966), writes:

> The humorist is similar to the depressive in so far as he resignedly accepts the fact that the good mother left him when he was expelled from the childhood paradise. But in contrast to the depressive, . . . he does something about it. He resolutely takes over the role of the good mother and himself plays it to the hilt for his own benefit. He is friendly and kind to himself and tries to develop a similarly tolerant and humorous attitude toward others. The grief over the loss of the good mother shows occasionally in the sadness of the humorist, who always seems to smile through tears.(55)

For Freud, this humor "that smiles through tears" is "broken" (that is, feminine) since it "only partially" economizes on the expenditure of pain, anger, pity that provokes it (*Jokes,* 232).

26. Cited by Freud in *Jokes,* 230.

27. The following psychoanalytic readings sensitive to gender difference have crucially informed my understanding of the preoedipal and its potential richness in thinking about a feminine use of humor: Nancy Chodorow, *The Reproduction of Mothering: Psychoanalysis and the Sociology of Gender* (Berkeley: University of California Press, 1978); Julia Kristeva, *Desire in Language: A Semiotic Approach to Literature and Art,* trans. Leon Roudiez (New York: Columbia University Press, 1980); Luce Irigaray, *Speculum of the Other Woman,* trans. Gillian C. Gill (Ithaca: Cornell University Press, 1985); and particularly Janine Chasseguet-Smirgel, *Sexuality and Mind.*

28. Jane Gallop notes in *Thinking through the Body* (New York: Columbia University Press, 1988) that this exchange mimics the socioeconomic exchange of women in patriarchal cultures; in ethnic jokes, the contempt for the female body expressed is replaced by a similar contempt for the body of the other. Steven Marcus, in *The Other Victorians: A Study of Sexuality and Pornography in Mid-Nineteenth Century England* (New York: New American Library, 1974), was perhaps the first to notice that the "imagery in which sexuality was represented in consciousness was largely drawn from the sphere of socioeconomic activity" (xiii).

29. In "The Relation of Humor to Masochism," *Psychoanalytic Review* 28 (1941): 37–46, Dooley notes that "since the great primary narcissistic needs are two—to be allowed aggression and to be loved—humor does indeed provide a triumph of narcissism" (45).

30. D. W. Winnicott, *The Maturational Processes and the Facilitating Environment: Studies in the Theory of Emotional Development* (Madison, CT: International Universities Press, 1965), 41.

31. Plato, *Symposium,* trans. Alexander Nehamas and Paul Woodruff (Indianapolis: Hackett, 1989), 27. I thank Nicholas Pappas for pointing out to me the maternal/fetal suggestiveness of Aristophanes's myth, especially evident in the navel as marking the wound of detachment from the other and in the awkward sphericalness of the perfect original state as emulating the condition of late pregnancy.

32. D. W. Winnicott, *Playing and Reality* (1971; rpt. Harmondsworth: Penguin, 1980), 27. Subsequent references to this edition appear parenthetically in the text.

33. George Eliot, *The Lifted Veil* (Harmondsworth: Penguin, 1985), 57. According to Chasseguet-Smirgel, the wish for the preoedipal mother is at least as psychically powerful as the wish for the phallus. This mother represents "a universe without obstacles, without roughness or differences, entirely smooth, . . . an interior to which one has free access. Behind the fantasy of destroying or appropriating the father's penis . . . can be detected a more basic and more archaic wish, of which the return to the smooth maternal belly is the representation" (*Sexuality and Mind,* 77).

34. Chasseguet-Smirgel, *Sexuality and Mind,* suggests the terms *linear* to indicate "nonhistorical" or primary process thinking associated with the maternal principle, and *causal* to indicate the secondary process thinking characteristic of the paternal order, where "thought in itself constitutes an obstacle" (81) to the archaic mother.

35. Jane Austen, *Emma* (1816; rpt. Harmondsworth: Penguin, 1966), 418.

36. J. G. Millingen, *The Passions; or, Mind and Matter* (London: John and Daniel Darling, 1848), 157.

37. Ruskin writes:

> The temperament which admits the pathetic fallacy, is . . . that of a mind and body in some sort too weak . . . , over-dazzled by emotion.
>
> A poet is great, first in proportion to the strength of his passion, and then, that strength being granted, in proportion to his government of it; there being, however, always a point beyond which it would be inhuman and monstrous if he pushed this government, and, therefore, a point at which all feverish and wild fancy becomes just and true. Thus the destruction of the kingdom of Assyria cannot be contemplated firmly by a prophet of Israel. The fact is too great, too wonderful. It overthrows him, dashes him into a confused element of dreams. (Quoted in Ruskin, *The Genius of John Ruskin,* ed. John D. Rosenberg [London: Routledge and Kegan Paul, 1963], 67, 69–70)

38. See *A Philosophical Enquiry into the Origin of Our Ideas of the Sublime and Beautiful,* ed. James T. Boulton (Notre Dame, IN: University of Notre Dame Press, 1968). Although Burke classifies sympathy among the "passions of society" rather than as a passion of "self-preservation," he nonetheless relies heavily upon it in describing the experience of the Sublime, which he classifies among the latter. For an illuminating discussion of Burke's mascu-

line appropriation of sympathy in both the *Enquiry* and *Reflections on the Revolution in France,* see Claudia Johnson, *Equivocal Beings.*

With its snobbishly masculine pedigree and particularly in its Burkean articulation, the Sublime has attracted very few female users. Indeed, if Fanny Burney's diary entry, quoted below, is any indication, its utter disdain for the material, its sustained self-seriousness, and its tumescent style rendered it antipathetic to a femininely humorous sensibility and an easy target of ridicule:

> "No 'tis impossible! this style is too great, too sublime to be supported with proper dignity—the sublime and beautiful how charmingly blended! yes! I *will* desist—I *will* lay down my pen while I can with . . . [B's ellipsis] It would be miraculous had I power to maintain the same glowing enthusiasm—the same— on my word I can *not* go on, my imagionation [*sic*] is rais'd *too* high, it soars above this little dirty sphere, it transports me beyond mortality—it conveys me to the Elysian fields—but my ideas grow confused—I fear you cannot compre- hend my meaning—all I shall add, is to beg you would please to attribute your not understanding the sublimity of my sentiments to your own stupidity and dullness of apprehension, and not to my want of meaning—which is only too fine to be clear.
>
> After this beautiful flow of expression, refinement sentiment and exaltation of ideas, can I meanly descend to common life? can I basely stoop to relate the particulars of common life? can I condescendingly deign to recapitulate vulgar conversation? I can!" (*The Early Diary of Frances Burney, 1768–1778,* ed. Annie Raine Ellis [Freeport, NY: Books for Libraries Press, 1971], 7)

39. Still worse, the culturally abnormal can sometimes serve double-duty as the feminine norm, as Poovey *(Uneven Developments)* has pointed out to be the case with hysteria ("hyste- ria was simultaneously the norm of the female body taken to its logical extreme and the medical category that effectively defined this norm as inherently abnormal" [36]) and as Freud and Deutsch argued frequently to be the case with masochism. Even in our contem- porary culture, Lynn Chancer in *Sadomasochism and Everyday Life: The Dynamics of Power and Powerlessness* (New Brunswick: Rutgers University Press, 1992) maintains, women are routinely and ideologically "situated in a predominantly masochistic position" (129).

40. So argues Janice Porteous, "Humor as a Process of Defense: The Evolution of Laugh- ing," *Humor* 1, no. 1 (1988): 76. Mary Noel Evans, in "Hysteria and the Seduction of Theory," *Seduction and Theory: Readings of Gender, Representation, and Rhetoric,* ed. Dianne Hunter (Urbana: University of Illinois Press, 1989), 73–85, suggests that hysteria quite literally embodies an insulting resistance to the regularization of (Freudian) theory, making it, like humor, a Certeauian "tactic of consumption."

41. Charles Darwin's *Expression of the Emotions in Man and Animals* (New York: Apple- ton, 1898), which postulates that bodily expression of feeling results from an overflow of excitation, is largely devoted to elaborating the physical manifestations of emotion.

In *The Philosophy of Laughter and Smiling,* George Vasey disputes Darwin's findings that laughter "'primarily expresses mere happiness or joy'" and, being present even in "idiots," points to a "natural" if not instinctual function (163). Rather, Vasey makes the remarkable claim that laughter, the etiology of which he traces to the tickling inflicted upon infants in European cultures, is nothing more than "an involuntary agitation of the diaphragm and pectoral muscles, causing a considerable derangement in the respiratory functions" (167) and "not unfrequently end[ing] in death" (34). Vasey does usefully note, however, that "we find it difficult to refer [laughter] to the class of either pleasure or pain" (30).

42. Josef Breuer and Sigmund Freud, *Studies on Hysteria* (New York: Basic Books, n.d.), attribute this rescue of affect to the "psychotherapeutic procedure" (17). Subsequent page references to this edition are noted in the text.

43. Monique David-Menard, *Hysteria from Freud to Lacan* (Ithaca: Cornell University Press, 1989), 45, 33.

According to David-Menard, hysteria is not a symptom of pathology but "the signifying material of a psychical conflict" (40), a bodily expression of the pleasurable pain produced in the conflict between desire and its negation. In this view, hysteria is more accurately described as a sign rather than a symptom of "a painful delight" (53). Signs of hysteria are produced when "drive is actualized" (62) on the terrain of the body, when the erotogenic body appropriates, so to speak, a somatically compliant organic body as its means of expression.

44. In *Thinking through the Body*, Gallop goes so far as to argue that the desire for "the unfulfilled mother-child union" (66) is not a substitute for the maternal phallus but in fact "the missing phallus" itself. According to Gallop, the desire for maternal union, which occurs prior to the fear of castration or to penis envy, leads the child to endow the mother with the phallus: the "idealized, transcendent" (132), universal signifier of desire. Hence, the desire for maternal union, represented by the maternal phallus, is the original, determining desire for which all others—including the desire for the phallus proper—are inadequate substitutes.

45. Arnold M. Cooper, "The Narcissistic-Masochistic Character," *Masochism: Current Psychoanalytic Perspectives*, ed. Robert A. Glick and Donald I. Meyers (Hillsdale, NJ: Analytic Press, 1988), 126.

The controversy over the proper denotation of *masochism* is largely concerned with whether the term should be used to refer specifically to sexualized suffering or whether it may serve as a rubric for "a number of self-motivated, self-destructive behaviors . . . , which are sought after in obligatory connection with a variety of pleasurable goals or gratifications" (Glick and Meyers, *Masochism*, 14). Among the "crucial concepts" of this second, more ecumenical form of masochism are "the role of the preoedipal mother and her phallic power," a "history of maternal loss in the victim," the "negative oedipal triangle," and "the fear of object loss" (3). Under this dispensation, humor, which entails "subjugation" to the maternal imago in an attempt to achieve a "pleasurable goal," qualifies as a "related dynamic" of masochism (14).

46. Galenson, "Protomasochism," in *Masochism*, 191.

47. "The Economic Problem in Masochism" (1924), in *CP,* 2:263, 257.

48. Like Freud, Helene Deutsch, *The Psychology of Women*, vol. 1 (New York: Grune and Stratton, 1944), readily concedes that environmental factors encourage a masochistic urge in women, but she still points accusingly to the "reproductive function" (277), which "requires toleration of considerable pain," as evidence of a biologically based feminine masochism. Defloration, menstruation, childbirth, and menopause demand that a woman "have a certain amount of masochism if she is to be adjusted to reality" (276). Her "destiny . . . as the servant of reproduction" (278), indeed, depends on her successful psychic "compromise between self-injury and self-love" (273). Qualifying Deutsch, Helen Meyers in "A Consid-

eration of Treatment Techniques in Relation to the Functions of Masochism" (in Glick and Meyers, *Masochism,* 175–88), points out that there is a crucial difference between a woman's conscious acceptance of "unavoidable discomfort . . . for the sake of an ideal or conscious goal" (labor pains, for example) and her pathologically seeking out such pain for its own sake and "taking pleasure in its severity" (178–79). Arnold M. Cooper reminds us of the many "constructive uses of pleasure in pain" utilized by both genders, including "the pleasurable fatigue after a day's work, the ecstasy of an athlete's exhaustion, the dogged pursuit of distant goals, the willingness to cling to a seemingly absurd ideal" ("The Narcissistic-Masochistic Character," 125). The last of these is, one could argue, the operative principle in feminine humor itself.

Even Karen Horney, "The Problem of Feminine Masochism" (in *Psychoanalysis and Women,* ed. Jean Baker Miller [Harmondsworth: Penguin, 1973], 21–38), doesn't dispute the existence of a feminine masochistic urge: "[C]ultural factors exert a powerful influence on women; so much so, in fact, that in our culture it is hard to see how any woman can escape becoming masochistic to some degree, from the effects of culture alone, without any appeal to contributory factors in the anatomical-physiological characteristics of woman, and their psychic effects" (36).

49. Glick and Meyers note B. Berliner's idea that masochism is "oral, not oedipal, in origin" (12), "an adaptive response" to a withholding environment.

50. R. Loewenstein suggests that the major motivation of masochism is the "desperate attempt . . . to revert to childhood, to the state when threats and dangers could actually be averted or minimized" (quoted by Glick and Meyers, *Masochism,* 12–13).

Freud debates at one point whether to call "feminine masochism" as such, since in fact "so many of its features point to a childish life" (*CP,* 2:258). But because he finds the passive role inherently feminine (the male masochist in his fantasies "is placed in a situation characteristic of womanhood, i.e. they mean that he is being castrated, is playing the passive part in coitus, or is giving birth"), he opts for the gendered label.

51. Deleuze argues that the "essence of masochistic humor lies in this, that the very Law which forbids the satisfaction of desire under threat of subsequent punishment is converted into one which demands" punishment in order to satisfy desire (88). Pain—a sense of frustration or suffering under the Law—is, in other words, the necessary component for the satisfaction of desire in both masochism and humor.

52. As Dooley in "A Note on Humor" long ago argued: "Irony is a forerunner of humor, has an admixture of sadism, and is mediated by the more punitive and sadistic superego" (56–57).

According to Deleuze, sadism is a consequence of the father-identified superego run amok. "What normally confers a moral character on the superego is the internal and complementary ego upon which it exerts its severity, and equally the maternal element which fosters the close interaction between ego and superego. But when the superego runs wild, expelling the ego along with the mother-image, then its fundamental immorality exhibits itself as sadism. The ultimate victims of the sadist are the mother and the ego" (*Masochism,* 124). Counterpoint to Deleuze's genealogy of sadism is Chasseguet-Smirgel's *Creativity and Perversion* (New York: Norton, 1984), which conceives sadism to be not the inflation of the Law but its abolition: sadism results when genitality fails developmentally to succeed anality, and the Law fails to take hold in the psychic chaos.

53. Helen Meyers, "A Consideration of Treatment Techniques," 178.

54. For a discussion of the preoedipal construction of the phallic (or terrifying) mother, see Melanie Klein, *The Selected Melanie Klein*, ed. Juliet Mitchell (New York: Free Press, 1986), especially 84–94, 211–29.

55. Dooley, "The Relation of Humor to Masochism," 45.

56. Bergler, *Laughter and the Sense of Humor*, 120. Bergler writes that the "real aim" of humor "is always deflation for the sake of diminishing inner fears." In the process of deflating such fears, however, "aggression which was originally directed outwards is diverted for use against the internal 'enemy'" (54–55); thus, the defensive use of aggression constitutes an expression of masochism.

Chapter Two

1. Simpson, unsigned review of Henry Austen's *Memoir* in *North British Review* 52 (April 1870): 129–52 (rpt. Southam, *Jane Austen: Critical Heritage*, 1:247). Despite the parsimonious praise here, Richard Simpson thought very highly of Austen's accomplishments overall and was among the first to recognize that Austen was more a humorist than an ironist.

2. Oliphant, extract from unsigned article "Miss Austen and Miss Mitford" (rpt. Southam, *Jane Austen: Critical Heritage*, 1:216).

3. William Hazlitt, "On Wit and Humour," *Lectures on the English Poets, and the English Comic Writers*, 3–9 passim.

4. Oliphant, "Miss Austen and Miss Mitford," 216. Oliphant's contemporary Julia Kavanagh similarly finds "Delicacy, Tenderness, and Sympathy" to distinguish feminine writing: see the extract from her *English Women of Letters* (1862; rpt. Southam, *Jane Austen: Critical Heritage*, 1:176). Although he does not note its gender, our contemporary Roger Gard, in *Jane Austen's Novels: The Art of Clarity* (New Haven: Yale University Press, 1992), identifies a "powerful sympathetic urge in English . . . fiction in the nineteenth century" (80) in "'gentle Jane,'" *Cranford*, Oliphant's Carlingford novels, "the profounder satire of George Eliot" (81), and "some of Henry James's gentler accounts" (80).

5. The term is, of course, F. R. Leavis's. Until the advent of feminist critical studies of Austen in the 1970s, however, his view was not only dominant but virtually hegemonic. See *The Great Tradition: George Eliot, Henry James, Joseph Conrad* (New York: New York University Press, 1960).

6. Oliphant, comparing *Emma* to *Pride and Prejudice*, observes that "it is not that the fun is less, or the keenness of insight into all the many manifestations of foolishness, but human sympathy has come in to sweeten the tale, and the brilliant intellect has found out, somehow, that all the laughable beings surrounding it . . . are all the same mortal creatures, with souls and hearts within them" ("Miss Austen and Miss Mitford," 223).

7. Jane Austen, *Pride and Prejudice* (New York: Norton, 1966), 1.

8. On the difficulty of even describing difference within humor, see Thomas Babbington Macaulay, who writes of the ineffability of Austen's style: "[A]ll this was done by touches so delicate, that they elude analysis, that they defy the powers of description, and that we know them to exist only by the general effect to which they have contributed" (extract from "The Diary and Letters of Mme D'Arblay"; rpt. Southam, *Jane Austen: Critical Heritage*, 1:122–23).

9. William Hazlitt, "The English Novelists," *Lectures on the English Poets*, 166–67. Court-

ney in *The Feminine Note in Fiction* follows Hazlitt's distinctions: men "create," women "reproduce" and "are happiest when they" do so (xxxii).

10. On the discomfiture caused by Burney's sometimes cruel humor, see Margaret Anne Doody, *Frances Burney: The Life and the Works* (New Brunswick: Rutgers University Press, 1988), who though partial to Burney's variety, admits that her "comedy is much more violent and disturbing than Austen's" (2).

11. One of the key features of such a tradition—the tension between "the acceptance of the established order and subversive protest against it"—pervades Burney's fiction, according to Katharine M. Rogers, *Frances Burney: The World of "Female Difficulties"* (London: Harvester Wheatsheaf, 1990), 4.

12. Fanny Burney, *Evelina; or the History of a Young Lady's Entrance into the World,* ed. Edward A. Bloom and Lillian D. Bloom (Oxford: Oxford University Press, 1968). Page references to this edition are noted parenthetically within the text.

Doody understands *Evelina* to be an admixture of the masculine and feminine rather than, as I do, incorporating two distinct strains of comedy: "She seizes a 'masculine' mode of comedy, largely derived from the public medium of the stage, wraps it up in the 'feminine' epistolary mode, and uses the combination for her own purposes" (48). Similarly, Ronald Paulson, in "Evelina: Cinderella and Society," *Fanny Burney's Evelina* (Modern Critical Interpretations), ed. Harold Bloom (New York: Chelsea House, 1988), 59–83, sees the text "as a careful balance of the old and the new, of Smollettian satire and a pre-Austenian ironic sensibility" (Bloom, "Introduction," 2)—thus adumbrating the distinction that Captain Mirvan and Mrs. Selwyn represent, though he places Selwyn in the Smollettian camp.

13. Doody, *Frances Burney,* 57.

14. For example, see Rose Marie Cutting, "Defiant Women: The Growth of Feminism in Fanny Burney's Novels," *Studies in English Literature 1500–1900* 17 (1977): 519–30; John Richetti, "Voice and Gender in Eighteenth-Century Fiction: Haywood to Burney," *Studies in the Novel* 19, no. 3 (Fall 1987): 263–72; Susan Staves, "*Evelina*: or, Female Difficulties," *Fanny Burney's Evelina,* 13–30; Patricia Meyer Spacks, "Dynamics of Fear: Fanny Burney," *Fanny Burney's Evelina,* 52; and Kristina Straub, *Divided Fictions: Fanny Burney and Feminine Strategy* (Lexington: University Press of Kentucky, 1987), 27. Julia Epstein, *The Iron Pen: Frances Burney and the Politics of Women's Writing* (Madison: University of Wisconsin Press, 1989), takes exception to the popular reading of Selwyn: though a "fast-talking country gentlewoman who teases as nastily and laughs as loudly as any of the men in her set," Selwyn is "sympathetically portrayed," according to Epstein, being "kind and compassionate to those who deserve it and . . . achiev[ing] independent status without compromising herself either socially or personally" (113).

15. For a thoughtful discussion of *Evelina* as a female *Bildungsroman,* see Susan Fraiman, *Unbecoming Women: British Women Writers and the Novel of Development* (New York: Columbia University Press, 1993).

16. Doody, *Frances Burney,* 150–51.

17. Staves, "*Evelina:* or, Female Difficulties," 27. Gina Campbell, "How To Read Like a Gentleman: Burney's Instructions to Her Critics in *Evelina,*" *ELH* 57 (1990): 557–84, points out that the idea of protection is introduced in the dedication to the "Monthly and Critical Reviewers" that frames the novel; here Burney not only pleads for their (masculine)

protection against critical contumely but disarms them by a feminine (and I would add humorous) posing of helplessness.

18. Epstein considers the footrace staged by Lords Merton and Coverley at Bristol Hotwell—in which two extremely elderly and enfeebled women are forced to compete "like dogs or horses"—as "the apotheosis of both physical violence and social violation against women" (*The Iron Pen,* 115).

19. Doody bases her argument for the maternal significance of Bristol Hotwell on the fact that Burney's much-loved, ailing mother had been sent there "in a futile effort to recover her strength" (46); Esther Sleepe Burney died shortly after her return to London, when Fanny was only ten years old. Doody, indeed, implies that the writing of *Evelina* itself might be an attempt on Burney's part to connect with the lost mother (see *Frances Burney,* 30–38).

Evelyn Farr, *The World of Fanny Burney* (London: Peter Owen, 1993), also stresses Burney's intense family attachment ("nothing was more important to Fanny Burney than her family" [13]) and suggests that the intimate affection she came to feel for her younger sister Susan compensated in part for maternal loss, especially considering that her stepmother "was almost certainly a lifelong enemy" (17).

20. Considering his propensity for joking, Mirvan's claim not to understand the meaning of grinning ("'tis a lingo I don't understand'" [97–98]) seems at first blush disingenuous. Yet, though a master of the practical joke, Mirvan is not humorously adept enough to combat Lovel's condescension successfully. Feeling belittled by the latter's attitude of superior sophistication, Mirvan threatens violence (a threat fulfilled in the monkey's attack on Lovel). Mrs. Selwyn, on the other hand, is never bettered by Lovel or anyone else on any issue.

21. Although Evelina—who never overtly laughs at Mirvan's joke—may be more exemplary in her sympathy than Mrs. Selwyn ("I was really sorry for the poor man, who, though an egregious fop, had committed no offence that merited such chastisement" [401]), we as readers are positioned in our response to Lovel's mishap in greater proximity to Selwyn than to Evelina (who is stranded atop a chair), since we, too, initially laugh at his comparison to the monkey. For discussion of the reader's "guilt in participating" in the "antimasculinist satire" of the monkey scene, see Doody, *Frances Burney,* 64–65.

22. Gerard A. Barker, "The Two Mrs. Selwyns: *Evelina* and *The Man of the World,*" *Papers on Language and Literature* 13 (1977): 80–84.

23. According to Annie Raine Ellis, editor of Burney's *Early Diary,* George Selwyn—an English banker in Paris—"was rudely discouraged by Mrs. Thrale [Samuel Johnson's friend], who had among other fantastic projects, one of marrying her to Mr. Thrale's nephew, the spendthrift Sir John Lade" (2:306n.). Burney "'could feel my whole face on fire'" when Mrs. Thrale lectured to Selwyn in Burney's presence on "the evil and absurdity of marriage between the old and the young" (1:lxxxii n.).

24. Unsigned essay, *The Times,* 7 December 1882, 9 (rpt. Donald Smalley, ed., *Trollope: The Critical Heritage,* [London: Routledge and Kegan Paul, 1969], 502).

25. David Skilton, *Anthony Trollope and His Contemporaries: A Study in the Theory and Conventions of Mid-Victorian Fiction* (London: Longman, 1972), 111; Henry James, "Anthony Trollope," *The House of Fiction: Essays on the Novel by Henry James,* ed. Leon Edel (Westport, CT: Greenwood Press, 1957), 107.

26. Unsigned notice, *Saturday Review,* 4 May 1861 (quoted in Smalley, *Trollope: Critical Heritage,* 124).

27. Smalley, *Trollope: Critical Heritage,* 199; James, *House of Fiction,* 92; Smalley, *Trollope: Critical Heritage,* 121, 123, 126.

28. *Saturday Review,* 3 February 1866 (quoted in Skilton, *Anthony Trollope,* 56); James, *House of Fiction,* 89. James, too, was sometimes gendered hyperfeminine. W. L. Courtney, who considered "literary reserve" a "feminine note" and a "real weakness," complains of James's reserve "trembl[ing] on the edge of the feeble" as well as of his "inertia and languor in style" (*The Feminine Note in Fiction,* xxx).

29. James, *House of Fiction,* 92.

30. Quoted in Skilton, *Anthony Trollope,* 56; James, *House of Fiction,* 112.

James R. Kincaid, *The Novels of Anthony Trollope* (Oxford: Clarendon, 1977), finds James's appreciation of Trollope to be disingenuous; indeed, he blames James for Trollope's second-rate status, since it was "primarily James" who "identified" Trollope "with a tradition" that the former "wished to reject" (7).

It is certainly true that James rescues Trollope from total feminization only by stressing his thorough mastery of the feminine:

> His great, his inestimable merit was a complete appreciation of the usual. This gift . . . would naturally be found in a walk of literature in which the feminine mind has laboured so fruitfully. Women are delicate and patient observers . . . They feel and perceive the real with a kind of personal tact, and their observations are recorded in a thousand delightful volumes. Trollope, therefore, with his eyes comfortably fixed on the familiar, the actual, was far from having invented a new category; his great distinction is that in resting there his vision took in so much of the field. (*House of Fiction,* 91)

George Meredith is more honestly appreciative of Trollope's feminine ways: he produces "a satire so cleverly interwoven with the story, that every incident and development renders it more pointed and telling . . . Mr. Trollope entrusts all this to the individuals of his story" (quoted in Skilton, *Anthony Trollope,* 6). Yet, despite such appreciation, Meredith nevertheless feels compelled to defend Trollope's masculinity: Trollope is "a caustic and vigorous writer, who can draw *men* and women, and tell a story that *men* and women can read"; he has "given us a novel that *men* can enjoy" (emphasis added).

31. James, *House of Fiction,* 111. James also comments on Trollope's lack of imagination (92) and irony (93). Furthermore, James recognizes that Trollope's humor (in feminine fashion) depends on its reducing satire and irony to mere "elements" in his work rather than developing them (in masculine fashion) as comprehensive strategies (92).

32. Richard Holt Hutton, quoted in Smalley, *Trollope: Critical Heritage,* 506–7. Victoria Glendinning, in her perspicacious and delightfully engaging *Trollope* (London: Pimlico, 1993), also frequently describes her subject's humor as suggestively feminine: "quiet humour and (good-natured) satire" (214); "romantic comedy . . . shot through with desolation" (136); "outrage like a chained bull behind his comedy" (221).

33. Skilton, *Anthony Trollope,* 32. Several studies published around the time that Skilton lodged this complaint (in 1972) have proved significant in redressing Trollope's critical neglect. Among these are J. Hillis Miller, *The Disappearance of God: Five Nineteenth-Century*

Writers (Cambridge, MA: Harvard University Press, 1963); Robert M. Polhemus, *The Changing World of Anthony Trollope* (Berkeley: University of California Press, 1968); Ruth apRoberts, *The Moral Trollope* (Athens: Ohio University Press, 1971); and Kincaid, *The Novels of Anthony Trollope.*

34. Limiting my discussion of Trollope to a handful of his popular early novels, though it may give unfair weight to one aspect of a very long and fruitful career, serves more than a practical purpose. Given his productivity, any discussion of Trollope must be selective, and the Barsetshire novels I consider, being among the most popular, are, from the point of view of their historical reception, also among the most representative: *Barchester Towers* (1857; rpt. New York: New American Library, 1963); *Doctor Thorne* (1858; rpt. Oxford: Oxford University Press, 1980); *Framley Parsonage* (1861; rpt. Harmondsworth: Penguin, 1984); *The Small House at Allington* (1864; rpt. Oxford: Oxford University Press, 1980); and *The Last Chronicle of Barset* (1867; rpt. Harmondsworth: Penguin, 1967).

35. In a letter to her publisher, George Smith, dated 23 December 1859, Gaskell comments that a story she is working on, while "not good enough for the C. M. [Cornhill Magazine] . . . might be good enough for H. W. [Household Words]." The former was edited by Thackeray; the latter, by Dickens. Although Gaskell apparently thought highly of the *Cornhill,* she had more than mixed feelings about its editor: "intended *for C.M.;* but delayed because of extreme dislike to writing for Mr T" (*EGL,* 595).

Gaskell's vexed working relationship with Dickens is discussed at greater length in my Chap. 4.

36. 1 March 1860, *EGL,* 602. Eliot, too, though somewhat less enthusiastically, expresses her gratitude for the restorative effect of Trollope's novels: "[T]hey are like pleasant public gardens, where people go for amusement and, whether they think it or not, get health as well" (Eliot to Trollope, 23 October 1863; quoted in Skilton, *Anthony Trollope,* 24). Oliphant also numbered among Trollope's fans, though she finds him to be weakest on the psychology of women: "It seems to be Mr. Trollope's idea that, so long as he is faithful to her, a woman can see no blemish in a man whom she has once loved . . . Women are neither so passive nor so grateful as they are made out to be" (Smalley, *Trollope: Critical Heritage,* 285).

37. If contemporary critics noted Trollope's debt to Thackeray, modern ones stress his imitation of Austen: see James Kincaid's Introduction to *Doctor Thorne,* xii, and Christopher Herbert, *Anthony Trollope and Comic Pleasure,* 165. Curiously, both Kincaid and Polhemus, while they perceive Trollope as questioning the "enclosed, almost idyllic milieu" (Polhemus, *The Changing World of Anthony Trollope,* 8) he shares with Austen, assume that she unambivalently "confirm[s]" it (Kincaid, *The Novels of Anthony Trollope,* 53).

Jane Nardin, *He Knew She Was Right: The Independent Woman in the Novels of Anthony Trollope* (Carbondale: Southern Illinois University Press, 1989), agrees that the earlier novels keep to this conservative narrative pattern, but she argues for a new feminist awareness in Trollope's plots, beginning with *SMAA.*

38. There is clearly a marked difference between treating anxiety as a joking matter and transforming anxiety into a joke. Trollope's mocking of the damsel in distress (quoted below) contrasts strikingly with Anne Brontë's in *The Tenant of Wildfell Hall,* quoted in my Preface. Whereas both recognize the suffering of the heroine, Brontë's joke recontextualizes the threatening situation so as to empower the heroine momentarily, while Trollope's in

Doctor Thorne encourages us—by locating his sympathy with Frank—to laugh at her quite palpable distress:

> [Seated awkwardly on a donkey as she is being proposed to by Frank, Mary] no longer bit her lips; she was beyond that, and was now using all her efforts to prevent her tears from falling absolutely on her lover's face. She said nothing. She could no more rebuke him now and send him from her than she could encourage him. She could only sit there shaking and crying and wishing she was on the ground. Frank, on the whole, rather liked the donkey. It enabled him to approach somewhat nearer to an embrace than he might have found practicable had they both been on their feet. (396)

39. The clearest exception may be Doctor Thorne, who is at least partially gendered feminine. He has a "manly, and almost womanly tenderness" exhibited not only in his radical childrearing theory that "the principal duty which a parent owed to a child was to make him happy" (*DT,* 41) but, more poignantly, in his willingly becoming a single adoptive parent to his niece, Mary.

40. For discussion of the subversive importance of Trollope's subplots, see Kincaid, *The Novels of Anthony Trollope,* especially 28–31.

41. Herbert, *Trollope and Comic Pleasure,* 98, 82. Despite Trollope's admirable ability to enter into the feelings of a "tormented woman with wholeheartedness and precision" (xix), Glendinning points out that he "continually fell back on an ideal of feminine helplessness, which flattered his sense of manliness" (*Trollope,* 239). "He understood absolutely about the death-in-life of middle-class female idleness, yet his terror of women abandoning the domesticity which sustained men over-ruled his intelligent sympathy" (446). In life, there was "no ambivalence . . . about his belief that masculine chivalry and babies were a fair exchange for women's subordinate role" (450).

42. Herbert, *Trollope and Comic Pleasure,* 165, 29. Herbert argues that Trollope is the only true comic novelist of the Victorian era—the legitimate heir to the English comic tradition of the Elizabethan and Restoration theater—although he also recognizes Trollope's occasional deployment of a humorous rhetoric characterized by its inconspicuousness, its recognition of the "childlike," its "affectionate mocking," and its "sympathy" (166).

43. It is this sort of detached affect that permits us to find funny the Mirvanesque scene in *The Small House at Allington,* where the indignant Mr. Lupex throttles Cradell for flirting with the former's wife (*SMAA,* 450).

44. Quoted in Skilton, *Anthony Trollope,* 119. Ironically, although he is critically effeminized, Trollope is nonetheless incapable, according to Hutton, of creating fully developed female characters, due to a deficiency of imagination (a masculine attribute). As a contemporary reviewer noted, "Trollope has never encouraged his readers to suppose that he himself has more than a ball-room acquaintance with his own heroines" (quoted in *Trollope: Critical Heritage,* 122).

45. On the avuncular quality of Trollope's narrator, see James, *House of Fiction,* 105: Trollope's "attitude throughout toward the youthful feminine" is "full of good humour" and "fatherly indulgence" that is "almost" but not quite "motherly sympathy." "He is evidently always more or less in love with" his heroine, but if "a lover, he was a paternal lover; as competent as a father" (109).

46. Despite the fact that Trollope's narrator enjoins us to fall in love with Lily (*SMAA*, 14), Trollope himself is on record in his *Autobiography* (Berkeley: University of California Press, 1947) as having resisted the temptation:

> In the love with which she [Lily Dale] has been greeted I have hardly joined with much enthusiasm, feeling that she is somewhat of a French prig. She became first engaged to a snob, who jilted her; and then, though in truth she loved another man who was hardly good enough, she could not extricate herself sufficiently from the collapse of her first great misfortune to be able to make up her mind to be the wife of one whom, though she loved him, she did not altogether reverence. Prig as she was, she made her way into the hearts of many readers. (150)

47. Juliet McMaster remarks in *Trollope's Palliser Novels: Theme and Pattern* (London: Macmillan, 1978) that "Lily's failure is more the fault of convention than of her own peculiarities: a social rather than a psychological tragedy" (105): see especially 3–19, for a discussion of the "daunting self-abnegation" of several characters in the novel, most notably Lily.

Although constancy may be a Dale family trait, Johnny Eames, in fact, proves more conventionally constant than Lily: Bell says that Lily's "pride would prevent her" from marrying Johnny Eames after having been jilted by Crosbie, "even if her heart permitted it" (*SMAA*, 579).

48. See *SMAA*, 74, 158 (these suggestions are proleptic), and 630, quoted below, in which Lily explains to her mother why she cannot marry Johnny Eames:

> "I should commit a great sin,—the sin against which women should be more guarded than against any other. In my heart I am married to that other man. I gave myself to him, and loved him, and rejoiced in his love. When he kissed me I kissed him again, and I longed for his kisses. I seemed to live only that he might caress me. All that time I never felt myself to be wrong,—because he was all in all to me. I was his own. That has been changed,—to my great misfortune; but it cannot be undone or forgotten. I cannot be the girl I was before he came here. There are things that will not have themselves buried and put out of sight, as though they had never been. I am as you are, mamma,—widowed."

49. In *The Last Chronicle of Barset*, Lily herself represents her relationship with Mrs. Dale as one that, while it retains elements of mother-infant union, has also acquired marital features: "'She always knows, by instinct, when I am coming. You must understand now that you are among us, that mamma and I are not mother and daughter, but two loving old ladies living together'" (116).

50. The narration of *Last Chronicle of Barset* makes explicit the symbiotic closeness that Lily regains with her mother: see 239–40 and 244.

51. Despite his greater political sympathy for the working classes, Trollope's narrator is more scandalized by Amelia Roper's looking out for the main chance than he is by Lady Alexandrina's. See 147–48, where the narrator not only expresses his scorn for Amelia's social aspirations but betrays a slight sadistic pleasure in doing so.

52. Trollope's failure of sympathy here is particularly disappointing when we simultaneously consider his own "self-flagellating nature," his extensive "practice in bearing pain"

(42), and what Trollope himself confessed was "'a certain weakness in my own character, which I may call a craving for love'" (Glendinning, *Trollope,* 88, 42, 296).

53. Edith Wharton, *A Backward Glance* (New York: Charles Scribner's Sons, 1933), 173. Subsequent page references to this edition are noted parenthetically in the text.

54. Edith Wharton, *The Fruit of the Tree* (1907; rpt. London: Virago, 1984), 12.

55. James letter to Wharton, 26 October 1900 (quoted in Lyall H. Powers, ed., *Henry James and Edith Wharton: Letters: 1900–1915* [New York: Charles Scribner's Sons, 1990]), 32. The portrait of Wharton laughing is attributed to Gaillard Lapsley (quoted in Percy Lubbock, *Portrait of Edith Wharton* [London: Jonathan Cape, 1945]), 76.

56. Lubbock, *Portrait of Edith Wharton,* 76.

57. I'm grateful to Priscilla Ferguson for pointing out to me that Flaubert often called George Sand "Cher Maître" (an epithet particularly resonant considering that the James-Wharton correspondence discloses a mutual, somewhat prurient interest in Sand's sexual history).

Lynn S. Chancer, *Sadomasochism and Everyday Life,* argues that the sadomasochistic dynamic is based on mutual striving for symbiosis; see especially 71–76. In their "closest of unions," James customarily played the sadistic role, Wharton the masochistic.

58. Letter dated 4 October 1907 (quoted in Powers, *Henry James and Edith Wharton,* 74).

59. Quoted in Millicent Bell, *Edith Wharton & Henry James: The Story of Their Friendship* (New York: George Braziller, 1965), 258.

60. Letter of 9 May 1909 (Powers, *Henry James and Edith Wharton,* 112). Quoted more fully below, this letter also makes clear James's Olympian image of Wharton:

> Dearest Edith!,
>
> Your letter gives me extraordinary pleasure—for my poor efforts don't meet with universal favour. Two American "high-class (heaven save the mark!) periodicals" declined poor John Berridge & the Princess—which was a good deal comme qui dirait declining *you;* since bien assurement the whole thing *reeks* with you—& with Cook, & with *our* Paris (Cooks & yours & mine): so no wonder it's "really good." [and then as an afterthought squeezed between the lines: "It wd. never have been written without you—& without 'her'"—meaning Hortense the car] At any rate, as I seem to be living on into evil days, your exquisite hand of reassurance & comfort scatters celestial balm—& makes me de nouveau believe a little in myself, which is what I infinitely need & yearn for.

It is worth mentioning perhaps that Wharton's collection of poems Olympically entitled *Artemis to Actaeon* was also published in 1909.

Henry James, "The Velvet Glove," *The Complete Tales of Henry James,* vol. 12, ed. Leon Edel (London: Rupert Hart-Davis, 1964), 233–65. Subsequent page references to this edition are noted parenthetically within the text.

61. Leon Edel, *Henry James: The Master: 1906–1916* (New York: Avon, 1978), 356. Edel, indeed, maintains that James, "Master and law-giver," apparently wrote "the tale in an open spirit of mockery" (354). See also Adeline R. Tintner, "James's Mock Epic: 'The Velvet Glove,' Edith Wharton, and Other Late Tales," *Modern Fiction Studies* 17, no. 4 (1972): 483–99; R. W. B. Lewis, *Edith Wharton: A Biography* (New York: Harper and Row, 1975), 254. In contrast, Allen F. Stein, in "The Hack's Progress: A Reading of James's 'The

Velvet Glove," *Essays in Literature* 1, no. 1 (Spring 1974): 219–26, argues that the story makes fun of the Berridge character, "a self-deluding hack" (219).

62. The first two quotations are familiar salutations in James's letters to Wharton; the others are quoted in Edel, *Henry James: The Master* (463, 352). The remark on the infirmity of *The Fruit of the Tree* was made to Mary Cadwalader Jones, quoted in Powers, *Henry James and Edith Wharton,* 79. To Wharton herself James wrote in a letter of 24 November 1907: "I have read The Fruit meanwhile with acute appreciation—the liveliest admiration & sympathy. I find it a thing of the highest and finest ability & lucidity & of a great deal (though not perhaps of a completely) superior art. Where my qualifications would come in would be as to the terrible question of the composition & conduct of the thing . . . The element of good writing in it is enormous—I perpetually catch you at writing admirably (though I do think here, somehow, of George Eliotizing a little more frankly than ever . . .)"; (quoted in Powers, 78).

63. In *A Backward Glance,* Wharton records that the first two times she was in company with James she dressed to dazzle him: "How can I make myself pretty enough for him to notice me? Well—this time I had a new hat; *a beautiful new hat!* I was almost sure it was becoming, and I felt that if he would only tell me so I might at last pluck up courage to blurt out my admiration for "Daisy Miller" and "The Portrait of a Lady" [as the Princess does with regard to Berridge's books]. But he noticed neither the hat nor its wearer" (172).

64. Lewis, *Edith Wharton,* 125.

65. Letters to Sara Norton [n.d.] and to A. John Hugh-Smith, 16 May 1909, quoted in Bell, *Edith Wharton and Henry James,* 136. Bell asserts that Wharton actually "felt a proprietary pleasure" in James's tale (135).

66. See Edel, *Henry James,* 359. Not only was Wharton extraordinarily generous and thoughtful about James generally (for example, giving him money conduited through Scribner's as an added advance), but she responded to the mockery of "The Velvet Glove" by helping to see into print Morton Fullerton's tribute to James: "Thus in an ironic way Edith Wharton reversed the situation of 'The Velvet Glove' and secretly repaid James with kindness. If the Master hesitated to 'puff' his acolytes, the acolytes could, with energy and sincerity, laud the Master" (Edel, *Henry James,* 420).

67. Wharton, *Fruit,* 33; Edith Wharton, *The Custom of the Country* (New York: Charles Scribner's Sons, 1913), 272; subsequent page references appear parenthetically in the text. There is, furthermore, a quiet joke directed toward James when Henry Langhope, sharing James's Christian name and recalling Lambert Strether, is told by the Maria Gostrey-like Mrs. Ansell: "'There's one thing you've never seen yet, Henry'" (*Fruit,* 593).

Chapter 19 of *The Custom of the Country* is largely devoted to a description of the Jamesian Charles Bowen, a "sociologist" (280) by imaginative inclination, who finds "endless entertainment" (275) in "the fantastic spectacle" (276) of "human nature's passion for the factitious, its incorrigible habit of imitating the imitation" (273): "During some forty years' perpetual exercise of his perceptions he had never come across anything that gave them the special titillation produced by the sight of the dinner-hour at the Nouveau Luxe." Bowen, who is "amused by Undine's arts" (280) and intellectually intrigued by her conduct, attributes her characterological failings to "the custom of the country" (206): the reifying treatment by American men of their women.

Wharton also borrowed heavily from James's "Julia Bride" (1908) for the location and plot complications of chap. 9 of *Custom of the Country.*

68. Edith Wharton, "George Eliot," review of Leslie Stephen, *George Eliot* (New York: Macmillan, 1902), in *The Bookman* 15 (May 1902): 247, 248, 250.

69. Seeing, at least since Rousseau, has been articulated as a feminine trait: "The social relationship of the sexes is an admirable thing. This partnership produces a moral person of which the woman is the eye" and "the man the arm"; he's good at "general principles," while she has "a mind for details" (*Emile: or, On Education,* trans. Allan Bloom, 377).

70. Quoted in Edel, *Henry James,* 418–19, 448.

71. Edel, *Henry James,* 38.

72. In *Epistemology of the Closet* (Berkeley: University of California Press, 1990), Eve Sedgwick touches on the notion of a homoerotic or homosexual poetics, characterized by a "bitchy" quality (192), a "proneness to parody and to unpredictable sadism" (192), and, using "The Beast in the Jungle" to illustrate her point, a "reifying grammar of periphrasis and preterition" (203).

Others have also noted a homoerotic component in James's fiction and correspondence. See, for example, Powers, who, in his introduction to the James-Wharton correspondence *(Henry James and Edith Wharton),* comments that James "clearly wanted a dash of the piquant, an element not physical but inescapably erotic" (13) in his relationships "with various attractive young men who admired him and whom he found bright and interesting" (12). William Morton Fullerton—Wharton's onetime, famously bisexual lover—was among the first of James's male followers: "Their friendship was further sustained from 1907 partly by their shared affection for Edith Wharton." In other words, the erotic element in James's relationship with Wharton was primarily voyeuristic: "[H]e was always interested in Wharton's affairs of the heart, actual or potential"; they "gave James a good deal of stimulation and gratification; it 'completed' the special relationship be enjoyed with Edith Wharton" (17).

On James's hysteria and its homoerotic content, Wharton herself bears witness. In a letter to Fullerton, she writes that James's chronic stomach problems "& the solitude of Rye—had brought on nervous depression, with 'almost hysterical' ups & downs" (199).

> He told me that, when he was in one of his "states," he had to take bromide to keep from "shaking all over"; & [his nephew] Harry James, who seems un esprit pondere, & judicious in the choice of words, used "hysterical" in its exact sense, I imagine.
>
> Henry asked for you with such tenderness that you wd write him a little word of congratulation & souhaite if you could hear the inflexion of his voice as he said: "Down there, alone at Rye, I used to lie & think of Morton, & *ache* over him." (R. W. B. Lewis and Nancy Lewis, eds, *The Letters of Edith Wharton* [New York: Collier Books, 1988], 200)

73. Henry James, "Daisy Miller," *Great Short Works of Henry James* (New York: Harper and Row, 1966), 43, 44, 42. Subsequent page references to this edition are parenthetically noted in the text.

74. This uncomfortable association between the narrator/ ethnographer and the population under investigation occurs as well in the descriptions of the social organization of St. Ogg's in *The Mill on the Floss,* especially in its rendering of the Dodson tribe. In both Eliot and Wharton, not only is the ethnographer's disinterested stance compromised by mordant humor, but the struggle for distance from a people to whom the narrator is affectively

bound and who are recorded with more abhorrence than affection suggests itself as a source of masochistic pain.

75. Letters to Howard Sturgis and Mary Cadwalader Jones (quoted by Edel, *Henry James*, 463–64).

76. "Dearest Edith" is James's usual epistolary salutation; "the Devastating Angel," quoted here by Edel, *Henry James* (450), is just one of many such references to Wharton as an Angel of Devastation; "beautiful and terrible" occurs in a letter to Wharton (Powers, *Henry James and Edith Wharton*, 50); and "Firebird" and "eagle"—both frequently used by James in letters to friends such as Howard Sturgis and Walter Berry— are here quoted from Edel, 460.

Critics who have remarked on the similarity of Wharton and her heroine include Lewis, *Edith Wharton*, and Cynthia Griffin Wolff, *A Feast of Words: The Triumph of Edith Wharton* (New York: Oxford University Press, 1977).

77. Quoted in Edel, *Henry James*, 352; quoted in Powers, *Henry James and Edith Wharton*, 125; quoted in Edel, 352.

78. Lewis observes that James "grew positively alarmed" by Wharton's "energy, her curious insatiable zest for life, and what seemed to him her 'fantastic freedom.' He felt inexplicably threatened by her, to the point where he missed the *capacity for suffering* which gentler-minded and less probing friends perceived rather quickly" (247; emphasis added). Lewis intimates, in other words, that though Wharton participated in James's mockery of her, she nevertheless found it deeply wounding.

79. On the reader's vexed relationship to Undine, see Cynthia Griffin Woolf, *A Feast of Words*, 233. The association of Undine with her legendary, famously soulless, namesake is made explicit several times in the text, by both the narrator and Ralph. Although Undine is sometimes figured here as a swan ("[S]he was always doubling and twisting on herself, and every movement she made seemed to start at the nape of her neck" [6]), Fouque's version of the myth (in which Undine is a water nymph) more fully informs Wharton's text, as Rachel Mann has demonstrated to me.

80. As Wharton's narrator observes in *The Fruit of the Tree*, identification is often at odds with pity: "[I]t was characteristic of Justine [the heroine] that where she sympathized least she sometimes pitied most" (227).

Readers like Bell, who see *The Custom of the Country* as a "picaresque comedy," can only do so by ignoring the difficulties of identification that Undine presents and by relegating Ralph's "subordinate tragedy" to a parenthetical fate: "Undine Spragg, the barbarian invader from the Middle West, rises . . . as she penetrates successive social elevations, and picaresque comedy emerges from her history (though there is a subordinate tragedy resulting for her victim, Ralph Marvel)" (*Edith Wharton and Henry James*, 278).

81. *Henry James: Literary Criticism, Essays on Literature, American Writers, English Writers*, ed. Leon Edel (New York: Library of America, 1984), 155. I am indebted to Eric Haralson for bringing this passage to my attention.

82. Sedgwick's comment about May Bartram of "Beast in the Jungle" is suggestively applicable to Wharton: "She seems the woman (don't we all know them?) who has not only the most delicate nose for but the most potent attraction toward men who are at crises of homosexual panic" (209).

Woolf (*A Feast of Words*) also addresses what might be called Wharton's "fag hag" status: "Possibly Wharton felt more comfortable with people whose notions of 'masculine' and 'feminine' were more flexible than those of society at large. Many of her closest friends were men whose sexual preferences tended to blur: Henry James, Howard Sturgis, Morton Fullerton," among others—men who found, as did Percy Lubbock, that "'she had a very feminine consciousness and a very masculine mind.'" Yet "intractabilities of language often betrayed the delicacy of her position all too well": Morton Fullerton, for example, "addressed her as 'cher ami'" (257).

83. Beth Kowaleski-Wallace argues in "The Reader as Misogynist in *The Custom of the Country,*" *Modern Language Studies* (Winter 1991): 45–53, that the reader, like Ralph Marvel, denies Undine her right to pursue her own desire and thus unfairly condemns her for her "failed maternity" (45) in relation not only to her son and husband but to the reader as well.

Chapter Three

1. Jane Austen, *Mansfield Park* (1814; rpt. Harmondsworth: Penguin, 1966), 75. Subsequent page references to this edition appear parenthetically in the text.

2. Austen, *Persuasion* (1818; rpt. New York: Norton, 1958), 68. Subsequent page references to this edition appear parenthetically in the text.

3. Susan Morgan, *In the Meantime: Character and Perception in Jane Austen's Fiction* (Chicago: University of Chicago Press, 1980), 5; and Paul Pickrel, "Lionel Trilling and *Mansfield Park*" (*SEL*, 27 [1987]): 618.

4. Most critics have overlooked this affective distinction of Austen's so-called irony. For example, Lionel Trilling, whose essay *"Mansfield Park"* in his *The Opposing Self* (New York: Harcourt, 1955), 181–202, is still a benchmark in Austen criticism, considers the peculiar, uncomic, (unmasculine) use of humor in the problem novels as evidence of a globalizing ironic perspective. See also Marvin Mudrick, *Jane Austen: Irony as Defense and Discovery* (Princeton: Princeton University Press, 1952). In *Jane Austen: Women, Politics and the Novel* (Chicago: University of Chicago Press, 1988)—a book I find otherwise enormously persuasive—Claudia L. Johnson writes, "Janeites confessed and unconfessed have lamented the ungratifying humorlessness of *Mansfield Park*" (94).

5. My discussion will henceforth consider only the humor of *Mansfield Park* and *Persuasion*. Although my argument about the gendermarked nature of the humor and its effect on the narrator-heroine relationship in the problem novels could (and in some sense does) include *Sense and Sensibility,* its pair of heroines complicates its homology to the other two novels. Because the narrative splits the heroine into two—one laughable, one not—the close, stable identification between Elinor and the narrator is undisturbed by the introduction of humor, which is heaped rather more lavishly and less mercifully upon Marianne than upon any other Austen heroine. Consequently, even when Elinor is sometimes susceptible to the overwrought romanticism she derides in her mother and sister, she is less narratively mocked than either Fanny or Anne. As a textual presence, furthermore, Elinor is even less distinct from the narrator than they: indeed, her humorous evaluations of Marianne, Mrs. Dashwood, and Willoughby, and her smiling at what would otherwise be an occasion of personal pain and frustration (such as her dealings with Lucy Steele)—are barely distinguishable in form and content, tone and import from the narrative humor. Compare Elizabeth's wit in *Pride and Prejudice,* which is sharper and more direct than her narrator's; Elizabeth's smiles work to hide contempt rather than to overcome frustration.

6. See, for example, Trilling, *"Mansfield Park"*; Marilyn Butler, *Jane Austen and the War of Ideas;* and Alistair Duckworth, *The Improvement of the Estate: A Study of Jane Austen's Novel* (Baltimore: Johns Hopkins University Press, 1971).

7. When the novel opens, Julia is 12, Maria 13, Edmund 16, and Tom 17. By the time the Crawfords arrive they are 20, 21, 24, and 25, respectively.

8. Mary Crawford's confusion as to whether Fanny is "out" or not—a confusion that fills three pages of text (81–83)—indicates the degree to which Fanny's adolescent status is in question. The fact, too, that Fanny, when grouped with Mary and Edmund at Sotherton (125, 127) and at the window at Mansfield (135, 139), in no way interferes with their courtship (cf. Julia, Maria, and Henry) suggests that she is considered too young to be an equal participant or a serious hindrance to their conversation and flirtation, especially since Fanny's class difference is not an issue for Edmund or Mary as it is for the others.

For discussion of Fanny's childishness, see Paula Marantz Cohen, "Stabilizing the Family System at Mansfield Park," *ELH* 54 (1987): 669–93; Jane McDonnell, "'A Little Spirit of Independence': Sexual Politics and the Bildungsroman in *Mansfield Park*," *Novel* 17 (1984): 197–214; and Louise Flavin, "*Mansfield Park:* Free Indirect Discourse and the Psychological Novel," *Studies in the Novel* 19 (1987): 137–59.

9. Tanner, for example, maintains that Fanny "is never, ever, wrong. Jane Austen, usually so ironic about her heroines, in this instance vindicates Fanny Price without qualification" (*MP,* "Introduction," 8). For a discussion of Austen's irony toward Fanny, see Martin Price, *Forms of Life: Character and Moral Imagination in the Novel* (New Haven: Yale University Press, 1983).

It is worth remembering that Elinor Dashwood is very seldom treated ironically either, though being a wit herself, she is implicated in the narrative humor in ways that Fanny is not.

10. Other readers have noted the Cinderella reference as well. See, for example, Margaret Lenta, "Androgyny and Authority in *Mansfield Park*," *Studies in the Novel* 15 (1983): 169–82; D. W. Harding, "Introduction," *Persuasion* (1818; rpt. Harmondsworth: Penguin 1965): 7–26; and McDonnell, "'A Little Spirit of Independence.'"

11. Clearly, the fact of Fanny's being a farmed-out poor relation, subject to Mrs. Norris's continual accusations of presumption and ingratitude, has at least as much to do with forming her character and her low self-esteem as does her training as a middle-class daughter, with its insistence on duty and selflessness. However, since middle-class ideology conceptually infantilizes middle-class women as well as the working classes, expects both groups to accept and abide by the structures of authority that deny them recognition of their own desire, and judges (or reifies) them according to their usefulness, the inferiority that Fanny feels on account of her class shares its etiology with the inferiority she experiences on account of her gender. For a discussion of how "the new ideology of bourgeois competition merely provides a useful vocabulary for [familial] hostility" (59), see Tara Ghoshal Wallace's *Jane Austen and Narrative Authority* (New York: St. Martin's Press, 1995).

12. Henry's love for Fanny is suspect, however, not only because of his elopement with Maria but because of its origins in a game of deception. Like Laclos's Vicomte in *Les Liaisons Dangereuses,* Henry is attracted by the heroine's virtuous innocence ("It would be something to be loved by such a girl, to excite the first ardors of her young unsophisticated mind!" [245]), titillated by Fanny's pure, unguarded, blushing, eye-dilating affection for her brother (244) and aroused by her resistance ("A little difficulty to overcome, was no evil to

Henry Crawford. He rather derived spirits from it. He had been apt to gain hearts too easily. His situation was new and animating" [326]).

For discussion of the incestuous aspects of male regard for Fanny, including Henry's, see Johanna Smith, "'My Only Sister Now': Incest in *Mansfield Park,*" *Studies in the Novel* 19 (1987): 1–15; Glenda A. Hudson, *Sibling Love and Incest in Jane Austen's Fiction* (London: Macmillan, 1992); Johnson, *Jane Austen,* 116–17, argues in a similar vein.

13. For a discussion of the importance of gratitude in eighteenth-century moral theory, see Johnson, *Equivocal Beings.*

Gratitude is also the fillip to Edmund's early attentions to Fanny: "[H]er countenance and few artless words fully conveyed all their gratitude and delight, and her cousin began to find her an interesting object" (53). See Morgan, *In the Meantime,* for a discussion of gratitude as the basis of romantic love for many of Austen's characters (Elizabeth's love for Darcy, Marianne's for Brandon, Henry's for Catherine).

14. McDonnell, "'A Little Spirit of Independence,'" considers "the very qualities which most readers find so distressing in Fanny . . . —her shrinking temperament, her passive, subservient nature, her very 'goodness'"—to be "the psychological result of profound neglect" (202). See also Bernard J. Paris, *Character and Conflict in Jane Austen's Novels: A Psychological Approach* (Detroit: Wayne State University Press, 1978) for a diagnostic discussion of Fanny's personality as shaped by her experience as an abused child.

15. Note Mrs. Norris's rather extended comment (165) on the ingratitude of the Jacksons, whom she considers beholden to Sir Thomas for their employment as servants, as she herself is less admittedly indebted to his charity, and whom she accuses of freeloading—a sin of which she is continually guilty.

16. Although William certainly cares for Fanny, the reason for his interest lies in their history of shared early affection, not in his admiration of her passivity. His investment in her (which is evidently less than hers in him) is, moreover, not as decisive for the narrative as that of Sir Thomas, Henry, or Edmund (nor is it tinged with the erotic component that characterizes theirs).

17. Although passivity may theoretically be an ideal of feminine behavior, when practiced in financially straitened circumstances it is intolerable to a bourgeois society. Even though Lady Bertram is Mrs. Price's sister and much like her, her extreme passivity is culturally appropriate (if narratively mocked), being located in a petty aristocratic home with ample means of supporting an efficient domestic staff, while Mrs. Price's similar passivity incurs vituperation.

18. For a discussion of Fanny's relationship to the Antiguan slave trade, "the sinister aspects of benevolence," and the issue of gratitude, see Johnson, *Jane Austen* (107); for a more extensive treatment of Austen and imperialism, see Maaja A. Stewart, *Domestic Realities and Imperial Fictions: Jane Austen's Novels in Eighteenth-Century Contexts* (Athens: University of Georgia Press, 1993).

19. Fanny, in contrast to Mary, is so "incumbered by refinement" (243) as to be "little equal to Rebecca's puddings" (404) or to the "half-cleaned" state of the cutlery and plates at Portsmouth and is consequently unable to eat at table. Her looks suffer accordingly.

20. For a discussion of Fanny as mirror to Henry, Edmund, and Sir Thomas, see Smith, "'My Only Sister Now.'"

21. Trilling in *"Mansfield Park"* views Fanny's eagerness to please as an expression of her religious belief, her moral "struggling against discontent and envy" (104), and her devotion

to principle: "Fanny is a Christian heroine" (188). While granting that Fanny's desire to please may well be bolstered by her religiosity, I would argue that its origins lie in a more basic desire for parental affection and approval—that is, that her desire for maternal affection (and paternal approval) are at the heart of her desire for the Father. For a discussion of the cultural pressure of Evangelicalism on Austen and *Mansfield Park,* see Oliver MacDonagh's *Jane Austen: Real and Imagined Worlds* (New Haven: Yale University Press, 1991), 1–19.

22. "For her own gratification she could have wished that something might be acted, for she had never seen even half a play" (*MP,* 156). Even though she knows Sir Thomas would disapprove of amateur theatricals at Mansfield, and therefore disapproves herself (she also objects to the particular play on moral grounds), there's no indication that her principled opposition would interfere with her watching the staged performance: it certainly doesn't interfere with her viewing—and participating in—the rehearsals.

23. For a thought-provoking discussion of General Tilney as a version of the tyrannical father popular in turn-of-the-century gothic novels, see Johnson, *Jane Austen,* who considers Sir Thomas as an emblem of the Sublime. As the narrative humor emphasizes, there are clearly parallels between the awful power of the Sublime and the power of the parental tyrant.

24. Fear of her father's tyranny is what drives Julia into eloping: "[H]ad not her sister's conduct burst forth as it did, and her increased dread of her father and of home, on that event—imagining its certain consequence to herself would be greater severity and restraint—made her hastily resolve on avoiding such immediate horrors at all risks, it is probable that Mr. Yates would never have succeeded" (*MP,* 451).

25. The association of Mansfield with nursing (being "nursed up at Mansfield") and of Portsmouth with weaning (or being "hardened") illustrates how thoroughly Fanny's preoedipal emotional investment has been displaced from the mother-associated environment of the one to the father-dominated society of the other. Mansfield, despite its patriarchal principle, provides Fanny with more luxury and attention to her needs than does Portsmouth, which, conversely, represents her most severe confrontation with the reality principle. Expecting to find a renewal of lost parental love and a sense of belonging upon her visit to Portsmouth, Fanny is vastly disappointed by her parents' indifference. Confronted with the failure of her family romance, Fanny for the first time vigorously and wholeheartedly embraces Mansfield as home, redirecting the energy previously invested in maintaining her cherished, illusory connection to her absent (lost) mother into supporting and idealizing Mansfield. Her return to Mansfield, indeed, signifies in one sense a flight from the reality principle.

26. See Zelda Boyd, "Jane Austen's Must: The Will and the World," *Nineteenth Century Fiction,* 39 (1984): 127–43, for a discussion of Austen's use of modal auxiliaries as a way to establish and embed textual ambiguity.

27. Notice, for example, how Sir Thomas's lengthy confession of guilt about his rearing of Maria and thus his own responsibility in her adultery (occupying five pages of text) concludes with an amusingly caustic comment about Mrs. Norris:

> He had felt her [Mrs. Norris] as an hourly evil, which was so much the worse, as there seemed no chance of its ceasing but with life; she seemed a part of himself, that must be borne forever. To be relieved from her, therefore, was so great

a felicity, that had she not left bitter remembrances behind her, there might have been danger of his learning almost to approve the evil which produced such a good. (*MP,* 450)

28. Austen kept a tally of readers' reactions to *Mansfield Park,* paying particular notice to their opinions of Fanny: for example, "My mother—not liked it so well as P. & P.—Thought Fanny insipid.—Enjoyed Mrs. Norris" and "Anna [her niece] liked it better than P. & P.—but not so well as S. & S.—could not bear Fanny—Delighted with Mrs. Norris, the scene at Portsmouth, & all the humorous parts" (quoted in Southam, *Jane Austen: Critical Heritage,* 1:48–49). Although not all the recorded opinions find Fanny unappealing, they tend to "admire" or to be "pleased" with her character rather than with her personality. With the exception of her brother Frank ("Fanny is a delightful Character! and Aunt Norris is a great favourite of mine"), not only do those who like Mrs. Norris tend to dislike Fanny, but vice versa: "Miss Lloyd perferred [*sic*] it altogether to either of the others.—Delighted with Fanny.—Hated Mrs. Norris."

For examples of modern readers who find Fanny difficult to warm to, see Nina Auerbach, "Jane Austen's Dangerous Charm: Feeling as One Ought about Fanny Price," *Jane Austen: New Perspectives,* Women & Literature, n. s., vol. 3, ed. Janet Todd (New York: Holmes and Meier, 1983), 208–23); and Kingsley Amis, "What Became of Jane Austen? *[Mansfield Park],*" in *Jane Austen: A Collection of Critical Essays,* ed. Ian Watt (Englewood Cliffs, NJ: Prentice Hall, 1963), 141–44.

29. Mary's sense of duty is not only masculine but morally corrupt, as evidenced by its association with the sense of duty attributed to William Elliot by Mrs. Smith in *Persuasion:* "'To do the best for himself,' passed as a duty" (202).

30. D. A. Miller, *Narrative and Its Discontents,* 77, 83. For additional discussion of the narrator's deep ambivalence about Mary, see Poovey, *The Proper Lady* (220).

31. For a catalogue of points of comparison between Fanny and Mary, see Pickrel, "Lionel Trilling and *Mansfield Park.*" We might add that while Fanny is the slave to all, Mary is not even "the slave of opportunity" (353), and that whereas Fanny is persistently asexual (despite being eroticized by her male admirers), Mary, precociously inducted into sexuality (thanks to her exposure to the Admiral), is overwhelmingly sensual.

32. For an important, extended discussion of Fanny's exemplary propriety and its titillating aspect, see Poovey, *The Proper Lady,* especially pages 15–30.

33. D. A. Miller, *Narrative and Its Discontents,* argues in a similar vein (60).

34. Angela Leighton, "Sense and Silences: Reading Jane Austen Again," *Jane Austen: New Perspectives,* 128–40, discusses the suppression of speech in *Sense and Sensibility,* particularly Marianne's, as overdetermined silence; the suppression of laughter in *Mansfield Park* is, I would argue, equally significant.

In contrast to *Mansfield Park,* smiles occur everywhere in *Sense and Sensibility,* particularly Elinor's, as a means of emotional concealment or in an effort to transform anxiety.

35. Fanny is less of a wit than even the self-admittedly witless Edmund (121), two wry observations filtered through the narrator being her closest approximation to a joke (see *MP,* 269, 329).

Although there is never any direct mention of Fanny's laughing, there are two instances where Fanny is present when laughter takes place and is not specifically excluded from participation (279, 288).

36. D. A. Miller points out that this is the most damning evidence against Mary, largely because, being her own text, and free from even narrative commentary, it comes to us and our judgment unfiltered and undistorted by another's interpretation (*Narrative and Its Discontents,* 85–89).

37. Mary, like the narrator, is most recognizable as a voice and laugh. Fanny, for example, detects Mary's unseen presence at Sotherton aurally: "[G]etting quite impatient, she resolved to go in search of them," when "the voice and laugh of Miss Crawford once more caught her ear" (130). Yet unlike the narrator (and to her own undoing), Mary has an obvious bodily presence as well.

38. Fanny is a Romantic heroine as well as a romantic one. Not only does she demonstrate a Romantic resistance to authority on the issue of love in marriage (opposing the will of Sir Bertram in refusing Henry and insisting upon the immorality of a loveless marriage), but following Edmund's instruction, she reveres "the sublimity of Nature" (139). Indeed, her devotion to "nature, inanimate nature" (110) borders on the extravagant (if not the ludicrous), leading her into paroxysms of enthusiasm on the subject of evergreens:

> "I am so glad to see the evergreens thrive!" said Fanny in reply . . . The evergreen!—How beautiful, how welcome, how wonderful the evergreen!—In some countries we know the tree that sheds its leaf is the variety, but that does not make it less amazing, that the same sun should nurture plants differing in the first rule and law of their existence. You will think me rhapsodizing; but when I am out of doors, especially when I am sitting out of doors, I am very apt to get into this sort of wondering strain. One cannot fix one's eyes on the commonest natural production without finding food for a rambling fancy." (222–23)

39. Fanny does experience a kind of *class* conflict about the love she bears Edmund. She would rather die than own the truth of her love for her cousin (317), not because she finds anything improper in eroticizing the (initially) fraternal/maternal love she bears Edmund but because she feels that the difference in class between Mary and herself makes her affection for Edmund "excessive" (271), selfish, and, according to bourgeois standards, morally wrong: "To call or to fancy it a disappointment would be a presumption; for which she had not words strong enough to satisfy her own humility. To think of him as Miss Crawford might be justified in thinking, would in her be insanity."

40. Anne's meritocratic opinions are evident in the following two passages:

> "My idea of good company, Mr. Elliot, is the company of clever, well-informed people, who have a great deal of conversation; that is what I call good company." (150)

> Anne, satisfied at a very early period of Lady Russell's meaning to love Captain Wentworth, had no other alloy to the happiness of her prospects than what arose from the consciousness of having no relations to bestow on him which a man of sense could value. There she felt her own inferiority keenly. The disproportion in their fortune was nothing. (251)

Johnson's political reading of *Persuasion* in *Jane Austen* concentrates in large part on this aspect of Anne's character.

41. Thomas Lockwood in "Divided Attention in *Persuasion,*" *Nineteenth-Century Fiction*

33 (1978): 309–23, goes so far as to assume not only a close identification between narrator and heroine but between author and heroine as well, suggesting (incorrectly, I think) that whatever "distinction" can be made between Austen and Anne "comes wordlessly and tonelessly out of slight differences . . . between a novelist and a character whose interest and sensitivities overlap everywhere without quite matching" (131).

Richard Simpson, one of the best nineteenth-century readers of Austen, notes the importance of Austen's handling of "high-wrought love" in her novels:

> That predestination of love, that preordained fitness, which decreed that one and only one should be the complement and fulfillment of another's being—that except in union with each other each must live miserably, and that no other solace could be found for either than the other's society— she treated as mere moonshine, while she at the same time founded her novels on the assumption of it as a hypothesis. (*Jane Austen: The Critical Heritage*, 1:246)

42. See Fanny Burney, *Cecilia, or Memoirs of an Heiress* (1782; rpt. Oxford: Oxford University Press, 1988), 286.

The narrative reference to Matthew Prior's "Henry and Emma, a Poem, upon the Model of the Nut-brown Maid" (1708), reprinted in *The Literary Works of Matthew Prior*, vol. 1, 2d ed., ed. H. Bunker Wright and Monroe I. Spears (Oxford: Clarendon Press, 1971), 278–300, occurs shortly after Louisa's fall at Lyme. Although she finds herself on the Cobb to be happily, if unexpectedly, appreciated by Wentworth, Anne is later greeted by her former lover in such a way as "must at least convince her that she was valued only as she could be useful to Louisa" (116):

> She endeavored to be composed, and to be just. Without emulating the feeling of an Emma towards her Henry, she would have attended on Louisa with a zeal above the common claims of regard, for his sake.

In Prior's poem, Henry tests his beloved Emma's "eternal constancy" by falsely declaring himself, first, a murderer and, later, in love with another woman. Emma—in over 500 lines of heroic couplets—exhaustively (and ludicrously) proclaims her undying love, regardless of its return, as well as her wish to serve her rival so as to be near Henry.

43. Chapter 12, a few pages of chap. 11, and the canceled penultimate chapter of *Persuasion* exist in manuscript form at the British Library. Although R. W. Chapman's edition (1923), upon which virtually all modern editions are based, is generally considered a model of textual scholarship, it introduces (or permits silently to stand from early published editions) a number of changes to the manuscript text. In the first paragraph of chap. 12, these changes are "young people" for "Young People," "pretty" for "*pretty*," and the elimination of a dash before "be they ever so poor." Although slight, all these changes weaken both the narrative distance and the humor of the passage.

The variants between the manuscript and Chapman's edition of the canceled chapter are especially pronounced. There are over twenty words emphasized (by underlining) in the manuscript that Chapman records without emphasis, as well as a number of capitalized nouns (for example, "Nobody," "Duty") that Chapman renders in lower case. Since in many instances the capitalization or emphasis of a word reinforces the humor of a passage (and sometimes the joke hinges on one of these devices), the manuscript version of the canceled chapter is considerably funnier than Chapman's.

44. That Mrs. Clay's self-seeking manipulative behavior is mistaken by Anne's family as devotion ("'You have been here only to be useful,'" declares Sir Walter [145]) while her own able willingness to serve is repulsed constitutes one of the wryest "jokes" of the novel.

45. I am indebted to Jonathan Arac for having pointed out to me that *Peitho,* attendant to Aphrodite, is a female spirit.

46. Although usefulness tops the list of Harville's "domestic virtues" (252), he is feminine in a number of other ways as well. Not only does he apparently share in childminding duties while on shore, but he eagerly engages in the feminine art of interior decorating (they were "all the ingenious contrivances and nice arrangements of Captain Harville, to turn the actual space to the best possible account" [98]). His lameness marks his "difference," as does the bent of his activity: "[A] mind of usefulness and ingenuity seemed to furnish him with constant employment within. He drew, he varnished, he carpentered, he glued; he made toys for the children, he fashioned new netting-needles and pins with improvements; and if every thing else was done, sat down to his large fishing-net at one corner of the room" (99).

47. In "The Achievement of Persuasion," *Studies in English Literature* 11 (1971): 687–700, Thomas P. Wolfe notes that in this episode Anne's behavior "is not capable of doing justice to the strength of mind it is supposed to represent," and then he excuses the "discrepancy" as "an unavoidable result of [Austen's] undertaking to render a consciousness that perhaps no 'public activity' available to her could adequately express" (696). The discrepancy, however, is critical rather than pardonable. Anne's behavior, being socially circumscribed, *is* incommensurate not only in this scene but throughout *Persuasion* with "the strength of mind it is suppose to represent"—which is precisely the point to which the narrative humor continually returns.

Stuart Tave in *Some Words of Jane Austen* (Chicago: University of Chicago Press, 1973) points out that "one of the improvements of the revised ending" is that it emphasizes her agency: "[I]t is Anne's *action* . . . that brings her and Wentworth together, as it was her action that years earlier had separated them" (284; emphasis added).

48. See, for example, Julia Prewitt Brown, *Jane Austen's Novels: Social Change and Literary Form* (Cambridge, MA: Harvard University Press, 1979), who sees in both this passage and that of "purification and perfume" an "aberrant and uncontrolled" quality that "suggests, perhaps above all, the pathology of disillusion" (134).

Austen, apparently, found even Dick Musgrove's given name exceptionable, if her following joking comment to Cassandra is any indication: "Mr. Richard Harvey's match is put off till he has got a Better Christian name, of which he has great hopes" (*JAL,* 6).

49. Anne's naive assessment of Nurse Rooke ("'Women of that class have great opportunities'" [155])—and her propensity for romanticizing—extends to her fantasized view of sickroom activities:

"What instances must pass before them of ardent, disinterested, self-denying attachment, of heroism, fortitude, patience, resignation—of all the conflicts and all the sacrifices that ennoble us most. A sick chamber may often furnish the worth of volumes."

"Yes," said Mrs. Smith doubtingly, "sometimes it may, though I fear its lessons are not often in the elevated style you describe." (156)

50. Although Anne apparently finds it characterologically impossible to take advantage of "the exquisite relief" of speech, she "could perfectly comprehend" (210) it as well as "the comfort" Mrs. Smith feels in "telling the whole story" of William Elliot's wickedness in "her own way" (211).

51. Park Honan, *Jane Austen: Her Life* (New York: St. Martin's, 1987), 58. For a discussion of "Austen's Francophobia" (33), see Warren Roberts in *Jane Austen and the French Revolution* (New York: St. Martin's, 1980).

52. Rachel Brownstein, "Jane Austen: Irony and Authority," *Last Laughs,* ed. Regina Barreca (New York: Gordon and Breach, 1988), 57.

Mary Evans in *Jane Austen & the State* (London: Tavistock [Methuen], 1987) and Margaret Kirkham in *Jane Austen, Feminism and Fiction* (London: Harvester P, 1983) argue for Austen's radicalism; Johnson in *Jane Austen,* for her progressivism. Recent feminist readings of Austen universally owe a large (not always acknowledged) debt to D. W. Harding's groundbreaking "Regulated Hatred: An Aspect of the Work of Jane Austen," reprinted in *Jane Austen: A Collection of Critical Essays,* ed. Ian Watt (Englewood Cliffs, NJ: Prentice-Hall, 1963), 166–79, which, more than any prior study, has worked to spring Austen from her critical imprisonment as a Johnsonian moralist.

53. See above, n. 21.

CHAPTER FOUR

1. Elizabeth Gaskell, *Cranford/Cousin Phillis* (1853; rpt. Harmondsworth: Penguin, 1976), 167. Subsequent references to this edition appear in the text.

2. Quoted from Thurstan Holland's letter to Charles Elliot Norton (18 November 1865), reprinted in *EGL,* 971.

3. *Cranford, Wives and Daughter, Cousin Phillis, My Fair Ludlow,* and several of Gaskell's short stories—all portraying village life in England of a generation or more before—are commonly referred to as the "Knutsford stories." Knutsford also lends its name to the complete edition of Gaskell's works edited by A. A. Ward.

4. The foremost among these is Lord David Cecil, *Victorian Novelists* (Chicago: University of Chicago Press, 1935). Cecil locates Gaskell's charm in "her femininity" (183), expressed not only in *Cranford* but in her married state and soft facial features.

5. See, for example, Nina Auerbach, *Communities of Women: An Idea in Fiction* (Cambridge, MA: Harvard University Press, 1978), 79.

6. See Introduction n. 25 for helpful studies on married women's legal disabilities in nineteenth-century England.

7. The term *redundant women* was apparently coined by W. R. Greg in his article, "Why Are Women Redundant?" *National Review* (April 1862): 434–60, and popularized by the press. The concept of unmarried women being superfluous or redundant, however, was in circulation long before 1862.

8. Critical thought often stumbles, so to speak, on this issue. Auerbach, for example, in *Communites of Women,* sees Cranford as "an organic community rooted in the past and containing the future, . . . taking what it needs of masculine reality and defeating what remains with its communal faith" (89, 90–91). In so doing, however, she is forced to ignore the humorous treatment of the Amazons almost entirely, though she does see humor when

it is directed at the male characters. See also Coral Lansbury, *Elizabeth Gaskell: The Novel of Social Crisis* (New York: Barnes and Noble, 1975), 83–94, who holds that the "delight of the novel is that a group of middle-aged and old women can order a society to their own pleasure" (93).

On the other hand, Martin Dodsworth—who, in his now notorious "Women without Men in Cranford," *Essays in Criticism* 13 (April 1963): 132–45, has eyes only for Gaskell's "ironic" handling of the Amazons—claims that Cranford is a dystopia filled with bitter women who, "either widows or spinsters, are obliged to do without men, and therefore pretend to be as good as, or even better than, men" (133).

9. Gaskell criticism has lately begun to acknowledge the importance of the narrator. See, for example, Hilary Schor, *Scheherazade of the Market Place: Elizabeth Gaskell and the Victorian Novel* (New York: Oxford University Press, 1992); Tim Dolin, "*Cranford* and the Victorian Collection," *Victorian Studies* 36, no. 2 (Winter 1993): 179–206; and Wendy K. Carse, "A Penchant for Narrative: 'Mary Smith,' in Elizabeth Gaskell's *Cranford*," *Journal of Narrative Technique* 20, no. 3 (Fall 1990): 318–30. For many years, Peter Keating was exceptional in paying particular attention to the narrator, whom he declares in his "Introduction" to *Cranford* (7–30) to be "by no means anonymous. Her individuality is fixed from the beginning and plays an important part in establishing *Cranford*'s distinctive tone" of "ironic distancing and affectionate concern" (14).

10. Historically, there has been a tendency in the criticism to treat the narrator and the author (Mary Smith and Elizabeth Gaskell) as one. Certainly there are parallels between them—like the equation of Knutsford and Manchester with Cranford and Drumble, which Gaskell herself readily acknowledged. Some readers have specifically associated Gaskell's relatives and friends with one or more of the Cranford ladies, the most surprising association being perhaps Auerbach's argument that Charlotte Brontë is the prototype for Miss Matty (*Communications of Wommen*, 91ff.). For other biographical prototypes, see John Geoffrey Sharps, *Mrs. Gaskell's Observation and Invention: A Study of Her Non-Biographic Works* (Fontwell, Sussex: Linden Press, 1970), 483.

Less, however, has been made of the fact that both the narrator and Gaskell are motherless and virtually fatherless, though subject in kind to the claims of a distant father and the surrogate mother(s) of Cranford/Knutsford. Like the narrator who as a child is yearly shipped to the care of Miss Jenkyns, Gaskell was sent as an infant, shortly after her mother's death, to be reared by Aunt Lumb (her mother's older sister, with whom she lived until her marriage). But unlike the narrator, who shuttles from father to surrogate mothers on at least an annual basis (more frequently when she is in demand by one party or the other), Gaskell was consigned to her aunt's care throughout her childhood and early adult life—her stay in Knutsford interrupted only by rare summonses (apparently only two) from her remarried father to his home in London. See Winifred Gérin, *Elizabeth Gaskell* (Oxford: Oxford University Press, 1976), 10–38.

11. Reconciling the dates and numbers of *Cranford* with those in Gaskell's sequel, "The Cage at Cranford" (1863; rpt. *Cranford*, 327–38) reveals that Mary Smith is roughly 12–15 years old in the opening two chapters of *Cranford* (comprising the initial "paper" published in *Household Words*), 18–21 in chap. 3, and 20–23 in the subsequent chapters. Though opinion varies, everyone seems to consider her somewhat younger than her hostesses. Keating, for example, states that Mary Smith is "two generations removed from the Amazons"

("Introduction," 15); Lansbury finds (rather remarkably) "that Mary Smith begins her narration as a young unmarried woman, but at its end has grown old with the women she has chosen to make her friends" (*Elizabeth Gaskell,* 87).

12. Although not self-narrated, Thackeray's *The History of Pendennis* (1848–50; rpt. Harmondsworth: Penguin, 1972) also invests its author's autobiographical details exclusively in the history of the title character rather than subsuming either the details or the personal history in a more widely focused narrative. Significantly, both *Pendennis* and *David Copperfield* (1849–50; rpt. Harmondsworth: Penguin, 1966) completed serialization the year before *Cranford* began publication.

The most striking contrast to Gaskell's absent female narrator is Charlotte Brontë's Jane Eyre, who is more forcefully present in her narrative than either Copperfield or Pendennis is in his and whose intense subjectivity and perspective determine the events related more narrowly than do theirs. Yet, because *Jane Eyre* (1847) is not a comic novel, as *David Copperfield, Pendennis,* or *Cranford* (broadly speaking) are, the issue of the narrating female's presence or absence has different significance. Brontë breaks with literary tradition and feminine decorum in writing a novel that voices female desire and insists on female selfhood. Gaskell, on the other hand, remains within the literary tradition of Dickens and Thackeray, but by exaggerating those aspects that marginalize or erase women and their desires, by literalizing in humor the trope of female voicelessness and invisibility, she undercuts it.

It is worth remembering that the best joke of *Wives and Daughters,* which shares many of its humorous particulars with *Cranford,* is that its plot is set into motion by the resignation of a governess named Miss Eyre.

13. With the exception of the narrator's using it to mention an idiosyncracy or a complaint, the *I* has a selfless quality even when it does occur, functioning more as the vehicle of discussion—and of humor—than as its subject. The *I* is seldom and exclusively used: (1) to report movement in and out of Cranford (for example, "the first visit I paid to Cranford, after I had left it as a residence" [44]); (2) to disclose an idiosyncrasy ("my pet apprehension," "my bugbear fault" [147, 163]); (3) to give voice to a personal complaint ("I was tired of being forgotten" [76]) or observation ("I notice that apathetic people have more quiet impertinence than others" [116]); or (4) to make a joke—a joke often founded on her difference from the Amazons, on her sudden, momentary emergence from the collective ("some of us laughed heartily. *I* did not dare, because I was staying in the house" [47]).

14. The narrator reinforces her bondage to Amazonian whimsy on other occasions by appealing to the reader's judgment. Rather than explicitly pointing out the peculiarities of Cranford customs, the narrator defers to her audience's (presumably sophisticated and urban) sense of propriety : "Do you ever see cows dressed in grey flannel in London?" (44) "Do you make paper paths for every guest to walk upon in London?" (53) This invocation of an urban reader also serves to imply a sociological distinction between the community under discussion (rural, female, "eccentric") and its urbane, knowledgeable, (male) readership.

15. The Amazonian indifference to Mary as an individual personality is poignantly—if associatively—illustrated by the following exchange between Miss Pole and Martha, occurring just after Martha has been asked to describe Lady Glenmire's appearance at church that morning:

"Well, ma'am! is it the little lady with Mrs. Jamieson, you mean? I thought
you would like more to know how young Mrs. Smith was dressed, her being a
bride." (Mrs. Smith was the butcher's wife.)

Miss Pole said, "Good Gracious me! as if we cared about a Mrs. Smith"; but
was silent, as Martha resumed her speech. (117)

It should be noted that. at this point in the text the reader has not yet been notified that
the narrator's last name is also Smith; thus, at least half of what is amusing about Miss Pole's
comment here is accessible only upon a second reading of the novel. The humor is also
enhanced when we recognize the intertextual echo of a similar vignette in *Persuasion:*

"Westgate-buildings!" said he [Sir Walter Elliot]; "and who is Miss Anne Elliot
to be visiting in Westgate-buildings?—A Mrs. Smith. A widow Mrs. Smith,—
and who was her husband? One of the five thousand Mr. Smiths whose names
are to be met with every where." (*P,* 157)

16. See, for example, Florence Nightingale's autobiographical *Cassandra: An Essay,* as well
as Breuer and Freud, *Studies on Hysteria.* Sarah Stickney Ellis's series of conduct books—
Women of England, Their Social Duties and Domestic Habits (London: Fisher, Son and Co.,
1839); *The Wives of England, Their Relative Duties, Domestic Influence, and Social Obliga-*
tions (New York: Appleton, 1843); *The Daughters of England, Their Position in Society, Char-*
acter and Responsibilities (New York: Appleton, 1844); and *The Mothers of England, Their*
Influence and Responsibility (New York: Appleton, 1844)—and others like them gave specific, detailed directions on how to most selflessly serve in the domestic roles available to
women. Ellis's advice is predicated on her belief that female self-interest lies in selflessness,
that women will best be appreciated and therefore be financially provided for, where they
perform the tasks associated with their roles as wife, mother, unmarried daughter most fully
and selflessly. In *Elizabeth Gaskell* (Brighton, Sussex: Harvester Press, 1987), Patsy Stoneman reports that "*The New Female Instructor, or Young Woman's Guide to Domestic Happi-*
ness, Being an Epitome of all the Acquirements Necessary to Form the Female Character . . .
went through six editions between 1811 and 1836, the period of Elizabeth Gaskell's girl-
hood" (53). Furthermore, like Deborah Jenkyns, "*The New Female Instructor* quotes Johnson's letters *verbatim* as models" (89).

17. Captain Brown is also selflessly devoted to the care of his family. He is, in fact, the
best mother in Cranford. However, he is not called upon to make the kind of particularly
feminine sacrifices that his daughters are. He is neither worn down by anxious care, as is
his daughter, in taking care of his family, nor put in the position of having to reject a lover
in order to nurse a chronically ill relative.

18. See Freud, "The 'Uncanny'" (1919), *CP,* 4:368–407; Jacques Lacan, *Ecrits: A Selec-*
tion (New York: Norton, 1977), 1–7 and 8–29, on the issue of primary aggression and
imagos; and Melanie Klein, *The Selected Melanie Klein,* 84–94 and 211–29, on object splitting and its relation to infantile rage.

19. Lacan's notion of the mirrored self as the first "other" (in both time and importance)
is relevant here. He argues in "The Mirror Stage" that identification with the image in the
mirror—the "specular I"—precedes identification with the other—the "social I." Such being the case, the "specular I," which totalizes pre-ego fragments, contradicts the later (false)
sense of an incipient, emergent self (associated with the "social I") and stands as evidence

that identity is by definition self-alienating, that the ego agency from the beginning is located in "a fictional direction," in its symbolization as the image in the mirror. For an interesting discussion of Gaskell's use of the Mother as mirror and of the mirror/Mother as the daughter's initiation into difference, see Homans, *Bearing the Word*, 251–76.

20. Gaskell, "The Poor Clare," in *The Works of Mrs. Gaskell*, 8 vols. (London: Smith, Elder and Co., 1906), 5:329–90. Subsequent page references to "The Poor Clare" appear parenthetically in the text.

21. Not only is the presence of Lucy's double signified in the same way as is the presence of Bertha Rochester in *Jane Eyre*— first as a laugh, then as a mirror image—but Bertha functions much in the same capacity for Jane as the IT does for Lucy. Moreover, the description of Lucy's first glimpse of her double in the mirror inverts that of Jane's first glimpse of her mirrored self in her bridal attire: "I saw a robed and veiled figure, so unlike my usual self that it seemed almost the image of a stranger" (252). For a discussion of Bertha as Jane's double, see Sandra Gilbert and Susan Gubar, *The Madwoman in the Attic: The Woman Writer and the Nineteenth-Century Literary Imagination* (New Haven: Yale University Press, 1979), 336–71.

22. Maureen T. Reddy, "Female Sexuality in 'The Poor Clare': The Demon in the House," *Studies in Short Fiction* 21 (Summer 1984): 259–65, discusses the angelic/demonic splitting of the female self in "The Poor Clare" as a comment on Victorian culture. See also Auerbach, *Woman and the Demon: The Life of a Victorian Myth* (Cambridge, MA: Harvard University Press, 1982), especially "Angels and Demons: Woman's Marriage of Heaven and Hell," 63–108.

Homans, too, points out the splitting of the female self in "The Poor Clare," though her emphasis is on how the mirrored Lucy *literalizes* the psychic split between female goodness and badness.

23. See Hélène Cixous, "The Laugh of the Medusa" (1975; trans. 1976; rpt. *New French Feminism: An Anthology*, ed. Elaine Marks and Isabelle de Courtivron [Amherst: University of Massachusetts Press, 1980]), 245–64.

24. *Dr. Fordyce's Sermons to Young Women*, quoted by Staves, in "*Evelina*: or, Female Difficulties," 27.

25. According to Oliphant in her *Literary History of England*, at the end of the eighteenth and beginning of the nineteenth centuries "Johnson still reigned there an autocrat of the severest sway, imposing the clumsy grandeur of his own mode of expression upon the language, and overawing all beginners into imitation of those defects of his ponderous genius which they had no better gift to redeem. He had given much to his generation . . . ; but in return he tyrannised over it, and permitted no voice to be heard in his presence . . . [A]nd literature, crushed under his weight, could only feebly moan out an allegiance to him, which in its heart it did not feel" (1:12).

26. Cf. Nightingale, *Cassandra: An Essay*, 42: "We can never pursue any object for a single two hours, for we can never command any regular leisure or solitude; and in social or domestic life one is bound, under pain of being thought sulky, to make a remark every two minutes . . . [T]o drop a remark, as it is called, every two minutes, how wearisome it is! It is impossible to pursue the current of one's own thoughts, because one must keep oneself ever on the alert 'to say something;' and it is impossible to say what one is thinking, because the essence of a remark is not to be a thought, but an impression."

27. Dickens's description of Mrs. Gowan and the royal servants imitates Gaskell here

(*Little Dorrit*, 359–60). Though perhaps because his subjects are so thoroughly disagreeable, Dickens' humor there is considerably less amused and amusing than Gaskell's.

28. According to the *OED*, the significations of "nut" as "the head of a person" (1858) and as being "out of one's mind" (1860) were in circulation during Gaskell's lifetime; the first citation it gives for "nut" as meaning "a person hard to deal with or conciliate" is 1888. Given Gaskell's use of Lancashire dialect in *Mary Barton* and her husband's published lectures on the subject, it is worth noting that "cran" is a Scottish form of "crane," that "crane" in one sense means "skull," and that "cran" is thus a synonym for "nut." The meaning of "cranky" as "of capricious or wayward temper, difficult to please" dates from at least 1821, and of "crank" as "an eccentric notion . . . ; a crotchet, whim, caprice" from 1848 (*OED*).

29. According to some, the Amazons, although admittedly lacking children, demonstrate their maternal instincts in their compassion and sisterly affection for one another. See, for example, Auerbach, *Communities of Women*, 77–97; Lansbury, *Elizabeth Gaskell*, 83–94; Patricia Wolfe, "Structure and Movement in *Cranford*," *Nineteenth Century Fiction* 23 (1968): 162–76; and Pauline Nestor, *Female Friendships and Communities: Charlotte Brontë, George Eliot, Elizabeth Gaskell* (Oxford: Clarendon Press, 1985), 43–56. For a more general discussion of the importance of sororal empathy to narratives of female community, see Sandra A. Zagarell, "Narrative of Community: The Identification of a Genre," *Signs* 13 (Spring 1988), 498–527.

30. In "The Cage at Cranford," the narrator admits her sense of perpetual youthfulness in the company of the Amazons: "I was past thirty, but did not object to being called a girl; and, indeed, I generally felt like a girl at Cranford, where everyone was so much older than I was" (329).

"The Cage at Cranford," first published 10 years after *Cranford* in Dickens's *All Year Round* (November 1863), takes place in the Cranford of 1856 (some ten to twelve years after Peter's arrival). Mary Smith, who is staying with Miss Pole, writes to Jessie Brown Gordon, traveling in Paris, to purchase "something pretty and new and fashionable" (327) for Mary to give to Miss Pole as a hospitality gift. What arrives is a dress hoop, which Jessie refers to as "a Cage" and which is consequently mistaken by Mary and Miss Pole as a cage for "Polly-Cockatoo" ("which was his grand name; . . . when she was speaking to the servants[,] . . . she always gave him his full designation, just as most people call their daughters Miss, in speaking of them to strangers or servants" [332]). It takes the "little stupid servant-maiden Fanny" (presumably different from the Fanny of *Cranford*), Mr. Hoggins, and Peter to set them straight (332). When Peter is appealed to by Miss Pole to state his opinion on the function of the cage, he replies, "'It is a cage,' . . . bowing to Miss Pole; 'but it is a cage for an angel, instead of a bird!'" (338). It is, in other words, a cage to imprison a domestic angel, an Angel-in-the-House (as well as an article of clothing that makes a "caged bird" of its wearer).

The seed story for *Cranford*, "The Last Generation in England" (1849; rpt. *Cranford*, 319–26), and "The Cage at Cranford" frame *Cranford*. Both are less accomplished and less humorous than the novel, but they help to clarify points about *Cranford* that, being humorously treated in that text, often escape notice: for example, the narrator's position of unappreciated, dutiful daughter ("The Cage") and the significance of the little umbrella-mobbing boys' violence ("hanging on the outskirts of society were a set of young men, ready for mischief and brutality, . . . [who] would stop ladies returning from the card-parties . . . and whip them; literally whip them as you whip a little child" [320]).

31. The issue of nurturance and its lack thereof—epitomized in the Cranford ladies' sobriquet—finds striking form as well in their method of eating oranges.

> Miss Jenkyns did not like to cut the fruit; . . . sucking (only I think she used some more recondite word) was in fact the only way of enjoying oranges; but then there was the unpleasant association with a ceremony frequently gone through by little babies; and so, after dessert, in orange season, Miss Jenkyns and Miss Matty used to rise up, possess themselves each of an orange in silence, and withdraw to the privacy of their own rooms, to indulge in sucking oranges. (66)

Although having "begged" Matty to remain with her, Mary is on these occasions abandoned at the dinner table—presumably without having an orange to suck. Before Deborah's death, she had succeeded occasionally in getting Matty to remain with her, but was obliged to hold up a "screen" and "not look" while Matty "tried not to make the noise very offensive." Apart from its illicitly sexual (and masturbatory) quality, this instance of "nurturing" (self-nurturing, really) in Cranford is noteworthy in that it specifically excludes the narrator. In addition, the surreptitiousness of this act of eating proleptically suggests the association of Matty with Aminé in the next chapter, in which gastronomical and sexual appetite are conflated.

32. See, for example, Auerbach, *Communities of Women;* Wolfe, "Structure and Movement"; and Edgar Wright, *Mrs. Gaskell: The Basis for Reassessment* (Oxford: Oxford University Press, 1965).

33. As the mother of four daughters, Gaskell was predictably concerned about the fate of unmarried women in her society. Contrary to the cultural view that maiden daughters were the logical candidates for family nursing and caretaking, Gaskell shows at least as much concern in her letters for the future of her daughters—"brotherless women" (*EGL*, 571), without masculine privilege, protection, or guaranteed financial support—as for family members in potential need of daughterly care (that is, her husband). Although believing that "unmarried life" could be "as full as happy, *in process of time*" as a married one—though "there is a time of trial to be gone through with *women,* who naturally yearn after children" (*EGL*, 598)—Gaskell fully understood the financial and social difficulties of such a life, and she secretly saved money to buy a house (remarkably near Jane Austen's, in fact) that her workaholic husband might "retire to & for a home for my unmarried daughters . . . The house is large . . . and in the middle of a pretty rural village, so that it won't be a lonely place for the unmarried daughters who will inherit" (*EGL*, 774).

34. See n.11 for citation; see n.30 for a brief summary of "The Cage at Cranford."

35. In her letter to Ruskin (already quoted), Gaskell remarks: "The beginning of 'Cranford' was *one* paper in 'Household Words'; and I never meant to write more, so killed Capt Brown very much against my will" (*EGL*, 748). *Cranford* began as a single sketch, which, due to its popularity (and Dickens's coaxing), was then extended. Having already eliminated Captain Brown, Gaskell introduces Peter at least in part to provide those qualities lost with Brown's removal.

36. On the issue of Peter as Mattie's adjutant, see Auerbach, *Communities;* Wolfe, "Structure and Movement."

37. The association between Peter and Mary extends beyond their characterological similarities to their semiotic significance. Both are marked by gender as "other": Mary in her native femaleness, Peter in "putting on" the accoutrements of such. Peter's transvestism, however, signals only one aspect of his representation of otherness. As the Aga Jenkyns, he is (like Brunoni and the Blue Beardian Hindu servant before him), "'so very oriental,'" a "cross-legged" Indian who mesmerizes the Amazons with his fantastically tall tales (he "was quite as good as an Arabian Night any evening") and conjures up the unbelievable: the appearance of Mrs. Jamieson and Mrs. Fitz-Adam at the same social event. His considerable appeal ("The ladies vied with each other who should admire him most") lies in his exoticism, with its undertones of sexuality and racial difference (the Amazons are "astonishingly stirred up by the arrival from India" [211]). Like Brunoni, Peter must be foreign in order to be considered *other* in Cranford; that is, in order for the females of Cranford to be normative, the males must be marked *other*wise. Since middle-class white men are the standard by which difference is judged, they necessarily dominate and define deviance in the context in which they appear (as Captain Brown, before he is killed off, is in danger of doing in Cranford). Thus, "Cranford" signifies a community of women only because its visible male inhabitants are racially or socially "deviant."

Cf. Auerbach, *Communities,* who sees the exoticism of Brunoni and Peter to be part of the general "aura of foreignness that surrounds all the men in the novel" (84).

38. On the importance of "incremental repetition" of event to the narrative structure of *Cranford,* see Joseph Allen Boone, *Tradition Counter Tradition* (Chicago: University of Chicago Press, 1987), 286.

39. Miss Pole's story of the bleeding sack is particularly memorable among these tales of violence in having as its aggressor a daughter who murders without guilt or punishment:

> "One of the stories . . . was of a girl, who was left in charge of a great house . . . when the other servants all went off to the gaieties. The family were away in London, and a peddlar came by, and asked to leave his large and heavy pack in the kitchen, saying he would call for it again at night; and the girl (a gamekeeper's daughter), roaming about in search of amusement, chanced to hit upon a gun hanging up in the hall, and took it down to look at the chasing; and it went off through the open kitchen door, hit the pack, and a slow dark thread of blood came oozing out. (How Miss Pole enjoyed this part of the story, dwelling on each word as if she loved it!) She rather hurried over the further account of the girl's bravery, and I have but a confused idea that, somehow, she baffled the robbers with Italian irons, heated red hot, and then restored to blackness by being dipped in grease." (141–42)

The daughter's phallic weapons and Miss Pole's relish in telling the story are memorable as well.

The popularity of gothic fiction—and its offspring, the ghost story—reached new heights during the late eighteenth through the nineteenth centuries (Gaskell herself produced many). For a discussion emphasizing the role of preoedipal fears in the construction and reception of the gothic, see Claire Kahane, "The Gothic Mirror," in *The Mother Tongue: Essays in Feminist Psychoanalytic Interpretation,* ed. Shirley Nelson Garner, Claire Kahane, and Madelon Sprengnether (Ithaca: Cornell University Press, 1985): 334–51. Ellen Moers, in *Literary Women* (Garden City, NY: Doubleday, 1976), is probably the first feminist critic to have suggested that the "fear of self" resides at the heart of the "feminine gothic" (107).

40. For a stimulating discussion of how the narrative's "loosely episodic" (193) form metonymically suggests a miscellany or "a woman's collection"—and in doing so radically revises the "formal authority of the masculine and the occidental in the writing of private life" (203)—see Dolin, "*Cranford* and the Victorian Collection." Andrew H. Miller also addresses the structural peculiarities of the narrative, in "The Fragments and Small Opportunities of *Cranford*," *Genre* 25 (1992): 91–111.

41. Gaskell asserts, in *"My Diary": The Early years of My Daughter Marianne* (London: privately printed by Clement Shorter, 1923), that "the dear and tender *tie* of Mother and Daughter" (5; emphasis added) "passeth every earthly love": mother's love, in other words, is supreme next to that of the Father. A remarkably progressive childrearer, Gaskell is nevertheless obsessed throughout *"My Diary"* with curbing her infant daughter Marianne's obstinacy, presumably because obstinacy, being prohibited by Law (especially in females), will result in her loss. Gaskell, that is, fears that the Father will punish her by prematurely reclaiming custody of her daughter's soul if either Marianne or she, in her too strong attachment to Marianne, is perceived as obstinate or otherwise Law-defying. Gaskell thus prays that she not make "an idol" of her daughter for fear of losing too severely when the Father calls the daughter (punitively or not) to Himself.

42. J. Hillis Miller, "Tropes and the Narrative Line in Elizabeth Gaskell's *Cranford*," paper presented at the Modern Language Association Convention, New York, 1986.

The exception within Dickens is, as I have already suggested, *Pickwick Papers*, which, although a strung-together narrative, is uncharacteristic of Dickens generally and in contradistinction to his "rubberband" style. If Gaskell, having once written a rubberband narrative, has temporarily sworn them off, Dickens, having once written a string-tied narrative, has conversely followed suit.

Prefiguring Miller's rubberband, Judith Little in *Comedy and the Woman Writer: Woolf, Spark and Feminism* (Lincoln: University of Nebraska Press, 1983) distinguishes between women's humor (which "mocks the deepest possible norms") and men's "rounded-off comic fiction" (1).

43. Auerbach, *Communities of Women*, 881–82.

44. For discussion of Gaskell's difficult negotiations with Dickens concerning the publication of *Cranford*, see Gérin, *Elizabeth Gaskell*, 125–26; A. B. Hopkins, *Elizabeth Gaskell: Her Life and Work* (London: John Lehmann, 1952), 135–57; and especially Schor, *Scheherazade*, 83–119, who writes in convincing detail of the complex figuring of Dickens in the text of *Cranford*.

45. In a letter dated 4 December 1851 (the first installment of *Cranford* ran in the 13 December issue), Dickens apologizes:

> I write in great haste to tell you that Mr. Wills [his subeditor], in the utmost consternation, has brought me your letter, just received (four o'clock), and that it is too late to recall your tale . . . (not hearing any objection to my proposed alteration by return post), and the number is now made up in the printer's hands. I cannot possibly take the tale out—it has departed from me. [note: the most generous explanation would be that letters crossed in the mail. Gaskell, who had gone on holiday after submitting the first "paper" about Cranford, had written

to Dickens of her holiday address, but the letter explaining the proposed alteration was nevertheless sent to her home address and from there forwarded.]

I am truly concerned for this, but hope you will not blame me for what I have done in perfect good faith. Any recollection of me from your pen cannot (as I think you know) be otherwise than truly gratifying for me; but with my name on every page of Household Words, there would be—or at least I should feel—an impropriety in so mentioning myself . . . I would do anything rather than cause you a minute's vexation arising out of what has given me so much pleasure, and I sincerely beseech you to think better of it, and not to fancy that any shade has been thrown on your charming writing, by—The unfortunate but innocent. (Quoted in Hopkins, 107)

As many of Gaskell's biographers and critics have noted, Dickens's editorial changes and suggestions were increasingly looked upon by Gaskell with annoyance. By the last installment of *North and South* (the last major work she would publish with him), their relations were known to be strained. Exasperated by her tardiness in submitting installments, Dickens exclaimed to Mr. Wills, "If I were Mr. G Oh Heaven how I would beat her!" (Quoted by Hopkins, 152). Gaskell, in turn, not only refused to write any faster but became less circumspect about her poor opinion of Dickens's critical judgment. According to Angus Easson in *Elizabeth Gaskell* (London: Routledge and Kegan Paul, 1979): "'[G]ood enough for Mr. Dickens' came to be a pejorative self-criticism" (41).

46. Dickens, letter to Gaskell of 25 October 1851; quoted by Gérin, *Elizabeth Gaskell,* 123. Like Scheherazade (the author of the Aminé and Sinbad stories), Gaskell spun installments of *Cranford* at Dickens's request, the first installment having been originally intended by Gaskell as a discrete story.

47. See, for example, Lansbury, *Elizabeth Gaskell;* and Wright, *Mrs. Gaskell.*

48. Margaret Ganz, *Elizabeth Gaskell: The Artist in Conflict* (New York: Twayne, 1969), 143. Although Ganz generally considers Gaskell's handling of conflict in her social problem novels less successful than in her humorous ones, curiously it is sometimes the very same conflict that occurs in both. Class difference, for example, figures throughout Gaskell's work. However, whereas in novels like *Mary Barton* and *North and South,* such difference gives rise to conflict that is dire, socioeconomically determined, oppressive and dominant, in *Cranford* it surfaces only occasionally in the humor, where its conflictual element is relieved: for example, in the fuss made by the Amazons over Lady Glenmire's marrying Hoggins the surgeon and in Mrs. Forrester's tale of her fastidious, snobby cousin who would only marry a woman similarly endowed with a surname beginning with "two little ff's."

49. Ritchie, "Preface" in Mrs. Gaskell, *Cranford* (New York: Thomas Y. Crowell, 1892), vi.

Chapter Five

1. George Eliot, "Woman in France: Madame de Sable," *Westminster Review* (October 1854; rpt. *Essays of George Eliot,* ed. Thomas Pinney (London: Routledge and Kegan Paul, 1963), 53. Some fourteen years later, having dropped the male persona of the reviews, Eliot expresses similar sentiments, though with less apparent assurance in the biologically determined nature of the feminine character. In a letter to Emily Davies of 8 August 1868,

she expresses her doubts about the feminine character being eroded by a masculine education:

> We can no more afford to part with that exquisite type of gentleness, tenderness, possible maternity suffusing a woman's being with affectionateness, which makes what we mean by the feminine character, than we can afford to part with the human love, the mutual subjection of soul between a man and a woman—which is also a growth and revelation beginning before all history. (*GEL,* 4:467–68)

2. Eliot, "Silly Novels by Lady Novelists," *Westminster Review* (October 1856; rpt. *Essays of George Eliot,* 324).

3. Eliot, "German Wit: Heinrich Heine," *Westminster Review* (January 1856; rpt. George Eliot, *Essays and Leaves from a Notebook* (New York: Harper and Bros., 1884), 66.

4. Furthermore, in "The Natural History of German Life: Riehl," *Essays and Leaves from a Notebook,* 179–225, Eliot attributes to the uncultured mind (and thus indirectly to barbaric humor) a loyalty to the Law that "*holds the place of sentiment, of theory, and in many cases of affection*" (196) and that thereby displaces any relation based on sympathy that barbaric humor might otherwise have held to the more advanced variety.

5. In a letter to her publisher, John Blackwood (dated 18 February 1857), Eliot writes: "My artistic bent is directed . . . to the presentation of mixed human beings in such a way as to call forth tolerant judgment, pity, and sympathy" (*GEL,* 2:298–99). This "maternal" attitude toward her characters—which is to some degree self-styled upon Cowper, who "presents the commonest objects 'truthfully and lovingly,' cherishing them in proportion to their nearness" (Haight, 217)—informs her ideas about "realism": "Art must be either real and concrete, or ideal and eclectic. Both are good and true in their way, but my stories are of the former kind. I undertake to exhibit nothing as it should be; I only try to exhibit some things as they have been or are" (*GEL,* 2:361–62).

Eliot, of course, is occasionally as guilty of idealization as any other writer, and while she may advocate "maternal" writing, strives herself, at least initially, to pass off her stories as "male": not only is her pen name masculine, but her narrators in *Scenes from Clerical Life* and *Adam Bede* are textually identified as men. Her humor, too, when pointed at institutions or other abstractions, leans more toward "masculine" satire than maternal sympathy. See Blackwood's comment, quoted by Gordon Haight in *George Eliot: A Biography,* that in *Janet's Repentance* Eliot writes about the Milby townspeople with a "harsher Thackerayan view of human nature" (234).

6. Although the narrator of *The Mill on the Floss* has often been identified as ungendered or masculine, N. Katherine Hayles, in "Anger in Different Voices: Carol Gilligan and *The Mill on the Floss,*" *Signs: Journal of Women in Culture and Society* 12, no. 1 (1986), 23–29, argues for a similarity between the "ethic of caring" addressed by the narrator of Carol Gilligan's *In a Different Voice* (Cambridge, MA: Harvard University Press, 1982) and that of Eliot's narrator and, in so doing, for the femininity of the latter.

7. Even normal—that is, nonmasochistic—experience of the preoedipal mother entails a sense of loss. As Janine Chasseguet-Smirgel puts it in *Sexuality and Mind,* in the Real "manifestation of feelings of grief . . . are necessary to the maintenance of bonds with the mother" (52). See, also, Julia Kristeva, *Black Sun: Mourning and Melancholia,* trans. Leon Roudiez (New York: Columbia University Press, 1990).

8. Eliot, *The Mill on the Floss,* ed. Gordon Haight (Oxford: Oxford University Press, 1980), 14. Subsequent page references to this edition appear parenthetically within the text.

9. Regina Barreca, in *Untamed and Unabashed,* argues that while Maggie as a child often intentionally solicits her father's laughter (and thus contributes to the humor of the text), "as an adult, she learns to suppress" her "defiance and wit," and "the narrator gradually absorbs the responsibility for the creation of humor" (94).

10. We shortly learn, however, that Scott is as inadequate a surrogate parent as the gypsies (306).

11. Mrs. Pullet also provides an excuse for one of the narrator's more scathing cultural commentaries: her satiric consideration of the "fashionably drest female in grief" [56]). Although the narrative humor is always comparatively mild when applied to individuals (being tempered by sympathy), it can occasionally become quite corrosive when touching upon social institutions, such as organized religion (280) or collective ethnographic subjects, like the Dodsons (451). It is worth noting that instances of both the most bitter and the broadest comic humor (the latter being applied to and produced by Bob Jakin, the packman) are relatively unmarked by gender.

12. Eliot, usually averse to admitting a contemporary's influence, acknowledged her debt to Gaskell in a thank-you letter:

> I was conscious . . . that my feeling towards Life and Art had some affinity with the feeling which had inspired "Cranford" and the earlier chapters of "Mary Barton." That idea was brought the nearer to me, because I had the pleasure of reading Cranford [*sic*] for the first time in 1857, when I was writing the "Scenes of Clerical Life." (*GEL,* 3:198)

The description of life "in Mrs. Glegg's day" (119) recorded in the chapter entitled "Mr. and Mrs. Glegg at Home" bears a remarkable resemblance to the early pages of *Cranford* as well (as, indeed, does the opening paragraph of Margaret Oliphant's "The Rector," in *The Doctor's Family and Other Stories,* ed. Merryn Williams [Oxford: Oxford University Press, 1986]: 35). There is mention, for example, not only of "gossip," outdated fashions, a country surgeon, and idiosyncratic customs but also of an "inherited . . . brocaded gown that would stand up empty . . . and a silver-headed walking stick" (which together rather vividly suggest the famous red umbrella or "stick in petticoats" of *Cranford*).

Aunt Glegg, furthermore, strongly recalls the Amazonian Deborah Jenkyns, even to her relationship with marginalized, crippled men of the community. As Eva Fuchs notes in "The Pattern's All Missed: Separation/Individuation in *The Mill on the Floss,*" *Studies in the Novel* 19 (Winter 1987): 422–34, "Aunt Glegg identifies Bob indiscriminately with a variety of deformed and malevolent characters: an itinerant whom she believes to have 'murdered a young woman in a lone place,' a legless cripple, a disfigured packman 'with a squint in his eye'" (429).

13. For discussion of *The Mill on the Floss* as a refutation of the "man of maxims" and the literary conventions with which he is associated, see Nancy K. Miller, "Emphasis Added"; and Mary Jacobus, "The Question of Language: Men of Maxims and *The Mill on the Floss,*" *Critical Inquiry* 8 (1981), 2:207–22.

14. Although Maggie's desire is a much discussed topic in the critical literature on the novel, most critics assume it to be a primarily sexual or ambitious desire that is thwarted by cultural circumstances rather than, as I do, an initial yearning for a preoedipal mother

that expresses itself in erotic transference: see, for example, Nancy K. Miller, "Emphasis Added"; and Jacobus, "Question of Language."

15. For discussion of author/narrator identification with Maggie's feminine experience of trying to read in a phallocentric culture, see Homans, *Bearing the Word,* 120–52; and Jacobus, "Question of Language."

16. Mrs. Tulliver's very first remark about Maggie is that she'll drown herself by "wanderin' up an' down by the water" [12]). For a discussion of the scene at the Round Pool as an evocation of the preoedipal, particularly in the context of Maggie and Tom's sibling relationship, see Homans, *Bearing the Word.*

17. Such a rendering leads in the first chapter to some narratological confusion: if the narrator's dream indeed begins from the first lines, as the fact that she wakes up seems to indicate, then the narrator's assertion that she "was going to tell . . . what Mr. and Mrs. Tulliver were talking about" *before* she "dozed off" assumes a prenarrative acquaintance with both the narrator and the characters that is otherwise unaccounted for by the text.

18. Nancy K. Miller discusses in "Emphasis Added" the mimetic break at closure as Eliot's only possible representation of a feminist alternative to the cultural plot in which Maggie is caught. Gillian Beer notes that Maggie's fate is a release "from the bounds of social realism"—a release that allows her "the plenitude which is nowhere available within her society" (*George Eliot,* 104).

19. As Chasseguet-Smirgel points out in another context, "the fantasy of dissolution into the cosmos" that Maggie experiences on the river is one with the wish for "fusion with the primary object, the Mother" (*Sexuality and Mind,* 2).

That Maggie's vulnerability to Stephen is largely preoedipal is seen in her rather violent reaction to his (oedipally) sexual overture at the ball and the description of her subsequent desire to retreat: Maggie "wished her mind could flow into . . . babbling current" and sought after "a childlike, instinctive relief" (434).

It is worth noting that the river has almost exactly the same maternalizing, consciousness-transforming effect on the eponymous heroine of *Romola* as it does on Maggie. In Romola's case, the maternally gendered river baptizes her, so to speak, into the cult of motherhood, with which she, as Madonna Romola, comes to be identified. In Maggie's case, her union with the maternal river is preoedipal desire fulfilled: that is, death. For sustained relief from consciousness is not available under the reality principle and can consequently be achieved only with the cessation of life. See George Eliot, *Romola* (Harmondsworth: Penguin, 1980).

20. Mrs. Tulliver's unprecedented display of affection for Maggie at this critical juncture (provoked by her being "frightened" by Tom's cruelty in enforcing the law) has strong markings of narrative/heroine wish-fulfillment:

> Slowly Maggie was turning away with despair in her heart. But the poor frightened mother's love leaped out now, stronger than all dread.
> "My child! I'll go with you. You've got a mother." (485)

21. On Philip as a double for Maggie, see Hayles, "Anger in a Different Voice"; on Philip as a figure for Eliot, see Janice Carlisle, "The Mirror in *The Mill on the Floss:* Toward a Reading of Autobiography as Discourse," *Studies in the Literary Imagination* 23 (Fall 1990): 177–96.

Maggie's (mostly) unconscious wish to be freed from her identification with Philip is even more starkly seen in the following fantasy:

Her imagination, always rushing extravagantly beyond an immediate impression, saw her tall strong brother grasping the feeble Philip bodily, crushing him and trampling on him. (344)

Curiously, Maggie, whom Wakem describes as "'dangerous and unmanageable'" (428), represents for Philip's father a threat to his *maternal* bond with his son (a bond that he's been "tightening" since Philip's mother's death).

22. For a deeply thought-provoking discussion of how the maternal "bears special relevance to women's empathic literary identifications, particularly the author's relationship to her character," see Judith Kegan Gardiner, "On Female Identity," who points out that "to mother maturely, a woman must develop an identity sufficiently flexible that she can merge empathically with her child and still retain an adult sense of herself as nurturing yet independent" (356). On this issue of the heroine as the female author's "daughter," see also Gardiner's "The Heroine as Her Author's Daughter," in *Feminist Criticism: Essays on Theory, Poetry, and Prose,* ed. Cheryl L. Brown and Karen Olson (Metuchen, NJ: Scarecrow Press, 1978): 344–53.

23. Peggy Ruth Fitzhugh Johnstone, in "Narcissistic Rage in *The Mill on the Floss,*" *Literature and Psychology* 36, nos. 1 and 2 (1990): 90–109, takes a harsher view of Maggie's conduct, considering her to be little more than a tease and the narrator to be overly tolerant.

24. It is significant that only after Maggie reaches actual adulthood and the humor toward her ceases is she frequently referred to as a child. Thus, when she is in the throes of her most adult conflict (that is, her struggle to renounce Stephen), we are told that the "poor child threw her arms round her aunt's neck, and fell into long, deep sobs" (450). Similarly, after her elopement, "her childlike directness" prompts her to confess "everything" to Dr. Kenn (494).

25. Not only does this joke about Philoctetes's sister underscore the Victorian expectation of unmarried women to cater to their brothers' domestic needs, but it reinforces by association the link suggested earlier in the text (when Mr. Tulliver is compared to the hero of *Oedipus at Colonus* [130]) between Maggie and Antigone, the prototype of the tragic heroine and dutiful daughter. For a somewhat different understanding of the figure of Antigone to Eliot's work, see Beer, *George Eliot.*

26. Many critics have noted the resonance of this reference to Defoe's text; see, for example, Beer (89). For an extended treatment of Maggie's association with witchcraft, see Nina Auerbach's "The Power of Hunger: Demonism and Maggie Tulliver," *Romantic Imprisonment: Women and Other Glorified Outcasts* (New York: Columbia University Press, 1986), 230–49.

Two of Philip's jokes also become a source of metanarrative humor: one about Maggie's stealing Lucy's beau ("'[P]erhaps you will avenge the dark women in your own person, and carry away all the love from your cousin Lucy'" [332]); the other about Maggie's "'selling her soul to that ghostly boatman who haunts the Floss . . . for the sake of being drifted in a boat for ever'" (459). There is, in addition, Stephen's peculiar, oddly amusing reference to Dr. Kenn's having done the "'very fine thing'" of "'taking into his house that poor lad Grattan who shot his mother by accident'" (379)—a reference perhaps most easily understood as a narrative projection of wish fulfillment on Maggie's behalf.

27. For an extended discussion of Hazlitt's ideas on humor, see Stuart Tave's *The Amiable Humorist: A Study in the Comic Theory and Criticism of the Eighteenth and Early Nineteenth Centuries* (Chicago: University of Chicago Press, 1960).

28. The narrator's sense of her maternal privilege is so strong that she refuses to allow Mrs. Tulliver her own moment of motherly pathos. Although apparently willing to share the maternal space, the narrator at the last moment turns Mrs. Tulliver's otherwise touching response to Maggie's tearful repentance into an opportunity for laughter: "'I must put up wi' my children—I shall never have no more; and if they bring me bad luck, I must be fond on it—there's nothing else much to be fond on, for my furnitur' went long ago'" (501).

29. On the powerful, Law-threatening appeal of the maternal principle not only for Maggie and the narrator but for the reader as well, note Dinah Mulock's comment that "in the whole history of this fascinating *Maggie* there is a picturesque piteousness which somehow confuses one's sense of right and wrong" (quoted in *George Eliot: The Critical Heritage,* ed. David Carroll [London: Routledge and Kegan Paul, 1971], 157).

30. Following Sandra Gilbert and Susan Gubar, Homans notes that "Maggie and Tom spend most of their precious time together making each other miserable" (*Bearing the Word,* 127). Although the narrator may occasionally assert to the contrary, roaming "the daisied fields together" (*Mill,* 521) has never been for Maggie more than one of those "illusory promises" of happiness common to both preoedipal and paradisaical thinking but "impossible to be fulfilled" in the Real: the "promises of our childhood" are "void as promises made in Eden" (*Mill,* 186).

31. On the longing for Eden as Maggie's motivating desire, see Ronald Schleifer, "Irony and the Literary Past: On *The Concept of Irony* and *The Mill on the Floss,*" *Kierkegaard and Literature,* ed. Ronald Schleifer and Robert Markley (Norman: University of Oklahoma Press, 1984), 183–216.

32. For a discussion of Eliot's appropriations of Wordsworth, see Homans, *Bearing the Word.*

33. The witch imagery that clings to Maggie and that Auerbach has provocatively explored in *Romantic Imprisonment* is another example of the narration making liberal use of implied metaphor.

34. Jacobus suggests that, more than playful self-deprecation, the lamentation-on-metaphor passage is a radical subversion on Eliot's part of "the realist illusion of her fictional world, revealing it to be no more than a blank page inscribed with a succession of arbitrary metaphoric substitutions" ("Question of Language," 217).

35. Dorothea Barrett, in her *Vocation and Desire: George Eliot's Heroines* (London and New York: Routledge, 1989), points out this pun on star (191). We might add that the "thick grove" of Latin rhythms in which Maggie's imagination happily wanders is impenetrable, not only by any star but by any Stelling as well.

Stelling's evaluation of Maggie as "quick and shallow," moreover, not only recalls Shakespeare's Mistress Quickly and Justice Shallow (as Steven Marcus has suggested to me in conversation), but it actually echoes the words of Shakespeare's Richard III—that most misogynist and despised of British monarchs—in his assessment of Elizabeth, Edward's widow, shortly after he has murdered her sons ("Your reasons are too shallow and too quick" [*Richard III,* IV.iv.361]).

36. Steven, introduced into the novel in the eternalizing present as a "Hercules" bedecked with a "diamond ring, attar of roses, and [an] air of nonchalant leisure" (363), never properly transcends his initial classification as a foppish lover.

37. Like the momentary relief provided by the good-natured mockery of Maggie as romantic object (see n.36), there is humor at a remove regarding Dorothea in the chapters where Celia and the Cadwalladers discuss the wisdom of Dorothea's marital choices: see

Colette Caraes, "Du Comique Dans *Middlemarch*," *Cahiers Victoriens & Edouardiens*, 26 (1987): 63–75.

38. Thomas à Kempis, *The Imitation of Christ*, trans. Leo Sherley-Price (Harmondsworth: Penguin, 1952), 29, 39. Subsequent page references to this edition appear parenthetically within the text. Haight notes in his "Introduction" to *The Mill on the Floss* that for Eliot as for Maggie, the à Kempis text was a "private manual of devotion . . . In describing the solace Maggie found in 'the little, cold, clumsy book' George Eliot was writing from experience" (x).

39. Ludwig Feuerbach, *The Essence of Christianity*, trans. George Eliot (New York: Harper and Row, 1957). Subsequent page references to this edition appear parenthetically within the text. Also in 1854, Eliot (in contrast to Maggie) actually did elope with her lover: Eliot and Lewes officially began their liaison by traveling together to Germany just two weeks after the publication of Eliot's translation of Feuerbach's text. About the importance of Feuerbach to her thought, Eliot commented to Sara Hennell: "With the ideas of Feuerbach I everywhere agree" (*GEL*, 2:153).

40. Feuerbach footnotes (*EC*, 292) à Kempis among others, in support of this particular definition of Christianity.

41. G. M. Young reminds us in *Portrait of an Age* (2d ed.; Oxford: Oxford University Press, 1960) that "the evangelical faith in duty and renunciation was a woman's ethic" (3). The notion of a female ethic of care (as opposed to a male ethic of rule) that Carol Gilligan articulates in *A Different Voice* is not far removed from Eliot's ethic of "wide fellow-feeling" (as opposed to the morality of the man of maxims).

For discussion of the relation between an ethic of care and masochism, see Hayles, "Anger in a Different Voice"; for discussion of the narrator's conscious advocacy of selflessness in tension with the suppressed anger of the characters, see Carlisle, "The Mirror in the *Mill*."

42. Both Homans *(Bearing the Word)* and Hayles ("Anger in a Different Voice") indirectly point to the painful attraction of Maggie's maternal connection.

In light of her masochism (and Lacan's theory of the mother's function as mirror), Maggie's renunciation of the mirror may be read as an attempt to repress her primary narcissistic needs, to do away with her desire for mother-love: "She wondered if he [Philip] remembered how he used to like her eyes; with that thought Maggie glanced towards the square looking-glass which was condemned to hang with its face towards the wall, and she half-started from her seat to reach it down; but she checked herself and snatched up her work, trying to repress the rising wishes by forcing her memory to recall snatches of hymns" (298).

43. Somewhat paradoxically, because the *pain* of self-sacrifice reinforces the very sense of separateness that self-sacrifice itself strives to undo, Maggie's masochism also acts as a defense against her wish for merger. Beer argues, in fact, that Maggie's renunciatory acts are primarily an expression of her desire for independence (*George Eliot*, 84). I would qualify Beer's reading by suggesting that what Maggie desires independence from is not (as is usually the case) the mother but the paternal order (and the punitive maternal object, which represents that order). Like St. Theresa and other female religious mystics, Maggie strives, through renunciation, for independence from the Real in order to connect with the source of life itself—represented, in Maggie's case, by the archaic mother rather than God.

44. Among those critics who read the ending of the novel as the textualization of Maggie's desire are Nancy K. Miller ("Emphasis Added"), Jacobus ("Question of Language"), Hayles ("Anger in a Different Voice"), and Barrett *(Vocation and Desire)*.

45. Cooper, "The Narcissistic-Masochistic Character," 135.

46. Haight's biography is the source of Eliot's complaints of illness (337). Haight also records that "Sara [Hennell] volunteered a suspicion that *The Mill on the Floss* seemed 'unfinished' because of Marian's intense sympathy with Maggie Tulliver, which, Sara thought, must have made her 'rush upstairs as you used to do, to give ease to the flood of passionate tears in your room'" (335).

For many years after her mother's death in 1836 (Eliot was sixteen years old), not only did Eliot enthusiastically embrace renunciation ("her religious zeal . . . , renunciation and asceticism" being "prolonged till she was past twenty" [Haight, *Biography*, 21]), but she occasionally suffered fits of hysteria as well. Attending a dance at the age of twenty, Eliot suddenly became aware "that I was not in a situation to maintain the Protestant character of the true Christian," and that "conviction . . . together with the oppressive noise that formed the accompaniment to the dancing, the sole amusement, produced first headache and then that most wretched and unpitied of afflictions, hysteria, so that I regularly disgraced myself" (*GEL*, 1:41; quoted by Haight, 28).

It is worth noting, furthermore, that despite her often-acknowledged affection for her father—he was "the one deep strong love I have ever known" (*GEL*, 1:284; quoted by Haight, 21)—Eliot's lifelong desire for someone "to lean on and be petted by" (*GEL*, 1:328; quoted by Haight, 77) suggests *maternal* anaclisis, however male a form the maternal substitute took.

47. Eliot, "Westward Ho! And Constance Herbert," *Westminster Review* (July 1855; rpt. *Essays of George Eliot*, 135. It is fitting that Eliot's most explicit psychological shift from patriarchal to maternal ethics occurs in the midst of writing *The Mill on the Floss:* "I have no longer any antagonism towards any faith in which human sorrow and human longing for purity have expressed themselves; on the contrary, I have a sympathy with it that predominates over all argumentative tendencies . . . [O]n many points where I used to delight in expressing intellectual difference, I now delight in feeling an emotional agreement" and a sympathy with "our struggling fellow men" (*GEL*, 3:231).

48. Eliot, *The Lifted Veil*, 63. This definition of woman—in emphasizing the connection between mother and daughter—suggests the indispensable importance of the maternal bond to female identity. In direct contrast to Maggie, who is completely misunderstood by her fellow characters but feels deep sympathy for their suffering anyway, the male protagonist/narrator of *The Lifted Veil* understands every thought and petty motive of his fellows and consequently feels affection for no one (except, momentarily, his father, whose deathbed suffering prompts the narrator's loving sympathy). Like the horror tales incorporated into *Cranford*, *The Lifted Veil* starkly presents—in the form of "split" objects—the same psychic conflict that more subtly informs *The Mill on the Floss*. While the "good" mother is represented by the narrator's aforementioned definition of woman, the "bad" or phallic mother is embodied by the "hard," "unloving" Bertha, the narrator's wife, who "looked like a cruel immortal, finding her spiritual feast in the agonies of a dying race" (63).

CODA

1. Anita Brookner, *Brief Lives* (1990; rpt. New York: Vintage, 1992), 82–83.

2. Poovey, *The Proper Lady and the Woman Writer*, 245–46.

3. Robert Emmet Long, *Barbara Pym* (New York: Ungar, 1986), 40.

4. *Jane and Prudence* (1953; rpt. New York: Harper and Row, 1981), 36; *Excellent Women* (1952; rpt. New York: Plume, 1978), 7. Like Jane Austen, Jane Eyre is often a background presence in the Pym canon, particularly in *Excellent Women* and *Less than Angels* (1955; rpt. New York: Dutton, 1990).

5. Anita Brookner, *The Debut* (1981; rpt. New York: Vintage, 1990), 7. Subsequent references to this edition are included in the text.

6. Penelope Fitzgerald, *The Bookshop* (1978; rpt. New York: Houghton Mifflin, 1997), 7. Subsequent references to this edition are included in the text.

Selected Bibliography

Amis, Kingsley. "What Became of Jane Austen? [*Mansfield Park*]." *Jane Austen: A Collection of Critical Essays*. Edited by Ian Watt. Englewood Cliffs: Prentice-Hall, 1963. Pp. 141–44.

apRoberts, Ruth. *The Moral Trollope*. Athens: Ohio University Press, 1971.

Apte, Mahadev. *Humor and Laughter: An Anthropological Approach*. Ithaca: Cornell University Press, 1985.

Armstrong, Nancy. *Desire and Domestic Fiction: A Political History of the Novel*. New York: Oxford University Press, 1987.

Auerbach, Nina. *Communities of Women: An Idea in Fiction*. Cambridge, MA: Harvard University Press, 1978.

———. *Woman and the Demon: The Life of a Victorian Myth*. Cambridge, MA: Harvard University Press, 1982.

———. "Jane Austen's Dangerous Charm: Feeling as One Ought about Fanny Price." *Jane Austen: New Perspectives*. Edited by Janet Todd. New York: Holmes and Meier, 1983. Pp. 208–23.

———. "The Power of Hunger: Demonism and Maggie Tulliver." *Romantic Imprisonment: Women and Other Glorified Outcasts*. New York: Columbia University Press, 1986.

Austen, Jane. *Jane Austen's Letters to Her Sister Cassandra and Others*. 2d ed. Edited by R. W. Chapman. London: Oxford University Press, 1952.

———. *Persuasion*. 1818. Edited by R. W. Chapman. New York: Norton, 1958.

———. *Persuasion*. 1818. Edited by D. W. Harding. Harmondsworth: Penguin, 1965.

———. *Emma*. 1816. Harmondsworth: Penguin, 1966.

———. *Mansfield Park*. 1814. Harmondsworth: Penguin, 1966.

———. *Pride and Prejudice*. 1813. Edited by Donald J. Gray. New York: Norton, 1966.

———. *Sense and Sensibility*. 1811. Harmondsworth: Penguin, 1967.

———. "Persuasion." MS. British Library.

Bahktin, Mikhail. *The Dialogic Imagination*. Austin: University of Texas Press, 1981.

Barker, Gerard A. "The Two Mrs. Selwyns: *Evelina* and the Man of the World." *Papers on Language and Literature* 13 (1977): 80–84.

Barreca, Regina, ed. *Last Laughs: Perspectives on Women and Comedy*. New York: Gordon and Breach, 1988.

———, ed. *New Perspectives on Women and Comedy*. New York: Gordon and Breach, 1992.

———. *Untamed and Unabashed: Essay on Women and Humor in British Literature*. Detroit: Wayne State University Press, 1994.

Barrett, Dorothea. *Vocation and Desire: George Eliot's Heroines*. London and New York: Routledge and Kegan Paul, 1989.

Beer, Gillian. *George Eliot*. Indianapolis: Indiana University Press, 1986.

Bell, Millicent. *Edith Wharton & Henry James: The Story of Their Friendship*. New York: George Braziller, 1965.

Bergler, Edmund. *Laughter and the Sense of Humor.* New York: Intercontinental Medical Book, 1956.

Bergson, Henri. "Laughter." *Comedy.* Edited by Wylie Sypher. Baltimore: Johns Hopkins University Press, 1956. Pp. 61–190.

Bloom, Harold, ed. *Fanny Burney's Evelina.* Modern Critical Interpretations. New York: Chelsea House, 1988.

Bodichon, Barbara Leigh Smith. *A Brief Summary, in Plain Language of the Most Important Laws of England Concerning Women, Together with a Few Observations.* 3d rev. ed. London: Trubner and Co., 1869.

Boone, Joseph Allen. *Tradition Counter Tradition.* Chicago: University of Chicago Press, 1987.

Booth, Wayne C. *A Rhetoric of Irony.* Chicago: University of Chicago Press, 1974.

Boyd, Zelda. "Jane Austen's 'Must': The Will and the World." *Nineteenth Century Fiction* 39 (1984): 127–43.

Breuer, Josef, and Sigmund Freud. *Studies on Hysteria.* New York: Basic Books, n.d.

Brontë, Anne. *The Tenant of Wildfell Hall.* 1848. Harmondsworth: Penguin, 1979.

Brontë, Charlotte. *Jane Eyre.* 1847. New York: Norton, 1971.

Brookner, Anita. *The Debut.* 1981. New York: Vintage, 1990.

———. *Brief Lives.* 1990. New York: Vintage, 1992.

Brooks, Peter. *Reading for the Plot: Design and Intention in Narrative.* New York: Knopf, 1984.

Brown, Julia Prewitt. *Jane Austen's Novels: Social Change and Literary Form.* Cambridge, MA: Harvard University Press, 1979.

Brownstein, Rachel. "Jane Austen: Irony and Authority." *Last Laughs: Perspectives on Women and Comedy.* Edited by Regina Barreca. New York: Gordon and Breach, 1988.

Burke, Edmund. *A Philosophical Enquiry into the Origins of Our Ideas of the Sublime and Beautiful.* Edited by James T. Boulton. Notre Dame: Notre Dame Press, 1968.

Burney, Fanny. *Evelina; or the History of a Young Lady's Entrance into the World.* 1778. Edited by Edward A. Bloom and Lillian D. Bloom. Oxford: Oxford University Press, 1968.

———. *The Early Diary of Frances Burney, 1768–1778.* Edited by Annie Raine Ellis. Freeport, NY: Books for Libraries Press, 1971.

———. *Cecilia, or Memoirs of an Heiress.* 1782. Oxford: Oxford University Press, 1988.

Butler, Marilyn. *Maria Edgeworth: A Literary Biography.* Oxford: Clarendon Press, 1972.

———. *Jane Austen and the War of Ideas.* Oxford: Oxford University Press, 1975.

Campbell, Gina. "How to Read Like a Gentleman: Burney's Instructions to Her Critics in *Evelina.*" *ELH* 57 (1990): 557–84.

Cantor, Joanne R. "What Is Funny to Whom? The Role of Gender." *Journal of Communication* 26 (1976): 164–72.

Caraes, Colette. "Du Comique dans *Middlemarch.*" *Cahiers Victoriens & Edouardiens* 26 (1987): 63–75.

Carlisle, Janice. "The Mirror in *The Mill on the Floss:* Toward a Reading of Autobiography as Discourse." *Studies in the Literary Imagination* 23 (Fall 1990): 177–96.

Carroll, David, ed. *George Eliot: The Critical Heritage.* London: Routledge and Kegan Paul, 1971.

Carse, Wendy K. "A Penchant for Narrative: 'Mary Smith' in Elizabeth Gaskell's *Cranford.*" *Journal of Narrative Technique* 20 (Fall 1990): 318–30.

Cecil, Lord David. *Victorian Novelists.* Chicago: University of Chicago Press, 1935.

Certeau, Michel de. *The Practice of Everyday Life*. Translated by Steven Rendell. Berkeley: University of California Press, 1984.

Chancer, Lynn. *Sadomasochism and Everyday Life: The Dynamics of Power and Powerlessness.* New Brunswick: Rutgers University Press, 1992.

Chasseguet-Smirgel, Janine. *Creativity and Perversion.* New York: Norton, 1984.

———. *Sexuality and Mind: The Role of the Father and the Mother in the Psyche.* New York: New York University Press, 1986.

Chesterton, G. K. Extract from *The Victorian Age in Literature.* 1913. Rpt. in *Jane Austen: The Critical Heritage,* vol. 2: *1870–1940.* Edited by B. C. Southam. London: Routledge and Kegan Paul, 1987. Pp. 239–40.

Chodorow, Nancy. *The Reproduction of Mothering: Psychoanalysis and the Sociology of Gender.* Berkeley: University of California Press, 1978.

Cixous, Hélène. "The Laugh of the Medusa." *New French Feminisms: An Anthology.* Edited by Elaine Marks and Isabelle de Courtivron. Amherst: University of Massachusetts Press, 1980.

Cobbe, Frances Power. "Criminals, Idiots, Women, And Minors." *"Criminals, Idiots, Women, & Minors": Nineteenth-Century Writing by Women on Women.* Edited by Susan Hamilton. Peterborough, Ontario: Broadview Press, 1995.

Cohen, Paula Marantz. "Stabilizing the Family System at *Mansfield Park.*" *ELH* 54 (1987): 669–93.

Cooper, Arnold M. "The Narcissistic-Masochistic Character." *Masochism: Current Psychoanalytic Perspectives.* Edited by Robert A. Glick and Donald I. Meyers. Hillsdale, NJ: Analytic Press, 1988. Pp. 117–38.

Courtney, W. L. *The Feminine Note in Fiction.* London: Chapman and Hall, 1904.

Cutting, Rose Marie. "Defiant Women: The Growth of Feminism in Fanny Burney's Novels." *Studies in English Literature 1500–1900* 17 (1977): 519–30.

Darwin, Charles. *Expression of the Emotions in Man and Animals.* New York: Appleton, 1898.

David-Menard, Monique. *Hysteria from Freud to Lacan.* Ithaca: Cornell University Press, 1989.

Davidoff, Leonore, and Catherine Hall. *Family Fortunes: Men and Women of the English Middle Class, 1789–1850.* Chicago: University of Chicago Press, 1987.

Deleuze, Gilles. *Masochism: Coldness and Cruelty.* New York: Zone Books, 1989.

Deutsch, Helene. *The Psychology of Women.* Vol. 1. New York: Grune and Stratton, 1944.

Dickens, Charles. *David Copperfield.* 1850. Harmondsworth: Penguin, 1966.

———. *Little Dorrit.* 1857. Harmondsworth: Penguin, 1967.

Dodsworth, Martin. "Women without Men at Cranford." *Essays in Criticism* 13 (April 1963): 132–45.

Dolin, Tim. "*Cranford* and the Victorian Collection." *Victorian Studies* 36 (Winter 1993): 179–206.

Doody, Margaret. *Frances Burney: The Life and the Works.* New Brunswick: Rutgers University Press, 1988.

Dooley, Lucile. "A Note on Humor." *Psychoanalytic Review* 21 (1934): 49–58.

———. "The Relation of Humor to Masochism." *Psychoanalytic Review* 28 (1941): 37–46.

Duckworth, Alistair. *The Improvement of the Estate: A Study of Jane Austen's Novel.* Baltimore: Johns Hopkins University Press, 1971.

Easson, Angus. *Elizabeth Gaskell.* London: Routledge and Kegan Paul, 1979.

Edel, Leon. *Henry James: The Master: 1906–1916.* New York: Avon, 1978.

Eden, Emily. *The Semi-Attached Couple.* 1860. Boston: Houghton Mifflin, 1947.

Edgeworth, Maria. *The Modern Griselda.* 1805. Rpt. *Tales and Novels.* Vol. 10. New York: Harper and Bros., 1856. Pp. 183–243.

Eliot, George. *Essays and Leaves from a Notebook.* New York: Harper and Bros., 1884.

———. *The George Eliot Letters.* 8 vols. Edited by Gordon Haight. New Haven: Yale University Press, 1954–78.

———. *Essays of George Eliot.* Edited by Thomas Pinney. London: Routledge and Kegan Paul, 1963.

———. *The Mill on the Floss.* 1860. Edited by Gordon Haight. Oxford: Oxford University Press, 1980.

———. *Romola.* 1863. Edited by Andrew Sanders. Harmondsworth, Penguin, 1980.

———. *The Lifted Veil.* 1878. Edited by Beryl Gray. Harmondsworth: Penguin, 1985.

Ellis, Annie Raines, ed. *The Early Diary of Frances Burney, 1768–1778.* Freeport, NY: Books for Libraries Press, 1971.

Ellis, Sarah Stickney. *Women of England, Their Social Duties and Domestic Habits.* London: Fisher, Son and Co., 1839.

———. *The Wives of England, Their Relative Duties, Domestic Influence, and Social Obligations.* New York: Appleton, 1843.

Ellis, Sarah Stickney. *The Daughters of England, Their Position in Society, Character and Responsibilities.* New York: Appleton, 1844.

———. *The Mothers of England, Their Influence and Responsibility.* New York: Appleton, 1844.

Emerson, Ralph Waldo. Extract from the *Journals of Ralph Waldo Emerson: 1856–1863.* Edited by E. W. Emerson and W. E. Forbes. Rpt. *Jane Austen: The Critical Heritage.* Vol. 1. Edited by B. C. Southam. London: Routledge and Kegan Paul, 1968. P. 28.

Epstein, Julia. *The Iron Pen: Frances Burney and the Politics of Women's Writing.* Madison: University of Wisconsin Press, 1989.

Evans, Mary. *Jane Austen & the State.* London: Tavistock (Methuen), 1987.

Evans, Mary Noel. "Hysteria and the Seduction of Theory." *Seduction and Theory: Readings of Gender, Representation, and Rhetoric.* Edited by Dianne Hunter. Urbana: University of Illinois Press, 1989. Pp. 73–85.

Farr, Evelyn. *The World of Fanny Burney.* London: Peter Owen, 1993.

Ferrier, Susan. *Marriage.* 1818. London: Eveleigh Nash and Grayson, 1929.

Feuerbach, Ludwig. *The Essence of Christianity.* Translated by George Eliot. New York: Harper and Row, 1957.

Fitzgerald, Penelope. *The Bookshop.* 1978. New York: Houghton Mifflin, 1997.

Flavin, Louise. "*Mansfield Park:* Free Indirect Discourse and the Psychological Novel." *Studies in the Novel* 19 (1987): 137–59.

Flint, Kate. *The Woman Reader, 1837–1914.* Oxford: Clarendon, 1993.

Fraiman, Susan. *Unbecoming Women: British Women Writers and the Novel of Development.* New York: Columbia University Press, 1993.

Freeman, Barbara Claire. *The Feminine Sublime: Gender and Excess in Women's Fiction.* Berkeley: University of California Press, 1968.

Freud, Sigmund. *Collected Papers.* Vols. 1–5. New York: Basic Books, 1959.

———. *Jokes and Their Relation to the Unconscious.* New York: Norton, 1960.

Fuchs, Eva. "The Pattern's All Missed: Separation/Individuation in *The Mill on the Floss*." *Studies in the Novel* 19 (1987): 422–34.

Gagnier, Regenia. "Between Women: A Cross-Class Analysis of Status and Anarchic Humor." *Last Laughs: Perspectives on Women and Comedy*. Edited by Regina Barreca. New York: Gordon and Breach, 1988. Pp. 135–48.

Galenson, Eleanor. "Protomasochism." *Masochism: Current Psychoanalytic Perspectives*. Edited by Robert A. Glick and Donald I. Meyers. Hillsdale, NJ: Analytic Press, 1988. Pp. 189–204.

Gallagher, Catherine. "Who Was That Masked Woman? The Prostitute and the Playwright in the Comedies of Aphra Behn." *Last Laughs: Perspectives on Women and Comedy*. Edited by Regina Barreca. New York: Gordon and Breach, 1988. Pp. 23–42.

Gallop, Jane. *Thinking through the Body*. New York: Columbia University Press, 1988.

Ganz, Margaret. *Elizabeth Gaskell: The Artist in Conflict*. New York: John Lehmann, 1952.

Gard, Roger. *Jane Austen's Novels: The Art of Clarity*. New Haven: Yale University Press, 1992.

Gardiner, Judith Kegan. "The Heroine as Her Author's Daughter." *Feminist Criticism*. Edited by Cheryl L. Brown and Karen Olson. Metuchen, NJ: Scarecrow Press, 1978. Pp. 344–53.

———. "On Female Identity and Writing by Women." *Critical Inquiry* 8 (1981): 347–61.

Garner, Shirley Nelson, Claire Kahane, and Madelon Sprengnether, eds. *The Mother Tongue: Essays in Feminist Psychoanalytic Interpretation*. Ithaca: Cornell University Press, 1985.

Gaskell, Elizabeth. "The Poor Clare." *The Works of Mrs. Gaskell*. Vol. 5. London: Smith, Elder, 1906.

———. *"My Diary": The Early Years of My Daughter Marianne*. London: privately printed by Clement Shorter, 1923.

———. *The Letters of Mrs. Gaskell*. Edited by J. A. V. Chapple and Arthur Pollard. Manchester: Manchester University Press, 1966.

———. *Wives and Daughters*. 1866. Harmondsworth: Penguin, 1969.

———. *Mary Barton*. 1848. Harmondsworth: Penguin, 1970.

———. *North and South*. 1855. Harmondsworth: Penguin, 1970.

———. "The Cage at Cranford." 1863. *Cranford/Cousin Phillis*. Harmondsworth: Penguin, 1976.

———. *Cranford/Cousin Phillis*. 1853/1863. Harmondsworth: Penguin, 1976.

———. "The Last Generation in England." 1849. *Cranford/Cousin Phillis*. Harmondsworth: Penguin, 1976.

Gérin, Winifred. *Elizabeth Gaskell*. Oxford: Oxford University Press, 1976.

Gilbert, Sandra, and Susan Gubar. *The Madwoman in the Attic: The Woman Writer and the Nineteenth-Century Literary Imagination*. New Haven: Yale University Press, 1979.

Gilligan, Carol. *In a Different Voice*. Cambridge, MA: Harvard University Press, 1982.

Glendinning, Victoria. *Trollope*. London: Pimlico, 1993.

Glick, Robert A., and Donald I. Meyers, eds. *Masochism: Current Psychoanalytic Perspectives*. Hillsdale, NJ: Analytic Press, 1988.

Greg, W. R.. "Why Are Women Redundant?" *National Review* 14 (April 1862): 434–60.

Grotjahn, Martin. *Beyond Laughter*. New York: McGraw-Hill, 1966.

Haight, Gordon S. *George Eliot: A Biography*. Oxford: Oxford University Press, 1968.

Hamilton, Susan, ed. *"Criminals, Idiots, Women & Minors": Nineteenth-Century Writing by Women on Women.* Peterborough, Ontario: Broadview Press, 1995.

Handwerk, Gary J. *Irony and Ethics in Narrative: From Schlegel to Lacan.* New Haven: Yale University Press, 1985.

Harden, Elizabeth. *Maria Edgeworth.* Boston: Twayne, 1984.

Harding, D. W. "Regulated Hatred: An Aspect of the Work of Jane Austen." *Jane Austen: A Collection of Critical Essays.* Edited by Ian Watt. Englewood Cliffs, NJ: Prentice-Hall, 1963. Pp. 166–79.

———. Introduction to *Persuasion* (by Jane Austen). Harmondsworth: Penguin, 1965.

Hayles, N. Katherine. "Anger in Different Voices: Carol Gilligan and *The Mill on the Floss.*" *Signs: Journal of Women in Culture and Society* 12, no. 1 (1986): 23–29.

Hazlitt, William. *Lectures on the English Poets, and the English Comic Writers.* 1819. Edited by William Carew Hazlitt. London: George Bell and Sons, 1984.

Herbert, Christopher. *Trollope and Comic Pleasure.* Chicago: University of Chicago Press, 1987.

Hirsch, Marianne. "Female Family Romances and the 'Old Dream of Symmetry.'" *Literature and Psychology* 32, no. 4 (1986): 37–47.

Holcombe, Lee. "Victorian Wives and Property: Reform of the Married Women's Property Law, 1857–1882." *A Widening Sphere: Changing Roles of Victorian Women.* Edited by Martha Vicinus. Bloomington: Indiana University Press, 1977. Pp. 3–28.

Homans, Margaret. *Bearing the Word: Language and Female Experience in Nineteenth-Century Literary Imagination.* Chicago: University of Chicago Press, 1986.

Honan, Park. *Jane Austen: Her Life.* New York: St. Martin's, 1987.

Hopkins, A. B. *Elizabeth Gaskell: Her Life and Work.* London: John Lehmann, 1952.

Horney, Karen. "The Problem with Feminine Masochism." *Psychoanalysis and Women.* Edited by Jean Baker Miller. Harmondsworth: Penguin, 1972.

Hudson, Glenda A. *Sibling Love and Incest in Jane Austen's Fiction.* London: Macmillan, 1992.

Hunter, Dianne, ed. *Seduction and Theory: Readings of Gender, Representation, amd Rhetoric.* Urbana: University of Illinois Press, 1989.

Irigaray, Luce. *Speculum of the Other Woman.* Translated by Gillian C. Gill. Ithaca: Cornell University Press, 1985.

Jacobus, Mary. "The Question of Language: Men of Maxims and *The Mill on the Floss.*" *Critical Inquiry* 8, no. 2 (1981): 207–22.

James, Henry. *The House of Fiction: Essays on the Novel by Henry James.* Edited by Leon Edel. Westport, CT: Greenwood Press, 1957.

———. "The Velvet Glove." 1909. *The Complete Tales of Henry James.* Vol. 12: *1903–1910.* Edited by Leon Edel. London: Rupert Hart-Davis, 1964. Pp. 233–65.

———. "Daisy Miller." 1879. *Great Short Works of Henry James.* New York: Harper and Row, 1966. Pp. 3–55.

———. *Henry James: Literary Criticism: Essays on Literature, American Writers, English Writers.* Edited by Leon Edel. New York: Library of America, 1984.

———. "Julia Bride." 1908. *Henry James: Complete Stories, 1898–1910.* New York: Library of America, 1996 [1908]. Pp. 661–96.

Jauss, Hans Robert. *Aesthetic Experience and Literary Hermeneutics.* Translated by Michael Shaw. Minneapolis: University of Minnesota Press, 1982.

Johnson, Claudia L. *Jane Austen: Women, Politics and the Novel.* Chicago: University of Chicago Press, 1988.

———. *Equivocal Beings: Politics, Gender, and Sentimentality in the 1790s: Wollstonecraft, Radcliffe, Burney, Austen.* Chicago: University of Chicago Press, 1995.

Johnstone, Peggy Ruth Fitzhugh. "Narcissistic Rage in *The Mill on the Floss.*" *Literature and Psychology* 36, nos. 1 and 2 (1990): 90–109.

Kahane, Claire. "The Gothic Mirror." *The (M)other Tongue: Essays in Feminist Psycho-analytic Interpretation.* Edited by Shirley Nelson Garner, Claire Kahane, and Madelon Sprengnether. Ithaca: Cornell University Press, 1985. Pp. 334–51.

Kaplan, Deborah. *Jane Austen among Women.* Baltimore: Johns Hopkins University Press, 1992.

Kavanagh, Julia. Extract from *English Women of Letters.* 1862. Rpt. *Jane Austen: The Critical Heritage.* Edited by B. C. Southam. London: Routledge and Kegan Paul, 1968.

Keating, Peter. Introduction to *Cranford/Cousin Phillis* (by Elizabeth Gaskell). Harmondsworth: Penguin, 1976. Pp. 7–30.

à Kempis, Thomas. *The Imitation of Christ.* Translated by Leo Sherley-Price. Harmondsworth: Penguin, 1952.

Kierkegaard, Søren. *The Concept of Irony: With Continual Reference to Socrates.* Edited and translated by Howard V. Hong and Edna H. Hong. Princeton: Princeton University Press, 1989.

Kincaid, James R. *The Novels of Anthony Trollope.* Oxford: Clarendon, 1977.

Kirkham, Margaret. *Jane Austen, Feminism and Fiction.* London: Harvester Press, 1983.

Klein, Melanie. *The Selected Melanie Klein.* Edited by Juliet Mitchell. New York: Free Press, 1986.

Kowaleski-Wallace, Beth. "The Reader as Misogynist in *The Custom of the Country.*" *Modern Language Studies* (Winter 1991): 45–53.

Kristeva, Julia. *Black Sun: Mourning and Melancholia.* Translated by Leon Roudiez. New York: Columbia University Press, 1990.

———. *Desire in Language: A Semiotic Approach to Literature and Art.* Translated by Leon Roudiez. New York: Columbia University Press, 1980.

Lacan, Jacques. *Ecrits: A Selection.* New York: Norton, 1977.

Laclos, Choderlos de. *Les Liaisons Dangereuses.* Translated by P. W. K. Stone. Harmondsworth: Penguin, 1961.

Lang, Candace. *Irony/Humor: Critical Paradigms.* Baltimore: Johns Hopkins University Press, 1988.

Langland, Elizabeth. *Nobody's Angels: Middle-Class Women and Domestic Ideology.* Ithaca: Cornell University Press, 1995.

Lansbury, Coral. *Elizabeth Gaskell: The Novel of Social Crisis.* New York: Barnes and Noble, 1975.

Lauter, Paul, ed. *Theories of Comedy.* New York: Anchor Doubleday, 1964.

Leavis, F. R. *The Great Tradition: George Eliot, Henry James, Joseph Conrad.* New York: New York University Press, 1960.

Leighton, Angela. "Sense and Silences: Reading Jane Austen Again." *Jane Austen: New Perspectives.* Edited by Janet Todd. New York: Holmes and Meier, 1983. Pp. 128–40.

Lenta, Margaret. "Androgyny and Authority in *Mansfield Park.*" *Studies in the Novel* 15 (1983): 169–82.

Lewis, R. W. B. *Edith Wharton: A Biography.* New York: Harper and Row, 1975.

Little, Judith. *Comedy and the Woman Writer: Woolf, Spark and Feminism.* Lincoln: University of Nebraska Press, 1983.

Lockwood, Thomas. "Divided Attention in *Persuasion.*" *Nineteenth-Century Fiction* 33 (1978): 309–23.

Long, Robert Emmet. *Barbara Pym.* New York: Ungar, 1986.

Lubbock, Percy. *Portrait of Edith Wharton.* London: Jonathan Cape, 1945.

Macaulay, Thomas Babington. Extract from "The Diary and Letters of Mme D'Arblay." *Jane Austen: The Critical Heritage.* Edited by B. C. Southam. London: Routledge and Kegan Paul, 1968. Pp. 122–23.

MacDonagh, Oliver. *Jane Austen: Real and Imagined Worlds.* New Haven: Yale University Press, 1991.

Marcus, Steven. *The Other Victorians: A Study of Sexuality and Pornography in Mid-Nineteenth Century England.* New York: New American Library, 1974.

Martineau, Harriet. *Harriet Martineau on Women.* Edited by Gayle Graham Yates. New Brunswick: Rutgers University Press, 1985.

McDonnell, Jane. "'A Little Spirit of Independence': Sexual Politics and the Bildungsroman in *Mansfield Park.*" *Novel* 17 (1984): 197–214.

McGhee, Paul E., and Jeffrey H. Goldstein, eds. *Handbook of Humor Research.* 2 vols. New York: Springer-Verlag, 1983.

McMaster, Juliet. *Trollope's Palliser Novels: Theme and Pattern.* London: Macmillan, 1978.

Meredith, George. *The Egoist.* 1879. Harmondsworth: Penguin, 1968.

———. "An Essay on Comedy." 1877. *Comedy.* Edited by Wylie Sypher. Baltimore: Johns Hopkins University Press, 1980.

Meyers, Helen. "A Consideration of Treatment Techniques in Relation to the Functions of Masochism." *Masochism: Current Psychoanalytic Perspectives.* Edited by Robert A. Glick and Donald I. Meyers. Hillsdale, NJ: Analytic Press, 1988. Pp. 175–88.

Miller, Andrew H.. "The Fragments and Small Opportunities of *Cranford.*" *Genre* 25 (1992): 91–111.

Miller, D. A. *Narrative and Its Discontents.* Princeton: Princeton University Press, 1981.

Miller, J. Hillis. *The Disappearance of God: Five Nineteenth-Century Writers.* Cambridge, MA: Harvard University Press, 1963.

Miller, Jean Baker. "Tropes and the Narrative Line in Elizabeth Gaskell's *Cranford.*" Paper presented at the Modern Language Association Convention, New York, 1986.

———, ed. *Psychoanalysis and Feminism.* Harmondsworth: Penguin, 1973.

Miller, Nancy K. "Emphasis Added: Plots and Plausibilities in Women's Fiction." *PMLA* 96 (January 1981): 36–38.

Millingen, J. G.. *The Passions; or, Mind and Matter.* London: John and Daniel Darling, 1848.

Moers, Ellen. *Literary Women.* Garden City, NY: Doubleday, 1976.

Morgan, Susan. *In the Meantime: Character and Perception in Jane Austen's Fiction.* Chicago: University of Chicago Press, 1980.

Mudrick, Marvin. *Jane Austen: Irony as Defense and Discovery.* Princeton: Princeton University Press, 1952.

Mulvey, Laura. *Visual and Other Pleasures.* Bloomington: Indiana University Press, 1989.

Mundorf, Norbert, Azra Bhatia, Dolf Zillman, Paul Lester, and Susan Robertson. "Gender Differences in Humor Appreciation." *Humor* 1, no. 3 (1988): 231–43.

Nardin, Jame. *He Knew She Was Right: The Independent Woman in the Novels of Anthony Trollope.* Carbondale and Edwardsville: Southern Illinois University Press, 1989.

Nestor, Pauline. *Female Friendships and Communities: Charlotte Brontë, George Eliot, Elizabeth Gaskell.* Oxford: Clarendon Press, 1985.

New Female Instructor; or, Young Woman's Guide to Domestic Happiness; Containing General Rules for the Regulation of Female Conduct, and the Formation of Moral Habits; Together with The Elements of Science, as Geography, Astronomy, Natural History, Botany &c. and Important Hints in Regard to Domestic Economy; Also, Examples of Illustrious Women: to Which Are Added, Advice to Servants; A Complete Art of Cookery, with Plain Directions for Carving; and a Great Variety of Medicinal and Other Useful Receipts; Being an Epitome of all the Acquirements Necessary to Form the Female Character, in Every Class of Life. Illustrated with appropriate Engravings. London: Thomas Kelly, 1835.

Nightingale, Florence. *Cassandra: An Essay.* Old Westbury, NY: Feminist Press, 1979.

Norton, Caroline. *English Laws for Women in the Nineteenth Century.* London: privately printed, 1854.

Oliphant, Margaret. *The Literary History of England; in the End of the Eighteenth and Beginning of the Nineteenth Century.* Vol. 3. London: Macmillan, 1882.

———. "Miss Austen and Miss Mitford." *Jane Austen: The Critical Heritage.* Vol. 1. Edited by B. C. Southam. London: Routledge and Kegan Paul, 1968. Pp. 215–25.

———. "The Rector." *The Doctor's Family and Other Stories.* Edited by Merryn Williams. Oxford: Oxford University Press, 1986.

———. *Miss Majoribanks.* 1866. New York: Virago (Penguin), 1989.

———. "The Grievances of Women." 1880. *"Criminals, Idiots, Women and Minors": Victorian Writing by Women on Women.* Edited by Susan Hamilton. Ontario: Broadview Press, 1995.

Omwake, Louise. "A Study of Sense of Humor: Its Relation to Sex, Age and Personal Characteristics." *Journal of Applied Psychology* 21 (1937): 688–704.

Paris, Bernard J. *Character and Conflict in Jane Austen's Novels: A Psychological Approach.* Detroit: Wayne State University Press, 1978.

Patmore, Coventry. *The Poems of Coventry Patmore.* Edited by Frederick Page. London: Oxford University Press, 1949.

Paulson, Ronald. "Evelina: Cinderella and Society." *Fanny Burney's Evelina.* Modern Critical Interpretations. Edited by Harold Bloom. New York: Chelsea House, 1988. Pp. 59–83.

Peacock, Thomas Love. *Nightmare Abbey.* 1818. Harmondsworth: Penguin, 1969.

Pickrel, Paul. "Lionel Trilling and *Mansfield Park.*" *SEL* 27 (1987): 609–21.

Plato. *Symposium.* Translated by Alexander Nehamas and Paul Woodruff. Indianapolis: Hackett, 1989.

Polhemus, Robert M. *The Changing World of Anthony Trollope.* Berkeley: University of California Press, 1968.

Poovey, Mary. *The Proper Lady and the Woman Writer: Ideology as Style in the Works of Mary Wollstonecraft, Mary Shelley, and Jane Austen.* Chicago: University of Chicago Press, 1984.

————. *Uneven Developments: The Ideological Work of Gender in Mid-Victorian England.* Chicago: University of Chicago Press, 1988.

Pope, Alexander. *Alexander Pope: Selected Poetry & Prose.* Edited by William K. Wimsatt, Jr. New York: Holt, Rinehart and Winston, 1967.

Porteous, Janice. "Humor as a Process of Defense: The Evolution of Laughing." *Humor* 1, no. 1 (1988): 63–80.

Powers, Lyall H., ed. *Henry James and Edith Wharton: Letters, 1900–1915.* New York: Charles Scribner's Sons, 1990.

Prerost, Frank J. "Reduction of Aggression as a Function of Related Content of Humor." *Psychological Reports* 38 (1976): 771–77.

Price, Martin. *Forms of Life: Character and Moral Imagination in the Novel.* New Haven: Yale University Press, 1983.

Priestley, J. B. *English Humour.* New York: Stein and Day, 1976.

Prior, Matthew. "Henry and Emma, a Poem, upon the Model of the Nut-brown Maid." *The Literary Works of Matthew Prior.* Vol. 1. 2d ed. Edited by H. Bunker Wright and Monroe I. Spears. Oxford: Clarendon Press, 1971. Pp. 278–300.

Pym, Barbara. *Excellent Women.* 1952. New York: Plume, 1978.

————. *Jane and Prudence.* 1951. New York: Harper and Row, 1981.

————. *Less than Angels.* 1955. New York: Dutton, 1990.

Raskin, Victor. *Semantic Mechanisms of Humor.* Boston: D. Reidel, 1985.

Reddy, Maureen T. "Female Sexuality in 'The Poor Clare': The Demon in the House." *Studies in Short Fiction* 21 (Summer 1984): 259–65.

Reiss, Erna. *The Rights and Duties of Englishwomen; A Study in Law and Public Opinion.* Manchester: Shervatt and Hughes, 1934.

Richetti, John. "Voice and Gender in Eighteenth-Century Fiction: Haywood to Burney." *Studies in the Novel* 19 (Fall 1987): 263–72.

Ritchie, Anne Thackeray. Preface to *Cranford* (by Mrs. Gaskell). New York: Thomas Y. Crowell, 1892.

Robbins, Bruce. *The Servant's Hand: English Fiction from Below.* Durham: Duke University Press, 1993.

Roberts, Warren. *Jane Austen and the French Revolution.* New York: St. Martin's Press, 1980.

Rogers, Katharine M. *Frances Burney: The World of "Female Difficulties."* London: Harvester Wheatsheaf, 1990.

Rousseau, Jean-Jacques. *Emile, ou de l'Education.* Paris: Carnier-Flammarion, 1966.

————. *Emile.* Translated by Barbara Foxley. London: Dent, 1976.

————. *Emile; or, On Education.* Translated by Allan Bloom. New York: Basic Books, 1979.

Ruderman, Anne Crippen. *The Pleasures of Virtue: Political Thought in the Novels of Jane Austen.* Lanham, MD: Rowman and Littlefield, 1995.

Ruskin, John. *The Genius of John Ruskin: Selections from His Writings.* Edited by John D. Rosenberg. London: Routledge and Kegan Paul, 1963.

Schleifer, Ronald. "Irony and the Literary Past: *On The Concept of Irony* and *The Mill on the Floss.*" *Kierkegaard and Literature.* Edited by Ronald Schleifer and Robert Markley. Norman: University of Oklahoma Press, 1984. Pp. 183–216.

Schor, Hilary M. *Scheherazade of the Market Place: Elizabeth Gaskell and the Victorian Novel.* New York: Oxford University Press, 1992.

Scott, Walter. *Waverley.* 1814. New York: Dent, 1969.

Sedgwick, Eve Kosofsky. *Epistemology of the Closet.* Berkeley and Los Angeles: University of California Press, 1990.

Shakespeare, William. *The Riverside Shakespeare.* Boston: Houghton Mifflin, 1974.

Shanley, Mary Lyndon. *Feminism, Marriage and the Law in Victorian England, 1850–1895.* Princeton: Princeton University Press, 1989.

Sharps, John Geoffrey. *Mrs. Gaskell's Observation and Invention: A Study of Her Non-Biographic Works.* Fontwell, Sussex: Linden Press, 1970.

Simpson, Richard. Unsigned review of Henry Austen's *Memoir. Jane Austen: The Critical Heritage.* Vol. 1. Edited by B. C. Southam. London: Routledge and Kegan Paul, 1968. Pp. 242–65.

Skilton, David. *Anthony Trollope and His Contemporaries: A Study in the Theory and Conventions of Mid-Victorian Fiction.* London: Longman, 1972.

Smalley, Donald, ed. *Trollope: The Critical Heritage.* London: Routledge and Kegan Paul, 1969.

Smith, Johanna. "'My Only Sister Now': Incest in *Mansfield Park.*" *Studies in the Novel* 19 (1987): 1–15.

Southam, B. C., ed. *Jane Austen: The Critical Heritage.* Vol. 1. London: Routledge and Kegan Paul, 1968.

———. *Jane Austen: The Critical Heritage.* Vol. 2: *1870–1940.* London: Routledge and Kegan Paul, 1987.

Spacks, Patricia Meyer. *Gossip.* Chicago: University of Chicago Press, 1985.

———. "Dynamics of Fear: Fanny Burney." *Fanny Burney's Evelina.* Edited by Harold Bloom. New York: Chelsea House, 1988. Pp. 31–57.

Staves, Susan. "*Evelina:* or, Female Difficulties." *Fanny Burney's Evelina.* Edited by Harold Bloom. New York: Chelsea House, 1988. Pp. 13–30.

———. *Married Women's Separate Property in England, 1660–1833.* Cambridge, MA: Harvard University Press, 1990.

Stein, Allen F. "The Hack's Progress: A Reading of James's 'The Velvet Glove.'" *Essays in Literature* 1 (Spring 1974): 219–26.

Stewart, Maaja A. *Domestic Realities and Imperial Fictions: Janes Austen's Novels in Eighteenth-Century Contexts.* Athens: University of Georgia Press, 1993.

Stoneman, Patsy. *Elizabeth Gaskell.* Brighton, Sussex: Harvester Press, 1987.

Straub, Kristina. *Divided Fictions: Fanny Burney and Feminine Strategy.* Lexington: University Press of Kentucky, 1987.

Sypher, Wylie, ed. *Comedy.* Baltimore: Johns Hopkins University, Press, 1980.

Tanner, Tony. Introduction to *Mansfield Park* (by Jane Austen). Harmondsworth: Penguin, 1966.

Tave, Stuart M. *The Amiable Humorist: A Study in the Comic Theory and Criticism of the Eighteenth and Early Nineteenth Century.* Chicago: University of Chicago Press, 1960.

———. *Some Words of Jane Austen.* Chicago: University of Chicago Press, 1973.

Terdiman, Richard. "Counter-Humorists: Strategies of Ideological Critique in Marx and Flaubert," *Diacritics* 9 (1979): 18–32.

Thackeray, William Makepeace. *Vanity Fair.* 1848. Edited by Geoffrey and Kathleen Tillotson. Boston: Houghton Mifflin Co., 1963.

———. *The History of Pendennis.* 1850. Harmondsworth: Penguin, 1972.

Tillotson, Geoffrey, and Donald Hawes, eds. *Thackeray: The Critical Heritage*. London: Routledge and Kegan Paul, 1968.

Tintner, Adeline R. "James's Mock Epic: 'The Velvet Glove,' Edith Wharton, and Other Late Tales." *Modern Fiction Studies* 17, no. 4 (1972): 483–99.

Todd, Janet, ed. *Jane Austen: New Perspectives*. New York: Holmes and Meier, 1983.

———. "Life after Sex: The Fictional Autobiography of Delarivier Manley." *Last Laughs: Perspectives on Women and Comedy*. Edited by Regina Barreca. New York: Gordon and Breach, 1988. Pp. 43–55.

Trilling, Lionel. "Mansfield Park." *The Opposing Self*. New York: Harcourt, 1955.

Trollope, Anthony. *An Autobiography*. 1883. Berkeley: University of California Press, 1947.

———. *Barchester Towers*. 1857. New York: New American Library, 1963.

———. *The Last Chronicle of Barset*. 1867. Harmondsworth: Penguin, 1967.

———. *Doctor Thorne*. 1858. Oxford: Oxford University Press, 1980.

———. *The Small House at Allington*. 1864. Oxford: Oxford University Press, 1980.

———. *Framley Parsonage*. 1861. Harmondsworth: Penguin, 1984.

Van Buren, Jane Silverman. *The Modernist Madonna: Semiotics of the Maternal Metaphor*. Bloomington: Indiana University Press, 1989.

Vasey, George. *The Philosophy of Laughter and Smiling*. 2d ed. London: J. Burns, 1877.

Vicinus, Martha. *A Widening Sphere: Changing Roles of Victorian Women*. Bloomington: Indiana University Press, 1978.

Walker, Nancy. *A Very Serious Thing: Women's Humor and American Culture*. Minneapolis: University of Minnesota Press, 1988.

Walker, Nancy, and Zita Dresner, eds. *Redressing the Balance: American Women's Literary Humor from Colonial Times to the 1980s*. Jackson: University of Mississippi Press, 1988.

Wallace, Tara Ghoshal. *Jane Austen and Narrative Authority*. New York: St. Martin's Press, 1995.

Warhol, Robyn R. *Gendered Interventions: Narrative Discourse in the Victorian Novel*. New Brunswick: Rutgers University Press, 1989.

Watt, Ian, ed. *Jane Austen: A Collection of Critical Essays*. Englewood Cliffs, NJ: Prentice Hall, 1963.

Webb, R. K. *Modern England: From the Eighteenth Century to the Present*. 2d ed. New York: Harper and Row, 1980.

Wharton, Edith. "George Eliot." Review of Leslie Stephen, *George Eliot*. *The Bookman* 15 (May 1902): 247–51.

———. *The Custom of the Country*. New York: Charles Scribner's Sons, 1913.

———. *A Backward Glance*. New York: Charles Scribner's Sons, 1933.

———. *The Fruit of the Tree*. 1907. London: Virago, 1984.

———. *The Letters of Edith Wharton*. Edited by R. W. B. Lewis and Nancy Lewis. New York: Collier Books, 1988.

Wharton, John J. S. *An Exposition of the Laws Relating to the Women of England; Showing Their Rights, Remedies, and Responsibilities, in Every Position of Life*. London: Longman, Brown, Green and Longmans, 1853.

Williams, Anne. *Art of Darkness: A Poetics of Gothic*. Chicago: University of Chicago Press, 1995.

Wilt, Judith. "The Laughter of Maidens, the Cackle of Matriarchs: Notes on the Collision between Comedy and Feminism." *Gender and Literary Voice.* Edited by Janet Todd. New York: Holmes and Meier, 1980. Pp. 173–96.

Winnett, Susan. "Coming Unstrung: Women, Men, Narrative, Masterplot." *PMLA* 105 (May 1990): 505–18.

Winnicott, D. W. *The Maturational Processes and the Facilitating Environment.* Madison: International Universities Press, 1965.

———. *Playing and Reality.* Harmondsworth: Penguin, 1980.

Wolfe, Patricia. "Structure and Movement in *Cranford.*" *Nineteenth Century Fiction* 23 (1968): 162–76.

Wolfe, Thomas P. "The Achievement of *Persuasion.*" *Studies in English Literature* 11 (1971): 687–700.

Wolff, Cynthia Griffin. *A Feast of Words: The Triumph of Edith Wharton.* New York: Oxford University Press, 1977.

Woolf, Virginia. *To the Lighthouse.* New York: Harcourt Brace and World, 1927.

———. *A Room of One's Own.* New York: Harcourt Brace and World, 1929.

———. *Death of the Noth and Other Essays.* New York: Harcourt Brace and World, 1942.

Wright, Edgar. *Mrs. Gaskell: The Basis for Reassessment.* Oxford: Oxford University Press, 1965.

Yeager, Patricia. "Toward a Female Sublime." *Gender & Theory: Dialogues on Feminist Criticism.* Edited by Linda Kauffman. Oxford: Basil Blackwell, 1989. Pp. 191–212.

Young, G. M. *Portrait of an Age.* 2d ed. Oxford: Oxford University Press, 1960.

Zagarell, Sandra A. "Narrative of Community: The Identification of a Genre." *Signs* 13 (Spring 1988), 498–527.

INDEX